JUGGERNAUT

JUGGERNAUT

WHY THE SYSTEM CRUSHES
THE ONLY PEOPLE WHO CAN SAVE IT

ERIC ROBERT MORSE

NEW
CLASSIC
BOOKS

For information, contact:
New Classic Books
www.newclassicbooks.com

ISBN 1-60020-049-4
978-1-60020-049-6

For the future generations.

CONTENTS

I. WEALTH

II. COMPETITION

III. GOVERNMENT

IV. AUTARCHY

AUTHOR'S
NOTE

ECONOMICALLY SPEAKING, WE HAVE a surplus of troubles. From the whimpering job market to corporate scandals and industrial pollution, from childhood malnutrition to a deteriorating education system and skyrocketing debt, the critic has his choice of problems to focus on.

But perhaps the most glaring sign of trouble can be found, not in the problems themselves, but in the way we attempt to solve them. Sincere analysis and thoughtful proposals are rare these days; most people simply point their finger at the group supposedly responsible for a problem and do everything in their power to ridicule, denounce, and censure them. It's the Republicans or Democrats, capitalists or socialists, corporations or labor unions that are to blame, and everything is their fault. In short, constructive discourse has been replaced by mere contempt.

Of course, defeating others is necessary in any competitive situation. But defeating others has become the new standard, replacing productive ends as the central goal in all social interaction. Browsing public fora will offer an abundant sample, whether in the comments section of popular YouTube videos, on Amazon.com message boards, on radio and television talk shows, or even in published books and political debates. The discussion appears to be aimed at the betterment of society—the economy, religious practice, education, the arts—but under the surface lies nothing more than sarcastic, petulant, and often downright hateful squabbling. Civility is thrown out the window; so too is cooperation. All the participants manage to produce is irrelevant factoids, sophistry, and name-calling, all aimed at beating the other side no matter what.

If viewed objectively, the whole enterprise can be pretty comical and would doubtless make the crew from Monty Python proud. But few if any view it objectively. Most take these arguments personally, as a kind of battle for survival—us against them, good versus evil—in which any and all maneuvers must be applied to ensure victory. They will try childish games, psychological trickery, illiteracy, and vulgarity (even though their words are replaced by dollar signs, percent symbols, and pound signs). As it seems, no one believes they can work with 'the other side' to attain a mutual goal, even if they have a good point or reveal the truth in some way—they are the enemy and must be defeated.

What this means is that truth, itself must be discarded in the interest of self-preservation. When it becomes

Man: I came here for a good argument.

Mr Barnard: No, you didn't; no, you came here for an argument.

Man: An argument isn't just contradiction.

Mr Barnard: It can be.

Man: No, it can't. An argument is a connected series of statements intended to establish a proposition.

Mr Barnard: No, it isn't.

Man: Yes, it is! It's not just contradiction.

Mr Barnard: Look, if I argue with you, I must take up a contrary position.

Man: Yes, but that's not just saying 'No, it isn't.'

Mr Barnard: Yes, it is.

Man: No, it isn't!

Man: Argument is an intellectual process. Contradiction is just the automatic gainsaying of any statement the other person makes.

Mr Barnard: No, it isn't.

—"Argument Clinic" sketch,
Monty Python

more profitable to make fun of someone or berate them for their beliefs than it is to offer a constructive alternative, intellectual discourse is threatened. And, when a people can no longer rely on intellectual discourse, the society is bound to fall.

If there is a sign of the looming Juggernaut at all, it is this kind of bitter discord. Infighting and power struggles are the only recourse in a situation as confined and oppressive as the modern world. It is not a coincidence that the term 'civil war' has been uttered by credible sources.

This book aims to break free from this standoff in two ways: First, this argument attempts to present all sides of the great debates and understand the validity behind each. There is, after all, legitimate rationale behind all major political postures these days, and it can only do good to appreciate each side the way practitioners do. Some may find it satisfying to call Michael Moore a 'fat loser', for instance, but it does no good to disregard his claims against corporations. Calling Glenn Beck a 'psycho elitist' may make one feel better about one's own beliefs, but it is not constructive to ignore his arguments against the state. Both have valid insight and both can be valued as such.

Second, the point of this book is to get to the root of the discord—the Juggernaut, itself—and formulate a viable solution. This book intends to explain why it is assumed that one cannot win unless someone else loses, and why everything is geared to making that other side lose. Such a mentality affects the entire civilization and has many sources, but it is accessible and ultimately comprehensible. The key rests in understanding the system as a whole. For quick reference, the thesis can be found in the introduction as well as in the compendium toward the back of the book.

As anyone can tell, this is an economics book. Seeing as how economics has been labeled the 'dismal science', the author can only hope that this does not deter potential readers from the study in search of more lively material. After all, as a slew of writers have shown in recent years, economics can be a very interesting topic. At the very least, economics is a science of the decisions we make on a daily basis, and so it affects each of us in very immediate ways. As such, no one can deny its relevance. But it is also the belief of the author that economics holds a much more important place in life generally and comprises the most fascinating material known to popular study. At its root, choice is the very substance of human action, and so economics is really the science of everything we do. From conducting business to creating art, from raising families to playing casual games on Facebook, everything is based in this fundamental study.

That is why economic trends lend insight into the great cultural trends of history, and why they provide a glimpse into the very character of mankind. Economics is not just the study of aggregate supply and demand charts; economics is the science of life, and nothing can be more interesting than that.

Certainly, the reader will find fair helpings of formulas and diagrams, all aimed at conveying the general concepts surrounding economics; but he will also find large doses of cultural and historical investigation, as well as references to literature, business practice, cinema, video games, sports, the fine arts, relationships, love, music, and religion, as well as a topic that the author considers to be one of the most interesting of all—breakfast cereal.

To be sure, this book is a theoretical study that contains little if any empirical analysis. This is not to say that such analysis would be unwelcome in defense of the thesis, but rather to reflect the author's belief that a theory is best conveyed in a conversational style rather than through mathematical equations. While the latter may eliminate doubt on a given issue, understanding may well remain lacking. Anyway, it is believed that a theoretical survey can connect with a much wider audience than an empirical study can, which is a goal that all writers strive toward.

Ultimately, this book aims at the mesmerizing and lively. It is for those who try to connect their daily activities with the big picture and wonder how it all works; who love to examine social trends and see how they shift over time; who love science, industry, technology, and the other practical arts; who enjoy thinking about the human psyche and the culture it produces; who love a good paradox and want to see it explained.

Above all, perhaps, this book is for those who still find value in the human intellect and seek an arena where it can flourish and bring about ingenuity. Ours is possibly the most fascinating age in all of history, when the complex intricacy of the social fabric leads constantly to new challenges and fresh perspectives. In an age of vast technical and sociopolitical changes, we are increasingly faced with mysteries and riddles that confound the status quo. Those mysteries long to be solved. This book is for those who are willing to engage in the intellectual endeavor required to do so.

INTRODUCTION

The System

DURING THE RUN-UP to the mid-term election in 2010, as it became apparent that scores of Democrats would be replaced by a troop of Republican 'Tea Party' candidates, a bystander was almost guaranteed to hear a steady chant of lament from the left side of the political spectrum. It was a familiar chant, one that included such claims as 'If those yahoos get into office, this country is ruined!' and the old standby, 'If they get hold of power, I'm moving to Canada!'

It was familiar because we actually heard it from the other side of the spectrum in 2008, when it had become clear that Barack Obama and the Democrats were poised to win power. Conservatives and Republicans from across the country shouted that 'If that guy gets into office, this country is ruined!' They too threatened to move to a different country, though it was to New Zealand or Singapore or some other place known to have reduced taxes and government intervention in recent years.

To the thoughtful participant, making such claims seemed like the only recourse. In fact, during every election, and especially the presidential ones, the mantra is always the same—'If the other side gets ahold of power, the only thing left to do is move.'

Of course, in 2010, as it was in 2008 and other election years before, no one actually moved. As the protesters quickly learned, there was nowhere to move that could provide an escape from the newly elected officials and still offer all the benefits of living in the United States. What troubled voters found upon reflection was that no other country in the world provided a better situation than that which could be found at home—all had their drawbacks, and none provided the kind of deliverance that might be imagined.

For example, modern liberals saw Canada as enticing because of its universal health care, its anti-war posture, its progressive stance on same-sex marriage, and other liberal causes célèbres of the time, but Canada has always had high unemployment, relatively limited culture, and, no matter how warm their poutine is, it's just really cold up there. Conservatives found places like New Zealand and Singapore appealing because they have reduced taxes and governmental bureaucracy in recent years, but they still maintain no small amount of strict rules and state intervention, which make them less appealing than they might have seemed on the surface—not to mention the 18-hour flight it would take to get there.

And so the typical disgruntled American voter really has no alternative in the situation. As corrupt as Dick Cheney and George W. Rex might have seemed, the leaders of France or Italy proved to be no more principled. As socialist and radical as Obama seems, the conditions in Germany or Australia provide no reprieve—all advanced countries suffer from the ills of the modern system, quite as if they are endemic. By moving away from America, one might be able to escape the threats to freedom and well-being present under its new regime, only to face new threats abroad. And who wants to eat Vegemite all day, anyway?

The fact is that there is no place to go that would provide a frustrated American with a viable escape. Certainly, there is no place to go that would improve the situation enough to justify changing citizenship, packing up, and actually making the move. It would be too much trouble for too little gain, and so, though such a move is often promised, it never happens.

* * *

This subtle truth is more troubling than it may seem. Simply, there is no place to move if things don't go the way one wants them to go. This means that the citizens of this country, as passionate and idealistic as they are, must endure whatever policies and ventures the few in power decide to assume, even when those policies and ventures completely contradict the people's core beliefs and ideals.

Throughout the Bush presidency, for instance, modern liberals had to tolerate eight years of foreign wars, crony capitalism, and bad public speaking; throughout the short Obama presidency, conservatives have had to endure third-world-style nationalization, deficit spending that would make Keynes' head spin, and really good speeches that make it all sound like grapes and sunshine.

Americans are not used to this sort of thing. To them, it seems illogical and even unnatural to accept anything that is disagreeable or contradictory to one's principles. If one is faced with a war that he finds objectionable or a government health care mandate that he considers to be unconstitutional, the American believes he should just reject it, turn away, and go find something that he does agree with—that is the American way; that is the way of a free people.

But that's not the way it works anymore. For some time now, the party in power has been able to dictate what everyone must do, whether or not those dictates coincide with what everyone wants or believes to be in their best interest. We live in what might be called a 'closed system', one where there are no real alternatives or means of escape. If one disagrees with the war or cannot come to accept the government-run health care system, too bad. Everyone must deal with it and carry on as if there is no problem at all.

Now, one might argue that the average citizen does not have to just sit by and deal with it—he is given a means to correct the situation by voting. And, certainly, the kind of elections that we have seen in the last decade or so show that an agitated public can and will take their concerns to the voting booth to change the officials in power. It is thought that by doing so the people can improve their situation and actually make the system work.

But this is to neglect the contingencies inherent in the system itself. A closer look shows that it is designed in such a way that every action a voter makes or attempts to make through his representatives to correct the system basically undoes or prevents an action that someone else wanted or aimed for through other representatives. In the modern system, one side's victory is the other side's loss.

And so a citizen's action necessarily invigorates a slew of others—Republicans stir up Democrats; the clean air advocates rile the tobacco lobbies to further action; environmentalists agitate the oil companies for more protection; financial regulations give banks incentive to find new ways to capitalize on their consumers. In a closed system, one group's action always leads to another group's reaction, and the process continues until everyone is affected.

Politically minded individuals will simply view this condition as a challenge. If we face a closed system with no real alternatives, then the only thing to do is to join in the fracas and get as much of the action as possible. The idea is to form some sort of lobby, ignite a campaign, or organize a special interest to extract as much funding, underwriting, or subsidy from the system as can be mustered.

These days, no one can afford to sit by and do nothing, and so everyone takes part and forms a special interest to gain political power. Manufacturers, teachers, engineers, farmers, secretaries, accountants, doctors, bankers, and so on—everyone must take part or else lose out. Indeed, this football fan recently learned that the NFL has a political action committee. Apparently, no one is exempt.

Anyone can see the trap that is set. By attempting to control the system through lobbies, campaigns, and special interests, these few politically minded activists only agitate others to join in and do the same. So more lobbies are initiated, more campaigns are run, and more special interests are formed in order to get more from the system, ultimately inducing even more of the same action. The more diligent and persuasive a group is, the more power they can obtain. Everyone involved is compelled to jump in on one side or the other and compete for control of the system that no one can afford to reject or deny. Since everyone has a stake in the game, and no one can deny the benefit of joining in, it becomes a massive tug-of-war that can only end in lots of muddy participants.

*   *   *

This vignette shows us in capsule form what happens when alternatives are eliminated from a given situation. Like clockwork, the powerful end up dictating, and so everyone is forced to compete for power, which only leads to an ever-escalating quest for control over others. This is the condition in which we live in early twenty-first century America. Without viable alternatives, everyone must adhere to the dictates of those in power, whether it is the Democrats or Republicans, the corporations or the unions. Given such a predicament, it is only reasonable to strive to achieve control, and so ensues a never ending struggle to obtain and hold power over everyone else.

The goal of this book is to examine this condition, how it came about in our society and how it comes about in general, the major consequences of such a situation, and, in the end, potential solutions. The primary source of reference is Western Civilization in the last five hundred years. As we will see, this slice of culture shows us exactly what happens when a closed system opens and then closes again. During the last five hundred years, we have experienced a wave of change that has taken us from one extreme to the other and back again, as if in a great tragedy.

The Western story is emblematic primarily because its signposts are so vivid in our historical imagination. At the end of the fifteenth century, the system was closed with nowhere to go, much like it is today. With the discovery of America, the system suddenly opened up, after which came an era of revolution and growth. Toward the end of the nineteenth century, however, the frontier closed, and a sort of cultural reversal set in. In our age, the West again finds itself locked in a closed system, not unlike that from which it emerged around 1500, and braces for what critics have warned will be another Dark Ages.

The plan of this book follows this rough sketch: The first part examines the discovery of the New World and the economic significance of its exploration and colonization. The second section opens with a survey of the close of the frontier, which occurred around 1890 and more or less brought an end to the era of expansion and growth, followed by an examination of the consequences of the close, namely interdependency and the competition for wealth and resources. The third part looks at the rather logical solution to this problem: the development of a welfare statist system and the large-scale control of wealth by central governments. It concludes with an appraisal of Statism and its moral effect. Finally, in the fourth part, having examined the root problem and the failed solution of government intervention, the text aims at a viable solution, which centers largely on self-sufficiency and independence—a moving forward to the new kind of life first experienced after the discovery of the New World.

* * *

If nothing else, this argument should be seen as a way to understand current troubles as more than just the intentional conspiracy of some group of malicious others. These days, it is all too easy to assign the ills of the world to some political party or contingent of the population, such as the corporations or the unions. All of the elements of the modern system arose from valid aims and are sustained by human beings. They are no more malicious or devious than the average voter or consumer or worker, and they should shoulder no more of the blame than anyone else.

That is to say that the average voter, consumer, and worker is no more exempt from blame than the great political parties, corporations, or unions.

Indeed, individuals and families are as responsible as those hated organizations, if not more so, because it is from the actions and desires of individuals that large companies and government bureaucracies derive their power. What reckless manufacturer, for instance, would be able to continue its egregious pollution if no consumer bought its products? What politician could curtail freedoms and aid a special interest if the citizens of the country refused to put up with a system that enabled such corruption? It is a truth widely recognized that tyranny stems from the consent of the governed as much as democracy does.

The fact is that consumers value highly the nearly infinite supply of cheap, reliable goods available at Walmart and Target; they enjoy McDonald's delicious, fatty foods and Microsoft's highly functional software. If these great corporations did not provide what consumers wanted, then the corporations couldn't act as they wished. Voters want 'free' health care and social security, protection and the removal of risk in financial investments. If the government didn't provide what the people wanted, then it would not have been able to grow so dominant in the first place. There isn't a conspiracy—everyday people are just getting what they're asking for.

Of course, exploitation does exist, and so do shady back-room meetings of twelve fat men—one such meeting took place in 1910 on Jekyll Island. But even so, the U.S. and other world economies are too large for any limited conspiracy to control completely, and must rely on everyone else to be carried through. This is to say that the problems we face as a people are not the intentional plans of some devious plot, but rather a natural manifestation of the system as a whole.

The system—what a concept! In common usage it implies a swollen leviathan that regulates the status quo and dictates the actions and thoughts of everyone in sight. In reality, it is nothing more than the complex organization of all social, political, and economic institutions—institutions that we, the average citizens, comprise almost wholly. At first glance, one might assume that these institutions are controlled by those at the top—the politicians, the CEOs, the bankers, the twelve fat men, and so on—but those figureheads only wield power because the populace is so willing to be over-powered. The fact that the large majority of Americans are largely content with their standard of living is proof of the system's appeal. And so it must be said that the people are as responsible for their condition as the fat men in shadowy rooms; indeed, they are just the instrument, and *we* are actually the system.

The Catch

Most citizens are content to let things go in Washington and New York if only because they are content with the standard of living they have been afforded by the system. One naturally feels the urge to stand up, protest, and revolt in some way when seeing the corruption at the top, but the insti-tutions that he would have to strike out against and reform are the same ones that he relies on for basic needs—food, shelter, security, and so on. A shopper might despise the way Walmart crowds out mom-and-pop stores, for instance, but cannot argue with the lower prices and convenience the behemoth offers; a parent might disapprove of Chinese labor policies, but cannot dispute the value of his child's clothes; a voter might frown on his congressman's earmarks, but cannot possibly vote for the other party—that would be defection.

Modern living props up the society that everyone knows is corrupt, and yet nobody can imagine living in any other way. Spending more for home-made items puts a consumer at a disadvantage; voting for the other party means that one's interests won't be looked after. One is encouraged to wake up to the iniquities being thrown upon him by the system, but he cannot overturn that system because he relies upon it for his well-being. He is the system that he would overturn.

And so there is something of a catch inherent in modern civilization. Everyone knows that the system is fraudulent and corrupt, but no one dares to try to reform it because it gives him what he wants. Any attempt at revolt or reform would disrupt and threaten his own well-being, which most people cannot afford. Reform in general is like trying to move a rug that you're standing on—doing so will only knock you down. It is better to stabilize yourself and let someone else try the move if they are so inclined. Of course, stabilizing yourself makes it more difficult for others to make the move, as they now have to contend with extra weight. In the end, no one attempts the reform and the system just grows more and more cumbersome.

This brings to light a troubling fact about the modern system that makes the predicament seem rather hopeless indeed. To accomplish anything in today's system, especially in the case of reform, one must address the problem with his own form of a lobby group, political action committee, or an actual political campaign. One can see the catch here in full view: To fix the ills of the modern system, one must support it and foster its ways, thus exacerbating those ills. To solve the problem, one must become a part of it and thus make it worse.

Given such a paradox, it is no wonder that most people simply stay away from it. Most Americans want nothing to do with the vast bureaucracies that make up our sprawling politico-economic system; they would rather focus on their personal endeavors, their jobs, their families, and so on. Of course, their staying away from the bureaucracy tends to make matters even worse.

They are the ones that the system needs most to come in and straighten things out. The more decent persons are repulsed by the system, the more corrupt the system becomes and thus requires their help. The more the system requires their help, the more repulsed they become.

And so the system continues to grow more complex and less stable, and at the same time makes it impossible for anyone to do anything to fix it. It is a self-perpetuating, uncontrollable Juggernaut that can only lead to catastrophe. The irony of our condition brings to mind Doc Daneeka's assessment of Catch-22 in Joseph Heller's classic satire, in which one condition leads automatically to its contradiction: "Orr would be crazy to fly more missions and sane if he didn't, but if he was sane he had to fly them. If he flew them he was crazy and didn't have to; but if he didn't want to he was sane and had to." Likewise, everyone knows that it is irrational to get involved in politics, so, as a matter of course, the rational stay away and only the irrational get involved, thus making government more and more irrational and making it more and more necessary for rational people to get involved to save it. It is some catch, indeed.

* * *

By the same token, there are those who claim that the ever-growing state is simply a necessary evil in the modern world, and that its costs are hardly a dear price to pay for the high standard of living we experience in America today. And no one can deny that Americans are very well off. Regarding conditions in Mexico, Russia, China, and Iran, for example, and even in other first-world nations such as Italy, Spain, and Sweden, one can easily see how much luxury we take for granted here, even in the midst of a deep recession. If, the thought goes, the enormous bureaucracy we call the system is necessary for our standard of living, then it is a price we should be eager to pay.

However reasonable, this is to focus on the standard of living and material luxuries of our culture to the neglect of intellectual and political necessities. It is to say that a comfortable life is more valuable than anything else, even the ability to choose what kind of comforts to enjoy. It is my belief that, if given the choice, most Americans would be willing to give up a little political freedom to guarantee the high standard of living they have grown to depend on. Such is the trade-off that a consumerist culture makes, the assumption being that we must suffer a great reduction in luxuries before we can enjoy full political freedom.

Whether or not we would have to suffer such a reduction, this mentality must be rejected on two counts. First, it is impossible to maintain the kind of deficit spending and debt that our country has incurred. The wealth we have invented to pay for all our luxuries and bailouts must come from somewhere at some point—it cannot just appear ex nihilo, out of thin air. Eventually, the liability will catch up to us and, when it does, there will be no way of meeting that obligation and a great fallout will result. Most people logically believe that such a crash couldn't happen in their lifetime, so they simply don't worry about it and instead encourage its perpetuation. Such a mentality is just kicking the can down the road and in the end will lead to much of the suffering we find so unacceptable now. It won't be in this generation, and possibly not the next, but it will come at some point and it will be cataclysmic.

Second, and more significant, the notion that material freedoms are more important than political freedoms is a fallacy whose importance cannot be stressed enough. Both are essential to human life and prosperity, and neither can be sacrificed for the benefit of the other. The belief that we can simply sacrifice a little political freedom for a wealth of material freedom is a contradiction in fact that amounts to an effort to provide liberty through coercion.

In the end, it cannot be said for certain that we must give up our material freedoms to regain our political liberty. One might well argue that the original goal of modern economics and civilization as a whole was to provide total freedom in both realms, and that gravitation toward one came only as an oversight, not as a necessary consequence. The solution to this problem has yet to be found, and it is unlikely that reform will come before it is. In the meantime, the system will continue to grow, and the people will continue to feed it with their souls.

* * *

To further explain this contradictory state of affairs and to help neutralize it is the purpose of this book. After all, the great towering system that reigns such hegemony over us has reasonable, defensible origins. The catastrophes that loom have been born of a logical progression from the very essence of our political and economic foundations. Understanding those foundations is essential if we seek to understand how they have evolved into the several crises we see throughout the world today.

The metaphor I have used to illustrate our condition is that of the Juggernaut, a term that has many connotations today, not the least of which is specifically suited for our aims. The legend of the Juggernaut originated during Far East travels of fourteenth-century British explorers, who returned with tales of a grand Hindu procession that drew devotees from hundreds of miles away. At the center of the march was a massive 45-foot chariot car that carried the local religious clerics as well as statues of Jagannath, the Hindu god known later as Krishna. With no little embellishment, the fable described how fanatics would throw themselves under the wheels of the towering structure as it passed in order to display their devotion and attain salvation. The more fanatics that threw themselves before the Juggernaut, the bigger and more powerful it became, making it all the more uncontrollable and unstoppable.

The legend was a mix of folktale and political commentary on the wretched condition of the alleged savages. It is not known whether it also served as criticism of the Western Juggernaut then growing in the form of the Holy Roman Empire. Comparisons are inescapable. Nowadays, the legend serves as an allegory of the condition of our own civilization, the Juggernaut being the system and the zealots being the average citizens who so willfully throw themselves under the crushing, moving monstrosity for the salvation that is the easy life.

To find solutions to our various problems, we must first understand what those problems are and how we arrived at them. That story, insightful and fascinating in itself, begins five hundred years ago, when the Holy Roman Juggernaut was at its pinnacle and the notion of Capitalism was just a faint glimmer on the distant horizon.

I
WEALTH

1. MUNDUS NOVUS

IF THE MODERN ERA can be defined by a single question, it would be whether or not man is capable of self-government. Of all the ages in history, the question of self-rule has never been asked more often and more sincerely than during the last five hundred years. From the expansion westward during the Age of Exploration to the English Civil War, from the Enlightenment and the French and American Revolutions to the rise of Industrialism, the question that continually surfaced was whether men were capable of ruling their own destinies and cooperating with each other in a civil, mutually beneficial way.

The theme is best seen in what might be considered the era's central event, both chronologically and symbolically—the creation of the United States of America. As Alexander Hamilton stated at the opening of "Federalist No. 1", the creation of the new nation was a process "to decide the important question, whether societies of men are really capable or not of establishing good government from reflection and choice, or whether they are forever destined to depend for their political constitutions on accident and force." That is, in short, the story of the modern era, and it can be seen in almost all major developments therein.

Of course, the concept of self-rule has always been a part of the Western tradition, with roots in early Judaism and Christianity, Athenian democracy, and the Roman republic. The Stoics were perhaps the greatest proponents of self-rule, dedicated as they were to discipline and self-control. But it was only in the modern era that the idea of self-governance became a driving force in culture, capable of shaping the hearts and minds of the public at large, guiding customs, and altering social organization altogether. Whereas self-rule had been promoted theoretically and rather disingenuously in the past, now people were willing to put it into practice. It had become compelling and real.

The catalyst for this breakthrough cannot be mistaken. Shortly after 1500, a small book had begun to circulate that included a letter from a little-known naval observer named Amerigo Vespucci. It recounted the recent westward explorations of Christopher Columbus and others, and bore the provocative title *Mundus Novus*—'New World'. The words alone ignite the imagination, but what did they mean? To be sure, Vespucci asserted that Columbus had been wrong when he claimed to have reached India on his voyages in the 1490s. According to Vespucci, rather, the islands that Columbus and his men discovered signified a new continent, which had previously been undiscovered and unsettled—it was, in a very real sense, a mundus novus.

Monumental as it stands in retrospect, this was the decisive event of the period, splitting into two distinct parts the age that preceded it and the age that followed. Prior to the discovery, there was Medieval Christendom, faith, feudalism; after, there was modernity, science, Capitalism. An entire culture had suddenly turned itself in a new direction.

This change was especially apparent with regard to the question of self-rule. Prior to the discovery, the question had been settled—men were incapable of self-rule and at least some form of hierarchical government was needed to maintain peace and order. Whence the feudal system of medieval civilization. After the discovery, however, critical doubts began to form about the legitimacy of the system as it stood, and almost as soon as word spread of the discovery of the New World, ideas of Individualism, personal autonomy, and self-governance flooded the Western spirit and forever changed the world.

The Law of the Land

To know why the discovery amounted to so much, it is first necessary to understand what life was like before the pivotal event. And, while it would take a lengthy survey to truly understand Medieval Europe, it is possible to grasp a few broad aspects of the culture here.

Prior to the sixteenth century, the West was rather fixed. Its social constructs, institutions, and customs were embodied in the monolithic Catholic Church and the Holy Roman Empire, which had dominated the civilization for more than a millennium. These pillars of culture had grown to become as immovable in their places as the earth itself was immovable in the universe, such that even gross corruption and injustice could not disturb their foundation.

In Medieval Europe, the big questions had all been answered, and life was relatively balanced and stagnant. A document dated 1493 expresses the sense of fixity well. In his *Nüremberg Chronicle*, German scholar Hartmann Schedel declared that the sixth age of man was coming to a close and offered several blank pages to record any notable events that might happen in the last days. The author's conviction was characteristic of a culture confident in its ways and certain that it comprised all that there was to consider in the world.

There were, of course, many reasons for this dual characteristic of confidence and fixity, but perhaps the most compelling was the limited availability of land. The system, from the church authority in Rome and Constantinople to the various fiefdoms throughout the continent, was based largely on the ownership of land. In medieval times, land was much like money in today's economy. Everyone needed food, shelter, clothing, and other resources to survive, and one could only satisfy these necessities by possessing and making use of land—by farming crops, harvesting timber, stone, iron ore, and so on. As such, whoever owned land owned competency and so could live and prosper in the medieval economy; whoever did not own land was left at a disadvantage.

Like money today, all efforts were made to secure and maintain land. Owners would hold onto it, seek to acquire more, and pass it down by lineage so as to ensure family possession of the plot. But, by the fifteenth century, all available land had been claimed. Beginning as far back as the third and fourth centuries, in a gradual, organic process, masses of people migrated from the cities of the late Roman Empire and settled throughout the European countryside, filling the continent with settlements.

Not long after this deurbanization took place, the entire countryside had been accounted for, and all available land was controlled. The fact that Medieval Europe was pressed for land could be seen in the Crusades of the eleventh, twelfth, and thirteenth centuries, which were launched in part as a way for Christian kingdoms to expand territorially. Simply, there was no more room on the continent, and so everyone had to make do with what they had.

Naturally, many people were left without possession of the essential soil and thus faced a tough proposition. To obtain competency, they relied on landowners. This resulted in a sort of long-term trade, a lifetime contract in which one would offer labor and services for the ability to live and work on the land with the possibility of becoming an owner himself. Landowners controlled their regions as lords and demanded labor from those who lived on it. The feudal system was born.

Feudal contracts typically took one of two forms based on the owner's two crucial needs. First, the landowner required military protection. Given the fact that land was scarce, the lord of a dominion lived under constant threat of invasion by rival lords. Similarly, he was always tempted to invade neighboring lands to increase his own holdings. As a result, military was indispensable. Local warriors—vassals or knights, as they were known—

could make a contract with the lord to provide military service and protection in exchange for a plot of land in the lord's dominion for their own use.

Second, the lord required a sizeable contingent of farmers and artisans to live on his land and produce necessary goods like food, clothing, shelter, furniture, tapestries, armor, and so on. Thus, peasants, or serfs, would trade manual labor and agricultural skills for land and protection by the local vassals. Just like the knights, the serfs formed a sort of contract, trading their services for sustenance and security.

Because the land was largely controlled, this system could remain unchanged for an indefinite time. Rarely could a vassal gain enough land to control a significant dominion, nor could peasants readily rise in status and become landowners themselves. For the most part, the lords in power could demand whatever they wanted from their knights and serfs, arranging their contracts in such a way that the lords were benefited to a greater degree than their counterparts. In effect, the lords used their possessions to gain more possessions. Landowners were more or less kings and ruled their dominion with their own laws, which were typically aimed at maintaining the order and hierarchy of the fiefdom.

These days, we would label this a form of exploitation and frown on the whole system for such an obvious denial of freedom. After all, 'serf' means 'slave'. Today, we take for granted the virtues of free choice and democracy and assume that without them life would be worthless. To us, the fact that Medieval Europeans did not embrace these virtues means that they were backward and therefore despicable.

But the brash critic fails to view feudal ways from the medieval perspective. To the average lord, vassal, or even serf, feudalism served as a workable arrangement between men who could provide each other mutual benefit—the lord provided land, vassals provided military support, and serfs and artisans provided food and practical goods. As such, the system was based on mutual need and a bond between men, not tyrannous exploitation.

Certainly, lords would at times exploit their vassals, and vassals would take advantage of their serfs. The infamous Primae Noctis as depicted in the film *Braveheart* illustrates the kind of exploitation that must have taken place throughout Medieval Europe. Even though the particularly heinous diktat has been proven largely fabricated, there is no reason to doubt that similar abuse did occur.

What is evident, however, is that exploitation, when it did take place, could not have persisted for any extended period of time. Lords needed military service and food production as much as vassals and serfs needed land. Everyone needed everyone else. It was a sort of interlocking puzzle with each piece necessarily holding up the others. Abuse from any one party would be detrimental to everyone, and so there was a natural impulse to limit exploitation. Ultimately, bondage was for all parties, not just the peasants. In any case, there was no real alternative to such a system, even if it was disagreeable. The kingdoms had been drawn out, and all land had been accounted for. Even if the serfs had mounted an uprising against their oppressors, they wouldn't have been able to change the geopolitical dynamic in any meaningful way, nor could they flee to the Mediterranean like Spartacus. Hierarchy was a fact of life in Medieval Europe, a fact which hinged on the limited availability of land.

A New Dawn

After 1492, all of that changed. With the discovery of the New World, the limits which had constrained the system were suddenly and irrevocably lifted, and a new way of life dawned in Western Civilization. No longer was power limited to the lord of the dominion, one of a few owners of land and the means of production; as the people of Europe would come to realize, everyone could own land and the means of production, and so everyone could be lord of his own dominion. This simple concept was to be the basis for a new paradigm.

Of course, this revolution in thought did not come about instantaneously. The date 1492 did not mean nearly as much to a Castilian or Portuguese of the time as it does to an American or Brazilian of today. Indeed, the magnitude of Columbus' discovery was not understood until decades after he first set foot on San Salvador Island. It wasn't until 1513, for example, when Balboa first crossed the Isthmus of Panama to view the Pacific Ocean, that Europeans could be sure an isolated continent rested between their home and Asia. Not until Magellan circumnavigated the globe in 1522 did anyone know how large the world really was.

And so, as a matter of historical fact, the cultivation of individual autonomy was a long and uncertain process. It took time for the people to understand that the New World was an entirely new continent, and even longer for them to realize that its discovery meant an alternative to their current situation; even then, most were unable to do anything about it. They may have longed to set sail for the Indies in order to make a new life, but had neither the money required for such a voyage nor the connections needed to facilitate it. It would be another 250 years before trans-Atlantic traffic was frequent enough to enable a typical Briton or Spaniard to hop aboard a ship and sail to America.

Still, a liberating force pulling westward was felt immediately throughout the Old World. To be sure, the expansionary push began decades before Columbus had even approached Isabella for his charter. The fall of Constantinople in 1453 meant that trade with the East had been effectively cut off, and Western kingdoms—especially Portugal—grew eager to find an ocean route. In the process, the Portuguese discovered a slew of smaller new worlds—the Cape Verde archipelago in 1456, Sierra Leone in 1460, the Gold Coast in 1471, and the Cape of Good Hope, which was named the Cape of Storms by Bartolomeu Dias in 1488. By the time Vasco da Gama first sailed to India in 1497 to '99, the sense was that the world was much bigger than had been previously assumed, and that it was somehow up to Western ingenuity to engineer a way to harness it.

After Columbus, there followed a flurry of exploration. Juan Ponce de León reached Florida in 1513, Balboa explored Panama and sighted the Pacific in the same year, and Magellan sailed around the globe between

1519 and '22. Hernán Cortés led a small army against the Aztecs in Mexico 1519-22, Francisco Pizarro conquered the Incans in Peru in 1532-33, and Pedro de Mendoza founded a colony near modern-day Buenos Aries, Argentina in 1536. Cabeza de Vaca journeyed into the American Southwest in the early-1530s, Hernando de Soto explored the Gulf Coast of Southeast America in the late 1530s, and Vásquez de Coronado discovered the Grand Canyon in 1540.

With all of these expeditions came some amount of settlement and colonization. It is estimated that, by 1520, there were already some 10,000 Spanish-speaking Europeans on the island of Hispaniola alone. Colonial Brazil was established as early as 1500, and the viceroy of New Spain flourished throughout Central and South America starting in 1521.

The influence of the early colonies was evident in Charles V's attempt to reign in Spain's increasingly powerful and largely autonomous satellites by establishing the Council of the Indies. His efforts were in vain. The western hemisphere was simply too distant to allow for consistent control and, at the same time, too rich in resources for the colonists to remain dependent on the crown. The consequence was twofold: As the flow of people and energy continued westward, the idea of freedom and self-rule burgeoned with it.

Exploration was a wholly European phenomenon, too, not simply limited to Portugal and Spain. France began expeditions around 1524 under the command of Italian Giovanni da Verrazano. New France dates from 1534 and, at its peak, stretched from modern-day Newfoundland and Northern Canada to Louisiana and the Gulf Coast. British exploration didn't begin until 1584, when Sir Walter Raleigh commissioned Philip Amadas and Arthur Barlowe to scout what is now the North Carolina coast. Those expeditions ended in failed outposts, but British colonization thrived the first permanent British settlement was established at Jamestown, Virginia in 1607. The Dutch followed in 1609 with Henry Hudson's founding of New Netherlands and the city of New Amsterdam, which soon became New York.

The names of the colonies are evidence of the Europeans' view of the endeavor. Exploration was a way to create their world anew, not simply to extend what had already been established. Everywhere across Europe, eyes turned westward. The discovery, exploration, and colonization of far-off lands stirred spirits and opened up possibilities for all, and the overwhelming sense amid the fervor was that of liberation.

Naturally, the first expeditions were crown endeavors, which meant they required sanction and funding from the royal sovereigns. The trouble Columbus encountered in obtaining a charter was characteristic of the first voyages—he was rejected at Portugal, Genoa, Venice, and twice at Spain before Isabella finally took a chance on him. But, once reports began to trickle in of the New World's abundance and fertility, everyone with the wherewithal became eager to invest in the prospect. The zeal for kings and queens to establish a presence in the New World meant that, by the mid-sixteenth century, any suitable group that was willing to undertake the adventure would likely be granted a charter. Raleigh's private capitalization paved the way for independent colonizers from across Europe.

Modern Americans will recognize the fervor experienced during the age of exploration as similar to the kind of enthusiasm witnessed during economic booms such as the dot-com frenzy of the 1990s or the housing boom of the aughts—everyone had to get involved. Perhaps the greatest hindrance to immigration was fear of the hardships of early colonial life. Stories of savages, of hot and humid summers and brutally cold winters, of disease and death, all dampened the spirits of potential immigrants. And yet the opportunity was there for anyone who could bear the adversity of such an adventure, and, as the drawbacks were alleviated over time, it proved increasingly inviting to any individual or group seeking a new life.

The quintessential example was that of the Separatist congregation in England, which sailed to America under the sponsorship of the Plymouth Company. After increasing ecclesiastical scrutiny, as well as constant derision from neighbors, the congregation attempted to migrate from London to the more tolerant Amsterdam. When that settlement failed and the English crown drew up charges on one member of the congregation, William Brewster, the group hastened their search for another alternative. The solution was to form a colony in the New World.

Their story is known to all—the Mayflower voyage, the landing at Plymouth Rock, the first winter and Thanksgiving feast, the arrival of John Winthrop, and the expansion of the colony. At its heart is the idea central to the American culture—a persecuted, oppressed people finding freedom and salvation in America.

It is the story of the age. Everywhere across Europe a new vision formed in the minds of men. It was no longer necessary to put up with the faulty and restrictive ways of the Old World. The New World provided an escape, an opportunity to make a new start.

In his "Reasons" for venturing to America, John Winthrop summarized the consensus mindset: "This, Land grows weary of her Inhabitants, so as man, who is the most pretious of all creatures, is here more vile and base then the earth we tread upon. We are grown to that height of intemperance in all excess of riot as no man's estate almost will suffice to keep sail with his equals; and who fails herein must live in scorn and contempt. Hence it comes that all arts and trades are carried in that deceitful and unrighteous course as it is almost impossible for a good and upright man to maintain his charge and live comfortably in any of them." In the Old World, life was harsh, restrictive, and corrupt; the New World was the only source of deliverance.

Discovering Utopia

The most fascinating aspect about this revolution is the fact that it was open to everyone, not just those who were willing to make the voyage westward. Even those individuals or groups who had no wherewithal to make the journey to America could rely on the mere prospect of leaving to improve their conditions. As Europeans who stayed behind found that the potential of the New World was alone sufficient to change the attitudes and principles of peasants and artisans as well as nobles and lords. Once the opportunity to migrate westward had been made known, everyone was given a freedom of choice that made it impossible for the existing order of bondage and servitude to persist.

To the Europeans longing for a new life, it did not matter that the New World was ready to be settled or even that it was easily accessible; what mattered most to the Europeans of the age was simply that the New World existed. From that vague starting point, man's fertile imagination was all that was needed to effect change.

The promise that this new horizon provided to optimistic Westerners can be glimpsed in the literary genre that blossomed in 1516 and flourished throughout the latter half of the sixteenth century—the Utopia. Beginning with Thomas More's groundbreaking work, which coined the term, the genre eventually came to define a culture coming to grips with the possibilities of an entirely new way of life. Through descriptions of imaginary societies, authors were able to explain the faults of their real-life societies and thereby posit solutions. To the visionaries who engaged in utopian literature, as well as to their readers, the New World not only represented a place where Christendom could grow and prosper, but also a place where new political and social structures could be built.

English translations of the complete title of More's classic book more fully describe the aim of the idealistic genre: *A Truly Golden Little Book, No Less Beneficial Than Entertaining, of the Best State of a Republic, and of the New Island Utopia*. Though the notion of designing the perfect society was not invented in the sixteenth century, the practice was given credence only with the opening of the New World.

After *Utopia*, there followed no fewer than 12 outstanding works in the genre, including Rabelais' 'Abbaye de Thélème' (1534), Lodovico Agostini's 'Repubblica immaginaria' (1583-90), Tommaso Campanella's *City of the Sun* (1602), Robert Burton's 'Utopia of Mine Own' (1621), and Francis Bacon's *New Atlantis* (1626). Even Shakespeare fell under the utopian spell with *The*

Tempest (1611), in which Gonzalo issues his vision of the ideal society he would like to establish on a remote island. Everywhere, the focus was on doing away with the old, the restrictive, and the oppressive, and producing a new life, ideal and virtuous.

Reform in this sense began almost as soon as the New World was discovered and affected nearly all aspects of early modern life. The area in which it was most significant and unambiguous was the most important aspect of life at the time—religion. If there was a consistent theme throughout the utopias of the age, it was that of religious practice and toleration. Naturally, religion dominated early modern thought and action, and so it was the centerpiece of the most prominent utopia of all, Martin Luther's *Ninety-Five Theses*, a vision of the Church's fundamental tenets and the basis for the reform needed to achieve them.

> **If you suffer your people to be ill-educated, and their manners to be corrupted from their infancy, and then punish them for those crimes to which their first education disposed them, what else is to be concluded from this but that you first make thieves and then punish them?**
>
> —THOMAS MORE, *UTOPIA* (1516)

The Protestant Reformation was, more than anything, a revolution that led to bloody sectarian wars that lasted no less than a century. At its root, however, was the simple idea that all men should be free to assert their beliefs and live under their own rule—a utopian ideal to be sure. And, like all utopias of the age, the idea could only have come about during the age of discovery. Certainly, the Reformation had many causes, most of which had been brewing in the Western mind for centuries. But only when the possibility of Utopia was introduced with the discovery of the New World could the revolution gain the energy necessary to move forward.

The fact that the Reformation had been spurred by a new mindset and not a new method could be seen in the acute trigger for the Reformation—the distribution of the *Ninety-Five Theses*. By posting such a work on the door to the Wittenberg Cathedral, Luther was certainly not being revolutionary—his action was a typical practice for anyone who wanted to spark debate. But the ideas were so potent that they were quickly reproduced, distributed, and printed in his native German, all without Luther's sanction. The message was rife, and soon it could be heard trumpeted all around Europe. The thunderous refrain could only mean an end to the old way of doing things—men were free, and the concept of self-rule was to be the driving force of the next five hundred years.

The Rebirth of the Natural Law

With our short survey, we begin to see a subtle truth about the Age of Discovery. As historian J. M. Roberts put it, the real discovery of the age did not take place in the Western hemisphere on San Salvador Island, but rather in the minds of men. It was there that the laws and constructs of the Old World existed and were maintained, and only there that new ones could be fashioned. If there was a New World at all, it was not in the Americas, but in the hearts and heads of the men looking on from Spain, France, Britain, and Germany.

What was this discovery? To understand it calls for a new theory of political economy. It can be assumed that men are born free and so are naturally capable of self-rule; but self-rule requires the ability to at least reject the prevailing hierarchy, which means that a people must be able to survive and flourish on their own. In short, self-rule is workable only when a people are *self-sufficient* enough to reject the hierarchic system as it stands. Prior to the discovery of the New World, men may have been capable of self-government, but without self-sufficiency they faced definitive barriers. After the discovery, men could be self-sufficient, and thus self-rule came quite naturally.

Now, 'self-sufficiency' is a somewhat ambiguous term that can mean different things to different people. These days, the term has come to mean 'isolationist' and 'positively resistant to cooperation of all kinds'. We think of the word 'autarky' as it is used to describe mercantilist states from the early modern era or China up to the late twentieth century. But, at their root, both 'self-sufficiency' and 'autarky' mean merely 'independence' or 'the ability to sustain oneself'. Indeed, it is possible to be self-sufficient and at the same time engaged in a high volume of trade and cooperation—as long as one has the ability to provide for himself, he can trade and interact all he wants. The key is personal autonomy, which can certainly take the form of isolationism, though it does not have to.

The political economist will find that this principle applies to all aspects of the social interaction. In order for any economic transaction to be sound and just, all participants must be self-sufficient, or able to provide for themselves. Only when one is self-sufficient can he reject a contract that he finds exploitative or disagreeable in any way. He can take or leave it depending on how valuable the exchange is to him. When he is not self-sufficient, on the other hand, when he is needy or lacking in any fundamental way, he is more or less forced to engage in the contract whether or not he finds the terms beneficial.

Thus, exchanges made when one or more parties is not self-sufficient, like those characteristic of the Middle Ages, tend to be exploitative and lead to a kind of hierarchy. On the other hand, exchanges made when all parties are self-sufficient, like those characteristic of the modern era, tend to be voluntary and thus mutually beneficial. Thus, the result of self-sufficiency is a basic form of self-rule, or 'autarchy' as it might be called.

It is reasonable that the terms 'autarky' and 'autarchy' are homonyms—after all, the concepts go hand-in-hand. Self-sufficiency (autarky) necessarily leads to self-rule (autarchy) and vice versa; one cannot exist without the other. To the early moderns, this concept became clear, if only subliminally. While the widespread social changes needed to bring about true autonomy in the form of democratic nations would require generations of work, the stage had been set in the sixteenth century, and many developments of the age reflected the growing standard.

Consider, as reference, the fundamental advances made in the West during the century that followed the discovery of the New World: the emergence of commerce, merchantry, and the bourgeois middle-class as the dominant socioeconomic force; the rise of autonomous artists, such as Michelangelo, Raphael, Leonardo, and Rubens, who were able to dictate their terms and often worked as ambassador for their patrons; the invention of unique human character in drama and psychology by Shakespeare and Montaigne, respectively; the rebirth of rationalism and self-determination in science, from which the work of Copernicus, Giordano Bruno, Galileo, and René Descartes could all blossom; the development of personal liberty and natural rights in political theory, on which John Locke's philosophy was founded; and, of course, the upsurge of Protestantism across Europe, the founding of hundreds of separate Christian sects, and the push toward a more personal connection with God.

These monumental developments in human thought signaled the beginning of an era of growth and refinement, and all were built on the notion of the autonomy of the individual. It is not a leap to suggest that all of the distinctive advances made between 1500 and today, for better or worse, were directly or indirectly brought about by the dissolution of feudal bonds and the rise of individual autonomy.

This freedom from bondage was, in essence, an economic event. Though the nascent individual was beginning to make use of his autonomy throughout the culture—in the arts, religion, and

> The world is not only what exists out there, it is also the picture we have of it in our minds, which enables us to take a grip on material actuality.
>
> —J. M. ROBERTS,
> THE TRIUMPH OF THE WEST (1986)

so on—all of these innovations were the fruit of self-sufficiency and economic independence. The reason sixteenth-century painter Paolo Veronese could demand license for his flourishes, the philosopher Descartes could publish his work without fear of persecution, and the solitary monk could ask forgiveness directly from God, was that they could all reject the prevailing system; they could reject the system because they were able to survive without it.

This liberation of thought and action is perhaps best seen in the most substantial economic development of the modern era—the resurgence of the Natural Law by Francisco de Vitoria and the Spanish Scholastics. Of course, not many readers today will recognize such an obscure name, nor are they likely to view the rebirth of the Natural Law as very significant, though its gates are wide indeed. If the rise of self-rule was the central event of the modern era, the argument for the Natural Law was its driving intellectual force.

The Natural Law asserted that all men had the same innate nature in that they all had access to God's law through right reason. As a result, all men shared the right to live freely and to do what they wanted with their own property so long as it did not infringe upon others to do the same. The concept of natural rights is prosaic today, but it was revolutionary in Vitoria's time. Feudalism had so dominated the public imagination that the concepts of natural rights and equal justice under a universal law were completely foreign. For most, the law of the land was the law of the king or lord. Serfs, artisans, and merchants were all peasants and thus beneath the law of the court.

Francisco de Vitoria was certainly no king. With a Jewish converso background, he studied at the Sorbonne in Paris before returning to Spain, where he taught theology at Valladolid from 1523 to '26 before becoming Prime Chair of Theology at the University of Salamanca in 1526. At Salamanca, Vitoria became nothing short of a legend. Through tracts, lectures, and debates, he formulated a body of ideas that reverberated throughout Charles V's empire, and he assembled a group of thinkers who would challenge the culture's long-standing traditions.

This School of Salamanca, as it became known, was founded on the concept of the Natural Law. Reviving thirteenth-century proofs made by Thomas Aquinas, Vitoria and his fellow Scholastics argued that the only true law was God's law and that no man—not even a lord—could know it completely. Men could access God's law through right reason, however, and since all men possessed the ability to reason, all men were capable of discerning

God's law. In short, Vitoria and his School of Salamanca put the case for self-rule into rational argument. Not only was self-rule now possible, thanks to the discovery of the New World, so too was it God's will.

With the Natural Law as their foundation, the Spanish Scholastics forged the way for nearly all economic progress that followed. From the concept of value to the notion of private property, from the foundations of industry to charging interest on loans, the Salamanca School covered the whole span of political economy, and, while the Scholastics were not able to devise a cohesive formula for political economy as a whole, certainly provided an adumbration of the theories that would later define the era.

The Scholastics' stress on the Natural Law, for instance, prefigured John Locke and the concept of the Social Contract; their ideas on property rights and profit-making anticipated Adam Smith and the eighteenth-century Enlightenment philosophers; and their concept of value was an early forerunner of Carl Menger and the Marginal Utility Theory of Value that arose in the nineteenth century. Altogether, the advances made by Vitoria and his Salamanca School amounted to a new political economy that introduced the era's most dominant form of social organization: Free-Market Capitalism.

For this reason, we can say that modern economics was born in the sixteenth century at the University of Salamanca. By most accounts, Adam Smith gets credit for the ideas that gave birth to Western political economy, mainly because he was able to consolidate those ideas into a single, coherent book of principles, which we know as *The Wealth of Nations*. But the central themes in Smith's work were conceived by the largely forgotten Spanish Scholastics centuries before Smith.

This is no discredit to Adam Smith, whose genius for clarity and eloquence is beyond question. Rather, it is to point out the fact that the ideas of industry and free trade had been circulating in the West well before 1776, when *The Wealth of Nations* was published, and that their flowering in the work of Adam Smith as well as the founding of the United States was a culmination and not a starting point, as it may seem. While Smith may have harvested the crops, the plant was being cultivated for some time.

The cultivation process took so long because culture is an intricate web of institutions and beliefs, and new ideas take time to penetrate the thick crust of custom. Old ways are hard to give up, especially when they have previously been successful. As cultural historian Jacques Barzun put it, "New ideas do not battle so much with ignorance as with solid knowledge°." That is why the ideas of the Salamanca School, revolutionary as they were, never convinced the powers in Madrid and were overlooked until Adam Smith became so renowned.

The Ills of Colonization

The effects of the new economic thought did not alter the face of Western Civilization right away. Indeed, throughout the sixteenth century and into the seventeenth, the ideas and practices that made up the free-market system were challenged incessantly by reactionary forces that upheld the longstanding beliefs of the feudal era. Taking advantage of the period's technical advances, these reactionaries were able to extend and multiply the ways of bondage, and, in so doing, successfully counteracted the liberating impulses of the age.

Here we find the root cause of a set of early modern contradictions. While the discovery of the New World made a new kind of freedom practical, we see in retrospect that this freedom was often used for ends that were restrictive, oppressive, and wholly unjust. At once, the early modern era saw an increase of both tolerance and fanaticism; of optimism for things to come and fear of the unknown; of unprecedented energy dedicated to the creative process and that dedicated to conquest and war. Altogether, the contradictory phase in the West's history can be characterized by the parallel trends of expanding freedom and intensifying enslavement.

While freedom ultimately prevailed, evenhandedness requires at least the acknowledgment of the cultural ills that came with the opening of the economy. And so, before concluding this survey of the effects of the New

World's discovery, it is necessary to touch on the various evils that came about as a result.

The main evil born of the age was the conquest and destruction of aboriginal peoples around the world. We are all familiar with the fact that Western expansion came mostly at the expense of the Amerindian and Afroindian peoples, the former being destroyed by war and disease, and the latter being humiliated and placed into chattel slavery.

It must be said that these developments were born of the age, not simply strengthened or exaggerated by it. After all, only with the colonization of the New World by the Europeans could a clash of cultures like that between the West and the Amerindians be so lopsided in favor of one or the other. Until the Age of Discovery, the only cultures that came in contact with one another were those that bordered each other or were otherwise engaged in frequent communication. This meant that all cultures were relatively uniform in technical abilities, military prowess, social constructs, and overall wherewithal. Witness the universality of feudalism, which stretched from Lisbon to Baghdad to Beijing at its height, and the general stalemate in martial conflict between the Occident and Orient.

By extending contact to peoples on continents that were formerly detached by impassable oceans and deserts, the period's exploration connected cultures that had advanced to vastly different degrees. By the sixteenth century, Westerners were far more powerful in nearly all aspects of life than the peoples of Africa, Southeast Asia, Australia, and America, and so they were practically granted free reign over their counterparts. To begin, the use of firearms, horses, and superior tactics meant that the colonists had a tremendous martial advantage over the native tribes. Only with this advantage could Westerners abduct slaves and conquer long-standing civilizations with minimal forces. The army Cortés used to conquer the Aztec civilization of around 25 million people, for instance, consisted of no more than 600 men.

What the military did not defeat, disease and other nonviolent intruders did. While the Americas had been isolated from much of the world's diseases before Columbus' discovery, the introduction of Europeans to the New World meant the introduction of smallpox, influenza, Bubonic plague, malaria, typhus, measles, cholera, tuberculosis, mumps, yellow fever, and the whooping cough, among other ailments. Europeans had fought these diseases and built up resistance to them over the previous centuries. Meanwhile, Amerind peoples, having built up no resistance, were utterly devastated by the illnesses. The coming of Europeans was in many respects like the Black Death, which had killed around one third of the people of Asia and Europe in the mid-fourteenth century. In the Americas, disease eliminated an estimated 90% of previous inhabitants.

By now, everyone knows the terrible injustices caused by African slavery and the invasion of America. Indeed, the story of European oppression over the natives of America, Africa, Asia, and Australia is so ingrained in the popular conscience that the typical grade-schooler might not realize that anything good came of the expansion.

However blatant these evils are considered today, there were harsh critics at the time as well. Neither the enslavement of the Africans nor the destruction of the Americans occurred as the result of a principled, unanimous effort by Europeans; both were promptly denounced and protested by a vocal many throughout the Old World.

As early as 1511, for example, the Dominican friar Antonio de Montesinos, who had studied at Salamanca and traveled as one of the first band of Dominicans to Hispaniola, preached ardently against the conscienceless brutality with which the natives were treated. His plea resonated with all who sensed the injustice: "Are these Indians not men? Do they not have rational souls? Are you not obliged to love them as you love yourselves?" To Montesinos and to others, the indigenous peoples had natural rights and freedom, just like Spaniards and Britons. And, even though the natives lived in a primitive 'prepolitical' state, Christians had no right to enslave them, make war against them, or take away their lands.

Montesinos was promptly censured and shipped back to Spain, where he attempted to argue his case before King Ferdinand. Eventually, with the help of other Scholastics, he was able to convince the king of the injustice in the situation and encourage some formal means of retribution. But the effort would ultimately prove futile. There was simply too much distance between the seat of power and the colonies. Formal restrictions were put in place, and yet mistreatment and enslavement continued. It was as if no voice of reason could be heard in the chaotic whirlwind of early colonization.

This is to bring to light one of the salient mysteries of the age, the contradictory nature of which has become clear upon centuries of reflection. The fact is that, while the New World represented a virgin continent to settle, thus providing Europeans with a new perspective on life and, ultimately, a new opportunity for freedom, it was in reality another people's land. And so, in order to make use of the new opportunity and secure freedom in the Occident, it was necessary to invade and conquer an innocent people.

The paradox could be seen most clearly in the efforts of Francisco de Vitoria to reestablish the Natural Law. He claimed that, for the Natural Law to be valid for any man, it had to be valid for all men, including natives of America and the other continents. Since the Amerindians were men and had reason by nature, they too owned the right to life, liberty, and property. With this rationale as a guideline, Vitoria pioneered the first concept of international law, which sought to govern actions between nations using the same principles of internal order. To Vitoria, all peoples were capable of, and thus deserved, self-rule.

Paradoxically, the most significant obstacle to the fair treatment of natives in the New World lay in the very argument used to defend them, as it was the colonization of the New World that allowed the Natural Law to return to the European conscience. In effect, Vitoria and other Spanish Scholastics were using the principle of the Natural Law to challenge and curb the expansion that had helped to justify it. It is the great irony of the age that the free land presented by Columbus' discovery, which made the Natural Law seem practical for the Western world was, according to the

Natural Law, actually not free at all. The very mechanism that allowed for Individualism, liberty, private property, and industry, existed only by means of conquering a foreign people and thus denying the Natural Law.

Two events during the year 1619 show the seemingly contradictory progress in stark contrast. In that year, the first truly democratic community in recorded history was built in the form of the Plymouth Colony in New England, and the first chattel slaves were brought from Africa to the North American coast in Virginia. In two distinct regions of the future United States, under vastly different conditions, two countervailing forces were established, both of which would grow to characterize the budding country. In the development of the nation, these two forces would expand to define the north and south of the country with two clashing sets of principles. Eventually, the clash would escalate until separation seemed like the only reasonable recourse, and the gruesome War Between the States became inevitable.

The objective spectator is left wondering how such a contradiction could form and how both forces could come to embody Western Civilization as they did. How is it that the concept of Natural Law could fill the conscience of the European people to the extent that they were able to build a new culture of freedom and individual autonomy, and, at the same time, not compel just action abroad? How is it that Europeans could argue for personal property and natural rights while trampling on the rights of others?

To be sure, there is no satisfactory answer. The contradiction is still a mystery to historians and political theorists alike. The only reasonably sufficient explanation is that society is a vast organism, and its culture is a varied and changing byproduct. Morals and ethics may comprise a given set of principles in one sector but a completely different set in another. Men react to their condition, and that condition changes over time and space.

However, a clue to the mystery may be found in politico-economic developments in the centuries following Columbus' discovery. In fact, during the sixteenth and seventeenth centuries, while economic freedom was starting to gain momentum throughout the West, most kings and nobles were unable to put feudal ways aside and push forward to the new concept of free markets. On the contrary, most sovereigns redoubled power over their subjects as a way to maintain their eminence despite the liberating forces. It is during this period, for example, that kings were elevated in their stature to monarchs with divine right, infallible in the eyes of their subjects and buttressed with all the pomp that we now associate with royalty. It is a premise that leads to the fact that the rococo style of the mid-era and the grandeur of Louis XIV would never have made sense in the fifteenth century and were only justified in order to confront the rising forces of self-rule.

Similarly, to counter the rising forces of equality and democracy, the lords and nobles had to augment their control over others. As in the cases of Afroindian slavery and Amerindian dispersion, this meant resorting to degrees of coercion and oppression that had been unnecessary for centuries. As nineteenth-century Italian economist Achille Loria put it, the discovery of the New World precipitated a return to chattel slavery that had been rather absent in the High Medieval Period: "We can also understand why the slave system of the ancient world and the serfdom of the middle ages were both re-introduced into our modern colonies; for it was only by resorting to such means that profits would be acquired during these epochs.°"

For the most part, attempts to grow wealth and secure power were limited to the same constructs that had fueled feudal economies for centuries—the accumulation of wealth by theft and hoarding. The notion that wealth could only be gained at the expense of others was a difficult concept to shed. And so, for the sovereigns and wealthy landowners of the early modern period, force was the only practical means of growing their power.

This concept was manifest throughout early modern society, most significantly in the specific economic policies that were later called Mercantilism. The thought was that, by setting tariffs on imports and encouraging exports, a nation could create a positive balance of trade and thus acquire more gold and silver. Though Mercantilism promoted the accumulation of wealth, it did so by means of increasing trade barriers rather than lessening them. It was not until Adam Smith and the moral philosophers of the Enlightenment pointed out that such tactics were actually harmful to overall wealth that Mercantilism truly began to subside. But, by that point, they were just reiterating and building on what the Economic School of Salamanca had already discovered.

2. THE ORIGIN
OF WEALTH

As an economic event, the discovery of the New World was perhaps the greatest in history. There can be no doubt that the new land and resources offered in the great virgin continent represented the single most extensive increase in real wealth ever gained by a society of men. To use a simple illustration, the amount of land in Western civilization per capita grew from around 24 acres in 1500 to around 148 acres in 1600. And not only was it inhabitable land, so too was it largely fertile and cultivable land. No thoughtful observer failed to recognize the latent power that rested in the new discovery.

The riches of the American continent were perhaps best captured by Tocqueville, who, on his early nineteenth-century voyage, said, "Those coasts, so admirably adapted for commerce and industry; those wide and deep rivers; that inexhaustible valley of the Mississippi; the whole continent, in short, seemed prepared to be the abode of a great nation, yet unborn."

But the bounty that the land's resources presented held merely a fraction of import compared with the freedom the new frontier represented. After all, Amerindian peoples had inhabited the land for millennia and were unable to grow their wealth in any fashion comparable to the Europeans. As Tocqueville put it, "The Indians occupied, without possessing it." Only a society of men poised to make use of the dormant land to its full extent could benefit from such a fount.

The moral was taught to the Europeans who attempted to exploit the lands and simply scavenge for gold as opposed to truly colonizing the New World. Those who sought to simply conquer and destroy, such as the Spanish Conquistadors, were of course rewarded with gold and wealth. But theirs was a fleeting wealth that was rather unsustainable. What could they do with the gold and silver once they pillaged it? Only the settlers who sought to build, farm, and organize a society around the abundant resources, such as the English, French, and Dutch colonies in North America, were able to thrive in the new environment.

It is a principle that was underscored throughout the sixteenth century in the development of the new economics and one that countered the long-standing beliefs of Medieval Europe. With a closed economy, the only way to grow wealth in the Middle Ages was to take it and withhold from others. The feudal system based as it was on vassalage was in large part founded in this notion.

Now, with a relatively limitless expanse of land into which settlers could migrate, the dynamic had changed. Not only had theft and exploitation become more difficult and obviously egregious, so too had wealth creation become an open endeavor for anyone to improve upon. With enhanced techniques, shortly after European expansion began in the sixteenth century, it had become clear that theft and exploitation was not nearly as profitable an endeavor as personal industry could be.

This novel perspective led to a subtle twist in the conception of wealth in general and what it took to create it. To the modern, wealth wasn't something that one could gain only by taking it from others and hoarding it or any form of mercantilist protectionism; wealth was the product of human industry, and so any endeavor that would increase human industry would increase wealth.

Private Property

The essential basis for this new conception was the early idea of private property. Directly descended from the Natural Law and self-rule, private property was a plausible heir. Simply, in order for one to maintain command over himself and his well-being, he must first be in command of his possessions. And, indeed, many Spanish Scholastics, including Vitoria, sketched out a basic defense for private property rights a century before Locke provided the definitive argument.

Like all new concepts of the age, private property was met with tremendous resistance, if for no other reason than the culture's imposing inertia. Prior to the sixteenth century, the notion of property existed, but it was limited in use. Objects could have properties—a chair could have the property of being sturdy, for example, a portico could have the property of being stately, and so on. Persons too could have properties in the form of their personal characteristics. One could have the property of being sanguine or phlegmatic, for example, honest or scrupulous. Property implied a form of ownership, but, for the most part, the ownership could only be of qualities inherent in the subject.

It wasn't until the sixteenth century that usage turned such that persons could have property in more than just their innate characteristics. Property still meant ownership, but now ownership could extend to the material things in one's possession—property as we understand it today—like furniture, tools, land, a house, et cetera. Prior to the sixteenth century, one could only rent these things from the true owner, the lord or king of the dominion, who had unlimited right of use to anything under his control.

In the sixteenth and especially in the seventeenth century, the attentive begin to see a shift away from this notion that the king owned everything. Spanish Scholastic Juan de Mariana, who participated in the School of Salamanca's great debates mainly from nearby Toledo, Spain, was perhaps the boldest in his attempt to define personal property rights. In anticipation of

Locke and the Enlightenment thinkers, Mariana argued that rulers, such as kings and lords, were only in power because of the consent of the governed, and that no ruler had the authority to take or make use of property unless the people gave their blessing.

The shift in thought that this represented was as powerful as any assertion could be, even during that volatile time. Mariana was basically saying that the kings' power, the divine right that they had claimed for a millennium, had been nothing more than tyranny, and that no ruler should hold sway unless sanctioned by the people.

Immediately, one can see the difficulties Mariana and other purveyors of this new theory would encounter. Not only did it imply the abolition of infinite royal power, such that kings could no longer do as they pleased, so too did it imply strict limits on those rulers, making them beholden to the people. It implied restrictions on taxation, price fixing, handling of currency, and the regulation of the people's activities and practices. The king's subjects owned the resources in question, and so they should determine how these issues would be handled. If any ruler's action was determined unjust by the people, the people had the right to rebuff and even depose the ruler—a thought unheard of before modern times.

> When the price is fixed by law, it is not lawful to increase this price by even a single farthing. If the excess be great, then it is mortal sin and a matter for restitution. A trivial increase, however, only constitutes a venial sin.
>
> —DOMINGO DE SOTO,
> *DE JUSTITIA ET JURE* (1553)

Mariana was perhaps the most extreme of all the Scholastics in this matter, due in part, no doubt, to his own property of frequent melancholy. Taking his policy to the ultimate conclusion, Mariana actually endorsed tyrannicide as a remedy for any ruler who adamantly opposed the people's wishes. This extremism can be understood, if not overlooked, by the fact that Mariana lived in a time during which a transfer of power was almost inconceivable without at least the threat of violence. No one would accept this policy today because we can comprehend transfer of power through peaceful elections. Because of Mariana's extremism, rulers were inclined to censure the obstinate man, and subsequent scholars were inclined to disregard his work.

And yet, the core of Mariana's ideas—the sovereignty of the people and the defense of private property rights—was seen as reasonable, and, in the end, served as the core of Western Civilization in the modern era. It was for this reason that his exaggerated conclusions were ultimately tolerated by the monarchs of the time. As a matter of fact, Mariana was made to stand trial only a handful of times and released from jail short of his sentence—unquestionably lenient punishment for such a mischief-maker.

It must be admitted that concerns with the notion of private property were not wholly based on the threat of tyrants. Even Mariana admitted that private property was a precarious scheme and that state intervention was necessary in certain instances. The feudal system had lasted for centuries, after all, and the standard of living was increasing, even if it was gradual compared to modern criteria.

Certainly, no king believed he should control all the goods and services in his domain, but it was assumed that most goods and services required some state supervision in the form of regulation, and that some components of the economy required explicit control. Without such oversight, the thought was that anarchy would ensue and no one's property would be safe, a reasonable premise given the barbarism dwelling beyond the kingdom's bounds.

One of the more prominent concerns had to do with goods that were considered to be of public benefit. These were resources that were so elemental to society's success that individuals could not be trusted with the power to control and distribute them, such as water supplies and medicinal plants. Holding those resources in common under the command of a neutral sovereign was the only way to ensure that everyone could obtain the necessities and that no one would be taken advantage of in times of need. If everyone owned the goods, it was thought, then everyone would be able to gain from them.

Take, for example, the ownership of medicinal plants. Given the social benefit offered by such plants, the prevailing notion was that they were public property and that, even if individuals owned the land on which the plants grew, they had no right to withhold the plants or sell them at a profit. To do so would be selfish, treacherous, and disastrous for the community as a whole. Better to have the state or the sovereign king decide who could use the plants and for what price.

With the light of a new economics, however, the Spanish Scholastics saw enduring problems in this system. To begin, who was to be sure that the sovereign power would distribute the property equitably? There was no way to know that the king would be exempt from favoring one group over another, or, in some cases, simply punishing a sector for no reason. The arbitrary nature of hierarchical rule was alone a threat to just distribution.

But there was still another, more fundamental problem with the notion of communal ownership. Luis de Molina, a Jesuit scholar who came to Salamanca toward the end of the sixteenth century, showed that communal ownership always tended to contradict its central purpose of equal distribution, even when the sovereign was dedicated to fairness. As Molina discovered, people used property differently depending on whether it was privately or communally owned. The main distinction rested in the pace of consumption. While people used private property with regard to the long term, most often they would use communal property with regard to the short term. The rationale is clear: Since private property is their own, they know it will benefit them if it lasts longer and so will take care of it and reduce wear and tear. By contrast, people know that they will probably not benefit from public property if it lasts longer, and so they will try to obtain as much of it as possible in quick order so that someone else doesn't take it instead. Helping to maintain a public good or to reduce wear and tear on it will just allow someone else to take advantage of the effort—essentially, it is working for someone else's benefit—and so it isn't even considered. As Molina found, the irony of collective ownership is that it spurs more selfishness than does private ownership.

To see this principle in effect, put a tasty treat out in a common room at a typical office, then watch how quickly ravenous coworkers raid the offering. Each office worker is compelled to trounce on it by compulsion of the mere risk of missing out. The faster one gets to the community treats and the more one takes, the better off one will be. As a result, the resource is promptly depleted.

Though different examples feature differing motivations, the overall effect is the same in all cases of communal ownership. Take, for instance, the modern health insurance scheme, which can be viewed as a pool of health resources owned by a community of patients. The typical mentality for each individual in the community is to take advantage of as many services as he can—to stock up on drugs, to make frequent if unnecessary visits to the doctor's office, and to undergo treatment, therapy, and surgery whenever possible. If one isn't able to take advantage of the services offered, then it is as if the others in the pool are gaining at his expense. The impulse is to raid the pool of resources, which naturally leads to their depletion, and, in this example, an increase in the cost of the services.

This tendency for people to take advantage of public goods leads to what twentieth-century ecologist Garrett Hardin called the 'Tragedy of the Commons', in which groups of individuals with no ill intentions will invariably harm and exhaust shared resources even when it is apparent that such behavior is not in anyone's long-term interest. In short, the group will cause its own downfall by devastating their common goods.

The traditional example of the tragedy is that of cowherds who each own their own fields but also share a common plot of land. In this scenario, it is in each herder's interest to graze his cows on the common land even to the extent of damaging the fields and depleting the resource. Each herder receives all the benefits of healthy cows, while the costs to the land are disbursed throughout the group, so it is assumed that no one really pays for it. For the individual cowherd, it makes complete sense to graze his cattle on the pasture until the grass is depleted. He sees plenty of gain and little risk in doing so. In fact, it would be riskier for him to withhold his cattle from the commons because others would benefit while he just depleted his own pasture. And so all cowherds will graze their cattle on the commons and none will fret about the pending tragedy.

As conveyed by the illustration, the cause of this dilemma is a condition in which individuals can gain at public expense. Whenever this is possible, the same tragedy will result. The solution, according to Molina and other Scholastics, is private property rights. By dividing the land between the cowherds so that each owns a share, the cowherds will keep to their own space and be relieved of the threat posed by others. When the owner receives all the benefits of his plot of land, he will make sure to ration the grazing so as to avoid excessive wear and will maintain the property so that it will keep supplying him and others a yield.

In other words, the solution is to bring costs to the private level so that both benefits and risks are localized. The union of the two compels prudent action and sustains the resources so that everyone is able to benefit from them indefinitely. Communal ownership means that all benefit for a short time; private ownership means that few people benefit over the course of an extended period of time.

At the dawn of the new era, the defense of private property took on an even more vital meaning. With the newly opened economy, it became clear that the only way to attain true justice was through autonomy; the only way for an individual to attain autonomy was by attaining self-sufficiency; and the only way to achieve self-sufficiency was, of course, by the possession of private property. Property rights, as such, became an essential ingredient of a just society.

While Scholastic work focused on the economic benefits of private property, an unmistakable link had been formed between those economic benefits and political benefits. Property rights were human rights, and human rights were property rights. This is why John Locke in the seventeenth century and Adam Smith and the Founders of the United States in the eighteenth all considered the ability to own and maintain property a fundamental, God-given right. Note that Jefferson's unalienable rights of "life, liberty, and the pursuit of happiness" were originally phrased "life, liberty, and property" and were only changed to suit a more general ardor. The Bill of Rights in the Constitution later reestablishes the standard of property as one of the three fundamental rights.

Political theorists in our day doubt sincerely whether personal property is necessary for the just life. Today, the norm is more like that of feudal times, in which the ruler—the state government—has the authority to take at least some portion of a citizen's income, usually by arbitrary decree. The income tax alone is proof of the stance, and arguments made to increase such a tax link the twenty-first century with the sixteenth. Between the era's bookends, the consensus was that the ability to own and distribute property was essential.

The Rise of Industry

Given property rights, the panorama changes completely. The ability to do what one wants with his own property means that the owner has the sole right to benefit from that property, which opens the door to an abundance of opportunity that had been closed off before. When one is guaranteed the entire output of his toil, it stands to reason that he will be inclined to make the most of it. This is especially true in the realm of producing and accumulating wealth.

Whereas profit had always been seen as usurious to a degree, and therefore reprehensible, the notion that one should be able to make use of his own property in any way he saw fit meant that he should also be able to produce goods and sell them at a profit or accumulate capital for future use.

Of all the developments in sixteenth-century economics, the notion of making a profit was the most highly contested. To convince the church and laypeople that profit was acceptable and, as the Spanish Scholastics argued, actually beneficial to society as a whole required a complete transformation of the concept of wealth. Like most economic matters of the time, the argument against profit rested in the fixity of the medieval ages. To a large degree, a kingdom's wealth was seen as a fixed sum and thus limited in amount. Since it was restricted in this way, the implicit understanding was that one could only extend one's wealth by hoarding it at others' expense or acquiring it through conquest, and neither method was quite acceptable to moralists of the day. For someone to be wealthy, to gain profit in any way, or to accumulate luxuries, it was assumed, someone else had to do without the necessities, to suffer destitution, or even starve; for one to win, in other words, someone else had to lose.

The moral stance on the issue had been made clear: Earning a profit on a sale was to prey on the buyer's needs and not make use of the seller's product. As Aquinas put it, "The usefulness that goes to the buyer comes not from the seller, but from the buyer's needy condition; and no one ought to sell something that doesn't belong to him." This was especially true since most did not have control over their needs. Entrenched in the web of feudal bondage, they were at the whim of others and so could not reject the price they were given even if it was exorbitant. What of a drought or a building fire? There was no moral justification for profiting on the disadvantaged when they had no recourse to prevent their needy condition.

As such, the church frowned on profit-making and condemned it outright in the instance of loans and other early forms of investment. The Second Lateran Council in the twelfth century and the Council of Vienne in the fourteenth condemned the charging of interest and any local legislation that tolerated it. This was the church's way of limiting the exploitation that any closed economy would engender. It is not a coincidence that we hear calls for similar condemnation today.

By giving the people alternatives, the discovery of the New World allowed for self-sufficiency. A move from a system of bondage to one of independence meant that a person's wealth was no longer contingent on others. That wealth could still be affected by disasters and bad harvests, but the ability to prevent these incidents and to prepare for them was no longer a function of the community. The individual had the freedom to avert loss;

if he didn't, it was his fault. He would determine the purchases he would make and the loans he would take out during hard times. No longer was he forced into either type of exchange, and so no longer was he innocent in the matter.

There was, therefore, no longer a moral concern with charging interest or earning a profit. If the consumer deemed it a trade fair, even with the profit and interest included, there was no reason to prevent its fulfillment. We see that, by Shakespeare's time, a sound case could even be made for Shylock's sadistic interest charged in *The Merchant of Venice*. Though the claim for "a pound of flesh" was irrational and motivated by revenge, the court and even the debtor were willing to uphold the recompense. The case against Shylock as presented in the play is based upon the villain's blind hatred, not on his inclination toward merchantry or even usury.

A subtler yet more momentous shift in thought was the realization that wealth could be gained by one person without necessarily causing others to lose. Just as the world had been opened with the discovery of the New World, so too had the market. The opened economy meant that one could build and accumulate goods without necessarily withholding them from those in need or by forcibly taking them from others—he just had to go to the open land and dedicate his efforts to the production. A person's wealth was no longer a social matter, gotten only through the help of others; rather, it was a personal matter, gotten through hard work and thrift. In a word, wealth was the product of industry.

Sixteenth-century thinkers and merchants were in no way prepared for a rise of industry like that witnessed in the eighteenth and nineteenth centuries. Much progress would have to be made before the widespread use of machines could make industry a driving force in culture. But it could be said that, in the sixteenth century, the most important barrier to that kind of progress had been removed. Moral apprehension of wealth, gaining profit, charging interest, and even possessing luxuries had all been subdued and, in the case of Catholic doctrine, officially reversed. The rise of industry followed as a matter of course.

Once the gates had opened, industry became an irresistible source of energy. By freeing individuals from bondage and allowing them to own and maintain private property with the incentive of profit, people were motivated to produce more goods at a higher rate, which could only lead to higher aggregate wealth. Individuals could save and thus add to their capital, giving them greater ability to produce even more and at an even higher rate. Ultimately, freedom would lead to greater production and more abundance all around. That abundance would become the characteristic result of the economic system later known as Capitalism and would ensure its triumph in the modern era.

An argument put forth by two early twentieth-century theorists summarized this concept by linking the rise of Capitalism with the Protestant Reformation. The theory, by Max Weber and R. H. Tawney, asserted that Protestantism promoted sober, hardworking individuals, and so was responsible for the great advances in industry and wealth that the West had enjoyed over the last five hundred years. Altogether, according to Weber and Tawney, the church reformers could be credited with all of the increase in prosperity that had come from this new mode of economy and all that had been good in the modern era.

And, certainly, the correlation can hardly be denied—the rise of Capitalism and all the industry that came with it did run parallel with the rise of Protestantism. A look at the output of nations in the twentieth century drove the point home: Protestant nations of the north—Scandinavia, Germany, Switzerland, the Netherlands, the United Kingdom, and the United States—displayed far more diligence, innovation, and reliable work ethic than any of the Catholic nations of the south—Italy, France, Spain, and Central and South America. By the twentieth century, the fact was clear.

A puzzling aspect of the theory, however, suggests that the cause of the Protestant work ethic is the core belief in predestination. With their souls in doubt, Weber and Tawney held, Protestants were encouraged to act as if they had already been chosen for Grace, as if their behavior alone would convince the Judge. It is not quite known how predestined souls would have maintained greater motivation to act on their faith than those for whom free will played a role. The skeptic wonders how fate would not quell motivation and produce more angst than material good.

Doubt is redoubled by the fact that, though both Luther and Calvin promoted hark work as a virtue, neither were great proponents of profit-making or the charging of interest on loans essential to Capitalism. Luther was actually vocal in imploring governments to end maneuvers by which Christians evaded usury laws, and Calvin was said to have dealt "with usurie as the apothecaire doth with poison". In essence, both contested the fundamental mechanism of industry—the accumulation of profit—and cannot be said to have instigated the rise of industry any more than the Catholic scholars at Salamanca.

What must be noted is that this essential capitalistic enterprise had its start in the High Medieval period, well before Luther, Calvin, or Vitoria began preaching, and only flourished after the discovery of the New World. Despite the resistance practitioners faced, the principal aspects of Capitalism had been called for by the adventurous for centuries and, in the case of Genoa and Venice, actually prevailed as the dominant form of political economy. If Protestantism did play a role in the rise in Capitalism, it was as a sibling and not a parent. Both Protestantism and Capitalism existed to some degree before the discovery of the New World and only flourished after. It took the rise of Individualism to bring both to fruition.

The Subjectivity of Value

The scope of economic changes taking place during the sixteenth century can best be seen in the fact that economics as a science had been more or less nonexistent beforehand, and only with the advances ushered in by the Spanish Scholastics and contemporaries like Jean Bodin was the field able to take form as a cohesive discipline afterward. Prior to 1500, economic thought was a function of political or moral thought; after 1500, economics was rapidly becoming an ordered system of thought in its own right.

The crux of this new science could be found in new theories on value that materialized in the mid-sixteenth century. If economics could be seen as a science of allocating resources, a systematic understanding of those resources and what makes them valuable was the necessary starting point. And so, in addition to the development of private property rights and the rise of industry, early modern thinkers saw it fit to devise a new theory of value, based in the new type of society that had been forming throughout the West.

This new theory of value was based largely on the experience of Spaniards during the Age of Exploration and was one of the first lessons Spain was taught in the sixteenth century. Formerly, it had been believed that the value of a good or service was rather static—that a wheelbarrow or loaf of bread, for instance, was worth the same to one person as it was to the next. Goods had a 'just price' or 'fair value' based on the cost required to produce them, the amount of labor involved, and so on. State price controls had been founded on this belief, and, to a large degree, it was what kept prices so stagnant during the Middle Ages.

Such a rationale made good sense in a closed economy. Since production costs had been about the same throughout medieval times, the value of wheelbarrows and bread could remain fixed. Value was objective—it didn't matter by whom a good was produced or by whom that good was purchased; its price would necessarily be consistent.

As with so many other aspects of the culture, events surrounding the discovery of the New World shed new light on this picture. The novel perspective came thanks to the sudden influx of gold and silver pouring in to Spain from the American colonies. From the moment explorers began to realize that San Salvador was an island off the coast of a new continent and not some uncharted land near Asia, the goal was to find El Dorado, the legendary city of gold, and bring back its treasures in glory. Hernán Cortés and his Conquistadors were the infamous examples of the rapacious pursuit, but, across the board, explorers were set on the mission to retrieve great new sources of the metallic treasures.

Though explorers never found El Dorado, they did find Potosí, the Peruvian (now Bolivian) city of silver, and, over the course of the sixteenth century, a fresh supply of precious metals gushed in from the Americas. As was expected, the influx initially made Spain much richer in the sense of gaining power to buy goods and services. But not long into the new paradigm, unexpected effects began to materialize.

Spanish Scholastic Martin de Azpilcueta showed in his *Review of Decisional Usury* (1556) how the influx of gold and silver made these precious metals so abundant in Spain that they actually became less valuable. A gold coin had been worth twice as much in 1500 as it was in 1550 simply because there were so many more in 1550 and so it took more to satisfy a person's wants. Spanish farmers, bakers, and tailors still accepted coinage for their crops, bread, and cloaks, but required more of it in exchange. As a result, prices rose and a severe shortage of money arose.

To be sure, other factors contributed to the rise in prices—reports of bad harvests in the early years of the century, a deterioration of industry, and the new financial stresses of world exploration all exerted an upward force on prices by lowering supply and increasing demand. Tracking the course of price inflation, however, shows that the most significant factor was the new American specie. Price inflation occurred first in Seville, the home port of the New World's treasure fleet, then spread to other ports and finally to the rest of Spain. The pattern shows how the rise in prices corresponded almost precisely to the rise in money circulation.

Meanwhile, in nearby countries such as Italy, where the people had no direct access to the new source of specie, prices remained relatively unchanged. By 1550, the effects of inflation were clear: The Italians, Swiss, and Germans could buy more with their gold and silver than the Spanish could buy with theirs. As Azpilcueta and the other Scholastics were astounded to discover, Spain's new riches had made that great empire seemingly—paradoxically—poorer than it had been. Contrary to the mercantilist wisdom, acquisition of more gold and silver had made the people of Spain more needy and, overall, less wealthy.

The gates of this subtle finding were wide, indeed. Generally, it meant that the previous belief that value was static was incomplete at best and probably wholly erroneous. If the price of money could fluctuate depending on the circumstances of its use, then the price of every good and service could fluctuate as well. The price of money affected the price of everything, and so no value was set or otherwise objective.

Looking more closely, the Scholastics began to formulate a more refined understanding of value in general. They could no longer put credence in the notion that goods and services had an objective value and were worth the same in all circumstances. They determined that all goods—even gold and silver coins—are valuable inasmuch as they can satisfy one's needs; and, since needs change, so too does value.

A loaf of bread, for example, is valuable because it satisfies one's appetite, a chair because it satisfies one's desire for comfort, a painting because it satisfies one's need for beauty, and so on. Money is valuable because it satisfies many needs indirectly by giving the owner the ability to purchase whatever is for sale. All of these have value according to their ability to satisfy needs one way or another.

If a good loses the ability to satisfy those needs, for whatever reason, then that good loses value. This can happen in a couple of ways. First, a good can lose particular qualities and thus be unable to offer the same level of satisfaction—if, for example, a loaf of bread grows stale or a chair breaks. These altered goods can no longer satisfy needs and so lose their value. Second, a good can lose value if a person's needs diminish or are satisfied by some other means—if, for instance, one is full on mutton or has at his disposal a variety of seats in which to relax. In either case, the value of the goods diminishes because they are needed less.

This means that the more abundant a good, the greater chance one will have at satisfying his needs and the less valuable the good will become. On the other hand, the scarcer a good, the lower chance one will have at satisfying his needs and the more valuable the good will become. This principle—that abundance plays a role in value—was developed by several of the Scholastics as well as contemporaries of theirs in France and Prussia with Jean Bodin, who was a forerunner in the development of what was later called the Quantity Theory of Money, and the multifaceted mind of Nicolaus Copernicus, who produced work in mathematics, medicine, the fine arts, justice, the military, diplomacy, and economics, in addition to his well-known work in astronomy. The concept of Subjective Value, it could be said, had universal appeal.

Azpilcueta showed how this principle applied directly to money. "All merchandise," he wrote, "becomes dearer when it is in great demand and short supply, and money, in so far as it may be sold, bartered, or exchanged by some other form of contract, is merchandise and therefore also becomes dearer when it is in great demand and short supply." Going on to reference the influx of specie from the New World, he said that "Even in Spain, in times when money was scarcer, saleable goods and labor were given for very much less than after the discovery of the Indies, which flooded the country with gold and silver. The reason for this is that money is worth more where and when it is scarce than where and when it is abundant°."

In our day, one can think of the flashy millionaire celebrity who tosses $100 bills around like they are nothing. To him, the bills come like rain and so he will feel no need to secure them in any way money is abundant. To the middle-class worker, these bills are scarce and so he will take care of them and protect them.

Throughout their work, the Scholastics showed how the value of every good is based, not on inherent characteristics, but rather on the conditions of its exchange. Why was wheat more expensive in the Indies than in Spain? Not because the nature of the wheat was different abroad, but because it was scarcer there than it was at home and so men esteemed it more in the New World than they did in the Old. Why was meat worth less than bread? Not because it was less essential to one's survival, but because it was more abundant.

This somewhat counterintuitive principle is the source of the so-called Diamond-Water Paradox, which puzzled Adam Smith though it had been correctly explained before *The Wealth of Nations* by French philosopher Étienne Bonnot de Condillac. The paradox is that diamonds are much more valuable than water, even though water is much more useful. Indeed, water is essential to health, and diamonds have little if any practical use at all. This was especially true in Smith's day, before diamonds were used in industry for cutting, grinding, drilling, and polishing. Why is it that something that has such great utility is so cheap and something that has such little utility is so expensive? A similar question has been asked about modern professions—teachers are much more important to society than NFL players, but the former get paid much less than the latter. How can this be?

The answer to the riddle rests in supply and demand. A drink of water is much more widely available than a diamond, and so the needs satisfied by water, though rather important, are much less urgent. And, because diamonds are so hard to come by, the needs they satisfy, though rather superfluous, are much more critical. Supply and demand, and not objective quality, dictate the price. The same goes for the teacher-sportsman paradox—teachers are much more abundant than qualified sports stars, so there is a much lower value placed on the former and a much higher value placed on the latter.

> Why should a bale of linen brought overland from Brittany at great expense be worth more than one which is transported cheaply by sea? Why should a book written out by hand be worth more than one which is printed, when the latter is better though it costs less to produce?
>
> —LUIS SARAVÍA DE LA CALLE,
> *INSTRUCCION DE MERCADERES* (1544)

> Music is good to the melancholic, bad to the mourning, and indifferent to the deaf.
>
> —BARUCH SPINOZA (1632-77)

> Price is what you pay; value is what you get.
>
> —WARREN BUFFETT (B. 1930)

Contrary to the dominant objective theory of value, the Scholastics' view suggested that value fluctuated depending on the conditions surrounding the exchange. Far from defining value on a strict supply and demand curve as is done in economics textbooks these days, Azpilcueta and his contemporaries simply argued that value is changeable and that certain conditions would affect any individual's desire to obtain a particular good. Since those conditions are personal and distinct, it can be said that value too is personal and distinct—value is subjective, as later economists would put it.

It wasn't until the nineteenth century that this concept was fully developed into a workable theory. In an effort to explain the Diamond-Water Paradox, among other issues, three economists, Austrian Carl Menger, Briton William Stanley Jevons, and Frenchman Léon Walras, all independently discovered what became known as the Marginal Utility Theory of Value. It is the 'marginal' theory because, as Menger, Jevons, and Walras explained, the value of any good or service is established with respect to the last unit of the good in question; that is, the unit in the margin. If one has thirty cattle, for instance, the value he places on each is based on the utility of gaining one more or losing the thirtieth one. Any time there is a wide abundance of a particular good, then the margin is far removed and value will be low; if there is a dearth of a good, then the margin is tight and value will be high.

Beneath all this lies the premise that value is based on one's needs, and, since needs are subjective, value itself must also be subjective. The value of any good or service can change depending on who is concerned or what the circumstances are in a given situation. This means that there is no such thing as a just price or a fair value—everyone sees it differently. If one were to define the just price at all, it would be the price that a seller and buyer agree on in a freely organized market; the just price is the market price. A loaf of bread or a chair is worth something different to someone who is hungry and in need of rest than to someone who is full and energetic, and so the former will be willing to pay more than the latter. As sixteenth-century Spaniards discovered, even the value of money can change given different supply and demand of the currency. Throughout the economy, prices of goods and services are mercurial, inconsistent measures that can reflect no two exchanges in the same way.

The upshot, as one might imagine, is a loss of control. Given a system of ever-changing supply and demand, the practices of setting fair prices, and even predicting future prices, become essentially impossible. There is no way of knowing what a given consumer will like or want from one day to the next, just as there is no way of knowing what new techniques a producer will employ to reduce his manufacturing costs. As such, there is no way of predicting what meeting point the two will agree on at any given time.

In response to such volatility, economists and sociologists alike have attempted to classify and group persons' needs in the vein of Aristotle's ethics so as to better understand and predict the market. Carl Menger, despite his lucid explanation of Marginal Utility, was one of the first to draw out a pattern of needs. He suggested that all needs fall into one of three categories—physiological, egotistical, and altruistic—and that each person would have to satisfy at least to some extent each category of needs. In the twentieth century, sociologist Abraham Maslow formulated a more elaborate version of this model, which he called the Hierarchy of Needs. In Maslow's diagram, there were five categories that persons would attempt to satisfy in order from base to peak: physiological, safety, belonging, esteem, and self-actualization.

Though they might shed light on the human condition, all such models are rather unproductive in the realm of economics. The idea in the models of both Menger and Maslow is that all men have the same set of fundamental needs, which they strive for in order from lowest to highest. They initially place more emphasis on the physiological needs such as food, sleep, and sex. Once these are satisfied, they can focus on more refined needs such as social and spiritual fulfillment.

As instructive as this may be with regard to man's psychology, it misinterprets the processes that go on in economic exchanges. Though all men might require food, shelter, and clothing to survive, there is an infinite variety of combinations of these needs, such that two very similar people will place completely different values on the same good or service. Two might share the same level of hunger, but one prefers fruit while the other prefers vegetables; everyone needs clothes, but clothes might mean Walmart brand for one and Valentino for another. Simply, we can never be sure what needs one is focusing on, to what degree, or how he seeks to satisfy them—only the individual can determine that, making value impossible to gauge objectively.

When considering the several categories of needs, determining the objective value of each becomes even more impossible. As Maslow pointed out, a person is entirely likely to strive to satisfy a higher need to the detriment of lower needs. He gives the example of Mahatma Gandhi, who endeavored to bring about freedom and social justice by means of hunger strikes and marches. Clearly the objective price-fixer would be befuddled by such an anomaly.

* * *

This is to point out a salient feature of a subjective notion of value and really all of the economic developments of the sixteenth and seventeenth centuries—the ascendancy of the individual and the decline of the state. Combined with private property rights as well as profit and industry, the emergence of subjective value cemented the individual as the elemental figure in social organization and made the role of the king or lord as overseer rather obsolete.

As could be expected, most sovereign kings and lords opposed the shift, and not entirely for selfish reasons. True, they sometimes benefited from the hierarchic system in the form of undeserved tributes, but most sovereigns were as loyal to the people as the people were loyal to their sovereign. Their rules often had good reason for being, not the least of which was the welfare of the people. And so good arguments had been made in resistance of the sweeping democratization. In the end, no one could know for sure whether any novel system would ensure the best outcome for the people.

To take a simple example: How could anyone believe that men would cooperate with each other and respect one another's property without the strong arm of the king in place to make sure no one stole or injured others? As English philosopher Thomas Hobbes explained, men are brutal and conniving and the only thing that can prevent an all-out war of every man against every man is the presence of an all-powerful 'Leviathan', a king that would ensure no one would be taken advantage of and peace would prevail.

And yet, as Hobbes was making his case, societies of men were actually beginning to form based on cooperation and mutual benefit. Cities in America were prospering wildly with almost no state at all. Perhaps the most fascinating aspect of modern economics is the fact that the countries and smaller communities which did reduce the presence of the king were the ones in which cooperation and civility grew most rapidly and comprehensively. In those lands, no hierarchy was necessary to get people in line and motivate them to act morally; they were doing so on their own, spontaneously, as if the social contract had been an expression of self-preservation. By the time of Locke, shortly after Hobbes, a sound case could be made that liberalism was not only the most moral form of social organization, but also the most economically promising.

3. LAISSEZ FAIRE, MORBLEU!

WITH THE FOUNDATION of a new economy established by the introduction of property rights, the defense of profit and industry, and a new theory of value, the Western world had opened the door to a freer and more productive system. The more countries were willing to allow for these developments to take place by lessening restrictions and eliminating controls, the greater their wealth increased. But all of these were secondary in terms of impact to the development of what became the defining characteristic of Capitalism, free trade.

The reason trade is so important rests in its innate ability to make use of surplus goods. Individualism, private property, and industry all increased production to a great degree throughout the sixteenth and seventeenth centuries, but there was always a limit to the amount of goods one could produce for himself. It was, for instance, foreseeable that one could produce 100 bushels of wheat in a week's work, but since he neither could nor wanted to make use of it, such production was hardly endeavored.

By granting producers the ability to trade freely, however, without tariffs or other restrictions, state governments of the period enabled producers to connect with consumers who would otherwise not have been available. Given a new supply of consumers, producers could now make use of industrial techniques that were previously useless or simply unimaginable and increase production to unprecedented degrees.

The key to unlocking the potential of trade was the inception of subjective value, which encourages trade in one distinct way: The fact that a person can value a good or service differently than another person means one person might own something that he doesn't necessarily want while another person wants something that he doesn't own. If that something is the same thing, then the two are encouraged to trade.

Assuming two people value goods or services differently, both will be able to benefit by exchanging the goods or services in their possession. They can both receive what they want by either getting rid of the good or service they offer or by acquiring the good or service that the other offers. One gets something that he values highly; the other gets rid of something that he doesn't value very highly. This is why, as a modern commentator has pointed out, the merchant and the shopper both say 'Thank you' upon the completion of a purchase—they both come out ahead.

An apple, for example, is worth less to a farmer who owns barrels of them than to a city dweller who lives in a fifth-floor apartment and hasn't seen a plant in weeks. It is only because these two individuals place different values on the apple that they are encouraged to make the trade. The farmer values the apple at 3¢ and the city dweller values it at $3. They agree on a price of $1.50 and both go away having gained about $1.50 in the trade.

If value were objective—if, for example, both the farmer and the city-dweller valued the apple at 3¢—then they would very likely not want to trade. Neither would gain in the equation since the items exchanged would be worth the same to both participants. With subjective value, on the other hand, the goods are worth different amounts, and so the parties are inclined to hold onto them to differing degrees and are thus given the incentive to make an exchange.

It bears repeating that this mutual gain has its source, not in the goods and services themselves, which all remain fairly static in their constitutions, but rather in the perception of those goods by the people involved. The apple is the same good to the farmer and the city-dweller, but, given the fact that they have different abilities and needs, the same piece of fruit is viewed as more or less valuable for each.

Disparity in needs and abilities gives us subjectivity in value and thus allows all involved parties to benefit from trade. Of course, in our egalitarian times, disparity is seen as a bad thing—unequal abilities and needs is a sign that people are unequal as people, and, when people are unequal, some can be taken advantage of. It is reasoned that disparity between people is the source of exploitation and so should be eradicated in favor of a 'level playing field'.

But without disparity, there would be no trade. It is important to note this consequence because, as we will see, by changing one's needs and abilities through specific techniques, one can effectively alter one's measure of value on related goods and services. In other words, the members of a group can increase profitability by simply cooperating with each other, making it possible to invent wealth through trade.

Specialism and the Division of Labor

Around the time of the Enlightenment, a few notable theorists discovered that, by dividing labor, specializing work, and trading, workers could focus on a limited number of tasks and thus become more productive. The more specialized an individual's work, the more he can concentrate and produce effectively, and the more of his product he will be able to offer. The farmer, for instance, specializes in producing apples in order to provide the best apples and the most abundant harvest. The more apples he can produce, the less value they have for him and the more profit he can make in trading them.

This feature of trade had been hinted at as early as the Spanish Scholastics and Jean Bodin, but its real magic was not uncovered until Bernard

Mandeville's 1714 classic, *The Fable of the Bees,* in the dialogues between Cleomenes and Horatio. Mandeville explained that any time people are able to conduct their affairs freely, they almost invariably end up dividing their labor and specializing in particular tasks, quite as if there was a natural pull to do so.

This allows each worker to fine-tune his skills and thus increase his output, the result of which is an increase in total wealth and a standard of living higher than it would be if everyone worked on their own. In short, the ability to trade makes for unparalleled productivity.

Cleomenes: If one will wholly apply himself to the making of Bows and Arrows, whilst another provides Food, a third builds Huts, a fourth makes Garments, and a fifth Utensils, they not only become useful to one another, but the Callings and Employments themselves will in the same Number of Years receive much greater Improvements, than if all had been promiscuously follow'd by every one of the Five.

Horatio: I believe you are perfectly right there; and the truth of what you say is in nothing so conspicuous, as it is in Watchmaking, which is come to a higher degree of Perfection, than it would have been arrived at yet, if the whole had always remain'd the Employment of one Person.

—BERNARD MANDEVILLE,
THE FABLE OF THE BEES (1714)

The benefits of specialism and the division of labor were famously demonstrated by Adam Smith, who illustrated the efficacy with the study of a local pin (nail) factory. According to Smith, a single worker could hardly make one nail given a full day's work and all the supplies necessary. The number of different tasks involved in the production process (Smith estimated eighteen operations in total) would require the sole worker to shift gears, prepare, and perform different actions some fifty times for each nail, extending the effort over a minimum of several hours.

Meanwhile, a small factory with ten workers who divided their labor and specialized on no more than two tasks each could produce upwards of 48,000 nails, or 4,800 nails per worker, all in the same amount of time. The fact that each worker could focus on the few operations he specialized in meant that they could all work more efficiently and produce an amount unimaginable without the division of labor.

The usefulness of this technique is based in the fact that every task includes a set of hidden tasks that are built into it. Pouring metal into a mold, for instance, consists not only in the pouring motion, but also includes setting the mold and adjusting the flask, as well as the mental task of figuring out the best method of such a procedure, not to mention the agility needed to administer the most precise degree of motion, among others. These hidden tasks all take time to master.

Altogether, the preparation for each kind of task can be much more time-consuming than the physical task itself. Of course, as the worker accustoms himself to an operation and gets in the mode of carrying it out, the mental preparation for each procedure takes less and less time, a trend that follows a learning curve familiar nowadays in all technical fields. The principle is the same for all repetitive processes: It takes less time to complete the hundredth procedure than it does the first or second because mental preparation is no longer needed.

It is for this reason that increasing the number of repetitions of a given task increases productivity. The more a worker operates a single task, the less mental preparation affects total output as its proportion diminishes. If a worker can focus on one task for an entire day, it is as if the mental preparation needed at the outset becomes negligible in comparison. On the contrary, if a worker must alternate between different tasks or conduct an entire series of tasks through the day, it is quite likely that the worker will have to undergo mental preparation for each task, thus reducing the efficiency for each manifold.

The Industrial Revolution

Specialism and the division of labor, designed for the production of goods for trade, encapsulate what has become known as the Industrial Revolution. Its practical manifestation could be seen throughout Britain and, to an increasing degree, on the continent and America beginning in the eighteenth century and lasting through to the early twentieth. In the second half of the eighteenth century, these techniques were used for a number of specific innovations that sped up production times, made better use of resources, and output higher quality goods than had ever been produced in the history of mankind.

To name the more significant inventions would focus on three areas: textiles, steam power, and iron founding. In textile production, there was Richard Arkwright's water frame, James Hargreave's spinning jenny, and, in 1779, Samuel Crompton's spinning mule (which combined the water frame with the spinning jenny). In 1793, American Eli Whitney introduced the cotton gin, which still stands today as the most effective mechanism for separating seeds from cotton fibers. In 1775, James Watt invented an improved steam engine, which enabled automation in factories and eventually locomotion. And in 1783, Henry Cort patented the puddling process for producing bar iron without charcoal, which made steel production easier and more reliable. All of these new processes provided unprecedented efficiency and effectiveness in the manufacture of goods, ensuring what would become the greatest explosion of industrial output ever.

The story of Eli Whitney is a quintessential look into the kind of improvements that were taking place during the Industrial Revolution. In addition to his design and assembly of the cotton gin, Whitney exercised his mechanical savvy in making muskets. His factory was one of the first to use the newly devised scheme of interchangeable, standardized parts, as well as a streamlined division of labor and assembly line. In promoting the value in his goods to the customer, the U.S. government, Whitney calculated the price per musket, factoring in fixed costs as well as those for parts and labor, thus making contributions to cost accounting in addition to efficiency in the modern manufacturing plant.

During the late eighteenth and early nineteenth centuries, this kind of technical advance had become characteristic of Western civilization. Building upon centuries of refined scientific thinking, the method was clear: mechanize, standardize, specialize, divide labor, and make use of capital implements to optimize production. The centuries following the Industrial Revolution made plain the benefit—simply, at no place in history had this kind of sustained economic growth ever occurred. Since 1800, population has increased sixfold—an astounding sign of increased wealth in itself—while income per capita has increased over tenfold. American Nobel Prize-winning economist Robert Lucas, Jr. put it in stark terms, saying, "For the first time in history, the living standards of the masses of ordinary people have begun to undergo sustained growth. Nothing remotely like this economic behavior has happened before." The credit, it must be said, rests largely with the techniques related to the Industrial Revolution and trade.

By the late nineteenth and early twentieth century, the widespread use of machines and replaceable parts had made the production process so complex and immense that the division of labor was impossible to avoid. For some evangelists, it was a godsend. To them, the employment of specialism and labor division was a way to usher in a perfectly efficient economy, from the start of the production process to the retail chain outlet.

Among others, Frederick Winslow Taylor and Frank Bunker Gilbreth Sr. put forth arguments that showed the division of labor to be effective in the minutest of actions—pulling a lever, reaching for a button, pouring a molten liquid, and so on—thus extending the division to scores of participants. In his 1911 book, *The Principles of Scientific Management*, Taylor convinced a generation that, through scientific analysis of each step in a given process, the whole system could be streamlined and layers of waste could be eliminated.

The benefits had already become evident. A few years before *Scientific Management* was published, Henry Ford utilized Eli Whitney's replaceable parts and mechanized the assembly line, making car manufacturing a science in Detroit. By dividing labor to the most incremental degree, Ford Motor Company become one of the top businesses in all of manufacturing and Ford one of the wealthiest people in America. And the benefits were not only extended to the company's owner—Ford's employees were some of the best paid and most loyal in the industry. The company as a whole flourished as Ford became a household name around the world.

The real winner, however, was neither Ford nor his workers, but the consumers. So streamlined was the production process, so efficient was the assembly line, and so minimal was the company's waste, that in 1908 Ford's legendary Model T could be sold for $850 (the equivalent of about $20,000 today). Previously, new cars would sell for $2,000 ($48,000 in today's prices), and in some cases for twice that. By 1915, improvements to the already industry-leading process cut the price even further, so that the Model T sold for a mere $440 ($9,400). Through the inventive use of scientific management, Ford was able to bring the automobile—and all the luxuries it afforded—to the masses. A drive to the beach for the day, a visit to the relatives upstate, a cross-country vacation—all were suddenly within reach of the average American. It is the kind of increase in efficiency that resembles that of the computer industry today, where over the course of two years a computer's power doubles and its price is cut in half. During the Industrial Revolution, it was happening across the board.

Taylor believed that such efficiency was possible for every company in America. The ideal of scientific management was to make twice as much money or more by selling products that were half the cost or less and superior in every way—just as it was at Ford. By streamlining the production process, eliminating waste, and perfecting the art of the division of labor, this ideal became the norm.

It could be argued in this light that the goal of specialism and the division of labor is not to make the people in a given community more equal in ability and needs, as the egalitarian ideal would have it, but to make them less equal in ability and needs; not to decrease disparity between individuals, but to increase it. Only when people are highly differentiated and thus value goods at different levels can they make the most out of trade. Specialism and the division of labor do exactly that—they ensure that workers, owners, salesmen, and consumers all optimize their disparity so that everyone benefits from trade to the greatest extent. The goal is to make a given individual's product so abundant that the marginal utility for each is infinitesimal, after which trade becomes highly profitable with anyone.

The Invisible Hand

At the heart of the Ford phenomenon and all such examples of scientific management was the central premise behind subjective value and free trade: By seeking one's own interests, everyone in a given exchange can benefit. The more diverse and varied personal interests are, the more people can gain throughout a community. As such, the members of a community will seem to be acting in a somewhat benevolent manner simply by seeking their own interests. They all realize that the best way to secure their own success is by making sure that others are also successful.

This is Smith's concept of the Invisible Hand, in which individuals, pursuing their own interests, are guided by a natural force toward civil society and just actions. As Smith put it in his *Wealth of Nations*, "It is not from the benevolence of the butcher, the brewer, or the baker, that we expect our dinner, but from regard to their own interest. We address ourselves, not to their humanity but to their self-love, and never talk to them of our own necessities but of their advantages. Nobody but a beggar chooses to depend chiefly upon the benevolence of his fellow citizens."

Henry Ford's management genius offers us the perfect real-life example of the Invisible Hand in action. No one can be certain of Ford's intentions, but we should not be far off to say that to some degree it was his ambition to make millions of dollars that compelled him to build such inexpensive automobiles. In order to get what he wanted, Ford had to offer the buying public something they wanted; in order to make millions, he had to provide the people with cheap, reliable automobiles. In the end, everyone benefited.

A particular account drives home the point. In 1914, upon noting a high employee turnover rate, Ford doubled the standard salary of his factory workers from $2.50 per day to an unheard-of $5.00. But, benevolent as it may seem, this measure wasn't taken just to make his employees happier—it was a calculated business maneuver aimed at increasing profit. And it paid off. Shortly after the raise, employee turnover decreased, production increased, and, within two years, Ford saw his profits double from $30 million to $60 million. Ford knew, as Adam Smith explained, that to succeed in an open economy, one must provide something that others want. Only by satisfying others can one succeed in one's own endeavors.

This notion of an Invisible Hand directing society made Mandeville declare before Smith that "private vices lead to public virtues". The pursuit of individual wants and needs, even when those wants and needs are hush-hush or naughty, invariably renders the people in a society highly fruitful and cooperative. Thus, what is thought to be bad or degrading for a given people actually leads to a productive and noble community, whence 'public virtues'.

Thus Vice nursed Ingenuity,
Which join'd with Time; and Industry
Had carry'd Life's Conveniencies,
Its real Pleasures, Comforts, Ease,
To such a Height, the very Poor
Lived better than the Rich before;
And nothing could be added more.

——Bernard Mandeville, "The Grumbling Hive", *The Fable of the Bees* (1714)

Laissez faire (leave it be), that should be the motto of all public powers, as the world is civilized. That we cannot grow except by lowering our neighbors is a detestable notion! Only malice and malignity of heart is satisfied with such a principle and our interests are opposed to it. Laissez faire, morbleu! Laissez faire!

——from the Marquis de Argenson's 1736 diary

No one can doubt that comprehensive laws and strict enforcement can ensure civility and just actions. But that old method is bulky, strains resources, and cannot be trusted against corruption and other natural tendencies. The thought occurs, why not rely on man's natural motives as they exist, and allow each man to assume responsibility for himself?

That way, a society can achieve civility and just actions without excess burden. Indeed, the society becomes much more efficient in the process—in a word, streamlined—and much more profitable as a result.

The fact is that no central planner, or monarch as it may have been, is capable of orchestrating the infinitely complex arrangement of interlocking parts of modern industry. Only the very individuals relied upon to perform the work can decide what they should or should not strive to produce. In an open economy, the variable price system serves as the Invisible Hand to direct individuals' time and efforts toward productive ends and away from destructive ends. Just as with a stream of cars in traffic, a group of people in an economy can operate efficiently and effectively by simply paying attention to the actions of those around them. A driver need not know what is going on miles down the road to decide where to exit; he need only know what the cars in front and in back of him are doing. By ensuring that they are moving in an appropriate way, the driver can ensure that his own commute will unfold without incident.

Likewise, an apple farmer (or potato farmer or wheelbarrow maker or any other producer) need not be concerned with anyone other than the buyers of his products and the suppliers of his necessary materials. By concentrating on his own needs and the needs of those around him, he can direct his time and effort to the most productive ends possible.

* * *

The benefits of specialism, labor division, and trade are far-reaching because their applications are nearly infinite. Every action in which cooperation is possible can make use of these three techniques—work, of course, but also household chores, study, sports, travel, sightseeing, dining out, entertaining, and more, can all make use of cooperation and thus of the triumvirate of trade.

To glimpse the extent of their application, one can reflect on any instance in modern life when specialism and the division of labor are for any reason taken away. The example that comes to mind is of Robinson

Crusoe, the fictitious sailor depicted in Daniel Defoe's classic, who is ship-wrecked and stranded on a deserted island in the Caribbean. Left without anyone else to work with, Crusoe is forced to provide for himself all the necessities for survival and luxuries he desires. His story is a fascinating account of all that it would take for a single person to procure and prepare food, to build tools and shelter, and to endeavor in the most basic of modern facilities such as agriculture, pottery, and baking. At one point, Crusoe shares with us the fact that he made a board "with infinite Labour". Anyone who has attempted amateur carpentry can relate to his struggles.

Or take the more recent illustration of Tom Hanks' character Chuck Nolan in the movie *Cast Away*, who is similarly stranded on a deserted island somewhere in the South Pacific. Like Crusoe, Nolan must provide everything for himself, including food, shelter, and clothing, using the various leftover tools he has found in washed up FedEx packages for help. Scenes of his attempts to create fire, to open a coconut, and to prepare a crab for dinner are indelible and bring to life the vast amounts of work that go into the various goods and services of modern living that are so easy to take for granted. The enormity of modern comforts is made all the more evident after Nolan escapes his island and arrives at a homecoming ceremony in which lavish fruit spreads, crab legs, and fire are all displayed for anyone to pick at.

The moral is clear: Modern civil society has made life so easy that we can be thoughtless and even wasteful with our goods and services. Even practices that would take a single person hours, weeks, or years to master can be taken for granted by the average citizen in a modern metropolis. Without specialism, divided labor, and trade, we would all be stranded on deserted islands; but with these techniques, we can afford to live like kings.

Given their efficacy, the techniques are employed whenever possible. Everywhere one looks, people are trading to save time, specializing to better allocate resources, and dividing labor to get more from a given supply. The fact that practically everyone in the modern society endeavors to learn a single salable skill through twenty or so years of school and embark on a lifelong career making use of that skill is perhaps the clearest evidence for this truth. But it is everywhere we look and not only in large, lifelong undertakings. Consider a night out at the bar. Everyone knows, consciously or otherwise, that it is much more efficient for a single person in a group to order and retrieve drinks for his whole entourage than it is for each person to go up and order his own drink. In the former scenario, there is only one trip to the bar, one order, one charge to the card, and, to the disgruntlement of the bartender, a much more proportionate tip. By specializing and dividing the labor, only one of the many friends must work at a given time. The group will then trade among themselves, one round now for the next round later, and so on.

Or consider a husband-wife duo that will divide, specialize, and trade duties for dinner. In order to avoid having each one cook his or her own meals, one of the pair will assume the task of cooking for both of them. The other will assume the task of washing the dishes. Since each individual can focus on a single task, both tasks are completed more efficiently and the couple can save time that would be occupied if they were single.

> **This will testify for me that I was not idle and that I spared no pains to bring to pass whatever appeared necessary for my comfortable support.**
>
> —Daniel Defoe,
> *Robinson Crusoe* (1719)

Larger families will attest that the system's expediency increases with the number of mouths to feed. The more persons involved in a given exchange, the more efficient each can be, and the greater number of tasks that can be provided for. Given seven family members who trade duties for dinner as in the illustration above, each could eat happily for a week while only having to cook once. The amount of cooking increases with more mouths to feed, but, as touched on above, the preparation needed to add a seventh dinner is much less than it would be to add the second or even third.

This truth leads to the paradoxical concept noted by scientific management pioneer Frank Bunker Gilbreth that children can be raised 'cheaper by the dozen'. Cost for clothing, food, and books may not be cheaper for the family in total, but it certainly is cheaper *per child* since all the hidden costs of purchasing the clothes, preparing the food, and teaching lessons are diminished proportionately. Since the return for each child remains the same, it can be said that raising children is not only cheaper but far more profitable by the dozen as well. This rationale was of course one of the primary reasons for large families before the twentieth century—the more kids in a family, the more help the parents got in raising crops, milking the cows, and so on. The large family format has lost its economic advantages in the modern city, dependent as society has become on atomistic workers and skyrocketing education costs, both of which are, ironically, offshoots of the overall effects of labor division, specialism, and trade.

But bulk transactions are not limited to large groups or families. Even a bachelor can benefit from the method, though he relies on time and preservation to a greater degree. The bachelor can cook for a dozen, as it were, as long as he doesn't mind refrigerating the leftovers and eating the same thing over the course of two weeks. His division of labor and trade can also be seen in the dishes that stack up in the sink, which can be cleaned much more efficiently after the pile has grown substantially and he can concentrate on the task of cleaning many at a time. The more dishes that need to be cleaned, the less time it takes to clean each one since the preparation time for each is reduced with the accumulated work. The practice is a real time-saver, though friends and relatives who visit might not appreciate the byproducts of that efficacy. It is not known whether this obscure rationale plays a role in some bachelors' ongoing solitude.

A conclusion we can draw, however, is that even a single person can utilize the methods of the division of labor, specialism, and trade in a similar way that a group does. To reference Smith's nail factory example again, it is reasonable to believe that a single worker could make the equivalent of 4,800 nails per day as long as he imitated the factory process. He could do this by completing only one task per day, as he would in the assembly line, and using the factory over the course of 10 days. He would be like 10 workers at different stations spread out over time as well as space. The only difference would be the need to store the unfinished nails during the interim.

Indeed, cooperation need not entail more than one participant to be effectual; it can be seen as an agreement between a single person and his future self. Personal industry is a kind of trade in time since the industrialist builds something for future use instead of instant consumption. He trades time and effort now for capital to be used later.

Carl Menger's student and fellow Austrian Eugen von Böhm-Bawerk described industry and the nature of building capital as this very process. He gave the example of a peasant who lives a great distance from the nearest spring. Needing water, the peasant must travel to the spring two or three times a day. As this method is inefficient and tedious, the peasant endeavors to build a runnel, or canal, from the spring to his house, where he can then collect a reservoir for use at any time. While he expends great effort to build the canal in the first place and does not profit directly during construction, he benefits upon completion by the time and effort saved from not having to make the trek to the spring every day. The peasant cooperates with his future self, specializing for the time being in order to gain later on.

Simply spending time to fashion a hammer or shovel to help with one's labor is a trade of current time and effort for capital to be used later. No one can deny that the initial outlay is worth the eventual yield, which is much greater than it would have been without the tools.

Cooperation, however, is much more practical between multiple persons since it does not rely as much on time and preservation. A Swiss Family Robinson, for instance, is much more efficient and productive than a Robinson Crusoe, since the former can coordinate efforts at the same time. Robinson Crusoe must divide his labor over time and is thus subject to the vagaries of nature. Similarly, the factory of 10 can produce 48,000 nails in a single day, while it would take a single worker 10 days to produce the same amount. One could surmise that a factory of 20 could reduce the production time to half a day or less, since further dividing the labor can increase efficiency exponentially. Given the strategies laid out in *The Wealth of Nations*, one might expect that the more workers there are in a given process, the higher their rate of production and the more exponential their output will be.

Economies of Scale

The triumph of specialism and the division of labor can be seen in the dominance of mass production over the course of the last 150 years or so. In every sector, the move has been to expand production lines, consolidate, and form conglomerations, all in attempt to take advantage of the division of labor to the greatest extent possible. The visible manifestation of this is the bevy of super corporations that have emerged in markets across the board. What was once Carter Oil, Imperial Oil, Standard of Louisiana, and Esso became Exxon, which merged with Mobile to become ExxonMobil. What began as Walton's Five and Dime in Bentonville, Arkansas, grew to become the gargantuan Walmart chain, the largest private employer in America. Throughout the history of modern business, the story is the same of expanding, reproducing, and growing to encompass higher quantities and a greater variety of products.

The tendency toward this method of trade is often subconscious, making its way into pretty much every activity where time and volume of goods and services play a role—which is to say pretty much every activity one undertakes. Not only do the division of labor, specialism, and trade apply to businesses and the production side of the equation, but consumers too can take advantage of the phenomenon by buying in bulk, whether at the supermarket, warehouse stores, or factory outlet malls. Both the supplier and the shopper benefit from conducting bulk transactions, where the amount of goods exchanged is increased and the overhead costs are diminished per exchange. When it is less costly for the store to sell a good, then that store can sell its goods at a lower price, and the savings is often handed to the consumer in the form of a sale.

As such, one cannot rightly blame the Walmarts of the world for the loss of mom and pop stores across the country. The proliferation of warehouse chains and the decline of smaller, family-owned shops is not some malicious business scheme devised in the back room as it might seem, but rather a logical manifestation of the very natural trade method. Doing things in bulk is much more efficient—for producer and consumer—and so it is only logical to apply this method to all endeavors.

Of course, savvy marketers have made use of this fact in just about every imaginable element of commerce, and they have become very successful in selling their products in bulk as a result. Executives at fast food restaurants, for instance, have learned that bulk transactions are so cost-effective that they can significantly reduce the price of larger portions and still make a profit. Whence the popularity of the super-sized portions that have become so infamous of late. The time it takes to procure the food and deliver it to the customer is the same whether the order is for the small, medium, large, grande, or über-humongus portion, and so it just makes good sense to boost the serving sizes in order to get more for the effort. It's not that the restaurant companies are devious scoundrels out to take advantage of hungry Americans, nor the consumers gluttonous pigs that don't know when to say when; it's just that both recognize a good deal when they see it. Neglect of waistlines is another story.

The efficiency of specialism and division of labor can hardly be doubted since the advantage has been shown in nearly every sector of society and every industry. Early economists found that the division of labor benefits participants even when one party is more productive at everything. If a woman is more efficient at both making dinner and doing the dishes, she is still better off specializing and dividing the labor with her husband. That is to say that the benefits of the trade outweigh the costs even if her husband is a lazy pig.

This is the Law of Comparative Advantage as described by British economist David Ricardo. He showed that even if one party in a given equation is better at the production of two different goods, it still benefits that party to specialize in one and trade for the other, as trading allows both parties to focus on their comparative advantage. The CEO of a company might be better than a maid at cleaning his house, but it is still advised that he focus on his forte and hire a cleaning crew. That way, he can spend more time on what he is best at and thus produce more in the long run. Likewise, one country might be better at producing both wine and cloth than another is, but it will profit by specializing in one good and trading for the other because it can focus on its comparative advantage.

A simple example (illustrated in the diagram below) shows the gain in numbers. We see that it takes France 50 workers to make one unit of cloth while it takes Italy 25 workers to produce the same unit of cloth; meanwhile, it takes France 200 workers to make one unit of wine while it takes Italy 25. Now, as we see in this simplified table, Italy makes both cloth and wine more efficiently than France. While France is better at making cloth than it is at making wine, it is still less productive than Italy at both.

	France	Italy	Total Output
Cloth	50 workers / 1 unit	25 workers / 1 unit	2 units
Wine	200 workers / 1 unit	25 workers / 1 unit	2 units

FIG. 1—Comparative Advantage, Diversified Production.

The total output when the countries are producing both goods is two units of each cloth and wine. As we will see, if we shift resources to allow each country to focus on its comparative advantage, both will win with a higher total output. If, for example, in France we take 100 workers from wine production and let them work on the more efficient production of cloth, and put all of Italy's workers into wine production, its comparative advantage, we will see total production expand for both.

Ricardo showed that when we allow the producers to work on what they do best, the volume increases substantially—three units of cloth as

	France	Italy	Total Output
Cloth	150 workers / 3 unit	0 workers / 0 units	3 units
Wine	100 workers / .5 unit	50 workers / 2 unit	2.5 units

FIG. 2—Comparative Advantage, Specialized Production.

opposed to two, two-and-a-half units of wine as opposed to just two. As we can see in the diagram, it benefits Italy to engage in the trade even though it is better at the production of both wine and cloth. Indeed, everyone benefits because total wealth—the total amount of cloth and wine—increases substantively.

Thus, one can rightly suggest that, in economics, the whole is greater than the sum of its parts. The amount of wealth created by cooperative individuals will be greater than the total amount of wealth created by uncooperative individuals simply because the former are able to make better use of their resources. If we are to use Lionel Robbins' definition of economics—the allocation of scarce resources which have alternative uses—then it is always in the interest of people to cooperate, divide labor, specialize, and trade because they will always be able to allocate their resources more efficiently.

The Costs of Trade

One might recognize the fact that in this example, as in all instances of trade, there must be an allocation for trade resources set aside in order for a profit to be made. Someone must actually conduct the trade once the goods have been produced. As such, the number of workers used for each task must be reduced to account for the additional specialized merchants and distributors. Instead of 100 workers producing wine, for instance, only 90 will be allocated, with the other 10 being used for transport and trade between the two nations.

This means that total output will fall since fewer workers are allocated to production. Given a tight enough margin, it might turn out that the benefit of dividing labor does not cover the cost of distribution and so would not be worth it in the end. For instance, it is possible that the amount of extra goods produced by specializing tasks is one unit. If the traders deprive the system of one or more unit of production, then it is not profitable. On a whole, we can conclude that this is rather unlikely. If the margin is anywhere near what it is in Adam Smith's pin factory example, the choice is plain. When the difference is between one and 4,800, it is clear that the margin is large enough to provide for the costs of distribution.

Applying this extra cost to the French-Italian trade illustration, we can offer a generous allotment of workers for trading and still realize gains in both cloth and wine.

	France	Italy	Total Output
Cloth	150 workers / 3 units	0 workers / 0 units	3 units
Wine	90 workers / .45 unit	45 workers /1.8 units	2.25 units
Traders	5 workers / 2 units	5 workers / 3.25 units	5.25 units

Fig. 3—Comparative Advantage, Specialized Production with Traders.

Taking a step back, one recognizes that there is another cost of conducting trade that is much less tangible than the price of merchants and distributors, and at the same time much more significant—the cost of interdependency. It may be an obvious corollary to the method, but its consequences are much dearer than might be expected. The fact is that, in order to take advantage of trade, one must be associated with others. Indeed, one is dependent upon others in direct proportion to his productivity. The more he concentrates on a single task, the more productive he is, but the less he is able to conduct other tasks. He can be a much more efficient metal pourer with this method, but he no longer has time to stamp out the head of the nail or apply the base. He relies on the work of other men to make his own work worthwhile at all.

All specialized workers rely on other people in the same way. A modern example shows the extent of the dilemma. One might be an excellent spreadsheet technician, but he cannot possibly live on spreadsheets alone. He relies on a whole slew of people, from the office clerk to the sales staff to the company executives, to make his work salable, without which his product could not garner even a penny, much less a loaf of bread or a jacket. This is not to mention all the people he requires to make the actual loaf of bread and the jacket that he aims to buy with the money he makes working on spreadsheets.

The implications of this phenomenon are various and can only be discussed fully on a later page. For present purposes, it is necessary to acknowledge the fact that the benefits of trade are all based in a network of mutual dependency that in effect counters the individualism born in the new economics of the sixteenth century. As soon as one establishes his freedom, the newly liberated individual finds that his well-being can increase exponentially—but only by resuming a form of bondage that he has just abandoned. In the extreme cases of modern super-specialism, one can see how trade could diminish the role of the individual altogether. To use the method to the greatest extent, one must become a single part in a complex enterprise that no more recognizes his abilities than can exist without his input. He is a cog in a machine—an essential cog, but a cog nonetheless.

On a larger scale, this is what happens over all industries and in every aspect of human life. An individual works as a spreadsheet technician, a hamburger flipper, a commercial airline pilot, or a Federal Reserve Chairman, for eight or more hours a day, producing no more than one or two things for the overarching company that is the system as a whole. He then trades his product for all the necessities and luxuries that he can afford, relying on other workers to provide him with what he wants, and thus trading his autonomy for dependence on others.

This interdependency is the driving principle behind the Juggernaut, which is something of a Chinese handcuff laid on the individual. The more productive one is, the more he relies on others; the more he tries to liberate himself, the more reliant he becomes. He believes that working hard and extending productivity grants him freedom in the ability to do what he wants, but as his access to goods and luxuries is increased, his ability to produce in other ways is decreased, and he thus becomes more and more dependent on the system.

A move from farm to city underscores the dilemma well. One might move to the city to find work at the highly efficient manufacturing plant there. His productivity increases and he gets high wages as a factory worker, but the move to the city means that he no longer owns a plot of land where he can grow his own food. He has become dependent upon other farmers and thus the distributors and produce merchants that are needed to deliver the goods. In specializing, he has excluded himself from self-sufficiency.

The mere fact that one must move to a congested metropolis to take advantage of the trade method these days is a significant cost in itself. While the luxuries that cities provide their inhabitants are clearly abundant, the drawbacks cannot go unnoticed. Crowded grocery stores and subway terminals, cramped living quarters at exorbitant rates, 30-minute tours to find parking, stacks of trash bags piled up on one's doorstep, et cetera, are circumstances that all city dwellers are bound to face on a daily basis. Either the city dweller becomes frustrated and angered by these aspects or grows desensitized to the largely uncivilized arrangement, of which neither option is particularly attractive.

It must be noted that this interdependency began, for the most part, as a voluntary interdependency. A farmer in Adam Smith's day could very well stay in the country rather than submerge himself in the intricate manufacturing process of the city. Likewise, the factory worker who was disgruntled by his increasingly tedious job was not obligated to stay and could fairly unceremoniously escape to the country and reclaim a life in nature if he so chose. Indeed, it might be argued that it was only this freedom to opt out that encouraged so many people to take part in the Industrial Revolution. Since they always had an alternative to it, they could demand from it all the wealth they thought they deserved; and since they had the freedom to leave, they most reliably got that wealth.

Still, the effects of the interdependent life were evident from the start of Industrialism, the greatest of which concerned the will and affected the very trade method that had given birth to specialism and the division of labor. As Adam Smith warned in his *Wealth of Nations*, the factory environment requires mechanical repetition that dulls the wit. Specialism is a technique that deliberately bypasses mental processes and so has the tendency to condition those involved to a rather mindless life. This is true for factory work, of course, but it applies to any specialized task that relies on repetition—pretty much every occupation in the modern world. As such, the typical citizen is as prone to this dulling of the wits as was the nineteenth-century factory worker.

Smith's solution was for workers to participate in a rigorous course of mental activity at home to reengage the soul. One can see how such a remedy has been neglected in modern society by the kinds of mindless entertainment that folks subscribe to after business hours. When one's mind is numb, his greatest tool for recovery is unusable.

As such, modern society has become a place where an individual must proceed mindlessly through the channels of school, career, and retirement, doing only as much as he needs to satisfy others and make a living. His will has been put aside because, after all, it is unnecessary in his daily interactions. Just as he relies on others to provide him with food, shelter, clothing, and so on, so too does he rely on them to provide him with guidance on what he is to produce himself. It is only for them and by their dictates that he can produce anything anyway, since it is only through them that he can obtain the money he needs to obtain food, shelter, clothing, and so on.

Marx used the term 'alienation' to describe this condition, which he feared was the inevitable consequence of any capitalist system. In general, alienation is a loss of the self, the process of becoming alien to oneself. A citizen works for others to carry out the tasks of others and attain the goals of others. He views his own product with ambivalence at best and often outright contempt.

One can see the effects throughout the business world. Aimless workers, lackluster efforts, misdirected enthusiasm, all help to create a condition of lower productivity. Recall any number of office scenarios, in real life or on television, in which workers irreverently waste time and goof off on the clock as if doing so is an assumed part of the job. When a worker's connection to the final product is displaced by scores of divides, he becomes incapable of understanding the significance of his trade, and thus incapable of putting forth a quality product.

This truth was acknowledged as far back as Aquinas, who observed that a good produced for sale will always tend to be of lower quality than one produced for consumption. If there is a cost in labor division, specialism, and trade, it is this simple fact of nature. And the more complex a given structure, the more prone to this degradation its product will be.

4. THE ABSTRACTION
OF WEALTH

As SHOWN IN THE ILLUSTRATIONS above, specialism, the division of labor, and trade help to increase productivity by minimizing overhead costs per transaction. The technique is so effective that the result is almost assuredly an increase in productivity in every process to which it is applied and an increase in wealth for all parties involved. But since there are multiple participants, the process does not come without its costs. As seen previously, the most basic cost is that of facilitating trade. At least a fraction of resources must be allotted to the merchantry and distribution of the goods once produced. This lessens the overall productivity and may nullify it in cases where the margin is low enough.

A corollary to the increase in these trends is the emergence of money as an essential component of daily life, which has its own benefits and costs. Of course, money has been around since long before the modern era, indeed, since perhaps the dawn of society, but it was the urgency of exchange in the new economy that thrust money into a central role, a place from which it has never retreated. It is in this central role that money has become something different altogether, not only a means for exchange, but a commodity which holds its own value. And so it is necessary to examine exactly what this commodity is, and how it affects the trade that has become so crucial to our modern way of life.

To examine this further, let us consider what trade was like before the new economy took shape. Prior to modern times, trade could be conducted smoothly without money in a kind of barter. Each participant had his own specialty goods and sought to trade them for other goods—a loaf of bread for a round of beef, a stool for a tapestry, and so on. But as trade became much more commonplace and at the same time much more complex, this system of barter grew insufficient and money had to be added to the equation.

Since Aristotle and the Greeks, it has been known that barter is restrictive. First, for barter to work, goods being traded must be exchanged evenly since it is often impossible to break up the bartered goods into fractions, as in half a tapestry or stool, for example. Second, the trading parties must have complementary needs and abilities, since the barter consists of one person trading wholly with another, a book for bread, a candle for a crucifix, and so on. Combined, these make trade rather cumbersome in any economy and practically impossible in the modern system.

To regard the second first, consider a fur collector who is hungry for apples. To engage in any trade at all, the fur collector must not only find an apple farmer, he must find an apple farmer who wants furs. The two parties must have complementary needs and abilities, what William Stanley Jevons has called a 'double coincidence', so that what one wants the other can provide and vice versa. Granted a diverse enough society and basic enough goods, this combination of needs and abilities is not inconceivable. A website designer, for instance, could easily barter with a woodworker or handyman for work that is equal in value.

But double coincidence is rare, even these days. The more homogeneous a society's production and the more eclectic its tastes, the more difficult a match becomes. As a contemporary economist put it, "People who own basketballs don't necessarily wish to exchange them for hats, and most newspaper vendors are not looking to unload their wares in order to hear someone speak about the War of 1812." The difficulty in finding a double coincidence limits the kind of trade that can be done and so is unsatisfactory in a growing economy.

Even if the bartering parties are able to find complementary partners, they face another obstacle in agreeing on terms. The fur trader, for example, may want only one or two apples, as any more would be excessive. But all he has to offer the apple farmer is a beaver pelt, which is worth no fewer than two hundred apples. To acquire an apple at all, the fur collector would have to acquire two hundred, and is thus forced to waste or figure out a way to trade the unwanted fruit. The difficulty might make the trade simply unworkable despite all that could be gained from the transaction.

Thus, an artificial, abstract form of accounting is wanted, a medium of exchange that allows different goods and services to be traded notwithstanding their differing values and their suppliers' differing needs. That abstract form of accounting is money. Whether it is a precious metal such as gold or silver, another commodity such as tobacco or wheat, or a piece of paper printed by a government, money allows for a fluid exchange of all goods and services between all people and thus frees the society to trade much more efficiently and effectively.

Materials used for money throughout history have varied widely, as one could suspect. Gold and other shiny metals have been used more than otherwise; so too have stones, shells, and even cigarettes, as in the case of P.O.W. camps during the Second World War. Lately, the standard paper bill money has evolved into mere numbers on a computer screen so that zeros and ones have become the predominant currency.

Despite such a range, all currencies since the dawn of exchange have featured the same general characteristics that make money what it is. Those characteristics can be summed up by the single notion of a stable supply. A currency could be anything that a people chooses to exchange as long as it can be obtained and possessed by persons involved, there is some limit to the amount available, and it doesn't fluctuate considerably. Anything with these qualities is a viable candidate and has most likely been used at some point as money.

The reason stability is the key ingredient in money has to do with its original purpose. People use money in order to trade. A given exchange can only be legitimate if the money used in it retains its value during the interim. If the total amount of money fluctuates, or if one of the traders somehow generates a large supply of the commodity, its ability to convey the value of the goods traded will change, and so it will cease to be of use as money.

We can see how important stability is for a currency throughout history in cases when the supply has suddenly changed. Sixteenth-century Spain offers a relevant example, but so too does Ancient Rome at the dawn of the empire and Germany after World War I. In all three cases, though for different reasons, the money supply increased dramatically within a short period of time; and in all of these cases price inflation soon followed with a slew of economic and political troubles. The value of the money changed, and so the price of goods and services also changed, leaving the system in disarray. As the famed monetarist Milton Friedman would have it, the primary cause of money mischief is a change in its quantity.

Wealth Abstracted

Efficiency in trade and a higher standard of living in general were doubtless the original intents behind the wide use of money. But, with the vast technical and social advances in the past several centuries, other consequences of money have become rather prominent throughout the economy. By its nature, money has abstracted wealth from its simple, relevant form, such as the value found in food, furniture, land, and so on, to a complex, intangible entity that can no longer be consumed or used in the old sense of the words. While the standard of living has clearly been improved by the widespread use of money, the way that those lives are lived has been altered altogether.

Being as familiar with money as we are, it is not easy to see just how far from reality this abstraction takes us. These days, when one thinks of the value of a good or service, one imagines a number that is usually attached to a dollar sign. An orange is worth $3.00, an orange Charger is worth $30,000, and so on.

We see the dollar amount even though we know that the true worth of these goods is a fuller concept that takes into account their ability to satisfy one's needs and wants. An orange's value is really in the satisfaction one would get from eating the delicious fruit; an orange Charger's worth is the satisfaction one would get from driving around in it. Viewing their worth as a numerical dollar figure is more convenient and easier to communicate, but it separates the value from the good itself and, at the same time, separates needs and wants from the individual.

To see how far from reality the abstraction of wealth has taken us, consider the confusion so common these days with regard to a person's occupation or job. When a person takes home a paycheck, we say that he is 'making money', which implies that he has done something that generates new money, ex nihilo. We don't necessarily mean to suggest that he is printing dollar bills at the office, but the implications are not far off. The thought is that the money is new and solely of the worker's doing. The reality is nothing of the sort. In fact, the worker is not making money, but rather 'earning an income', which is to say that he has done something that someone else has found worthy of transferring money to him. The money is not generated out of thin air, but rather transferred from some other person's possession.

This is a crucial distinction to make because these days it has become a granted assumption that we can just make money at a whim or whenever some powerful politician or banker believes it to be the best course of action. The assumption is that in so doing we can create wealth out of thin air, that the printing of money is equal to the creation of goods and services, food, clothing, shelter, and the like. Adam Smith himself spotted the trend in his own day, writing that "To grow rich is to get money, and wealth and money, in short, are, in common language, considered as in every respect synonymous."

As we will see, the two are not synonymous. The difference between three dollar bills and an orange is clear. An orange can satisfy a person's needs directly and three dollars can only do so indirectly—the latter relies on the presence of a grocer and his willingness to give up his orange in exchange for the money, a set of circumstances that cannot always be presupposed. While it is easier to assume all of the benefits one can get from a given amount of money, taking the intermediate steps for granted can and has been troublesome. Money is artificial, intangible wealth. It detaches value from the good and stores it in an imaginary vault outside of reality. This frees us to do much more with our wealth but, like all abstractions, complicates matters and introduces a level of precariousness that must be guarded against.

> **All the perplexities, confusion and distress in America arise, not from defects in their Constitution or Confederation, not from want of honor or virtue, so much as from the downright ignorance of the nature of coin, credit and circulation.**
>
> —JOHN ADAMS (1735-1826)

* * *

To examine a culture based on the widespread use of money, it is constructive to look at the differences between real wealth and its abstracted form. Those differences can be seen best in the specific ways in which thoughts and actions change when the concept of wealth shifts from the real and tangible to the artificial and abstract.

The first thing one might notice upon the abstraction of wealth is a kind of leveling among those who use it. Since money detaches value from a good or service, it can represent that value no matter where it comes from or who has previously owned it. In other words, it depersonalizes wealth. Some economists have speculated that this abstracting quality has helped to break down racial and religious prejudices that might have prevented trade otherwise. It has made possible a place like New York City, which sees every ethnic background intermingling in a 'melting pot' of culture, primarily because the city has always been dedicated to commerce and the exchange of money.

Real wealth, on the other hand, being tied directly to the producer, comes with the characteristics of that producer. And the consumer cannot help but take into consideration those characteristics, whether his reaction is rational or groundless, authentic or imaginary. As such, a blanket or brand of food or automobile can be more or less valuable to a potential consumer depending on where it came from.

Yet money is wanted no matter where it came from or who previously owned it. Money is wanted by prejudiced whites even if it is from blacks, by fundamentalist Muslims from Israelis, and by male chauvinists from independent career girls. In this light, money can be seen as a universal language that breaks down barriers and unites all people in a common goal—the goal of getting rich. An advertisement once quipped, "It doesn't matter if you're rich or poor, just as long as you have money." The same can be applied to all stations and creeds—it doesn't matter if you're white or black or Muslim or Jewish or male or female or anything else, as long as you have money, you can buy and sell, you can be a part of the community.

By the same token, money validates actions even when they carry with them rational disdain. Gambling, prostitution, and bootlegging are all perfectly acceptable in the eye of money-seekers since these can all make money and can do so to the same degree as more traditional pursuits. Crime in general can be seen as a valid enterprise when real value is neglected in lieu of monetary value. Consider crime in a society without money, for example. There, theft, vandalism, and murder garner little or no value and can thus not be redeemed for real wealth. No one will harbor or encourage such behavior because it is clearly harmful to all but one. In a money-less society, crime results in ostracizing oneself from a community, and those who engage in criminal pursuits lose influence and standing in the community.

In a society based on money, however, it doesn't matter how a person comes up with the cash so long as they obtain it in some way. As such, criminal action can become a sustainable endeavor. Rather than being ostracized from society, criminals have been some of the most powerful and even beloved figures in certain money-based communities. The kind of loyalty and reputation that mafia bosses attained during the twentieth century is a testament to the power of money over morality.

It is a short jump from the thought that anything could possibly be done for money to the impulse that one should be able to do anything for money. The subtle shift in perception represents the overall shift in the meaning of wealth. In a money-based society, practically anything can garner wealth, even if it has traditionally been seen as harmful to personal or social well-being—who would pursue a career in public school teaching, garbage collection, dangerous factory work, or politics if it weren't for the paycheck? These careers and others can be seen as tedious, degrading, harmful, and even life-threatening as a matter of fact, but they all acquire legitimacy in a money-based economy.

Thus, the abstraction of wealth can lead very directly to its contradiction and a sort of poverty. For example, the conscientious modern liberal might despise the big corporations that dominate the economy, but he is obliged to 'sell his soul to the devil' in order to earn the swollen paycheck the company offers for his services. And, while it is true that the teen pop star might be vulgar, immodest, and officious, the statement that 'she's making millions now' hushes any critics. It is as if the fact that she is a millionaire means that anything she does is sanctioned by society and thus represents a legitimate enterprise.

Indeed, one would be hard-pressed to find a single person these days who is willing to stand firm on his principles in the face of a sizeable monetary reward. The thought, perhaps, is that one's principles can be better served with a large enough income. Either way, it appears as though ideology has a price, and a large income is all the justification one needs to excuse reprehensible behavior. As Euripides is quoted as saying, "Among mankind, money is far more persuasive than logical argument."

The weakening of morals that accompanies the use of money is nothing new. It can be seen as far back as ancient times, Judas the Apostle being the quintessential 'sell-out'. And it is doubtless this ever-present tendency that has given money the timeless label 'the root of all evil'. All abstractions blur lines, and amorality, if not blatant immorality, is the inevitable outcome of this ambiguity. One will find that money's ability to distort the economy—and by turns, the moral constitution of the society—is increased as its use increases. Keen observers of the modern era recognize that, with soaring trade levels, the use of money has increased

> I smil'd to my self at the Sight of this Money, O Drug Said I aloud, "What art thou good for, Thou art not worth to me, no not the taking off of the Ground, one of those Knives is worth all this Heap, I have no Manner of use for thee, e'en remain where thou art, and go to the Bottom as a Creature whose Life is not worth saving." However, upon Second Thoughts, I took it away.
>
> —DANIEL DEFOE,
> *ROBINSON CRUSOE* (1719)

exponentially, and as such the economy and society as a whole have been altered in vast new ways unthinkable in ancient or medieval times.

The more a society offers in the way of goods and services, luxuries and comforts, the more that money can obtain for the owner. As this reward grows more and more powerful, the desire to own money grows that much more powerful.

The Accumulation of Money

Perhaps the most radical distortion caused by money has to do with its innate flexibility. Since money is by nature a plastic commodity, able to fit in different contexts and thus represent various kinds of property, it can behave in ways that real wealth cannot. For one, unlike goods and services, money does not lose value with its use. Real wealth, whether it is an automobile, a rug, or an iPod, necessarily loses value with each use. It acquires nicks and cracks and generally wears down after enough uses. New cars drop some 30% in value the minute they are driven off the dealer's lot. Some forms of wealth, such as foods and raw materials, actually cease to exist after they have been used once.

Money, on the other hand, loses no value with each use. Even when considering commodity money in the case of gold or silver coins, which certainly accumulate wear and tear like other goods, the money value will always stay the same. A shabby quarter from 1982 is worth the same as a newly-minted one; a two-dollar bill from 1976 is worth the same as two singles printed in 2010; and so on. While real wealth deteriorates or ceases to exist with use, abstract wealth remains, transferred, perhaps, like energy in the universe, but just as persuasive. As a figment of social intercourse, money is flawless even when it is in use.

A document from the early nineteenth century illustrates the longevity of money aptly and amusingly by tracking the path of a fictitious bill of paper money through its various owners, all the while recounting their sundry financial escapades. First, the bank note recalls his humble beginnings as a couple of rags found in the East Indies and Ireland. He then describes his brief yet painful makeover at the mill, followed by a sort of transubstantiation at the bank, where he was miraculously converted from rags into "gold or something nearly as valuable".

The new money then takes off on an adventure unlike any of the time. The bill recounts his travels first from the bank to a merchant, then to a shopkeeper, a director, and to another bank, before carrying on to a shoemaker, a tavern keeper, a farmer, the bank again, and finally to the president of a corporation, under whose ownership the bill witnesses a number of legal misdeeds and a trial for his owner's castigation.

The adventure is found in James Kirke Paulding's *Letters from the South* (1816), a collection of anecdotes and annotations on the world as it stood at the time. The exercise is pure fantasy but offers a vivid picture of money's abstract nature, durable even through the most tumultuous of social events and the cause of any number of morally questionable pursuits. The bank note is confounded by the various schemes people undertake to obtain more of the abstracted wealth, but he dares not contend the artificial glory lest he lose his own consequence in society and be reduced to rags again.

Because of its flexibility, money can perform two feats that no real goods can ever aspire to: It can be practically infinite in its productivity, and it can be stored and accumulated indefinitely. First, since money can be used without losing value, it is the perfect mechanism for lending and borrowing. While real goods lose value with each use, an owner is less inclined to lend them out. He will be sure to use them himself or hold on to them when not in use so as to hedge against depreciation. The frivolous lender of goods will learn quickly how costly it becomes. The last time I lent out my mountain bike, for instance, I got it back with a mangled front wheel.

Meanwhile, money can be borrowed, used for whatever purpose, and returned without an economic scratch. Quite often, it is returned with value added to it by means of interest earned. As a tool of lending and borrowing, money is much more productive than real wealth. When one isn't using it, someone else could be using it to buy productive capital goods or turn around and loan it again. In effect, it is as if several people own it and benefit from it at the same time. While one is inclined to let his mountain bike sit unused for an extended time, he might be more willing to loan out $20. That $20 can be productive while the bike must collect dust.

In the second place, most real wealth, whether it is in the form of foodstuffs, durable goods, or even lasting property, has some level of expiration inherent in it and can only be preserved through some elaborate storage system. Ice cream, for example, can only be stored by the use of a fair amount of resources. The refrigeration and storage space needed make it unprofitable to store and accumulate large quantities of the tasty treat, though many would probably find it very rewarding to do so. Even grains, which typically can be stored without much preservative, still occupy a good deal of space and thus make it unprofitable to store and accumulate beyond a given point. It could be said that the granaries of ancient and medieval communities were evidence of man's deference to nature more than his adherence to sound economics.

By contrast, money can be stored easily and without much expense. It was Locke who noted that money, unlike real wealth, allows for accumulation without spoilage, a feature which he saw as in accordance with God's law. While foodstuffs and even furniture and clothes would all perish over time, money would never perish and so made the accumulation of wealth an acceptable and even noble thing. Most coins and bills are moreover compact and can fit in a personal container. With the advent of digital currency and credit cards, money requires virtually no space at all. One can therefore accumulate money and save it over time without any real costs.

This fact is perhaps the most substantial way in which wealth is distorted, and perhaps the most influential in changing our lives. It is, after all, only through the widespread use of money that great amounts of wealth—in the order of millions or billions of dollars—can be amassed, and only with money that such wealth can be used in any particular endeavor. The fortunes of John Jacob Astor, Cornelius Vanderbilt, Andrew Carnegie, and John D. Rockefeller, for instance, would all have

> He that gathered a hundred bushels of acorns or apples, had thereby a property in them, they were his goods as soon as gathered. He was only to look, that he used them before they spoiled, else he took more than his share, and robbed others. And indeed it was a foolish thing, as well as dishonest, to hoard up more than he could make use of. Again, if he would give his nuts for a piece of metal, pleased with its colour; or exchange his sheep for shells, or wool for a sparkling pebble or a diamond, and keep those by him all his life, he invaded not the right of others, he might heap as much of these durable things as he pleased; the exceeding of the bounds of his just property not lying in the largeness of his possession, but the perishing of anything uselessly in it.
>
> —JOHN LOCKE,
> *TWO TREASTISES OF GOVERNMENT* (1680-90)

been impossible without the prevalent use of abstract wealth in the form of money. If all wealth were made of real goods, such fortunes would have to be consumed at some point or else rot away before it could be accumulated.

Take, for example, the fortune of John Jacob Astor, America's first multimillionaire. His riches were built on the fur trade, a business which he helped to perfect during the early 1800s in the expanding American Middlewest. As he demonstrated through expert trapping techniques and trade negotiations, it was possible to collect hundreds of millions of dollars worth of furs. Of course, no single person or family could possibly make use of so many pelts, nor could anyone find enough other goods to trade for such a bounty. The only way Astor's business acumen, trade procedures, and utter efficiency could be worth anything was by retaining the profits in the form of large quantities of money. Otherwise, the whole of his business prowess would necessarily be squandered.

The same goes for the other titans of nineteenth-century industry. The only way Vanderbilt's shipping and railroad lines, or Carnegie's steel manufacture, or Rockefeller's oil extraction and refining companies could be effectively employed and properly utilized was through the large-scale accumulation of abstract wealth in the form of money. Without it, no industry would be feasible or even desirable.

Just as industry is only fully utilized with the buildup of great stores of monetary capital, so too do great endeavors of all kinds require monetary capital. A million-dollar railroad cannot be built unless a million dollars of wealth can be accumulated beforehand; a multimillion-dollar skyscraper cannot begin construction until that kind of capital has been raised, and so on. Only when wealth has been abstracted from real, tangible goods into artificial, intangible means can these immense industrial projects be undertaken.

And the kind of outcome need not be limited to industrial products aimed at generating revenue. Indeed, the business savvy of the great nineteenth-century industrialists was perhaps matched by their philanthropy toward schools, churches, and other organizations, without which it could be argued that many of the great institutions of the twentieth century would not exist. John Jacob Astor, for example, used his wealth to support John Audubon's ornithology and the writing of Edgar Allen Poe. A large sum of his wealth was used to establish the Astor Library, which today assumes the name of The New York Public Library.

Vanderbilt's charitable giving can be seen in the university that bears his name. The Mellon family, from which several multimillionaires were bred, formed the Mellon Institute of Industrial Research, which later merged with a charitable contribution from Andrew Carnegie, the Carnegie Institute of Technology, to form Carnegie Mellon University. Carnegie was perhaps the quintessential industrialist-turned-philanthropist. His dictum was that one should spend the first third of one's life gathering all the education possible, the second third making as much money as possible, and the last third giving it all away to worthy causes. His other causes included the Carnegie Endowment for International Peace, Church Peace Union, and numerous public libraries around the world.

John D. Rockefeller was by many accounts the richest man to ever live. Being the first man to possess a nominal fortune of $1 billion, his wealth had grown to $1.4 billion by his death in 1937. Estimates for the inflation-adjusted equivalent range from $392 to $663 billion—some six times Bill Gates' peak wealth of $101 billion in 1999. By all standards, Rockefeller was exceedingly rich. He was also one of the most charitable men in the history of the United States, giving 10% of his income to his church from his very first paycheck. His donations helped to create what later became Spelman College for Afroind women, the Rockefeller Institute of Medical Research, the Rockefeller Foundation, and also supported Denison University and the University of Chicago among others.

The vast accumulation of wealth made possible by the widespread use of money means that more people can be persuaded in a single endeavor, bigger enterprises can be pursued, and more comprehensive organizations can be formed than ever imagined by the use of real goods and wealth.

Without money, hardly any of the institutions in our mass culture could be comprehended, let alone attempted.

The greatest recognition that one can give to money and the circulation of currency is perhaps the very fact that wherever in history free trade has occurred and vast amounts of coin has traded hands, there has always been a great upsurge in culture and civilization as a whole. Whether one considers ancient Athens, Rome, Constantinople, or Genoa, Venice, Amsterdam, London, Shanghai, New York, San Francisco, or Tokyo, free trade has led to riches in the arts, architecture, science, technology, social organizations, and standard of living. Wherever free trade and the circulation of money have been quelled, on the other hand, in places like Sub-Saharan Africa, the Middle East after the close of its Golden Age, late medieval China, Soviet Russia, and modern-day Cuba, technical advance has slowed or ceased, the arts have diminished, and social organizations have repressed enterprise and growth.

Theoretically, there is no limit to the amount of money that one can accumulate and utilize, which is to say that there is no limit to money's usefulness. While one might readily accumulate boxes of cereal, there is a limit to the amount that can be considered useful. A collection of 10 could be useful, while one of 80 is pushing it, and one of 10,000 is not only useless but cumbersome and thus costly. With money, a collection of $10 is useful, and one of $80 is even more useful; one of $10,000 is exponentially more useful. One could imagine that the pattern would continue at least until one reaches the upper limits of the entire money supply.

The Satisfaction of All

This survey calls to mind a false belief common when thinking of abstracted wealth: the idea that money is only good as a means of exchange. To be sure, money is only worth something if someone is willing to give the owner of the money something in exchange for it. Five dollars is only worth something, for example, if the delicatessen is willing to give the owner of the money a sandwich in exchange for it, the record store is willing to trade an mp3 for it, or the phone company to provide a five-minute call. In short, the money is only worth that which can be acquired in exchange for it; it is a means of exchange and nothing more.

But, with an inherent plasticity, money has the ability to take the shape of any good or service on the market, and so it is much more versatile than any real good could possibly be. This chameleonic quality is so unique and powerful that, at a certain point in the development of an economy, money actually becomes more than just a way to transfer value between goods. To the extent that money in itself is accommodating, convenient, and an all-around time-saver, it can satisfy needs by itself and is regarded as valuable in its own right.

Whence the pervasive love of money, a cliché to be sure, but one with sensible origins. Even though five pieces of paper with green print are in themselves not as useful to a person as, say, a sandwich or an mp3 or a five-minute call on a cell phone, in a complex, cooperative society, the paper becomes worth any one of these. Indeed, since the paper can turn into these and more, it is almost as if it is worth all of them combined because of the freedom it affords. The thought occurs that money is worth more than real goods because owning it is like owning the potential for owning everything. How much is the mere ability to collect and store wealth worth in itself? Being free from want, the constant threat of suffering, and wretched subsistence is alone worth a great deal in the peace of mind it provides.

Nineteenth-century German philosopher Arthur Schopenhauer said it best when he defended the love of money that had become so prevalent even in his day. "People are often reproached for wishing for money above all things and for loving it more than anything else," he wrote in his *Wisdom of Life*, "but it is natural and even inevitable for people to love that which, like an unwearied Proteus, is always ready to turn itself into whatever object their wandering wishes or manifold desires may for the moment fix upon. Everything else can satisfy only *one* wish, *one* need: food is good only if you are hungry; wine, if you are able to enjoy it; drugs, if you are sick; fur for the winter; love for youth, and so on. These are all only relatively good, (Greek: agatha pros ti). Money alone is absolutely good, because it is not only a concrete satisfaction of one need in particular; it is an abstract satisfaction of all."

Indeed, money offers even more. By its ability to accumulate and grow unlike real goods, money can satisfy not only one's needs but one's elaborate wishes and desires; it can satisfy one's greatest dreams. Since money's power is practically limitless, so too can the aspirations that it fulfills be. An Aston Martin, a 2,000-foot skyscraper, a flight to the moon—all are possible if only one has enough money. To some degree, five dollars is worth more than a five-dollar sandwich because the dollars can be added to more money and thus can provide a means to something greater, whereas the sandwich is always limited in its ability to satisfy.

It is in this way that money can supersede real wealth, goods, services, and even religion, ethics, and responsibility as the most important element in one's life. With a grand view, money is all of these things wrapped up in a neat package, ready to be stashed in one's wallet or purse and distributed. And so it is only reasonable that money has become the driving force in life and the bane of moralists from time immemorial.

In one of the most enduring proofs from *Das Kapital*, Karl Marx shows how the goal of money-based societies evolves from a traditional notion of wealth to the abstract. In this Money Nexus, societies begin with the straight barter of commodities, shown in Marx's equation of $C - C'$. To alleviate inefficiency in trade and the need for double coincidence, a medium of exchange is introduced in the form of money: $C - M - C'$, which includes a sale $(C - M)$ and purchase $(M - C')$ of commodities using money. In a more complex system, such as in our modern economy, the layers of exchange will multiply in the process from raw commodities to final product, though the pattern of sale-and-purchase remains the same: $C - M - C' - M' - C''$. At this point, money is still just a medium of exchange and useful only as a means to the end of useful commodities.

As suggested above, however, money can be accumulated and used as a form of capital. In this way, money becomes the primary goal in a given transaction rather than just its medium. Traders use commodities as the intermediary instead, represented by the equation $M - C - M'$. No longer does the trading party sell his goods in order to buy other useful goods; rather, he buys goods in order to sell them at a dearer price, in effect reversing the previous equation. As Marx further showed, this new equation is often pared down in financial markets to the simple exchange of money and money-based products such as stocks and treasury bills. The final equation in the evolution is $M - M'$, where commodities are eliminated outright.

	Circuit	Equation
1	Barter	$C - C'$
2	Money Exchange	$C - M - C'$
3	Commodity Arbitrage	$M - C - M'$
4	Financial Market	$M - M'$

FIG. 4—Money Nexus.

Here, we come upon the most distinct and potent way in which money abstracts wealth: by objectifying value. As is plain from experience, money differs from real goods by design. In order to serve as a means of exchange between goods, money must have a detached and neutral value, equal from one person to the next. The more constant the value of money between those who use it, the more functional the money; and likewise, the more the value differs between its users, the less it can function as money. Ultimately, as money becomes a form of wealth in itself, the value of that wealth grows objective.

Thus, Marx's transition from a system of barter to a strictly money-based exchange is really a transition in the concept of value in general. While commodity goods each have their own values, money is by design worth the same thing to everyone. The evolution from the former to the latter, then, is an evolution from a condition where everyone seeks different goods and services based on their varying tastes to one where everyone seeks the same good no matter what their varying tastes might be. The more important money becomes in a given economy, the fewer paths the pursuit of wealth can take and the more it gets funneled into a singular path leading to one end: the accumulation of money.

As one might imagine, the consequences of this are great. Brought to its logical conclusion, the evolution would undermine the entire structure of modern economics. Without subjective value, there can be no individualism, no property rights, no industry, and no trade; without subjective value, there cannot be any kind of advance like that which we saw in the centuries after the founding of the New World.

Of course, this transition can never be complete because money will never become the only good valued in a given society. People will always have differing needs and thus will always value things differently, whether it is a steak dinner, a cruise to the Bahamas, or a six-bedroom mansion. A person who really enjoys oranges, for instance, will value them more highly than one who prefers apples, no matter what the price. The first will see the price tag and jump on such a good deal, while the second will probably shrug off such an expensive sale. In this way, subjective value is never really reversed and money is just another good added to a given trade, a filter that transmutes one's perceived value rather than redefining it altogether.

In the end, the goal is always to obtain those real goods, and they are the substantive rewards for each trading party. But, as we have seen, money has become more and more necessary in attaining real goods, and so it has become an almost necessary conduit. As money grows more accommodating, useful, and powerful than real goods, individuals will think less in terms of the satisfaction of needs when considering value and more in terms of dollar amounts. Strange as it may seem, as it is in Marx, goods become simple means of exchange in the pursuit of more money.

Marx's account shows that by the mid-nineteenth century, money had already gained a prominent enough role that goods had begun taking on objective values. In what he called the Fetishism of Commodities, he argued that brokers gave an almost religious credence to trade goods, as if those goods could perform the personal, even spiritual, estimation necessary for determining value. In our day, money has grown so dominant that we take for granted the objective value of goods. The automatic price tag that flashes in our minds when thinking of a good or service is a sign of the pervasive mentality. Throughout the economy, we can see how producers and consumers alike fail to view goods in terms of the satisfaction afforded by them and rather by the abstract notion of a dollar amount—ironically, a figure that represents what someone else would be willing to pay for the good.

A new breed of sociologists called behavioral economists have endeavored to show how consumers in the modern marketplace make little or no use at all of their subjective values and simply buy goods according to the going rate, whatever that rate may be. Consumers are said to buy a good that can offer them no utility at all just because it is on sale or because it looks like a good deal next to a more expensive brand. One will buy a $70 bottle of wine, for instance, not because one believes the wine to be worth the time, effort, and resources necessary to satisfy a fair amount of needs, but because it is positioned next to a bottle selling for $52 and another selling for $120. Since the $70 bottle is moderately priced compared to the others, the buyer feels as though it is the best choice—not too cheap, but not exorbitant either.

Peculiarities like this are the norm when money supplants real goods as wealth. The more prevalent and necessary money becomes, the more subjective value is displaced and a universal, objective value takes hold of the economy. As such, true objectivity of wealth can only happen when money has become absolutely necessary to one's well-being. And, while Western civilization had not reached that point by the mid-1800s, it was fast reaching it, a fact that could be seen in the increasing use of exchange currency and the intricate mechanisms aimed at cultivating more.

Until the economy reached that point, it was possible for any given individual to reject money altogether, cultivate his own goods, and barter for anything else he needed. As long as one had the ability to live on his own and obtain all his needs through simple exchange, money could still be just an efficient method of trading goods and multiplying wealth to the greatest extent possible. But, as we will see, the lure of a money-based economy was more persuasive than could possibly be imagined, and the notion of self-sufficiency was drowned out by the brilliance of ever-expanding wealth.

5. COMPLEXITY

ONE ABSTRACTION CALLS FORTH a myriad. Money, being at the core of modern economics, becomes like a commodity itself, and so, like other commodities, begs a number of institutions aimed at the production, protection, and outlay specifically of money. Since it is so different from real goods, however, the money industry is vastly different from those based on commodities, such as corn, iron, timber, or fish. The result is an amplified abstraction of wealth and an exacerbated interdependency from which it is nearly unimaginable to escape.

The most essential aspect of this new wave of abstraction comes in the form of credit—the lending and borrowing made possible by money's inherent ability to be used and reused without losing value. While one person is storing money, another person can be investing that same amount of money in a company, for example, or buying productive goods, or lending it out again. As such, it can be said that money can be used in more than one place at the same time. This subtle feature makes it possible for money to be twice or three times as productive as real wealth, or even much more so.

The upshot, as anyone paying attention to the latest financial turmoil can attest, is a sort of multiplication of the money supply. Whereas the monetary base, or the amount of actual money in circulation, can be limited and controlled, the money supply, or the amount of money that is essentially being used at a given time, is an exponent of its base and rather uncontrollable as a result. To look further into this multiplication of money, it is necessary to examine in more detail exactly how abstracted wealth can be compounded.

Credit

Modern credit was devised no later than when the increase in global trade forced the widespread use of money during the seventeenth and eighteenth centuries. Higher volume of trade naturally spurred a higher use of currency and thus a greater demand for money storage and currency exchange. Early banks, such as the Bank of Amsterdam (founded in 1609 during the ascent of Dutch economic power), were established explicitly for these basic functions. Customers would deposit gold, silver, and other moneys for safe keeping, getting in return receipts on their deposits. These receipts were the original paper money and served as a primary form of exchange for smaller transactions outside the bank—at the market, for wages, and so on.

As the system grew more prevalent, bankers quickly began to note a subtle fact about it: Depositors tended to leave their money in the bank unused for long periods of time. Reasonably, they preferred to use smaller denominations for exchange and to withdraw large quantities only on rare occasions.

As such, the bank could take those deposits and loan them out to others in order to collect interest, or take the deposits and invest them in securities such as stocks and bonds in order to earn dividends. This way, the money that had been deposited by the customer could be used in two places: one by the depositor in the form of paper receipts and another by the bank in the form of a loan or investment.

This system of loaning out deposits has been called 'fractional reserve' or 'minimum reserve' banking because the institution keeps only a fraction of the deposits on hand, while loaning out or investing the rest. The effect is a sort of multiplication of the wealth.

To see how fractional reserve multiplies the money supply, consider an example of a simple loan. George has $100 in gold coins. He could use that money to pay for a number of useful goods including food, furniture, books, or anything else. But let us assume he does not want the goods just yet, and instead chooses to save it for future use. He deposits the $100 in the bank for safekeeping. At this point, the money is relatively dormant with no real production coming from it—no food, furniture, or books are being produced or consumed with its use. Let us then say that the bank loans out half of the $100 to John, who needs $50 to buy a set of chairs for his kitchen. John takes the $50 and gives it to the carpenter, Thomas, who, being quite pleased with his profit, then deposits it in the bank. By loaning out half of the money that George deposited, the bank materializes a sale that would not have occurred otherwise, and thus spurs productivity and greater wealth in the society as a whole.

Fig. 5—Simple Loan.

In effect, this system swells the money supply, since the money is theoretically in use by George and John (and eventually Thomas), whereas without the loan it would only be in use by George. It is as if the money is being used three times, more or less simultaneously. As can be plainly seen, the result is greater production—the sale of furniture where there would have been none.

Expanding from this simple scenario, one can see how fractional reserve banking can really increase a society's level of trade and overall production. With more money in play, more business endeavors can be undertaken, more people can be paid wages, and so more goods can be produced in turn. The effect is amplified by the fact that banks, by virtue of collecting large pools of deposits, can make loans and investments that individual creditors could not otherwise make. Like the wealthiest of entrepreneurs, the bank can take deposits from George, Benjamin, Alexander, and Chevy to provide a much larger loan to John in case he needs greater capital to pursue his endeavor. Instead of buying a table, John might rather like to invest in a startup company that looks to hire a dozen people and begin producing great new gadgets that would otherwise have been nonexistent. Because of the loan, twelve people will now have an income and millions of gadgets will be produced where there would otherwise be none.

Fractional reserve banking is only possible with the common use of money. In a commodity or goods-based economy, wealth can only be used once—food can only be eaten once, a cart can only be used by a single owner, land can only be occupied by a single inhabitant, and so on. Money, on the other hand, can be used over and over without diminishing value, and so can be used by more than one person at a given time. A grandfather in the seventeenth century can use the same shilling that his grandson uses in the eighteenth; a depositor in Paris can make use of money at the same time as does a trader in Singapore. Money's abstract nature allows for its varied use and thus, given the proper system, its expanded use as well.

The extent of this expansion can be illustrated by a hypothetical scenario in which deposited money is loaned out to debtors who turn around and deposit the money at other banks. Since the deposited money can then be loaned out yet again, the process can continue infinitely, thus expanding the money supply infinitely. The only control over this multiplication is the bank's rate of reserves. Let us assume the reserve rate for all banks in this scenario is 20%, so that every bank must keep 20% of their deposits on hand at all times. An individual deposits $100 in Bank A, which turns around and loans out $80, keeping $20 on reserve. The debtor then turns around and deposits the $80 in Bank B, which turns around and loans out $64, keeping $16 on reserve, and so on.

Bank	Amount Deposited	Lent Out	Reserves
A	100	80	20
B	80	64	16
C	64	51.20	12.80
D	51.20	40.96	10.24
E	40.96	32.77	8.19
F	32.77	26.21	6.55
G	26.21	20.97	5.24
H	20.97	16.78	4.19
I	16.78	13.42	3.36
J	13.42	10.73	2.69
K	10.73		
Total	457.05	357.04	89.26

Total Reserves + Last Amount Deposited	100

FIG. 6—Money Expansion through Fractional Reserve Banking.

At all times, the total amount of reserves plus the last amount deposited will always be equal to the amount of money first deposited (in this case, $100). This is the monetary base that the rest is built upon. From that base, as can be seen in the table, a succession of ten deposits and loans generates another $357.04. Granted, money that is loaned out is rarely deposited again at a bank—it is usually spent at the lumber yard, the manufacturing plant, the construction company, or the like—the principle of regeneration is still a valid concern since the lumber yard owner, manufacturing plant owner, and the construction company owner may themselves turn around and deposit the money in a bank. Ultimately, the regeneration of money can and does occur whether it is immediate or displaced.

As pointed out before, this process of loaning out deposits can continue infinitely because there will always be an amount that the bank can loan out again (80% in the above example). The nominal amount of money loaned out continually gets smaller since some percentage of reserves is retained, but the process could keep going indefinitely. The equation that shows the total amount of regenerated funds is aptly called the Money Multiplier since that is essentially what the fractional reserve system does— multiplies money. With an initial source of $100 and a 20% reserve rate, the ultimate relevant amount of money generated by this process ends up being around $400 extra for a total of $500.

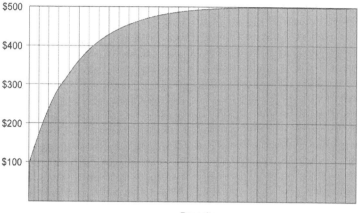

Deposits

Fig. 7—Money Multiplier Curve.

Economists have given the monetary base the label of 'high-powered' because of this very phenomenon. Since an addition or subtraction of the actual money in circulation can multiply through various forms of credit, its effect on the economy as a whole is exceptionally dynamic or high-powered. The designation goes to show how much of an effect the system of credit has on the economy. What may seem subtle and incremental might well have large-scale consequences.

Loans, Securities, Insurance, and Derivatives

The mechanism of credit as viewed here can take many forms, not all of which resemble the basic form at first glance. The original and most pervasive brand of credit is a loan, where a creditor (usually a bank) advances some amount of money to a debtor (usually an individual or a business), who makes use of it and then returns it later or incrementally over time with interest.

The core idea behind this transaction can manifest into any number of other structures, with three main kinds of financial instrument: regular loans, securities, and insurance. Loans in themselves can vary based on different amounts, repayment methods, interest rates, and durations. One website lists some forty types of mortgages alone. Other kinds of loans can be seen in simple store credits (which have been around since ancient times), installment buying plans (first popularized in the 1920s), and credit cards (which began to flourish with Diner's Club in the 1950s and American Express and Bank Americard—Visa—in the 1960s). The principle of a creditor advancing money to an individual or business to be paid back later is the same in all of these; so too is the resultant increase in sales and production. The credit card holder is able to purchase a washing machine, refrigerator, or vacation to Disney World, for example, when he would otherwise not have had the cash on hand to do so. And so there is economic growth with the use of these loans where there was none before.

In the same way, the purchase and sale of securities also make up a form of loan, though the arrangement of parties involved is rather flipped. With securities such as stocks and bonds, the individual is usually the one lending the money and the large corporation the one borrowing it, using it, and paying it back with interest, which takes the form of a dividend paid to the stock or bondholder. Here, one can see the similarities between securities and loans—both are a form of investment in which the creditor offers an initial sum of money to a party who believes it can make use of that money and thus provide some monetary return from which everyone can profit.

One last broad category of credit is insurance, a financial tool rarely considered to be a loan though its characteristics are quite similar indeed, albeit rearranged. The loan in an insurance policy is the amount allotted to the policyholder in case of some unseen event—$100,000 in case of a house fire, for instance. The policyholder pays back the loan over time as he would any other such advance, though he does not see the money at first and rather hopes that he never has to. The borrower makes use of the loan, not by employing it directly in a productive capacity, but rather in the leisure with which he can conduct the business surrounding the insured property. The owner of a Bentley Mulsanne, for instance, might be hesitant to drive it anywhere considering the automobile's extraordinary price tag. With insurance, he can feel a little more relaxed in taking it out for a spin. It is as if the insurance allows the owner to drive the automobile when and where he wouldn't otherwise drive it and so generates production just as a regular loan or investment can.

As the use of money can be productive, creditors can and should be able to charge interest for that use, a principle that goes back to the Spanish Scholastics. Since a borrower can purchase a productive good and thus create wealth with the money, it stands to reason that the lender should be granted some portion of that profit. The residual payment is seen in the interest charged for loans, the dividends yielded from stocks and bonds, and the premium paid on insurance policies.

Given the profitability of lending money, one cannot be surprised that the practice has flourished in modern times and increased as knowledge of markets and trading techniques have improved. Though lending, investing, and insurance were present in ancient and medieval times, they only became full-scale industries in the last five hundred years. It is also during this time period that one will find the extensive use of financial instruments based not on real wealth as it is with loans, securities, and insurance, but on money itself. These spin-off instruments are called derivatives because they are derived from underlying financial instruments, thus forming an abstraction of already abstracted wealth.

If banking, securities, and insurance can be considered efforts to make money on the production of goods, the idea behind derivatives is to make money on the effort to make money. Consider the typical farmer, who attempts to raise crops for sale. A bank will loan him money so that he can rent land enough to raise the crops and thus earn enough money to sustain himself and pay back the loan with interest. Here, the bank makes money on the farmer's effort to make goods.

Derivatives take the same form, though they are displaced from the actual goods. Seeing the profit that the first bank makes by loaning the farmer money, a second bank looks to loan the first bank money so that it can extend more loans to farmers and they can then produce more goods. In short, derivatives seek to profit by offering loans on loans, or a stock of a group of stocks, or insurance of insurers, or, as the case may be, a loan on stocks, or insurance on loans, or any other combination of these devices. By extending one's wealth in more complex forms of credit, lenders are able to increase the size and scope of their investments and thus take advantage of the economies of scale so expertly employed in the production of real goods. Ultimately, the multiplication of wealth increases in the same way that production increases.

The three categories usually associated with derivatives are futures, options, and swaps. The first form of derivative was developed as early as the seventeenth century and is simply a contract between two parties to buy and sell an asset at a future time for an agreed price. Futures are like guarantees for both the buyer and the seller, who are more or less betting on the future condition of the market. One might like to buy several steel futures, for example, if he believes the market for the commodity will go up. If there is a boom in construction, steel becomes more valuable, and the buyer can then cash in his futures at a low price and sell them on the market at a profit.

Options, which came into prominence around the 1960s, are similar to futures in that they designate a set time of sale in the future but leave the price up to the market. These derivatives also contain an option to buy or sell the asset before that time at an agreed price, making the process a bit more complex and giving the financiers more ways to try and make money. One might buy the steel options in the hope that construction will increase.

If it does not increase by a certain point, or if it goes down, he can exercise his option and sell at the agreed price.

The third form of derivative, a swap, was developed in the 1980s as a way to exchange particular benefits of given assets, the most common being one form of interest rate for another. A company might be obligated to pay some high variable interest rate on a loan, for instance, and want to swap a lower fixed rate with another company. The benefit to the first company is clear—relief from a higher interest rate. The benefit to the second company is that the variable rate might eventually fall below the fixed rate, thus opening the door to gains.

In short, swaps, like options and futures, and all trades really, are exchanges between parties with different abilities and needs. One party might benefit more from a consistent, fixed income, while another can bear the weight of greater volatility and risk. Since all three forms of derivatives include one part that is certain and one part that is variable, it can be said that they are trades in time for more or less certainty. While a struggling bank desires greater certainty, a larger, more secure investment bank might well want more variability, which could lead to the chance to make more money.

As with normal trades, both parties benefit. The first bank sees its interest payment decrease instantly; the second bank watches as its profits increase over time. Just as the apple farmer and city dweller both benefit from the sale of an apple, so too do the banks in a derivative contract.

After swaps, the deluge. Savvy traders noted that, just like the division of labor and specialism in machine industry, the financial industry could be sectioned off and distributed so that each bank, each investor, and each borrower can focus on his comparative advantage. The investment bank is the new assembly line, and computers, with their ever-expanding capacity for calculation, the new factory machines. The upshot, as it is in regular industry, is an extreme fine-tuning of mechanisms and a vast expansion in the production and reproduction of output. In recent years, the derivatives market has exploded in popularity as the number of variants have proliferated.

A brief perusal of available financial instruments will give the lay observer an idea of the immense complexity of modern finance: In addition to regular loans there are some dozens of variants of mortgages and home equity lines of credit. Stock and bond traders offer any number of precise methods of buying and selling, including market, limit, stop, stop limit, and trailing stop trades. Insurance has bred countless offspring that protect against any number of financial events, defaults on loans being one extremely popular brand these days.

Everywhere, it is the same scheme of taking financial instruments, slicing them up into various salable pieces, and sending them all over the world in the aim of better refining the process. Derivatives of financial instruments have been surpassed by derivatives of derivatives, and so abstract the abstracted wealth to the third and even fourth or fifth degree. Futures, options, and swaps are still being sold and bought, but the real market is in caps, floors, swaptions, repos, reinsurance, mortgage-backed securities, collateralized debt obligations, asset-backed securities, and credit default swaps.

In modern finance, the complexity is practically impossible to avoid. Only one company was conducting swaps in the early '80s; now, every bank takes part if only to stay relevant. The climate makes one wonder why the first principle in Warren Buffett's method of investing is simplicity, since his own company Berkshire Hathaway is made up of hundreds if not thousands of different interlocking parts and only became the powerhouse that it is on the profits of a reinsurer, a company that insured insurers.

The complexity of modern finance astounds even those close to it. Upon attempting to sift through the carnage of the 2008 financial crisis, U.S. Treasury Secretary Henry Paulson admitted that even he, with his Harvard M.B.A. and experience as CEO of Goldman Sachs, could not understand some of the more intricate financial instruments that had been built over the last decade. It is an indication of disarray when the person in charge of presiding over the country's finances is unable to wade through the convoluted mechanisms that dominate the economy.

Inventing Money

The premise behind all exchanges of credit, such as the loans in the above scenarios and even the more abstract derivatives transactions, is the existence of equivalent real wealth. Reasonably, banks will loan out money only if they believe the debtor to be worthy of paying it back. To be sure of credibility, lenders will make certain that the debtor has collateral equal to the amount being loaned. For example, the bank will only lend John $50 to buy a set of chairs if he can prove that he has $50 worth of goods, say a table, to back the loan with. Theoretically, the bank takes possession of the table until John pays back the loaned sum. The table is the collateral for the chairs. The collateral in a mortgage is the house itself. The bank gives out the money and theoretically holds the house until the loan is paid off.

In this sense, loans are just like any other sale—a trade of money for goods—though inherent in the deal is its reversal some time down the line. As such, the loan is not truly creating or multiplying wealth at all; it is rather transferring one form of wealth for another so that it can be more productive overall. By the same token, a debtor is not using money created out of thin air, as it might seem, but rather putting to use his land or building or machinery, which would otherwise not be as productive.

Using the example above, we can see how the amount of total wealth associated with a typical loan remains constant despite the increased money supply and increased volume of trade. When, for instance, a bank loans out $50, the money supply increases by $50 since the borrower has money that he didn't have before, but if the loan is backed by collateral, the increase in money supply is always a reflection of real wealth—the money supply increases by $50, but so too does real wealth. If that money is then multiplied through more loans, as in the above illustration, so that the money supply is equal to $500, real wealth is also increased to $500 as long as the loans are backed by full collateral. Any money in circulation is thus backed by real wealth and only a representation of that real wealth.

These loans are productive because the goods used as collateral are only capable of generating trade when they are transformed into collateral for a loan of money. The owner of a house, for instance, cannot trade part of it for groceries or tickets to the opera. As such, the house is wealth, but it is dormant wealth. The fractional reserve system allows the house to be turned into kinetic wealth, as it were, so as to allow the homeowner the ability to buy smaller useful goods and thus increase production.

Of course, lenders have not always been so particular as to how they loaned out or invested money. Lending, especially that which started around the 1920s with extensive home mortgages and installment plans, began to be offered to borrowers not based on collateral, but on the expectations of future income. In contrast to lending on collateral, this form of speculation is actually a way of creating wealth out of thin air. A business loan, for example, could be made based on the soundness of the business plan and the likelihood that the business will recoup the money loaned. Yet the business doesn't offer any real wealth as collateral for the money, and so it is as if the bank invents the money for the loan.

When this kind of credit is issued extensively throughout an economy, as one might guess, certain pressures begin to form. If several banks lend out money based on expected

> Credit is a system whereby a person who can't pay gets another person who can't pay to guarantee that he can pay.
>
> — CHARLES DICKENS (1812-70)

gains rather than real collateral, the pattern that arises is that of an upside-down pyramid, with the initial deposit sitting at the bottom and layers of artificial wealth built up above it. Taking the fractional reserve example from above, we can see that the further up the pyramid we go, the wider the layers can be, until they reach five times the width of the base investment (or more, given a smaller reserve requirement). Whereas a series of loans based on full collateral will contain supports on either side of the money supply, a series of loans based on little or no collateral will have no such supports. The image alone shows how top-heavy and precarious the system can be.

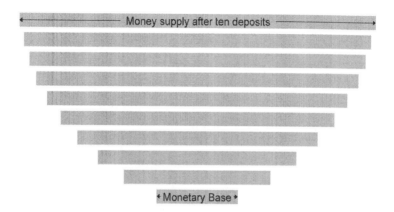

FIG. 8—Fractional Reserve Upside-Down Pyramid.

Even when loans are based on full collateral, fractional reserve banking naturally poses a risk since it takes relatively liquid assets (such as deposited money) and converts them into illiquid assets (such as a portion of a house). When money is loaned on speculation, as in the case of an installment plan or loan on expected income, liquid assets are converted into nothing at all. In all forms of credit, the money being loaned out is locked up in investments or production and so cannot be returned to the depositor in any easy way. If the initial depositor were to unexpectedly show up at the bank and demand all of his funds, thus revealing the deficiency, the scheme would break. His funds are no longer liquid; they are locked up in part of a house or in someone's business, and cannot be readily accessed. While the bank might be able to cover the withdrawal by giving the depositor someone else's reserves, the deficiency is only shifted to another depositor, and the problem persists.

It is like someone attempting to pull out the bottom rung of the upside-down pyramid. He might be successful in yanking it from its place, but in so doing, he will necessarily topple the teetering structure.

The threat of this happening is not terribly high. Typically, bank managers can count on most depositors keeping their funds in place and so do not have to worry about the deficiency created by their lending. Under normal economic conditions, a bank's reserves will be plenty to cover the rare withdrawals. But in times of economic downturn, when masses of people need to tap into their savings, or during economic turmoil, when masses of people begin to lose faith in their bank's ability to recoup its loans, a situation may arise where large-scale withdrawals will eclipse the reserves and render the institution insolvent.

The 'run' on the bank that results is the prototypical panic scene during economic crashes and can be seen as far back as the expansion of credit in the sixteenth century. Runs that took place during the Great Depression inhabit the public imagination. Recall the frantic scene in Frank Capra's *It's a Wonderful Life*, where George Bailey tries to salvage his savings and loan bank from the runs that are engulfing the economy. Pleading with his customers, who all demand that their deposits be returned, George explains that their money isn't locked in some vault in the back but rather invested in their neighbors' homes and businesses. Like a good fractional reserve system, the Bailey Building and Loan took deposits and loaned them out to needy borrowers. In so doing, it rendered itself liable for collapse.

Fear of runs during the Great Depression was warranted. Prior to the 1933 establishment of the Federal Deposit Insurance Corporation (FDIC), banks would return deposits on a first-come, first-served basis. Once they ran out of reserves, they would close their doors, and the remaining customers would lose their money. That system of get-what-you-can naturally fueled panics; depositors had extra incentive to withdraw their money, which only made the bank less stable and encouraged more people to withdraw their funds. With automatic insurance through the government, runs are practically nonexistent on the consumer level, and bank failures are less common. As we have seen in recent years, this safeguard has not done away with panics altogether. Instead, it has just shifted their epicenters further up the economic structure to the corporate level, where similar and yet more seismic runs jar the financial world every so often.

Booms, Bubbles, Panics, and Busts

Speculation occurs in all forms of credit and can best be seen in investments such as stocks and bonds, perhaps because these ventures are made by individuals, who can act more impetuously than structured banks or corporations. Like regular loans, stocks and bonds are likely to be purchased based not on the real wealth they represent or the guaranteed return that comes in the form of dividends, but rather on the projected increase in the price of the stock or bond—the anticipated capital gains. In fact, the more successful a company is, the more people will be interested in it and the more its stock price will rise, providing the investor with a much better prospect than the dividends would by themselves.

Once this switch occurs, the investment's success depends not on the quality of the company or even the ability of the company to operate as expected, but rather on the market's perception of the company's ability to do so. The speculation will pay off as long as others are willing to buy the stocks, bonds, or whatever the investment is at a higher price. And so it doesn't even matter what the company is or what it does as long as others find it promising.

Neglect of the real qualities of the company and a blind reliance on other investors make speculation very precarious. One can see the upside-down pyramid form here as well. At the bottom lies the real wealth, the value of the company; above it, several layers of speculation accumulate, widening the price of the stock just as it is with speculation loans. And, like speculation loans, the higher up the pyramid one goes, the more people must get involved for it to remain stable.

The first layer sees a few reasonable investors who look to gain on the more or less guaranteed dividends of the stock. Then, as the stock educes greater demand, the price rises. At a certain point, the rise in price becomes worth more than the dividends, and speculation ensues. The pyramid is forced to grow wider and wider for the investors to profit at all. More and more people must get involved for it to be worthwhile. When the investors finally realize that others are not inclined to join the frenzy and decline to buy more or actually start selling shares, it suddenly becomes a race to get rid of the investment, and the price plummets.

Here, we find the anatomy of an economic phenomenon characteristic of modern times: the bubble and its inevitable rupture. It is the likely and almost natural consequence of abstracted wealth to extend credit beyond the underlying wealth with the expectation that the superficial price will continue to grow. From the initial boom, the speculation takes on a life of its own and the bubble becomes something that everyone either has to be a part of or risk losing out on. The thought occurs, 'If we don't buy now, prices will continue to rise and we'll never be able to get in.' Gradually, it becomes more reasonable to borrow money to pay for the investment, from which it is assumed that one will easily profit and pay for the interest on the loan.

History offers us striking examples of this kind of irrational investing. Dutch Tulip Mania of the seventeenth century, and the South Sea and Mississippi bubbles of the eighteenth century, offer clear real-life examples in which whole communities invested in prospects tens and even hundreds of times beyond their rational scope only to watch that inflated sense of worth disintegrate before them. Each starts with a fad of sorts. In The Netherlands, it was the tulip, the flower that had been imported from the Near East and become the trendy luxury of the wealthy in 1635. Just like any fashionable decoration, the tulip had attracted attention to the extent that showing off a garden full of them became a status symbol. Hard to get, their demand skyrocketed.

Things changed when the bulbs themselves attracted attention as a way to make money. Tulip notaries were enlisted to facilitate the sale and purchase; exchanges were organized and tulip futures sold; one Haarlem merchant was said to have given half his property to obtain a single bulb—for resale, not to plant and display. Mass fortunes were made overnight, as it seemed, out of thin air. The thought took root that this passion would last forever, and that the wealthy from all over the world would convene in Holland to engage in the trade.

It could not last. At one point, when prices had reached upward of 6,000 florins for single bulbs, sales began to dwindle and prices began to fall. Investors sold their reserves to crystallize profits, and supply suddenly blossomed. As value decreased, so did demand, and the inevitable crash came abruptly and definitively. Months of debate and fierce struggle were not enough to straighten out the legal mess, and a generation was needed before the economy could return to its senses.

Two similar episodes occurred eighty years later featuring the stock of trading companies, the South Sea Company in England and the Mississippi Company in France. As with Tulip Mania, the investment in both companies was initially sound, and dividends provided the early income. When the ventures proved successful, speculation resulted, and bubbles were a matter of course. South Sea Company executives used profits to pay off debt, and at the same time issued too much stock, which investors used as collateral to take out loans for more stock. Led by the capable Scot John Law, the Mississippi Company also issued too many shares, and, when trade in the colony lagged, thousands of enlisted men were shipped from Europe to enliven commerce.

The objective bystander can instantly see the folly in such schemes. But when wealth is abstracted to the third, fourth, and fifth degrees, it is easy to neglect the real value of the goods at hand and look only at the rising price that appears to have no ceiling. As long as others show interest, the investment is a sure thing. This ideology underscores the self-perpetuating nature of speculative bubbles. Prices rise when demand is high. At the same time, demand is high when prices rise. When trapped in such a bubble, it is almost natural to believe that such a sequence can go on forever.

The allure of speculation is no alien concept to modern investors. Contemporary readers will recognize the pattern in any such financial boom and bust in the last two hundred years, the crash of 1929 being the most prominent, but also the crash of 1987, the Savings and Loan fallout in the early 1990s, the Asian crisis of the 1990s, the Dot-Com Crash, and especially the real estate bubble and meltdown of 2001-08. This last, the consequences of which are still being felt by most Americans, was no different than Tulip Mania or any other bubble. They are the same conditions, in which investors forget the value of abstracted wealth, that give license to schemes like interest-only mortgages, no-income loans, and upside-down financing, and sees stocks without dividends become the most profitable stocks in recent history.

> Not only in the cities, but in the country south of Connecticut River, are people losing their habits of industry, to become dependents on banks, and speculators in something or other; but what is perhaps still worse, men are daily more and more acquiring a habit of extravagance, supported by borrowing of the banks, and not by the regular profits of their estates, or their business.
>
> —BROTHER JOHN, *LETTERS FROM THE SOUTH BY JAMES KIRKE PAULDING* (1816)

Anyone familiar with the Wall Street crash of 2008 will know that there is such a thing as a credit default swap, a contract in which the buyer is protected against the default (failure to pay) of a credit instrument (a bond or mortgage loan, for instance). It is, in a way, a form of insurance against the default of a loan. It was invented in the 1990s as a way for banks to hedge against potential defaults, but ballooned in the beginning part of the aughts as a way to bet on the likelihood that certain companies or portfolios would suffer financial difficulties. The complexity of this kind of trade illustrates how convoluted the financial markets have become, and the prominent role credit default swaps played in the crash shows how severe the consequences of their failure can be. These forms of investment multiply the money that has already been multiplied several times over by the more elementary forms of investment and so swell the initial source of money at astronomical rates. Estimates on the notional value of credit default swaps in 2007 alone reached $45 trillion—more than three times the U.S. GDP and almost as much as the estimated total wealth of American households (around $50 trillion).

In the mid-aughts, everyone seemed to be investing in bubbles and borrowing large sums of money in order to do so. Homeowners, banks, investors, corporations—everyone was leveraged 32-to-1 (borrowing some $32 for every $1 in equity) in order to make their investments. The potential for gains, of course, was clear. The more one borrowed, the more he could invest. When the venture is thought to be a sure-fire win, as was the case with the housing market, it is assumed that no debt-to-equity ratio is too high and that the plan can only bring about greater returns.

Ultimately, these methods of contingent investments create an intricate system that becomes more precarious as it grows in size. The greater the volume of funds that is put into such a scheme, the more complex and layered it becomes; as the scheme's complexity increases, the more difficult it becomes to unravel; the more difficult it becomes to unravel, the less faith the persons involved will have in it; the less faith those involved have, the more likely they will be to withdraw from the scheme and the more imminent a collapse will be. Like a house of cards, these kinds of economic systems are pieced together with delicate precision based on fairly reasonable expectations of productivity, and a slight tremor in any sector will cause the entire structure to crumble.

At the same time, the modern financial system is rather like a game of musical chairs. Those people involved are encouraged to run around just like everyone else while the music is playing. As long as you're not the one left standing when the music stops, everything is fine. And so everyone runs and jumps around, taking on more debt and accumulating risk in the hope that they will find seats when the music stops.

Noting the extraordinary complexity of the new financial instruments, several economists and finance experts attempted to sound alarms. One University of Chicago professor practically explained the 2008 crisis before it happened: "While the system now exploits the risk-bearing capacity of the economy better by allocating risks more widely, it also takes on more risks than before. Moreover, the linkages between markets and between markets and institutions are now more pronounced. While this helps the system diversify against small shocks, it also exposes the system to large systemic shocks, large shifts in asset prices, or changes in aggregate liquidity." Anyone who had been familiar with the various bubbles in the past knew that the housing bubble was no different, and that the complex financial instruments used to build it up were just new ways of creating the same illusion of wealth.

The fact that the real wealth of these investments—the company or land allegedly being invested in—has little or no relevance in today's investment market reveals the level of abstraction that has taken hold of the modern economic system. Making money has become the primary concern, and one can make much more money much faster by simply doing away with the real wealth that the money supposedly represents. The standard for investing these days is to borrow money, invest it to make more money, pay back the principle, and earn an income with the profit made. It doesn't matter what the borrowed money is backed by or whether it is backed at all, because it is assumed that one will be able to turn that money into more money and thus make a profit.

> O Gold! I still prefer thee unto paper,
> Which makes bank credit like a bark of vapour.
>
> —LORD BYRON, *DON JUAN* (1823)

This is the mentality that swept through the housing market of the last decade and subsequently made a mess of the whole economy. The assumption was that anyone could borrow money, more or less created out of thin air and not backed by anything, to buy an overpriced house, make a few improvements, or do nothing at all, and watch as the property value continued to rise. Selling the house after a few years, the debtor could pay back the loan and keep the profit, which could be hundreds of thousands of dollars. It was Tulip Mania all over again.

Like Tulip Mania, the South Sea Bubble, or the Mississippi Bubble, the scheme would work if housing prices rose consistently as they did from 2000 to 2006. As long as someone was willing to pay a higher price, the values would continue to go up. But demand always has a limit. When that limit is reached, the willingness of others to join in the scheme will fall and so will prices. As prices fall, the return disappears, and folks are left without profit and, as shown in the real estate debacle of 2007 to 2008, without even the ability to pay back the loan.

The extreme of this form of speculation is seen in so-called Ponzi schemes, the brand of fraud named after Charles Ponzi, an Italian immigrant to New York around the turn of the twentieth century. In a feat of pure salesmanship, he was able to solicit investment money with the promise of huge returns. What he did not tell his investors was that he would garner the returns, not from any concrete business, but from the outlay of future investors. When the first investors were given their returns as promised, the word spread of Ponzi's great business deal. His ruse would continue to be successful and investors would continue to be paid as long as he could find more and more investors. Given the contingent nature of the plot, it was bound to fail—there would always be a last investor, and when that last one was found, the upside-down pyramid would collapse. Eventually, the authorities caught on before the last investor was found, and Ponzi ended up going to prison for his ploy.

The casual observer might wonder if there is a difference between this notorious example of fraud and that of the housing bubble in the last decade or any other complex financial scheme these days (Social Security comes to mind).

With respect to the fundamental substance of the schemes, this spectator can find no difference at all. By design, they all neglect the real wealth of the investment in the hope of creating more money, and they all rely on other people to come through with a higher bid or subsequent investment to make the machination work. Astute witnesses will recognize that, given the extreme effects of abstracted wealth, all economic structures these days are more or less Ponzi schemes, appreciably neglecting genuine wealth and relying on others for success.

The Business Cycle

The financial manias touched on here are not limited to the great crises we see plastered on front pages of newspapers and blogs. Indeed, they happen all the time to a much smaller degree throughout the economy as the normal result of a constant oscillation in supply and demand. Prices for all goods and services fluctuate and are thus prone to some level of speculation. Since no one can predict the supply and demand of a particular good or service, much less those for an entire economy of goods and services, the market will rise and fall like waves in a body of water.

Most of these waves can be compensated for and so disappear not long after they materialize. An overpriced stock, for example, will soon find its owners selling and watch its price fall back into equilibrium. Other waves, as with the aforementioned booms and busts, grow until they become so powerful as to defy individual corrective measures. Taken all together, the crests and troughs of these undulations may add up to create vast disturbances in the economy. This is the 'Business Cycle', or 'Trade Cycle', a process by which the entire economy goes through an extended boom and protracted bust as an almost natural reaction to its constantly jostling prices.

In the big picture, it is sensible that periods of excessive growth would be followed by periods of large-scale retraction. But, as early theorists determined, the cycle was a troubling sign that Capitalism, as an economic system, was unstable. Critics challenged the notion that economies guided by the Invisible Hand could adjust instantaneously, and that production slumps and widespread hardship were as fundamental to the system as higher productivity and efficiency.

Nineteenth-century Swiss economist Jean Charles Léonard de Sismondi was the first to investigate what he described as recurrent crises. Like all observant persons of the time, Sismondi recognized the fact that industrial advances were generating more and more wealth across the board, and that total well-being was rising as a result. But he also noted that this overall increase in wealth was punctuated by sharp upsurges and drastic declines that confused the average participants and left some worse off than they had been before.

"Let us beware," he said, "of this dangerous theory of equilibrium which is supposed to be automatically established. A certain kind of equilibrium, it is true, is reestablished in the long run, but it is after a frightful amount of suffering°." This suffering had been a going concern: If Capitalism and the output of machine industry were so productive, then why did they seemingly bring on 'poverty in the midst of plenty'? If there was such an abundance of goods and services in the new economy, why was there homelessness and hunger at all?

The answer had to do with the Business Cycle. As explained above, free enterprise encourages some degree of speculation in which artificial wealth is introduced for the sake of projected gains. When the market is keen, the investment succeeds and everything goes on normally. But when the market is saturated or otherwise unreceptive, that speculative investment is lost and the business retracts, leaving a hole in the economy where the artificial wealth had been.

Take for example a speculative business endeavor in which a capitalist borrows $50,000 to start a railroad line. Though he does not have $50,000 in collateral, the bank lends him the money because they know that the railroad business is booming and the venture will likely produce great returns. In order to pursue his endeavor, the entrepreneur must buy land, steel, and a factory with his loan, and hire hundreds of employees. Upon doing so, the artificial money has made an impression in that it has skewed the economy toward the railroad industry. Landowners and steel manufacturers raise prices in reaction to the higher demand, and workers gravitate toward the industry. In short, the economy adjusts to compensate for the new wealth.

Of course, if the railroad is successful and raises enough profit to pay back the loan with interest, the enterprise will be a success. The economic adjustments will have been fruitful, and everyone involved will flourish as a result. But if the railroad fails for any reason and the entrepreneur defaults on his loan, a sudden and cruel reality will set in. The landowners and steel manufacturers will see lower demand and thus lose business, and the workers will all be unemployed and searching for jobs in an industry that no longer needs them.

Certainly, everyone involved will return to their previous places, landowners and manufacturers will lower their prices, workers will all seek and find work elsewhere, and equilibrium will be found. Yet this return happens, as Sismondi explains, only with significant pains. Like the growing pains of an adolescent, an economy in transition is awkward, inefficient, and ultimately unproductive.

Now, it must be admitted that all failed businesses come with economic retraction, whether the businesses are supported by real wealth or by money created out of thin air. But speculative businesses naturally come in clumps—the more popular a given enterprise, the more speculation it will attract. And, just as these businesses are built up in clumps, so too are they dissolved in clumps. The result is a magnification of routine economic waves and an exaggeration of the booms and busts that occur naturally in the free market.

It is only when speculation has overemphasized the subtle shifts in the market that these large-scale tidal waves of economic growth are formed and that the equally sizeable trough can follow. As such, only when speculation has taken hold of the market can significant damage be done to the economy. When the occasional business fails, prices can shift easily if they need to at all, workers can find jobs elsewhere; the economy adjusts. On the other hand, when many businesses fail, prices have no standard, and workers face extended periods of unemployment.

This is why Austrian economist Ludwig von Mises declared that a reduction in credit does not cause the disaster but rather reveals the disaster that has already occurred. The real disaster is not the recession or the depression or the countless unemployed; it is the shape of the economy after being distorted by artificially generated money.

This is to say that, in a modern economy of infinite complexity such as ours, no one is safe from the false speculation of others. We may not be interested in the activities of investment bankers or financiers some thousands of miles away, but their various schemes distribute artificial money into the economy, which regular people end up depending on. Some banker sells $1 billion worth of collateralized debt obligations, for example, and makes $3 million in the transaction. He then buys a house from a broker, who uses his profits to buy a car, a dishwasher, and a refrigerator; the automotive and appliance companies then pay their employees, salesmen, engineers, technicians, managers, et cetera, who then go on to buy groceries, iPods, movie tickets, and so on.

All of this is begun by the creation of artificial wealth. When the scheme works and the investment is met with an increase in production, the distributed wealth stays put and everyone becomes that much richer. But when the scheme fails, all of that artificial wealth must be sucked back to its source as in a vacuum. The loss created by the failed speculation reverberates in the lives of everyone involved: the real estate broker, car salesman, appliance retailer and manufacturer, suppliers, vendors, and employees of those companies, and the grocery store and retail outlets and all of their suppliers, vendors, and employees. An incalculable amount of people is affected by the infusion of the artificial money, and so every one of them is affected by the retraction.

In a complex society, any interaction one endeavors might be affected by any number of other factors. The more complex it is, the more factors that potentially affect it. An investor has to take into account many different levels of transactions—not only the sale right before him, but the one beyond that in which the banker acts, and the one beyond that in which the broker acts, and so on. In the modern society, the average participant must consider an almost infinite number of transactions in order to make sound decisions, transactions that practically no one can find the time or energy to take into account.

By the 1890s, complexity was a fact of life. Westerners had come face-to-face with an intricate system that seemed only to grow more and more commanding. But as the nineteenth century drew to a close, the people of the West were beginning to face another, related phenomenon that would render the Business Cycle a mere harbinger.

II
COMPETITION

1. THE CLOSE
OF THE
ECONOMIC SYSTEM

IN JULY 1893, at the peak of the World's Columbian Exposition, 32-year-old historian Frederick Jackson Turner delivered a speech that brought to light a single, stunning point of consideration: The frontier had closed, and all of civilization was bound to change because of it.

The superintendent of the census had confirmed it in his report: "Settlements of the West lie so scattered over the region that there can no longer be said to be a frontier line." The free land had all been taken, settlement had all but been completed, and Manifest Destiny had been fully realized.

According to Turner, this meant an entirely new way of life. The frontier had always been an integral part of the American character. As he put it, "The existence of an area of free land, its continuous recession, and the advance of American settlement westward explain American development." Those conditions gave the American people qualities unique to frontier life, such as rugged individualism, adaptability, and inventiveness necessary for survival in the wilderness, and led to the kind of economic and industrial vigor that made the United States one of the greatest powers in the world.

But the frontier was much more than just a rough wilderness that gave the pioneers in Indiana, Iowa, and Idaho a rugged appreciation for life. The open frontier in the West was the key to an open economy throughout the Occident, and, as such, had a greater if subtler significance to Americans on the Atlantic seaboard and the Europeans of the Old World as well. As the door to free land, the frontier had been the door to freedom, giving anyone who chose to venture westward the ability to say 'No' to any prevailing system, to escape oppression or exploitation, and to make a life for himself. With such a threshold, all the bonds formed and enterprises undertaken at its foot would be on equal terms and so would be voluntary and just. As Turner put it in his treatise *The Frontier in American History*, "So long as free land exists, the opportunity for a competency exists, and economic power secures political power."

The American character, and that of the entire Western civilization, had been formed on the notion that if one did not like the constructs and institutions that he found himself in, or if he for any reason thought they were unjust or exploitative, he could move on and build his own. Just as it had been with John Winthrop and the Plymouth Colony, if society was restrictive or oppressive, the solution was to move west and found a new society that would better suit a people's convictions.

Even within the Plymouth Colony, this principle was exhibited. When one of the members, Roger Williams, found his morals to be in conflict with those of the colony's leadership, he was not persecuted and burned alive as might have been done in England. Rather, he was able to flee and start a life on his own. It was not in any way easy, but the principled man endured a harsh journey through the New England winter to settle miles away in what later became Rhode Island.

Such was the progress of America from the founding—whenever society would bear down and oppress its people, its people could always flee to make a better life somewhere else. Not only did this provide the people who fled with a sense of freedom and self-ownership, it also put stress on the society from which the people fled to be more tolerant and to sustain more just social contracts. Even the dictates of the consummate Puritan John Winthrop were subdued to some extent after the Roger Williams incident.

By Frederick Jackson Turner's day in the 1890s, the free land that had encouraged such civil accord had all gone. The frontier had closed and, with it, so had the economic competency that Americans and indeed all Westerners had come to take for granted. Without the frontier, Americans and Europeans as a whole no longer had a natural source of political sovereignty on which to depend. At some point in the following decades, Turner surmised, the choices and freedoms that Westerners had been granted with the discovery of the New World would diminish and take with them the dynamism of the modern era. Without self-sufficiency, there could be no self-government, and without self-government, none of the advances that the modern era had seen could remain viable. Individualism would lose its potency, and so too would private property, industry, subjective value, trade, and cooperation in general. Slowly and subtly, as the American West had been conquered, territory by territory, the Occident had arrived at the very place from which it had departed four hundred years before.

The End of an Era

It could be said that the close of the frontier in the 1890s was the reversal of Columbus' voyage and discovery of the New World in the 1490s. In effect, the close negated the revolution of thought and practice made around 1500 and returned the West to its previous condition of bondage. Without the option to strike out on one's own, volition itself would become obsolete. Soon enough, the people, like their predecessor serfs, would again have to accept the ways of those in power, the lords of modern times, without so much as an alternative.

Now, it must be said that the modern way of life, with its specialism, division of labor, trade, money, and complexity had always been a possibility. And, indeed, it was a possibility of increasing luster as it increasingly benefited its practitioners with abundant lives of necessities and luxuries. But it is important to note that, before the close of the frontier, this modern way of life was an option, one of many alternatives in which the individual could take part. One did not have to take part in the interdependent way of life if he for any reason did not want to. If an individual or group saw a given contract as unjust or exploitative, he could reject it and seek a solution elsewhere—he could, like Roger Williams, move to the next region and start his own community; he could move out West like the homesteaders. The ability for people to reject a particular way of life (or a particular contract) meant that there was a natural motivation for trade to be trustworthy and mutually beneficial.

In the 1890s, with the close of the frontier, this modern way of life became obligatory. While it had previously been possible to opt out of specialism, trade, and complexity, now it was rather impossible—after all, there was nowhere else to go. As such, it was less and less likely that an individual or family could reject a contract even if they found it unjust or exploitative. And thus the close of the frontier brought about a major shift in the economy as a whole. No longer was there a natural impetus for trade to be trustworthy and mutually beneficial—it would occur no matter what, even when it was unjust or exploitative.

The acute effect of the close of the frontier was the competition for resources. When the frontier was open and individuals and groups had the option to strike out on their own for a life of self-sufficiency, it was not necessary for them to compete with others for resources. They could, of course, compete with others for pastures or oil or gold, for instance, but they were not forced to. They always had the opportunity to say no to the system and just go somewhere else.

Once the frontier closed, this easy condition of social intercourse was eliminated. Around the 1890s, when the frontier was said to have evaporated in the West, the ability to strike out on one's own grew abruptly and significantly more difficult. The resources that had been discovered were all the resources that there were, and, as those resources had all been contained and controlled, it had become necessary to compete with others for them. Suddenly, scarcity became an urgent issue.

This phenomenon was forecast as early as the 1820s by Thomas Malthus, who argued that population increases strained resources and would ultimately be checked by limitations in the food supply. His thought was that suffering and crime were the inevitable consequences of a people that was growing too large for its environment. Later in the nineteenth century, American activist Henry George devised a theory on economic inequality later termed Georgism, which stated that, as population grew (and, one might add, as technology advanced), people grew more and more capable of holding land and thus monopolizing it. As a result, land became more and more scarce. George saw this scarcity of land as the primary reason for the class struggle and the exploitation of the poor by the wealthy. Ultimately, he launched a campaign to counter the monopolization of land by means of a land tax and the confiscation of economic rent.

In a later reflection, George recited the revelation he experienced upon an 1871 horseback ride overlooking San Francisco Bay: "I asked a passing teamster, for want of something better to say, what land was worth there. He pointed to some cows grazing so far off that they looked like mice, and said, 'I don't know exactly, but there is a man over there who will sell some land for a thousand dollars an acre.' Like a flash it came over me that there was the reason of advancing poverty with advancing wealth. With the growth of population, land grows in value, and the men who work it must pay more for the privilege.°"

While competition for land and other resources had always existed, throughout the modern era it had always been backed by the inherent ability for participants to opt out of the contest. This subtle possibility made the competition on all counts elective and therefore voluntary. Thus, there was a natural constraint to the rivalry that ensured at least some degree of civility in its practice. Once the frontier closed, this natural check was dissolved, and competition was bound to intensify.

Strain on resources was the primary energy during a period that witnessed a dramatic shift toward competition, struggle, and strife. And this shift in conditions did not take the form of a gradual process. Within a mere ten years of Turner's Columbian Exposition speech, Turner was able to document four major events that verified his conjecture and completely altered the United States' socio-political landscape. As he pointed out in 1903, the Occident had already begun to see the effects of this new paradigm. The first event was the exhaustion of the supply of free land and the close of the frontier; the second was a concentration and control of capital in several primary industries; the third was the introduction of American imperialism and the conquest of foreign nations; and the fourth was the division of American political parties along the lines of socialism. This last was just the precursor to even more profound changes that would take place in the following decade.

Altogether, the pattern during the twenty years between 1893 and 1913 is one of closure, confinement, and the inevitable reaction to these conditions in the form of competition and conflict. Throughout the West, escalating interdependency bred an intensifying feeling of being trapped, of there being no place to go, a feeling which invariably intensified the motivation to compete—with other people and other peoples. Borders were pressed, sovereignty questioned, and conflict brewed at home and abroad.

War is, of course, the most prominent expression of this sense of being trapped and of having to compete for survival. As such, it cannot be a surprise that the time in question saw a number of significant conflicts brew up seemingly out of nowhere, in contrast to the extensive period of relative peace and calm that preceded it.

The 1898 Spanish-American War, which spanned the globe with theaters in the Caribbean and Asia-Pacific and included the previously isolationist United States, was but a single marker. The Second Anglo-Boer War lasted from 1899 to 1902, crises in Morocco occurred in 1905 and 1911, a crisis in Bosnia occurred in 1908, and the Balkan Wars flared up in 1912-13. And all of this took place before the Great War of 1914-18.

Assassinations had become a trendy mode of political protest and agitation. Within five years, the president of France, Sadi Carnot; and of the United States, William McKinley; the Empress of Austria, Elisabeth of Bavaria; and the King of Italy, Umberto I, were all victims of the conscienceless deed by so-called 'anarchists'. In 1914, the assassination of Archduke Franz Ferdinand was the pivotal event that plunged all of Western civilization into a century of war.

After the 1890s and the close of the frontier, the sense of confinement had become a driving force. From that point on, peoples and nations were so restricted that it seemed the only way to grow and prosper was by expanding into already occupied territories. When this expansion could be done relatively peacefully, it took the form of imperialistic conquests of undeveloped nations; otherwise, it took the form of attacking and invading other civilized countries. Increasingly, the world was coming to grips with the notion that the only way to succeed was for others to fail. The buildup of military might and the incessant political posturing between the nations of the West in the period before the Great War were the direct and inevitable consequences of a culture accustomed to freedom and expansion suddenly cut off from growth.

Consider all the good minds that had expressed support for and actively engaged in the militarism and warfare of the day. Previously, salvation could be found in escaping society as it stood and making a life on one's own; now, the only way to find salvation was to ram up against neighbors and wage war with them. Roland N. Stromberg's *Redemption by War* provides a gripping account of the seemingly contradictory fact that, in 1914, intellectuals of all stripes found war to be the best and most justifiable means of growth, economically to be sure, bur also spiritually.

The conflict was not limited to geopolitical battles. It could be seen perhaps most clearly in the cultural arena, where the Occident's finest minds assumed the lead in an overt rejection of style and customs through support of the war, naturally, but in other, more veiled forms as well. In painting with the Impressionists and Cubists, in theater with the Symbolists, and in literature with the Naturalists, the theme was not only doing away with the culture that infringed from all around but taking to pieces all that had been built. The most earnest of the artists were the most destructive.

It is no wonder why the period begot a troop of artists who proudly called themselves the Decadents in honor of the cultural decay that they saw taking place around them. The double decade that straddled 1900 was the time of Oscar Wilde's literary manhandling, where everything is seen as its opposite; of Nietzsche's contradictory philosophy, where everything is its opposite; and of Rimbaud's positive cultural destructiveness, where only negation exists.

In the sixteenth century, the discovery of the New World had led to new rules, practices, and customs; in the late nineteenth and early twentieth centuries, the close of the frontier put an end to that new way of life. The possibilities and dreams that had marked the era would all conclude at some point in the following hundred years by either dwindling out or being intentionally cut off. It was as if the documents of that time were reflections of the socioeconomic transformation taking place all around.

Such a view naturally gravitated toward the pessimistic, and, just as the opening of the frontier brought about a new literary genre of optimism and possibility in the Utopia, the close of the frontier brought about the opposite genre of cynicism and limitations, the Dystopia. The foremost example, Samuel Butler's *Erewhon*, was fashioned after its sixteenth-century counterparts, though it maintained a sarcastic tone. *Erewhon* chronicles the discovery of a new land that is like the utopias of the early modern era but turns out to be a false discovery, only revealing the way things are in the England of Butler's time. As such, it is a mock utopia or, as it might be said, 'utopia' spelled backward.

While it is not known whether Butler intended to christen a new literary genre when he wrote *Erewhon*, the farseeing Briton drove home a convincing point: The era of Utopia had come to an end; it was no longer desirable to fashion a society in which everything could and did work properly—that dream had gone. In the late 1800s and beyond, it was only possible to denounce society as it was without the benefit of providing an alternative. In fact, there were no alternatives. The system had closed, and all that was left was what was already in existence.

Anatomy of the Close

It would be fallacious to suggest that after 1890 all hope and energy was suddenly crushed. On the contrary, the pivotal time seemed to be one of great dynamism and productivity. The artistic innovations brought about by the various pressures were fresh and creative despite their restless tenor, and they led many to regard the age as a 'belle époque'. With regard to the period's new techne alone—the automobile, the electric light, the radio, and the airplane, among countless others—there seemed to be no limit to the Western imagination. With these and other advances, it was as if civilization could improve indefinitely, and, as idealists William Godwin or Marquis de Condorcet might have had it, could actually reach perfection at some point.

At the turn of the century, an argument could well be made that, even though the frontier had come to a close, the new economy presented Westerners and especially Americans with an infinite galaxy of opportunities. As Joseph Schumpeter perceptively pointed out later, the rapid extension of technology constantly opened doors to new industrial frontiers, which afforded the typical American much more appealing prospects than the frontier of the Wild West ever could. The simple fact that one could innovate and expand into infinitely intricate arenas of technical growth meant that there was no limit to one's productive powers or those of the nation altogether.

The immense progress experienced in the period cast doubt on Turner's otherwise reasonable hypothesis that the close of the frontier meant the close of opportunity. As a whole, Western civilization was wealthier than ever before, people were richer than they had been in times past, and there seemed to be an endless supply of work for anyone who wanted it in the growing industrial metropolises. Opportunity seemed bountiful, even after the close.

But however limitless opportunity seemed, the West had arrived at a point where its prosperity had become contingent on undeniable factors of constraint. Specifically, since the frontier had closed and all the free land had been taken, an individual could only derive opportunity through other people, which meant that the prospects one had were limited at least by his ability to work with and for others. Of course his ingenuity and work ethic would play a role in his success, but it could not provide him with all that he needed. In order to take advantage of America's opportunity, one would have to work in a factory under a manager, or as a salesman for a large corporation, or as a banker at the local savings and loan, or in some other capacity for some other organization. In the highly interdependent society, an individual would have to work for someone else in one way or another to earn a living. As such, despite the fact that the economy's overall wealth was that much more abundant, it was all controlled by others and so was for all practical purposes limited.

It is ironic to think that, just as Industrialism had taken hold of the American spirit and delivered the country as a world power, forces were at work to undermine that great new authority. Just as America had offered near infinite capacity to her people, she had cut them off. Wealth had become a glowing beacon of hope and prosperity like the torch on the Statue of Liberty, seemingly close enough to touch, and yet, like the torch, practically impossible to obtain.

Exactly how this close took place could be seen in the pressure placed on money as a conduit of trade. When an economy closes, the people within that economy grow instantly interdependent on each other. In a highly interdependent society, one can only satisfy his needs and wishes through other people—his hair must be cut by the barber, his meat procured by the butcher, his bread made by the baker, and so on. And, since those other people require money in exchange for their goods, an individual can only satisfy his needs by first obtaining currency.

In short, one can only survive and thrive by obtaining and making use of money. And so money replaces goods and services as the only real source of well-being. With it, one is wealthy and can attain anything he wishes; without it, one is hopeless and destitute. Ultimately, wealth itself and the ability for any given individual to attain it are directly dependent upon money and one's ability to obtain currency. In the end, the close of the economy causes Marx's Money Nexus to be borne out to its ultimate conclusion, in which money is the all-important aim and its procurement the end purpose for all exchanges.

And this is how the close of the frontier brings about the close of the economy. Because the money supply is naturally controlled and limited, everything that is dependent upon it is effectively controlled and limited, including wealth itself, because the only way one can access it is through the use of a scarce supply of money. This is true notwithstanding the fact that wealth, in terms of goods and services, can be virtually boundless, just as it must have seemed in the 1890s and may well seem today. Yet as long as one can only gain access to that infinite supply through the use of money, then the wealth itself is controlled by other people and thus limited as well.

And so we see that the problem was not, as Malthus suggested, that the resources were limited and could not keep up with the growing population; it was rather that the resources were all controlled and that those in charge of them would reasonably check their use. Here we find the basis for concerns about overpopulation and the scarcity of necessary resources. Certainly, natural resources such as land, food crops, petroleum, and clean water are all quite abundant in the world and can be procured satisfactorily despite a nearly exponential growth in population. The fact is that they can all be contained and thus controlled, and so it seems as though they are limited and at risk of exhaustion.

This is why reports of the imminent expiration of natural resources are always granted such credence. Resources are plentiful and perhaps even limitless in all meaningful ways, but since they can be controlled, they can seem limited and thus scarce. For example, Americans have heard for forty years that oil reserves will run out within years; though, decade after decade, it hasn't happened. Despite the fears, reserves have increased to the extent that we now have more oil available to us than ever before. And yet, because the supply is wholly owned, and, in large part, owned by foreign countries, oil reserves seem limited and fears of exhaustion continue to plague us in an energy-mad economy.

What can be said is that scarcity is a function of accessibility, not necessarily of mere existence. When a resource's accessibility is limited for any reason, it is scarce, whether or not there is an abundance in nature. There might be an infinite amount of baobob trees in some garden on a faraway planet, but since that planet is unknown and inaccessible, baobob trees are understood to be endangered. The same goes for all resources—land, water, petroleum, and so on. Ultimately, scarcity begets fear of exhaustion, whether a resource is limited by Mother Nature or by the Organization of the Petroleum Exporting Countries.

The Effective Supply-and-Demand Problem

Since an interdependent society means that all resources can only be accessed through money, it is as if all resources are controlled and limited as money is. They could be infinite, but as long as it is only possible to access them through money, they are scarce, and the result is a closed economy.

The significance money plays in an interdependent economy can best be summarized by the paradox of effective supply and demand. In the early nineteenth century, French economist Jean-Baptiste Say had postulated a theory that stated that money was neutral in trade, that goods were exchanged for other goods, and that money served only as a conduit in the process. But, as society grew more interdependent, money grew more vital.

As the economy's exchange of wealth grew more dependent on money, its neutrality diminished.

It was Sismondi who first stressed the fact that it is not enough for one to simply want food, clothing, and furniture for a trade to occur; one must also have the ability to purchase them. In an interdependent society, that ability rests increasingly on the possession and application of money. In other words, it is not supply and demand that matters in a given economy, but rather the supply that is available for purchase and the demand that is redeemable through purchase. The close has meant that regular old supply and demand are basically meaningless and that *effective* supply and demand, or supply and demand accompanied by purchasing power, are what really matter. Without this effective supply and demand, producers cannot find buyers, buyers cannot find producers, and the economy cannot find its equilibrium.

At its core, the problem of effective supply and demand represents the source of one of the great paradoxes in all of social matters: poverty in the midst of plenty. It is a mystery apparently endemic to capitalist economies. From as early as Sismondi's time, the Business Cycle was seen as a precarious force that at times left many without means of income and therefore without the necessities. Even though the capitalist mechanism was busy producing goods in abundance, multitudes went without food, clothing, and shelter. The desperate question was rife: If Capitalism and machine industry were so productive, then why did so many people go hungry and homeless? If there was such an abundance of goods and services in the new economy, how could there be want at all?

The answer lies in the effective demand trap. In the modern economy, productivity is so high that only a very few need to work to produce food, clothing, shelter, and the like for the entire population. The better and more efficient the production process becomes, the fewer workers are needed. Moreover, what is typically a gradual evolution in the improvement of production processes is accented from time to time with excessive booms of investment and production that make output even more abundant and thus make workers even less necessary. The less workers are necessary, the fewer jobs there are and the more the working class suffers unemployment. Without income, the working class is unable to buy the goods that they have produced so efficiently.

One might assume that technical progress must be beneficial and rewarding to all—the more productive we are as a people, the less work needs to be done to attain the high standard of living we seek. The utopian dream of minimal work for everyone and hours upon hours of leisure becomes a simple matter of course. In the end, Capitalism and machine industry are the vehicles that get us to that utopia.

Of course, to obtain food, clothing, shelter, et cetera, consumers must be able to pay the producers who make them and so need money to that end. The plan, naturally, is for the consumers to work to obtain that money. But, after periods of excessive production, it is not always necessary for everyone to be employed. The result, as Sismondi and others found, was unemployment, which leads inevitably to a lack of income and thus the inability for the people to pay for the necessities they demand. Needs go unsatisfied while stockpiles of goods go to waste. Ultimately, the result is poverty in the midst of plenty.

The extent to which this problem can occur is seen in an historical sketch of American agriculture. One estimate has shown that, in 1776, no fewer than 19 of 20 workers in America were needed to feed its three million inhabitants. Two hundred years later, industry had so improved that fewer than one out of 20 American workers were needed to feed its population, which had blossomed to 300 million. If agriculture is in any way representative of industry in general, the trend is clear. Greater productivity means less need for workers, and less need for workers means fewer jobs and ultimately lower purchasing power. Goods are produced in increasing abundance, though there are fewer and fewer consumers able to buy them.

As Keynes later showed, the real scarcity in the modern economy is not in food, clothing, or shelter, which are all made abundant because of the efficient production techniques; rather, scarcity lies in employment and the wide diffusion of money, without which none of the necessities can be obtained. Though industrial economies can output goods in wild profusion, the producers still need to be paid money in return for those goods. So what is needed is not the production of more goods, but full employment and more money so that consumers can purchase those goods. Only with these, it is thought, can the economy as a whole work efficiently.

In the twenty-first century, we know how impossible the vision of a utopian society is because we have extended the principles of effective supply and demand to their extremes. To obtain leisure at all, to be able to afford a night out or a vacation in the Caribbean, one first needs to obtain money; but to obtain money, one needs to work; and when one is working, by definition, there is no leisure. The more leisure a people requires, the more they have to work and the less free time they can afford. And so the work-leisure catch is a self-perpetuating cycle in which a people must continually increase their workload to pay for the increasing demands of leisure.

Eventually, time becomes the scarcest resource there is. Swedish economist Staffan B. Linder showed mathematically how this dilemma materializes. In his 1970 work, *The Harried Leisure Class*, Linder makes the point that consumption takes time just like production does. In order for a people to enjoy all the fruits of their labor, they must allot a given amount of time for eating and relaxing, for travel and tourism. The more productive and efficient the people are, the more leisure they can afford. At the same time, the more productive and efficient the people are, the less time they have to participate in the leisure they have allowed themselves.

In the modern economy, as Linder points out, we hardly recognize the limits of consumption time. Like the nineteenth-century utopians, we assume that increased productivity will allow for infinite occasion to relax. Says Linder, "The very term free time suggests a failure to realize that consumption time is a scarce commodity." It is not free after all and comes only at the expense of work time, which is necessary to purchase free time.

The Objectivity of Value

As money grows more essential to a given society, its value grows as well until a point where it becomes the central focus of all economic actions. But this evolution from a simple means of exchange to the actual goal of exchange, as it is in Marx's Money Nexus, is more than just a shift in the perceived value; as touched on earlier, it is a shift in the notion of value altogether. That is, as money becomes the goal in a given economy, value in that economy changes from something that is subjective and personal to something that is objective and universal.

When this happens, the entire capitalist system is turned on its head. Generally, the upshot is the upheaval of the individualist framework in which all parties can gain from cooperative exchanges. When money is seen as an objectively valuable good, everything is viewed in relation to it and only one party can gain in a given exchange—the party which obtains the greatest amount of the objectively valued good. Anyone else in the exchange necessarily loses out. Ultimately, when value is objective, cooperation is no longer possible because gain for one means loss for all others.

As we will see, the more useful money has become as the means of economic exchange, the more the pursuit of wealth becomes a closed endeavor with a single aim. When everyone is striving for the same thing, the pursuit becomes competitive and one person can only get ahead at the expense of another.

The close of an economic system is illustrated expertly and entertainingly in the 1980 Jamie Uys comedy *The Gods Must Be Crazy*. The movie opens with a vignette about a tribe of primitive African Bushmen who live harmoniously on the lands of the Kalahari. They reside there happily unaware of the civilized world outside, until everything is turned upside down when an empty Coke bottle magically drops from the sky, as if it were from the gods. They immediately find the gift useful (they can cure snakeskins with it) and fun (one of the elders gets his finger stuck in it). Everyone in the tribe is thankful for the productive tool that the gods have given them, which to the tribe is the most useful and productive thing in the world.

But gradually, 'the thing', as the Bushmen call it, gains too high a demand, and fierce competition arises for its use. One of the tribesmen wants it to help with his cookery and another wants it to help with his art; the children all want to play with it. Shortly, the tribesmen discover that there is not enough usage to go around. Selfishness leads to antagonism, which ultimately leads to fighting. The conflict escalates until the Bushman who came upon the bottle is convinced that he must throw it off the end of the earth to return it to the gods.

The astute comedy shows how easily a tribe of gentle people can turn vicious. The only thing that changed in the Bushmen's situation was the Coke bottle—the sole item that everyone wanted. Prior to the discovery, the tribesmen all had what they needed and cooperated with one another in production and trade. With the addition of the bottle, cooperation became impossible. One person's use of it meant that everyone else necessarily could not use it. And so the conflict brewed.

Because it serves as a sole item that everyone wants, money works in a similar way. Money provides a single goal that can satisfy everyone's needs, whether it is curing a snakeskin or vacationing in the Bahamas. Whereas without money, a people can produce and trade harmoniously, just as it was before the African Bushmen found the bottle; a society dependent upon money necessarily begets competition, antagonism, and the occasion for fighting, just as it was after the discovery of the bottle.

Implications of this competitiveness are far and wide. In general, it can be said that the shift brings us to a condition where mutual gain becomes difficult and almost impossible. The broad brushstrokes in the earlier sketch of the turn of the century illustrate the kind of conflict that naturally developed as a result—upheaval in the arts, in literature, in science, as well as in the geopolitical sphere. Far from the harmonious overtures of the Romantic century, the tones of the early twentieth century were of antagonism and conquest. Upon reflection, it was the only way to advance.

During the lead-up to World War I, good minds across the board promoted war and destruction, quite as if it had been the only recourse; indeed, as if it had been the best possible recourse. This is why the objective historian cannot be surprised by the century of war that followed. The stage had been duly set. From the base economic relationships at the bottom of society to the sprawling national relations at the top, those involved had sensed that the system had closed, and so the only way to succeed and grow was by defeating others.

* * *

The argument was that, in a system such as the modern economy, encroachment and intrusion were inevitable. Only the powerful could succeed, and the weak would have to submit. In the early twentieth century, the thought was that might made right. Of course, the thoughtful recognized that this was nothing new. Indeed, it was nothing more than a return to the premodern hierarchy of power laid out in the feudal kingdoms. Just as it was in medieval Christendom, so too would the confinement of the new age bring about a defined chain of power. At the top were not kings and lords, but rather financiers and industrialists, so-called 'robber barons' by twentieth-century American commentator Matthew Josephson. At the bottom were not serfs but rather the 'proletariat', the impoverished working class named by Sismondi in reference to the Ancient Roman proletarius, the lowest class of the empire.

No fewer than three excellent Belle Époque treatises endeavored to demonstrate this return to feudal ways: Achille Loria's *The Economic Foundations of Society* (1899), Vilfredo Pareto's *The Rise and Fall of Elites* (1901), and Hilaire Belloc's *The Servile State* (1912). All three dealt with the themes so dominant in politico-economic discourse at the time—the close of the economic system and what that meant for the capitalist way of life.

In a treatment that echoed Henry George and Malthus before him, Italian economist Achille Loria argued that the newly closed system was the major influence on all central institutions of modern civilization. With a focus on three cultural institutions in particular—morality, the law, and politics—Loria showed how the close limited alternatives and conformed behavior so as to favor those in power. "The normal increase of population," he asserted, "eventually results in the appropriation of all lands cultivable by labour alone, and the economic system then undergoes a radical transformation. The labourer now loses that liberty of choice which up to this constituted his safeguard against the usurpations of capital, and henceforth he has no means of livelihood other than to sell his labour to the capitalist for the wages which it pleases the latter to determine." In the confines of the closed system, the worker is bound to the owner, the proletarian to the robber baron, as serf to lord.

Bound as he is, the worker has no real alternative to the owner's dictates. Even if he is politically free, he is economically restrained to the will of the men in power; he is a servant with or against his will. Naturally, the worker has the freedom to refuse his labor and in so doing sway the terms of the working agreement, a freedom that the slave technically lacks. But, in the case of the worker, there is a limit to his ability to bargain since he is bound by time and place to come up with subsistence. Whereas the owner has no pressure to make the deal, the worker has the threat of hunger or homelessness. Like the serf, the worker has no real alternatives, and so must accept the owner's terms or else.

This is the principle behind Pareto's notion that the rise in authoritarian rule is only possible with the sanction of the victims. They are the ones who drive the exploitation because, after all, they are the ones who are making the choices. Modern economics is of course made of contracts between workers and owners, who conduct business as partners in a company as it might seem. As Belloc puts it, however, "The vast bulk of so-called 'free' contracts are to-day leonine contracts: arrangements which one man was free to take or to leave, but which the other man was not free to take or to leave, because the second had for his alternative starvation." In a closed system, even voluntary actions are to some extent involuntary.

Nor were the new restraints limited to the economic realm. Loria, Pareto, and Belloc all saw the emerging hierarchy as the threshold to an absolutely polarizing system. Not only would the lower and upper classes be separated by comparative wealth, but that divide would become institutionalized and eventually lead to differing legal and administrative rights altogether—a truly feudal system in the modern economy.

As a sort of reversal of Turner's dictum, it was argued that the absence of free land would mean a lack of competency, without which political freedom would be rendered indefensible. Just as economic freedom secures political freedom, so too would economic bondage secure political bondage. Belloc makes the point clear: "To control the production of wealth is to control human life itself. To refuse man the opportunity for the production of wealth is to refuse him the opportunity for life; and, in general, the way in which the production of wealth is by law permitted is the only way in which the citizens can legally exist."

By 1912, when Belloc published *The Servile State*, he could already document at least one major step toward formalized exploitation in his home of Britain in the form of the progressive income tax. Though it was designed as a way to redistribute wealth in favor of the lower classes, the income tax was the first major comprehensive legislation established across the liberal West that converted a largely spontaneous economy to a planned political system. The following century would be in large part a continuance of that process, with the political class growing ever more powerful until it controlled all aspects of daily economic life and therefore all aspects of political life as well.

As Marx had predicted, Loria, Pareto, and Belloc viewed the ascent of the State and ultimately the victory of Socialism as the rather imminent consequence of the closed economic system. A distinction lay in their perceived causes. While Marx attributed society's march from Capitalism toward Socialism to deterministic material forces, Loria, Pareto, and Belloc saw the movement as being a logical progression given the confinement of the modern economy, which, in some ways, made the path to serfdom even more disheartening. It was only natural for men, once exploited, to desire a formal incarnation of their servitude, to control their slavery by whatever minimal means they had available. They paid attention to the crisis itself, and the crisis was one of volition.

Prospects for the Individual

Granted the fact that true freedom is based on the ability to say 'No' to the system, the question remains whether that ability remained after the close. Many would argue that the abundance of choices available to average Westerners of the time, especially Americans, proves that they were perhaps the freest people in all of history, both economically and politically. In the twentieth century, one could look down the aisle at the local market and see a number of brands of bread, tools, laundry detergent, and so on, and bask in his unrivalled freedoms. By many accounts, the dawn of the twentieth century was the dawn of plenty and not, as the case was made, the dawn of restriction and servitude.

One fails to notice, however, that of all the choices, the one missing was the most important—the choice to reject them all. In the end, the average Westerner only had the ability to choose from what was given to him, abundant as it might have been, and this is the definition of restriction. His dependence on others meant that he relied on those others to satisfy his needs and so had no way of rejecting them.

Of course, few would claim that modern industrial living was anything but accommodating and comfortable. Most would have said that it was overwhelmingly pleasant, and it is assumed that anyone who wanted to escape from it must be mad. But let us for a moment consider the possibility of someone who did want to reject the modern industrial life. Let us consider, for example, a thought experiment in which the great individualist philosopher Henry David Thoreau lived in the early twentieth century and tried to live in the woods fifty or sixty years after *Walden* had been published, perhaps with the same intentions of getting closer to nature and escaping the confines of society. Whatever his rationale might be for breaking free, could he do it? In the twentieth century, does he have the freedom to say 'No' like he did in the mid-nineteenth, or is that freedom just a chimera?

Politically, the twentieth-century Thoreau does have the freedom to say 'No' to the system—he is politically free to do as he pleases and has been granted a Bill of Rights that secures the freedom to move where ever he sees fit and to turn away from the advances of the day. He can avoid the new inventions of the day, the electric lights, the automobiles, the planes, the radios, et cetera; he can avoid the bustle of the subway and the crowds at the local bar and any other disagreeable gathering place if he is so inclined.

But, if he is to live in the world at all, he must live somewhere, and that means he must occupy some amount of land and produce at the very least some sort of sustenance. In a closed economy, these simple needs mean that he must obtain some amount of money for housing and groceries, which means he will need a full-time job. To get a job these days, he must go to school and thus fund his education in some way, either by loan or some kind of part-time employment. To secure these types of occupations, he must engage in some level of communication for which the radio, phones, cars, and other techne are essential. This is not to mention the clothing and other accessories he needs to impress potential employers and school administrators. And so on, in the modern industrial city, one's needs multiply ad infinitum.

In short, to exist at all these days, one must take part in the system as it stands. He must participate in the various channels of development from school to career to retirement and all the in-betweens that have developed in the modern world. Even if he were extreme and moved out into the country to live on the land like Thoreau did at Walden away from the things of man, he could find no haven in his flight. Out in the country, he would still be affected by the industrial world—by the pollution and development that would constantly encroach on his property, not to mention the taxes and regulations that would be imposed on him by the government some thousands of miles away. Most likely, he'd eventually be kicked off whatever piece of land he chose or required to pay some sort of fee for it. No matter where lived, the system would be there, waiting for him.

The joke around election time rings true: Voters fearful of their candidate's defeat threaten to move to another state or country if the other side wins. Of course, no one moves, and the reason is clear—they have no place to go. Other countries offer no real shelter from American ways, as they've all become Americanized anyway. The frontier had closed a century before, and there was no longer free land to which one could escape. The disgruntled voters have to stick it out and accept what they know is a corrupt system. As Milton Friedman expressed in his *Capitalism and Freedom*, "If I do not like what Washington imposes, I have few alternatives in this world of jealous nations."

As long as the land is all controlled, the choices an individual has will be limited and subject to the owners' dictates. Faced with such a predicament, our Thoreau finally arrives at the only conclusion possible, deciding that as long as he is going to be burdened by the system, he might as well put himself in the place where he can profit most from it. That is, he will try to take advantage of the system to the greatest of his abilities. He will go to the best schools and get the best jobs and arrange the best life possible, quite as if his choices could be judged on their objective merit. In the end, however, he is only choosing between this or that fixed option and can only succeed in the way that the system has arranged.

The consumer culture that seems so abundant in freedoms is not unlike the child psychology technique that urges parents to give their children choices between two options when, for instance, dressing for school, in order to make the child feel engaged in the decision-making process. The child is the one putting his finger on the outfit, and so he feels as though he has a choice. In reality, the two options are just two versions of the same thing—both of the parent's design—and the child is no more engaged than he would be if the parent made the decision by himself. Similarly, modern day consumers and voters must feel like they are making choices, but in reality they are just adhering to the system's design.

The problem with this psychology is that the façade of decision-making has replaced true discretion. The child is conditioned to refine his taste by judging superficial elements in relation to others—this color or that, this style or that. But he is not taught how to administer sound judgment—what would be appropriate in this situation or that. Sound judgment can only be harnessed if the child looks at the purpose of the decision objectively, outside of his confined selections. It may well be that the parent has given the child the best two options, but unless the child knows what makes them the best, he will not be able to appreciate them or replicate the decision on his own.

Consumers in the modern economy reflect this pseudo-decision-making in that few if any look at the choices they are making objectively. Most will base their decisions on the surrounding alternatives and be content that they have the freedom to do so. They will most certainly not look to the real value of a certain decision or consider how it relates to life in general. Recall the behavioral economics example from before: The wine connoisseur buys the $75 bottle, not because it is worth $75, but because it is next to a bottle selling for $60 and one selling for $120. He doesn't know what makes it a good choice, just that in comparison to his other choices it stands out as the best.

The phenomenon is seen throughout our culture, in practically every retail situation imaginable, but also in other business interactions, social and romantic relationships, education, the arts, media, religion, and, naturally, government. A prospective college student knows that going to Harvard, Yale, or Princeton will give him a good education, for example, but he has no idea what a good education entails or why these institutions provide it over others; a voter knows that electing this politician will help this or that industry, but he has no idea what makes a good public official or whether they should help any industry at all.

The modern citizen is not concerned with what is proper, what is good, what is just; he is concerned with what is acceptable, what is better, what is workable. When a system is closed, an individual's decisions are not made from the ground up; they are made under relational pretexts and cannot possibly be based in one's perceived value.

* * *

Now, it must be said that the notion of free land has never been absolute. There has always been a cost to setting out on one's own and making one's own living. The frontier life requires one to do without luxuries, for example, and possibly necessities such as vitamins and nutrients. As can be construed from accounts of the eighteenth and nineteenth centuries, frontier life was as dependent upon the whims of nature as city life was dependent upon the whims of bureaucrats and public officials. It could be said, then, that the cost of saying 'No' to the system is having to rough it.

Moreover, there has always been an initial cost to moving in the form of securing supplies for the journey and for settlement once there. Pioneers had to raise enough funds to buy food, tools, the steamer and coach ride, and the actual land that they were to settle in order to successfully take advantage of the so-called free land. In this way, the land was not completely free, and there was to some extent a limit as to who could take advantage of it.

In this light, one sees that, so long as there is unoccupied land somewhere in the world, there is always the opportunity for one to break free from one's current environment and move to that open space. All one must do is raise enough capital to purchase the property and guarantee the payment of taxes and the like. What we are seeing since the close of the frontier, however, is that the cost of doing so is increasing exponentially. One must not only raise funds for the food, tools, transportation, land, et cetera; he must also account for ongoing taxes and most likely ongoing lobbying to nullify the regulations that continue to multiply around his property. Before the close, free land required some sort of startup capital, but once that initial payment was made, it was essentially free, and one didn't have to be part of a system; now, free land requires startup capital and what might be called maintenance capital as well, the fee demanded for belonging to the system.

Ultimately, these extra costs are paid to those in control of the system as it stands, making them wealthier and more powerful. In short, one must buttress the system if he hopes to leave it. But, by paying this tribute, he only bolsters the behemoth and ties himself more intimately to the web of controlling interests.

2. INTERDEPENDENCY

THE IMPLICIT GOAL IN modern economics has always been to increase production so as to better satisfy the needs of mankind. By the late nineteenth century, progress was undeniable—life expectancy was up, production of necessities was up, and luxuries had become commonplace for nearly all. But once the chief manifestations of the pursuit had been realized, one could see that something unexpected, almost paradoxical, had happened at the same time. Certainly, thanks to industry, trade, and the large-scale multiplication of wealth made possible by the use of money and credit, most people throughout the world and mankind in general had experienced a rise in the quality of life that had never been witnessed before. Parallel to this progress, however, there was such an increase in specialism, a reduction in self-sufficiency, and a concentration of people so as to provide a countervailing force equal to if not greater than the rising standard.

While the goal had always been freedom from the fetters of nature, the modern man had found himself increasingly dependent on others and so enslaved by the system designed to liberate him. In a word, he had traded the chains of the natural world for the chains of the system, the latter being no less oppressive or damaging than the former. This second is the phenomenon of interdependency, as it can be called, and it stands as the great coup of modern economics.

Our Interconnected Lives

Interdependency was always a corollary of modern economic cooperation, foreshadowed as early as Aquinas and warned of by Smith. Toward the end of the nineteenth century, however, as the frontier began to close and the alternatives to the modern system dwindled, Americans and Europeans began to realize that specialism, labor division, trade, and complex intricate networks of people and organizations were the only way to live. Without one's own land or the ability to set out on one's own, one had to engage in the system as it stood. And that meant interdependency would expand to every sector of society and one's daily life.

These days, we take for granted the premise behind interdependency. In order to make use of the vast possibilities of cooperation and trade, one must specialize and thus limit his functions in life. Brought to its logical conclusion, the modern system leaves individuals completely incapable except for the ability to perform one task, which he then trades for everything else. Simply, the modern man cannot do anything other than one or two things, and even those are usually dependent on others to be useful. One needs others to produce, store, and prepare his food; to build and maintain his shelter; to sew his clothing, design and manufacture his furniture, accessories, and household appliances.

In order to acquire all these things, moreover, one needs to buy them with money, a commodity that can only be obtained by providing a good or service that someone who already has money is willing to pay for. In other words, one needs others to even position himself to be able to get the things he needs from others. And the more complex the economy is, the stricter this dependence becomes.

An increase in the number of labor divisions in a manufacturing plant, for instance, will mean that each component is that much less crucial to the whole and that much more dependent on the other parts to be useful.

The more specialized and complex the whole, the more dependent each individual becomes.

An essay written fifty years ago by Leonard Read titled "I, Pencil" shows how even the simplest aspects of one's day-to-day activities require the work of countless others. The tale is a first-person account of the genealogy of a pencil—a normal, everyday pencil with which every schoolboy and girl is acquainted. It begins with the provocative statement that "not a single person on the face of this earth knows how to make me." And then the pencil goes on to prove it, describing where his various parts come from and how each is made by its own unique and meticulous process.

The pencil's family tree, as the pencil explains, begins with a tree. He depicts the elaborate procedure used to harvest and procure the wood and does not fail to mention all the tools and machinery needed for that task, in addition to all the work needed to create those tools. "Think of all the persons and the numberless skills that went into their fabrication: the mining of ore, the making of steel and its refinement into saws, axes, motors; the growing of hemp and bringing it through all the stages to heavy and strong rope; the logging camps with their beds and mess halls, the cookery and the raising of all the foods. Why, untold thousands of persons had a hand in every cup of coffee the loggers drink!"

The pencil then goes on to describe the processes used to procure the lead, which is not really lead at all but rather graphite mined in modern-day Sri Lanka, a procedure which requires its own set of support tools, instruments, and techniques. The reader is enlightened to know that the pencil's yellow paint requires six coats of lacquer, which is made possible by growers of castor beans and refiners of castor oil, among incalculable others. Then there is the labeling, the metal ring, and the eraser, which all require their own sets of complex and involved systems to be made ready for use.

Read summarizes the notion that millions of human beings have a hand in creating the typical pencil, reiterating the fact that not a single one of them knows how to perform all the tasks necessary to make it on their own. Most do not even know that they are helping to make a pencil at all. They simply carry on their duties—felling timber, mining ore, shipping packages, growing plants, and so on—completely oblivious to the ultimate product that has been so integral to the daily activities of so many schoolchildren and adults.

No one would think twice about the simple if fundamental writing utensil, but when considered in this light it is clear that even the use of something so minimal requires a complex network of individuals and organizations. Imagine a single person trying to produce one of these simple writing utensils—the number of processes it would take and the amount of resources is almost unfathomable, all for something that you can buy at the corner store for five cents. Basically, it is impossible to do it all oneself and yet almost negligible when done in an intricate network of people. Such is the miracle of a modern economy.

The more complicated a product is, as one can imagine, the more intricate the supply chain and labor force would have to be. The Apple iPod, for instance, is a consumer electronic device that has garnered much praise over the last decade for its simplicity and ease of use. Still, no one can quite imagine the amount of interconnected systems needed to bring it all together. There are some 450 parts in the iPod, and each one has a unique production process that is similar to if not more multifaceted than that of the pencil.

To even contemplate all the people involved in the manufacture of the parts, the shipping and assembly, the refining of raw materials, the harvesting and amassing of those materials, and all the various work needed to provide the tools and mechanisms for these tasks, would be a monumental feat in itself. It would not be a stretch to suggest that a billion people had a role in the production of every one of the 250 million iPods sold worldwide, each person diligently focused on his own task and happily harmonizing with the other hundreds of millions of people to produce one of the most popular devices ever.

Granted, a change in any one of these individuals' lives would not mean the discontinuation of the line. Others would fill in to ensure that the production continued as planned. But every role in that inestimable supply chain must be filled for the system to work. To use an iPod at all, and to receive the limitless musical and visual joy that it brings, one depends on an absolute mass of humanity. To use a pencil, to cook a meal, to wear the latest fashion (or even the not-so-latest fashion), to get an education, to work for a living, to earn an income, to do just about anything these days, one relies on countless others. Detaching from them for whatever reason would bring not only discomfort and a passé wardrobe, but real suffering and potentially death. It has come to the point in the modern economy where one's very survival is tied inextricably to the billions of people around him.

So what exactly does this interdependency mean? In general terms, it means that everything in one's life becomes a function of other people. In order to do what one wants—to eat the food one wants, watch the movies one wants, and listen to one's favorite songs on an iPod—one must first do what others want. It is quite a paradox.

In the modern economy, where one's actions are bound to several if not hundreds of people and possibly everyone around, it is impossible to conduct oneself without at least considering those others. A survey of a major metropolis illustrates the condition clearly. Everywhere one turns in the big city, one encounters some form or other of restriction or inconvenience made necessary by the proximity of others. At least some measures must be taken, for example, to wind around slower walkers on the sidewalk, to allow other cars to go through an intersection, and to account for the nincompoop who thoughtlessly runs the red light, crashes into the median, and holds up traffic for 45 minutes. We all encounter these cumbersome and somewhat tedious situations as parts of our daily lives. To take part in the great modern complexity and to benefit from the higher standard of living that it provides, one must also put up with its assorted inconveniences.

More than likely, this submission to the masses extends to the point where one must conduct himself expressly in reflection of others. It isn't just that one has to move around others or make room for them on his commute; in order to survive in the modern world, one must positively conduct business with them, do things with them and for them, and arrange his life according to their dictates.

This is more or less what all people do these days with regard to their careers, which are their only sources of livelihood and depend almost entirely on what other people want. The lament of the bored office worker is apt—he has no idea what he is working on or why he must do it, but he knows that if he does he will get a consistent paycheck, which will allow him to eat the food he wants, entertain himself the way he wants, and spend time with people he likes. To reiterate, in order to do what he wants, he must do what others want.

Even if this worker enjoys his job and is eager to produce, his work must be channeled through other people before it is made useful. He might have an excellent idea for a new product, for example, but in order to see it through, he must first present it to his boss, who will take his time in dissecting the proposal before sending it on to the oversight committee, who will take their time analyzing it. If and when it passes inspection, the idea can be implemented into the production plan, which requires its own set of procedures and policies to be followed. Once production starts, the idea is almost completely out of the creator's hands and into the control of the system.

Whether it resembles the original concept when it is finally produced is a matter of pure conjecture. Even the head of the company is powerless without the rest of his staff—he can't produce the many books, cars, iPods, et cetera all by himself; he too is dependent on everyone else.

Long gone are the days of the discrete genius inventor who sees his product through from conception to retail shelf. In the 1850s, lone adventurers could make a fortune by traveling to the American River Valley in California and panning for gold; today, nothing less than a multimillion-dollar industry with scores of scientists and engineers can profit from gold discovery. The kind of hands-on engineering that Samuel F. B. Morse employed for the telegraph, that Michael Faraday used on his conductors and motors, or that Edison used for his stock ticker, automobile battery, electric generators, musical records, and motion pictures, has become wholly impossible these days, as practically all inventions require fleets of researchers working on distinct problems in a minuscule corner of the whole enterprise.

Similarly, it was not long ago that a well-off individual could maintain his business affairs and keep tabs on all his finances; nowadays, it is basically impossible for one to do so by himself—financial planners, accountants, and lawyers are essential to keep on top. The immense complexity of the modern economy has made it nearly impossible for one to cross disciplines in work at all without the help of scores of specialists and advisors.

Economies of Service

If there is a convincing sign of growing interdependency, it is in the rise of the service economy across the West. Throughout the twentieth century, industrialized countries have steadily shifted their economies from agriculture and industry-based output such as farming and manufacturing to service-based output such as sales and finance. The transition has been a move from a simple economy to a complex one; or from independent, self-sufficient production to interdependent, other-sufficient production.

The economies of the United States and the United Kingdom provide the most prominent examples. Statistics show that, in the 1870s, services accounted for around a 20% share of employment° in the United States, with the rest consisting primarily of commodity production. Today, services account for around 80% of employment. A look at the global economic picture reflects this evolution from agriculture and industry to service in a gradient from the least developed nations to the most industrialized.

Like a cross-section in the history of the Information Age, we can see the progress from undeveloped countries based heavily in agriculture to complex, developed countries based heavily in services. But the difference

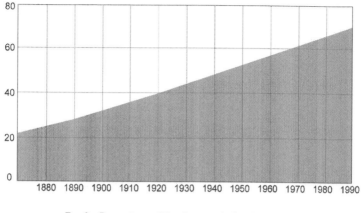

FIG. 9—Percentage of Employment in Service Sector.

between an economy based in agriculture and industry and one based in services rests in more than just its historical stage. It is a very substantive difference between product-oriented work and relationship-oriented work; it is the difference between real wealth and abstract wealth dependent upon others. Those countries that have remained heavily agricultural and industrial are largely focused on producing real wealth—commodity goods, food stuffs, automobiles, and so on—while those countries that have leaned significantly into services are producing less real wealth proportionate to their population and relying more heavily on the abstract wealth of services—financial planning, physical therapy, graphic design, management, and so on.

Of course, it may well be that the United States produces more real wealth than any other country nonetheless. It would not be a surprise, since the U.S. maintains the highest GDP in the world by several trillions of dollars. Still, it must be recognized that the abstract wealth that some 80% of our population depends on for livelihood is only worth something if others demand it, which is to say that the wealth generated by the service economy is dependent upon other people.

Quite unlike the output of agriculture and industry-based economies, which to a large degree is useful no matter who wants what, the output of a service economy is only useful if there is someone else out there who wants the service. Put in another way, a country could survive and prosper without the service economy; without the agricultural and industrial economies, it could not.

As financial analyst Peter Schiff has explained, Western nations' focus on services has left them at a disadvantage to emerging agriculture and industry-driven economies like China, India, and Brazil, who have accumulated real wealth in recent decades while Western nations have accumulated debt. The trade deficit that has resulted is the statistical manifestation of the Western nations' disadvantage.

In modern economies, the distinction between goods and services itself is actually being blurred. One aspect of this shift to a service economy is what has been called the 'servitization' of products. The notion is that, in a modern economy, products cannot exist on their own and some degree of service is needed to make those products useful. Consider the automobile, which is of course a real good. It is only useful, however, over an extended period of time if the owner submits it to continual checkups, fills it with gas and oil, and pays for insurance, registration, and taxes so that he can operate it on community roads. The car is a real good, but it is not necessarily useful unless one also includes the many services that accompany it.

IBM provides a pertinent example. Here is a company that was at the forefront of computer production throughout the middle of the twentieth century. In its maturity, however, the company has shifted focus to a more service-oriented business model featuring solutions consulting (id est, is dependent on others). While IBM still sells machines, computer sales represent only a fraction of its revenue. In this service economy, the company has found that consulting provides longer-lasting contracts and lower price elasticity for greater and more reliable income.

Similarly, some of the fastest-growing businesses these days are those that have done away with the single payment option and established a subscription-style pricing model. For example, phone service comes at a monthly cost, with texting, picture mail, Internet, and all the other bells and whistles incurring their own monthly fees. Apple used to be a manufacturer of computers and now sees the future of its business dwelling in the sale of content sold through iTunes. Likewise, companies that provide DVDs, video games, Internet radio, magazines, books, and even clothes via a rental system have grown immensely popular in recent years.

Modern economics have practically disposed of the product-service distinction in lieu of a continuum that connects pure services with pure commodity goods in a spectrum of varied servitized products. The result is a snapshot of a modern economy.

Pure Service

Teaching

Investment Banking

House Cleaning

Plumbing Repair

Restaurant Service

Tailored Clothing

New Car

Radio

Soft Drinks

Salt

Pure Good

Fig. 10—Good–Service Continuum.

Of course, to suggest that services have only recently been instituted is inaccurate. Services have been a part of all economies since ancient times. So too do non-service businesses incorporate services within their realm. Take, for example, machine industry, the prototype of which can be seen on the assembly line in Adam Smith's nail factory. Individuals on the line were not really producing the nails that were ready for use, or any fraction thereof; they were merely applying their techniques to the iron as it passed.

And, as their work was not useful until it was joined with the work of the others, it could be said that they were only providing a service for the company, which was no more a single person than a city or state's economy would be.

*   *   *

Our modern service economy reveals the same interdependency, except we have just expanded the notion by about a billion products and a billion workers and consumers, none of which could function or survive without the help of every other one. The service that one individual offers these days is only worth something if it is attached to the work of the other hundreds or thousands in his company. And it is only valuable in exchange if it is attached to the work of every other company in the world.

One recognizes the extent to which the economy has become interconnected by the rhetoric alone—the language surrounding every vital action or thought today is steeped in connotations of interdependency. Regard talk of prosperity and the American way: It is almost always about getting a job, climbing the corporate ladder, or providing something that everyone else suddenly cannot do without—the next iPad, the next Segway, the next great American novel. All of the major milestones of success are dependent upon other people, and the greater the success, the greater the number of others one is dependent upon to achieve it. It has come to the point where the average American cannot possibly imagine making a living, much less making it big, if it is not through the system and according to the dictates of the masses.

This is in large part why employment has become such a major focus of economics and, by extension, politics. The notion is that a person cannot survive or do anything unless he has a job working for someone else, and so jobs have become something of a God-given right that the state is obligated to provide the populace. Worker's unions will clamor about the 'right to work' and, ever since Keynes, the notion of 'full employment' has become the underlying goal of all economic policies. Less concern is spent on whether that employment is geared toward something productive, the assumption being that all jobs must be productive by nature. But the bottom line is not whether jobs are productive, only whether people have jobs and income in the first place.

By the same token, it is assumed that an individual cannot retire unless it is via a pension; one cannot maintain good health unless it is through an amalgamated insurance and health care system; one cannot start a business unless it is through a set channel of bureaucracy outlined in some far-away office; a woman can't have a baby without the proper disability insurance, supervisor approval, and paid maternity leave; one cannot hold a small group meeting without some formal petition from the community, and so on. As such, it is no longer up to the individual to attain sustenance and security; it is up to society at large. It is no longer a matter of self-sufficiency or industry; it is a matter of benevolence. The standard has been established: Communities that provide well-being are generous, and communities that do not are cruel and ruthless.

The Ineluctable Crowd

The effects of interdependency received great attention around the turn of the last century, though it was not called by that name. Industrial society had become a way of life, and crowded cities were a fact of that new condition. As a result, a new mentality became the norm, less based on the individual and more reliant on a collective frame. French sociologist Gustave Le Bon found in his treatise *The Crowd* that individuals lost their rationality as a function of becoming part of a crowd, a phenomenon that intensified with the size of the group. It only makes sense: When every single action one can possibly conduct is dependent on the crowd around him, the inevitable result is the abdication of thought, reason, and judiciousness, and the assumption of a simple reaction to the crowd's motion.

This sort of mania was said to extend beyond situations normally associated with crowds, namely, mobs and riots, to affect all group settings, including public events, juries, electoral bodies, and parliaments as well. Wherever groups form, the tendency is to abandon one's psychological independence and just go with the flow.

It can be witnessed in the way decisions are compromised when considering others or in the way options are limited by the mere presence of the multitude. The individual becomes, as José Ortega y Gasset put it, a 'mass-man', a person who exists solely in the multitude, in the capacity and character of the multitude. While there had always been groups, and men had always been impressed upon by them, he had managed to stay independent of mind. By the late nineteenth century, the crowd had become too dominant to deny.

With good reason, both Le Bon and Ortega y Gasset focused on crowds as they existed in physical arrangements. But one can be a mass-man not only at sporting events, political rallies, subway terminals, high school hallways, and during riots, but also when he is alone, studying, for instance, or when he is figuring out what to wear or what computer to buy, or even when he is deciding on what career he would like to pursue. He knows that society is looming somewhere beyond the walls, and eventually it will have the final word in everything he does in his life.

> The disappearance of the conscious personality, the predominance of the unconscious personality, the turning by means of suggestion and contagion of feelings and ideas in an identical direction, the tendency to immediately transform the suggested ideas into acts; these, we see, are the principal characteristics of the individual forming part of a crowd.
>
> —GUSTAVE LE BON, *THE CROWD: A STUDY OF THE POPULAR MIND* (1895)

It is only in the Information Age with the advent of the Internet that we can plainly see how the mob mentality exists where there is no physical gathering. The Internet brings about the added phenomena of participating in online discussions, siding with political or other groups in comment boards, and of course being connected to others at all times with e-mail and social networking sites like Facebook. The knowledge that society is out there and will ultimately determine one's success is all that is needed to make every one of our activities and beliefs fundamentally social. In the end, it is more influential than a crowd's physical presence would be by itself anyway.

The upshot of all this for the individual is loss of autonomy and personal volition. When one's livelihood is dependent upon others, it is as though his choices are made for him. When he goes to school, to work, to the store, or to social gatherings, his decisions are necessarily and fundamentally skewed to accommodate the masses. Certainly, he can choose what kind of job to occupy and what to buy with the money he earns, but when it comes down to it, his client, his boss, the market, or society as a whole are really the decision-makers. They are the forces that determine what is most profitable, most accessible, or most feasible, and so they are the forces that encourage him in one direction or another.

Ultimately, since his very health is dependent upon these choices, it is as though the masses are in charge of his survival and ability to flourish. No longer does he have a choice in doing what he wants or producing what he believes to be rewarding, good, or just—all his actions must reflect the will of others, the society at large. The modern individual is, as it could be said, at the mercy of the masses.

The power of the public over the individual can be seen most clearly in the effects of the Business Cycle, which oscillates with no regard for the good or misguided actions of individuals, rewarding and punishing all at different occasions no matter what any single person has done. A perfectly reasonable entrepreneur, for instance, might have a brilliant business plan and follow the best business practices in establishing his company; but if the market runs into a slump, he could lose everything. At the same time, someone who is completely reckless with his business could by chance make it big. While sound business decisions can and do typically lead to success, just as wastefulness can and does typically lead to failure, in an increasingly interdependent society, both success and failure are based more and more on luck.

Amateur stock investors realize how little control the individual has when dabbling in the market. One might make a sound investment in a company's stock, an investment that shows all the promise of a profitable return. But even when the company is sound and all the financial bases have been covered, the stock price can still go down. One watches as a company announces bad news and the stock price goes up, and then, thinking it will continue, buys the stock, at which point the price goes down. The investor might hold on to the stock in the hope that it will resume its upward path, only to end up watching it continue to fall. Finally, when the price begins to fall precipitously, the investor sells, at which point the price rebounds and begins to rise again.

One cannot help but wonder: Is this unpredictable fluctuation a conspiracy against the little guy? A way the elite can manipulate independent investors? The best analysis is not in need of such hyperbole. The modern stock market, like any other social organization these days, is, as American statistician Karl Pearson first called it in 1905, a 'random walk', in which various inputs over the course of time will direct the price of a good or service randomly in any number of directions. It is not a plot; it's just the natural development of things in a highly complex, interdependent system.

The trick in the stock market these days is realizing that every investor affects the market as much as the others do, and together they can affect it as much or more than actual company performance. The act of buying a stock increases demand, and selling it decreases demand, both of which are reflected in the price. And so, to a large degree, it is the collective conscience that dictates the success of a given investment. If a substantial contingent of investors believes that the stock will do well, it very well might. Likewise, if that contingent believes that it will do poorly, it might as well. In this direct way, the confidence of the participants affects the outcome of the situation. Considering the role of the innumerable investors, one might focus on the people's view of the company and neglect the company outright. As this approach has grown more and more pervasive, the market has become little more than an exchange of bets on how the investors will react to given events.

One recalls Keynes' beauty contest analogy. In it, a newspaper displays a set of attractive young women and holds a contest in which entrants are encouraged to choose who they think is the most beautiful. The winners of the contest will be all the entrants who choose the most beautiful girl. But, since there is no impartial judge, the most beautiful woman is determined by the number of votes she receives. The winners, then, are those who choose the woman who is chosen by the majority—id est, the winners are the majority. As such, a rational entrant will not pick the woman he thinks is most beautiful, opting instead to pick the woman he thinks everyone else will think is most beautiful. His choice would be based, not on his own tastes, but rather on his perception of the average taste of all the entrants.

This strategy does not end there, however, since the rational entrant will realize that the other entrants will base their choices on the average taste as well, and so he would then base his choice on his perception of the average perception of the average taste. As Keynes explained, "It is not a case of choosing those that, to the best of one's judgment, are really the prettiest, nor even those that average opinion genuinely thinks the prettiest. We have reached the third degree where we devote our intelligences to anticipating what average opinion expects the average opinion to be. And there are some, I believe, who practice the fourth, fifth and higher degrees°."

All I have to do is divine from what I know of you—are you the sort of man who would put the poison into his own goblet or his enemy's? Now, a clever man would put the poison into his own goblet, because he would know that only a great fool would reach for what he was given. I am not a great fool, so I can clearly not choose the wine in front of you. But you must have known I was not a great fool, you would have counted on it, so I can clearly not choose the wine in front of me.

—Vizzini analyzing the test of wits in *The Princess Bride* by William Goldman (1973)

To a large extent, the stock market is no longer focused

on the buying and selling of ownership in companies. Investors have found that there is much more money to be made—and at a much quicker rate— in the buying and selling of the public perception of the companies, just as it is in the beauty contest. It is a sort of bet on the direction in which the public will sway—whence the expanding market of derivatives of securities. An entire sector is dedicated to the purchase and sale of futures contracts, which is a way to invest in the future exchange price of a stock or commodity, something of a bet on a bet. A credit default swap is something of a bet that the bet on someone else's bet will go awry. It would be an instructive exercise to see how many layers of bets the most complex derivative on the market is made of.

The Loss of the Individual

The interdependent climate naturally favors opportunists who can be successful no matter what they do, as well as those who care little about the consequences of their actions. Without care for goods or products that hold the greatest virtue or value on a moral plane, they simply seek out prospects that elicit interest from the largest crowd and produce goods that generate the highest customer traffic. The path is paved for the opportunist in a way that it is not for the considerate. All he has to do is follow the crowd—go to the most esteemed school, take the most highly regarded classes, undertake the most salable extracurricular activities, interview for the big-name corporations, and climb their ladder as everyone would expect. In the end, he makes tons of money doing so.

Opportunists pursue this course whether or not they believe it has any intellectual or moral merit at all. These days, it might be more successful if it is explicitly hostile to the intellect or morality. As it is with the abstraction of wealth, one will be willing to sell his soul to the devil in order to make a big enough salary. In fact, the highly interdependent architecture of the modern economy is the ultimate manifestation of the abstraction of wealth because it eliminates subjective valuation of goods and actions in lieu of an objective, socialized mentality that says 'that which is popular is good'. The inclination is to 'go with the flow' since of course the flow of the masses is the only real engine of success anyway. The individual's mind and will are stowed for the sake of the public's, and, naturally, the individual doesn't even realize this is occurring.

The average citizen, however, conscientious of the moral effect of his actions, will struggle with the lack of economic control. Without the freedom to do what he wants with his own resources, he lacks the freedom to use them toward moral ends. He is, like John Winthrop in sixteenth-century England, faced with a condition where "it is almost impossible for a good and upright man to maintain his charge and live comfortably in any of them". Coupled with the explosion in material wealth, this sense of restriction has put a strain on the average citizen that is easily sensed but hard to define. It is the paradox of progress: The wealthier we become, the more trying the society that surrounds us becomes; the better off we are, the more difficult life is.

A 1999 *New York Times* article illustrates the paradox succinctly. The photo depicts a middle-class family seated in front of a ranch home with two bedrooms, a full kitchen, a carpeted living room, two stately oaks in front, and a swimming pool in back. It is a typical display of American affluence, a middle-class family with nearly all the comforts of life, which, by most accounts, exceeds that of any eighteenth-century king's. They have cozy winters, cool summers, biannual trips to the dentist, and all the luxuries they could possibly want. But despite this abundance of wealth, the family is not happy. As the article's headline declares, this American middle-class family is actually "Just Getting By".

How could this be? How could a family, whose material well-being would have placed them among the richest people in all of ancient or medieval times, be just getting by? The reason is that their wealth, comfortable as it might seem, is not necessarily real. Like most other middle-class American families, their wealth is artificial, created out of thin air and rather dependent on others. As the husband and wife explained, they were struggling to make ends meet with their budget. Thanks to a modest income of around $50,000, they were unable to distance themselves from their mortgage and monthly bills. They had all the comforts they could possibly have dreamed of but lacked the freedom to truly enjoy them.

The more a family has, the more ties and expenses they must incur. A car requires insurance, the house needs furniture and a mortgage, an electric bill, a water bill, et cetera. As a wife in another family was quoted as saying, "I want my house set, so that when I come to it I have it the way I want it. But if we make a wrong move, the pressure we had from the bills will come back, and that is painful°." In other words, the property and goods they have accumulated are not their real concerns—the lack of money is their real concern. These families are barely getting by, not because they are short on wealth, but because they owe that wealth to their creditors, the landlords, and their companies; it is not the level of comfort that puts them on edge, but the fact that they have no real control over their lives.

The helplessness sensed in the article is more than just a matter of a few families not being grateful for what they have. As economist Thomas Sowell puts it, "Even millionaires can have a hard time making ends meet if they try to live like billionaires." It was not as though these families wanted more wealth, just that they longed for control over the wealth they did have. Without it, all the money in the world could do no more to satisfy their needs or provide for their well-being.

It is for this reason that one of the peculiar facts of modern times arises: As we have seen an exponential increase in production and quality of output, we have seen a decline in happiness. While the standard of living has skyrocketed, the quality of life has plummeted. Though all the riches of the world are ours for the taking, we are constantly bombarded from every direction by demands, restrictions, curbs, and ultimatums.

To witness the effects of this paradox, simply regard a civilian in the typical modern city. He lives there, presumably, to have access to a good job, a high standard of living, and cultural institutions, and to be close to a community of friends and family. It doesn't take long for him to realize, however, that in order to obtain this way of living, he must put up with uncomfortable crowds on the subway, tedious lines at the grocery store, hour-long commutes, and other people's trash piled up on the sidewalks. Due to temporal and financial constraints, it is practically unthinkable for him to live in a spacious condo, eat healthily, and foster lasting relationships.

He might escape to suburban communities, where constraints are assumed to be less demanding. But even there, the city life absorbs him. His commute lasts that much longer, and so there is less time to spend with his family, which inevitably dissolves into alienated factions. Each member goes his or her own way in hopes of finding the bond that the other family members should have provided but could not afford. Society's impression on the individual is even more compelling in the suburb because institutions and facilities are distorted to accommodate farther stretches of community. Schools house thousands; churches, tens of thousands; and shopping malls, hundreds of thousands of people. Everything is mass-produced, mass-marketed, uniform, specialized, and sprawling; everything is cold, plastic, synthetic, and contrived. In short, everything is the exact opposite of what he lives there for.

Civilized man refused to adapt himself to his environment. Instead, he adapted his environment to suit him. So he built cities, roads, vehicles, machinery. And he put up power lines to run his labour-saving devices. But somehow he didn't know when to stop. The more he improved his surroundings to make life easier, the more complicated he made it. So now his children are sentenced to ten to fifteen years of school, just to learn how to survive in this complex and hazardous habitat they were born into.

And civilized man, who refused to adapt to his surroundings now finds he has to adapt and re-adapt himself every day and every hour of the day to his self-created environment. For instance, if the day is called Monday and the number 7-3-0 comes up, you have to dis-adapt from your domestic surroundings and re-adapt yourself to an entirely different environment. 8-0-0 means everybody has to look busy. 10-3-0 means you can stop looking busy for 15 minutes. And then, you have to look busy again.

—*THE GODS MUST BE CRAZY* (1980)

Ultimately, the city-dweller faces the great irony that, in attempt to satisfy his innate human desires, he has enrolled in a society that is hostile to his humanity—one that has grown so substantial that the individuals that make it up have grown insignificant—and that in order to live, he must surrender his life to the collective. With any task he assumes or enterprise he endeavors to undertake, he must turn to other people for guidance, assistance, and approval, which come only on their terms, at their convenience. As a minimum, he requires them to do the most basic things in life, such as earning a living, feeding his family, and putting a roof over his head.

> Her green plastic watering can
>
> For her fake Chinese rubber plant
>
> In the fake plastic earth.
>
> That she bought from a rubber man
>
> In a town full of rubber plans
>
> To get rid of itself.
>
> It wears her out, it wears her out
>
> —RADIOHEAD,
> "FAKE PLASTIC TREES" (1995)

The rules that bind at every turn, explicit or implied, and the traps around every corner are all that one can see in the civilization he finds himself in. These traps are the source of Freud's 'discontents', people defined by their rejection of the civilization that they have grown to depend on. It is a self-supporting, self-contradictory situation, its parts as reliant on the whole as much as they are repellent from it.

The word that best describes the modern state can be found as the title to Book IV of Dostoevsky's *The Brothers Karamazov*—'Nadryvy'. The literal translation is 'Ruptures', though the motif in the book is a much richer concept of 'strained conditions about to break'. The novel's innocent protagonist Alyosha leaves the monastery and embarks on a trek to endure the challenges of modern society. It is only there that he can truly test the teachings of his mentor, Father Zossima. Alyosha suffers an encounter with his father in which he listens to a slew of vulgar stories, he is introduced to a number of intrigues that include sour marriages and infidelity, and he is attacked by a schoolboy, who lays upon Alyosha his own grief. On the whole, it is a portrait of the modern world as the typical bystander witnesses it.

Father Zossima's charge for the young Alyosha summarizes the interdependent condition, explaining that each man is responsible for every other man, and, what's more, that "He is responsible to all men for all and everything, for all human sins, national and individual°." The English variations of the book's title offer a glimpse of the kind of stress that this interdependency produces, growing prominent in Dostoevsky's time and finally consuming mankind in our own: 'Strains', 'Torment', 'Crises', 'Crack-Ups', 'Lacerations'.

The Logic of Competition

Granted interdependency creates strains on a given social body, the optimist will argue that there are positives involved in the condition as well. The mere fact that two or more people depend upon each other for necessities can and reasonably does bring about a kind of harmony between people with otherwise conflicting interests. Austrian economist and champion of the free market Ludwig von Mises underscored this very notion in his work titled *Liberalism*. When one is dependent upon others for food, shelter, and clothing, for example, he is more inclined to treat them with respect and help to ensure their well-being, since doing so will help him secure his own well-being. Countries that trade with each other will be less inclined to go to war because doing so will eliminate the benefits of specialism and thus harm their overall well-being. On the contrary, they will foster solid relations and encourage greater interaction. In short, interdependency leads to cooperation, peace, and harmony.

In his popular survey of human history, *Nonzero*, Robert Wright reiterates this thesis. Using contemporary examples, Wright shows how the interests of interdependent individuals or groups become correlated such that benefit to one means benefit to all. An economic boom in Japan, for instance, means that Japanese products can be bought at lower costs, the country's stocks go up, and Americans invested in the country's industry generally enjoy a higher standard of living as well. As Wright puts it, "increasingly, good foreign news is good domestic news". Similarly, parties in an interdependent system will all be worse off if any one of them does poorly. The spread of AIDS in Africa puts greater strain on industries there, prices go up, and so Americans are thus burdened in turn—"bad foreign news is bad domestic news". In both cases, since the parties are all dependent upon each other one way or another, each has incentive to improve the lot of others and cooperate with them so as to better facilitate their relationships.

This theory has its basis in Adam Smith and the fundamentals of modern economics. Through a more effective method of exchange, individual and aggregate productivity can increase, thereby offering everyone involved greater material well-being. Wealth as a whole increases so that everyone can benefit.

But, as Wright points out, interdependency does not always lead to cooperation. Parties involved in potential exchanges may well have other motives and might find it in their interest to take from others what they need rather than offering something in exchange. As such, the fact that the parties are dependent upon one another does not necessarily mean that they will seek cooperation, but that they might also resort to exploitation as an alternative. To be sure, interdependency does not guarantee any particular action at all, whether it is cooperative or non-cooperative. It does, however, guarantee certain limitations. Since the parties involved have needs and can only satisfy those needs through the other parties, they must in one way or another engage in some action with those other parties. The action they choose is not predetermined, but it is certainly limited, this being the premise behind interdependency.

In fact, one can only imagine two possible outcomes in an interdependent system—trade or theft, cooperation or exploitation. In the first outcome, the two parties may have realized that it is better to engage in a civil exchange and stay on good terms with one another; in the second, one of the two parties may have come to the conclusion that it is better to simply take the goods at the expense of the other, thinking for whatever reason that the other would not or could not defend himself from the raid, or that the costs of such a struggle would be less than those of an attempted trade. The first is a cooperative equation and the second is a non-cooperative or exploitative equation; both are possible given an interdependent system.

Mises and others have concluded that the only long-lasting, reasonable course of action in an interdependent system is for the parties involved to trade and continue on good terms with one another. That is, it behooves them to find cooperative solutions to their economic problems. But this is not always as straightforward a conclusion as it seems. Take, for example, the case in which one of the two parties is for some reason unable to fulfill his end of the bargain because he can only do so at the expense of his own well-being. Such a condition would leave those involved in a tricky position, in which trade is not necessarily more economically sound or otherwise beneficial at all, and competition for resources is the only reasonable recourse.

One will find that the key to cooperative situations is self-sufficiency. When an individual or a people as a whole are able to take care of themselves, their decisions are of their own volition and thus can be made intentionally and willfully. The benefits of specialism and labor division make cooperation the likely and almost inevitable path. If, on the other hand, an individual or a people are not able to take care of themselves, their decisions are not made of their own volition and are rather forced. Without active consciences, competition is likely and, as we will see, almost inevitable.

Through the development of modern economics, this latter condition is the one that we find ourselves increasingly faced with, and, contrary to the logical approach of cooperation, the standard in modern times has become one of intensifying competition, where all those involved will seek to benefit themselves at the expense of others. No matter how reasonable cooperation seems on the surface, the pressures of modern times have meant that competition is the rule of the day.

3. THE TRANSFORMATION OF WEALTH

OF THE MANY DIRECT CONSEQUENCES of interdependency, one stands out as the most significant in terms of economic impact: the transformation of wealth from real goods and services into money. On a previous page, we found that money's abstract nature makes it valuable in itself and so encourages people to seek it out and to accumulate it. Simply, money can do things that real wealth, such as food, furniture, and automobiles, can never do, and so it offers its owners something that cannot be gained by real wealth. In the end, money has always been just a means to those goods. The goal was always to attain the food, furniture, and automobiles, and money was just the most expedient way of doing so.

In an interdependent society, however, the urgency of money changes. No longer can one make a life on his own; in order to get what he needs and wants, he now has to participate in the system. This is so whether he sees the system fit or not.

As a result, he must adhere to the standards of that system, especially with regard to the system's standard means of exchange. Since an individual's well-being is dependent upon the vast, interconnected system that is the modern economy, it is thus dependent upon the lifeblood of that system, and that lifeblood is money.

As Friedrich A. Hayek put it in *The Road to Serfdom*, "The more complicated the whole, the more dependent we become on that division of knowledge between individuals whose separate efforts are co-ordinated by the impersonal mechanism for transmitting the relevant information known by us as the price system." To get anything these days, whether it is a house or a Blu-ray copy of *The Incredibles*, one must first obtain money. Likewise, if one wants to get something in return for his labor or production, he is limited in practically all instances to getting money as payment. It is for this reason that money has more or less become the focus of all economic endeavors; it has become, as Marx would have it, both the cause and end of all exchanges.

As a thought experiment, consider all the things that a modern man might want in life—three square meals a day, a crafty wind chime from the fair, a nice walk in the park, whatever it is that he might desire—and imagine possibly attaining it without money. For most things, it is obvious that one needs money to obtain them, the square meals and wind chime being typical examples. Others aren't so straightforward. It may seem as though it requires no money, for example, to take a walk in the park. After all, there is no money being exchanged at the entrance. But, if it is a typical park, it could only have been built by some elaborate construction company, hired by the municipal government or a private firm which required money to facilitate, and it could only be maintained by a crew of landscapers who all require money as payment.

Even as the imagination is let loose, one will still find it difficult to identify a single desirable thing in society these days that one can do without money. Love is perhaps the greatest of all human experiences, and, while it is true that a penniless and homeless couple can manage to fall in love and share their affection over an extended period, no one can doubt that the ability to buy a bouquet of flowers or a box of chocolate candy will add to the man's chances of wooing his mate.

While it is true that the ends sought have always been the satisfaction of human needs, and those human needs can only be satisfied by the use of real goods and services, in an interdependent world, the only way one can obtain those goods and services is through the acquisition and application of money. Goods and services are useful, of course, but money is the only way to access those goods and services. And so it is not unreasonable for an individual to simplify the equation and strive directly for money, not goods and services, as the central goal of his economic endeavors.

On the surface, this is a subtle shift. Money, for all intents and purposes, seems to be the mere representation of real goods and services and not wealth in itself, just as it has always been. The thought is that we only use it during the meantime in our pursuit of the things we really want—BBQ pulled pork sandwiches, a new Wii game, a 70-foot yacht. But, since all of those real goods and services are only available by first obtaining and making use of money, they are all seen in light of possessing and spending money; they are, as it might be said, functions of money. Ultimately, this fact creates a shift in the perception of wealth in general. Since money is seen as necessary for all goods and services, and those goods and services are all seen as functions of money, money and wealth become synonymous. The process consists in a sort of transformation of wealth, from real goods and services to plain old money.

This transformation is monumental because of the differences between real wealth and money. As was explored on an earlier page, money abstracts the notion of wealth and does with it that which is absolutely impossible with real goods and services. The ability to accumulate and store money alone makes it vastly different from real wealth in very pertinent ways. The most important facet of money is that it takes what was a rather open system in the pursuit of wealth and confines it to specific boundaries. As we observed in the previous part, these abstracting qualities of money make it considerably useful in the pursuit of wealth; but, at the same time, its economic usefulness makes money a desired end for everyone—it is an objective and social goal rather than one that is subjective and personal.

Altogether, as we will see, the more necessary money becomes in the pursuit of wealth, the more that pursuit of wealth becomes a closed endeavor with a single aim. When this occurs, something very strange and powerful happens to that pursuit. When everyone is striving for the same thing, whether it's money or the Coke bottle in *The Gods Must Be Crazy*, the situation becomes confined and one can only gain at the expense of another.

* * *

Now, to say that the concept of wealth has transferred from real goods to money is to make a tremendous claim. The bizarre conclusion met with upon reflection is that all goods and services have completely lost value, and that only money is of any use to its participants. This is of course an exaggeration and cannot possibly be the case. The shift toward a closed system, where money is the only goal, has been a gradual process marked by degrees, and one might reasonably argue that real goods like iPads, electric MINI Cooper convertibles, and ShamWows will always maintain some value as long as we have physiological and psychological needs.

The dramatic rise of consumerism over the last century alone shows that there is at least some increasing value in goods and services in the modern economy—why else would we constantly want to buy so many things?

By taking a step back, however, one can see just how far the gradual process has taken us in the hundred years since the close, and just how meaningless goods and services have actually become. The *New York Times* article mentioned above illustrates how the middle-class family residing in a ranch home with all the amenities of modern life is, as the headline suggests, just getting by. In other words, the property and goods that they have accumulated are not their real concern; the lack of money is their real concern. They have real wealth in goods and services, but that does not matter. What matters is their cash flow—or lack of it.

It cannot be denied that the modern society is made of a consumerist economy, that people of all socioeconomic statuses are largely driven by the consumer goods they buy, and that the buying of consumer goods at the retail and wholesale levels are a dominant aspect of the total economy. And yet, at the same time, the objective observer will note that this undeniable feature of the economy is largely disdained and even despised. Everyone participates in the weekly trip to the shopping mall, the online spree, and of course the melee during the holidays, but hardly anyone can admit feeling totally justified in doing so. It is like it is just another duty that one must add to the list.

In principle, the notion is that the consumer and the sales clerk will both say 'Thank you' upon the completion of an exchange. These days, a courteous nod is perhaps all that is offered. Most likely, the exchange elicits frustration and even contempt from the buyer, who is seemingly involved in the shopping against his will, and the clerk who couldn't care less what the customer wants and needs.

When money becomes the only real form of wealth that people care about, then even voluntary exchanges, in which money is traded for a good or service, become rather one-sided. On the surface, the exchange seems fair: One person trades \$3 in bills for \$3 worth of milk. The \$3 worth of milk is certainly valuable to the customer, and so the exchange seems fair in that both parties get what they want. Yet the consumer good is only valuable to the consumer because it allows him to eat cereal and thus survive in order to work and make more money. In other words, it is only valuable because of its ability to generate more money. The immediate exchange is seen as a loss for the consumer because, at least in the interim, it is thought that he is giving up wealth while the grocery store is gaining it.

Normal is getting dressed in clothes that you buy for work and driving through traffic in a car that you are still paying for, in order to get to the job you need to pay for the clothes and the car, and the house you leave vacant all day so you can afford to live in it.

—ADVICE COLUMN CURRENT°
(CIRCA 2000)

In this case and in others, the store owner is seen as the winner since he is the party in the transaction that gains money. All stores, corporations, banks, and so on, are the only ones seen as gaining in the modern system, despite the fact that consumers always get something in return for their money. Even though they get real goods and services—food, iPads, automobiles, cell phone coverage, and so on—these are seen as obligatory and even insignificant gains, and so it seems like a loss. This weird state of affairs is doubtless the source of the almost mechanical antipathy felt toward every big business in the world today. Though the large majority of Americans buy their goods from large corporations, getting their necessities and vast supplies of luxuries directly from Walmart, Starbucks, Ikea, and the like, all while paying bargain basement prices for them, they cannot help but to despise the sprawling companies that get so much of their money. The consumers will enjoy their cheap clothing, delicious lattes, stylish furniture, and video chatting with family on the other side of the continent, but then turn around to criticize the financial behemoths for accumulating such great masses of what they really want—money.

Use-and-Throw-Away Society

The perspective is held on a macroeconomic as well as a microeconomic level. Consider, for example, trends that have arisen in the last several decades in parallel to mass consumerism, most notably a greater propensity to waste and the introduction of disposable goods. Everywhere one looks, people are casually tossing aside soft drink bottles, fast food containers, gum wrappers, and other disposable goods. And this goes for the actual products themselves, not just for their containers. Never do I go out to a restaurant with others and witness everyone either cleaning his plate or taking home all the leftover food. Far from it, the norm is to buy as much food as looks appetizing and only eat some fraction of the portion. The scraps are naturally discarded, and no one ever questions the waste. It occurs to the mindful conservationist that no one mentions the 'starving kids in China' anymore, as my grandfather was known to do. The thought that throwing away the scraps is wasteful hardly comes to mind in a vibrant social setting.

Even when goods are kept for the long term, they are treated poorly, as if they hold no value in themselves whatsoever. One will note the destructive behavior of the younger generations, who are among the greatest consumers in all of history and yet constantly warrant scolding from their parents on how they neglect their clothes, electronic goods, and even automobiles and homes.

In *The Harried Leisure Class*, Staffan B. Linder explains that the rise of this 'use-and-throw-away' system is the inevitable consequence of the modern economy. When there is a proliferation of inexpensive goods and a rise in salaries, it actually pays to throw away perfectly functional items when they have accumulated a little wear. When one's time can be used in the pursuit of more money, it costs to package the leftovers, wash the plates, and store unused goods. Today, it's just cheaper—more economic—to simply dispose of everything and buy a replacement when hungry. Linder argues that we have come to a point in our modern culture where it is economically sound "to reduce the maintenance per product and instead devote a corresponding amount of time to highly productive work that will offer income to replace the goods that needed service°." Given high enough incomes, for instance, it is profitable to save the time it would take to clean and reuse a plate and silverware after dinner and just buy a new dining set. The move to disposable baby diapers is another example—why spend time and resources washing and pinning when Huggies are available?

Those familiar with life on college campuses will recognize the phenomenon clearly. There, almost nothing is kept for the long term. Food and containers are all highly disposable; so are books, clothes, furniture, and living space in general. On the time-starved campuses, even goods that are kept for the long term are hardly kept in shape. As a result, deft marketers have been quick to satisfy the careless students' needs with replacement goods and services of all kinds, from promotional T-shirts to disposable books and journals. Soon enough, one might speculate, diapers for college students might be seen as an economically sound product.

Time is the essential matter here, it must be stressed. But this is not to suggest that money is unimportant in the equation. Indeed, according to Linder, the reason why time is so valuable is because of one's opportunity costs—the amount of money one could make by doing something else in that time. If one could be making $30 an hour by working, it pays to simply throw away a book or container or scarf that would cost $12 to replace. As scientific management pioneer Frederick Winslow Taylor aptly put it, time is money, and so saving time is equivalent in the modern society to saving money.

Services too take time to consume, whether it is a one-hour massage or a smog check. The pleasure or utility gained from the given service might well be worth the dollar amount at which it is priced, and so it seems like a fair deal, as in the case of an exchange for goods. With regard to opportunity costs, however, the service becomes increasingly less profitable the higher one's income. For a Westerner earning $50 or $60 an hour, for example, every moment must be used in the pursuit of money, even if one is also obliged to use the time allotted for the pursuit of pleasure as well. This is doubtless why one will see salesmen, contractors, and executives on the phone conducting business while on vacation at some tropical destination. The notion that one cannot escape work in a modern economy is a fact that has left most 'on call' at all hours of the day.

One finds workers constantly mixing business with pleasure to optimize time spent, and, when necessary, it is not uncommon to mix one pleasure with another or more pleasures in order to maximize the yield. Multitasking has become a skill of incomparable value as the need for combining several activities into one dictates daily schedules. One will chat while studying, watch TV while eating and playing a game, and various other combinations. It has come to the point where some might venture to eat breakfast while shaving, brushing teeth, and talking on their cell phone during the morning commute.

The effect, as one could expect, is a lowered capacity to enjoy each activity. One cannot enjoy a concert fully while constantly sending and receiving text messages; one cannot wholly take pleasure in the warm sands of Tahiti while e-mailing frantic clients. It occurs to the typical multitasker that the value in each service has fallen such that the act of receiving it is not what matters anymore—all that matters is the fact of having received it, the satisfaction of being able to tell other people of the event or trip or entertainment. The quality and substance of the service is of no importance because one has no occasion to fully enjoy it anyway. As Linder poses, only partly in jest, "Who has time these days for intimate lunches in conversation with an attractive woman?", as if such a rendezvous could not possibly be worth the time spent.

Consider the ubiquity of music as a sign of the phenomenon. Music is played everywhere one goes, no doubt as a way to maximize the yield one receives during each unit of time. To make reading more enjoyable, for instance, one turns on some Mozart; to make a dinner party more enjoyable, one flips on some Miles Davis; to make lovemaking more enjoyable, one turns on some Mott the Hoople.

It has come to the point where new music is designed with this kind of preoccupied usage entirely in mind, such that it intentionally lacks musical consequence and only gratifies the listener by enhancing the activity that it is presumed to accompany. Rhythm and bass are emphasized and sensational effects are strewn throughout, while the lyrics and themes are more or less abandoned.

Despite the popularity of music, one cannot help but question whether music as an art form is being appreciated nearly as much as it could be. In *The Decline of Pleasure*, American critic Walter Kerr describes the condition well: "We have had Music to Read By, Music to Make Love By, Music to Sleep By, and, as one humorist has had it, Music to Listen to Music By. What is interesting about these titles is that they so candidly describe the position of the popular arts in our time. They admit at the outset that no one is expected to sit down, for heaven's sake, and attend to the music. It is understood that, while the music is playing, everyone within earshot is going to be busy doing something else°.'"

The Decline of Service

The diminution in the value of goods and services can best be seen in the service industries through the kind of effort and dedication demonstrated by those professionals providing the services themselves. When wealth is regarded as money only, the actual service that is provided for that money is no longer viewed as worth the time and effort, and that goes for those producing the service as much as anyone else. Just as the consumer has not the time to enjoy high quality services, the provider has not the time to produce them.

Observe the workers at an average restaurant or retail store. More and more these days, one will find the attendants involved in providing these services more and more ambivalent of the tasks set before them. Even though it is their job to serve, they could not care less whether the customer would like a glass of water or extra tartar sauce. It is not uncommon for a paying customer at a restaurant to feel as if he is rather burdening the waiter by asking for what might have been considered essentials in previous ages—things like silverware and ketchup. When ordering, the customer feels obliged to make it easy on the server so as to not put him out, and, ultimately, upon the close of the burlesque, the perfunctory 18% tip is paid to no great appreciation—it is assumed, just like the $1.50 refills.

Or consider the modern office scenario. Gossiping, games, and outright goofing off are often more common than actual work, no matter to what industry the services are dedicated. Internet-savvy readers will note the prevalence of workplace Facebook usage. There are those who spend nearly half their time at work simply browsing social networking websites, filling out quizzes, and making their mark on message boards. The popularity of comedies such as *Office Space* and *The Office* prove how easily relatable the absurdity of modern office life really is. Practically no one in these situations cares about or even knows very much about what their work tasks are; they simply trudge along doing what they need to do for their paycheck without a modicum of pride in their work.

Indeed, with a decline in the quality of service and goods, craftsmanship has become a lost art. It is nearly impossible to find a restaurant, retail store, or other service provider that will consistently come through with the level of service it promises to provide. Of course, haggling over the bill is unthinkable these days since it simply takes too much time and does not even guarantee a monetary reward. Going above and beyond, as some providers would tout in the past, is practically unheard of in the modern service industry. These days, it is just easier—and more cost-effective—to do the least work necessary to get the money and get on with things.

This is the predictable and inevitable outcome of a situation in which jobs are only valued as a means of getting money to survive and not for the actual work the job entails; it is the necessary result of the pursuit of effective demand and full employment. Everywhere one looks, one will see waiters neglecting their duties, attendants turning away customers that they could be helping, and customer representatives bouncing the customer to the next representative instead of solving the problem himself. To help the customer would create new work, which is regrettable to anyone these days. Meanwhile, the money will come in no matter what. The customer still needs to pay for the goods and will do so whether the service is shoddy or not.

Not coincidentally, the diminishing value of services has occurred at the same time as our economy has grown more and more dependent on those services. It is with this fact in mind that Linder and others have spoken of the 'decline of service in a service economy'. With reference to the propensity for higher salaries to issue a more ambivalent view of services, Linder concludes that "Economic development involves both an increase in the quantity of service and a decline in the quality[°]." The upshot is that the modern economy is more and more service-oriented and yet less and less capable of sufficiently providing those services.

It is easy to speak of the rise of the service industries as proof of an improvement therein—more waiters on staff means that the restaurant is better equipped to serve its customers, more nurses equal better health care, and so on. But when those waiters are rude or incompetent and those nurses are careless or unknowledgeable—situations that one faces with increasing frequency these days—the result must be a decline in the overall product. There can be no doubt that the modern economy has rendered a condition of elevated output and consumption of real goods and services. A look at annual national output statistics will convince the average observer that our system is heavily based in goods and services. But as those goods and services become more and more plentiful and inexpensive, the money used to buy them becomes more and more valuable, until the goods and services themselves become mere ways to obtain more money.

And so we arrive at the point where the evolution of Marx's Money Nexus is completed such that only money serves as the primary purpose for trading and obtaining commodities and not the other way around. Though the middle-class family featured in the *New York Times* article is surrounded by real wealth—the house, the car, the swimming pool—they lack the one asset that signifies wealth these days—money—and so are on the brink of poverty.

The Ascent of Money

Parallel to the depreciation of goods and services, and in contrast to it, the significance of money has appreciated throughout the twentieth century to an equal and opposite degree. Just as the value of goods and services has fallen to the tune of extreme waste and slapdash service, so too has the value of money skyrocketed such that cash is the only thing one thinks of when wealth is mentioned.

The transformation of wealth into money is seen most clearly on the local, microeconomic plane in the materialism of the age and the seemingly limitless greed displayed by individuals in all spheres of society. The greed is limitless because, unlike goods and services, there is no ceiling to money's usefulness. As was touched on earlier, the more money one has, the more power it provides. And so the quest for money is a nonstop, relentless effort that consumes as it grows.

Greed is nothing new, of course, but it is a sign of unprecedented audacity that the concept has been promoted in the twentieth century and even vindicated as a virtue. Whereas the millionaires of the 1870s and '80s were conscientiously discreet with their wealth, all subscribing to the Victorian pressures of 'inconspicuous consumption', the millionaires of today flaunt their wealth. Far from the stuffiness of the nineteenth century, the rich of the modern age have been as indiscreet as they dare—the more showy, the more respect they seem to garner. Everyone knows it is gaudy and uncouth, yet at the same time it is also very rewarding. At one point in the 1980s, the mantra of American finance echoed the sentiments of the fictitious broker Gordon Gekko from the film *Wall Street*: 'Greed is good.'

Of course, whether the Gordon Gekkos of the world have convinced the rest of us that greed is actually a virtue, their underlying point is legitimate: Everyone can agree that the aim of greed—money—makes, as it were, the world go around, and the active pursuit of it energizes industry and serves as the sole driving force behind a rising standard of living. It is hard to deny that the eager chase has marked, as Gekko famously noted, the upward surge of mankind. Ultimately, money's dominance cannot be denied, and everyone must contend with it one way or another.

Consider the rise of macroeconomics as a sign of the import of money. As a field of study, macroeconomics has become the central focus of the modern political sphere and heavily dictates the course of public policy in every Western government. But as any freshman Econ student will tell you, macro is aimed at the tracking and reporting of general trends in wealth and socioeconomic movements in general and, as such, relies heavily on statistics of sales and income—statistics which are only possible with the widespread use of money. The exchange of goods, rent, labor, and so on, are only able to be handled and understood on a large scale if they are abstracted into some objective, calculable means. That means that to a large degree the way we track well-being and guide public policy is through statistics of the circulation of money.

This is to say that macroeconomics is impossible without the pervasive use of money. Unless the great majority of economic transactions are made through the exchange of currency, it is impossible to track the ups and downs of a large-scale economy such as a county, state, or nation. As such, it can be said that the shift toward a macro view of the economy reflects the shift from a goods-based system to a money-based system.

Regard the pervasive use of the Gross Domestic Product, or GDP, as a fundamental guide of a country's well-being and power. It is not a stretch to suggest that whenever the condition of the economy is mentioned, the speaker will reference in some capacity the figures that this measure represents. News reports are quick to incorporate data received and translate it into salable headlines: 'U.S. Recovery Continues at its Slow Pace, GDP and Other Data Show', 'Stock Futures Up on GDP Report', 'Consumers Bounce Back, but GDP Still Weak', and so on. From these and other reports such as the Gross National Product (GNP), Consumer Price Index (CPI), and Producer Price Index (PPI), consumers and policy experts make their decisions and choose whether to buy or save accordingly.

All of public policy and, increasingly, personal financial planning is guided by these statistics in one way or another, which means that all of public policy and a good deal of personal financial planning is based solely on the ebbs and flows of monetary exchange. As the GDP is only capable of relaying information on goods and services that are produced and sold with money, all the production that does not use money goes neglected. Work done around the house, home gardening, trades between neighbors, exercise, cooking, and cleaning are all accomplished without exchange of money and are thus nonexistent in the view of the GDP. This is to overlook what might be the most important of productive activities—amateur composition of music, poetry, scholarship, philosophy, or religion, none of which are truly measured unless they are sold in a major market.

The difficulty in tracking non-monetary production is best seen in the kinds of jerry-rigging done around tax time to make sure one's efforts are counted. The tax system, like all good government programs, relies on statistics and thus on the use of money to work successfully. As such, the state's encouragement of particular activities through the tax code, especially tax breaks, is skewed heavily in the direction of activities that involve monetary transactions. Of course, not all worthy activities include such transactions, and so it is incumbent upon taxpayers to finagle a way to put a monetary value on their activities. Time spent volunteering at the local homeless shelter, for instance, is not tax-deductible since it naturally does not include the transfer of money.

To be able to write something off, one needs a tangible expense, which volunteering does not provide. One must hire a babysitter during volunteer work or actually donate money to the shelter in order to register the charitable contribution for tax purposes.

The fact that tangible, monetary exchanges are the only elements that can be counted toward GDP in itself presents a contradiction. The purpose of GDP statistics and other such measures is to calculate the wealth of a nation and thus the well-being of its people. But these figures necessarily omit elements of life that can bring the greatest sense of pleasure and well-being—the thrill of a well-composed sunset, the security of a warm Floridian night, the bliss of figuring out a problem. None of these can be tracked and reported in any reliable way. While all of these intangible things can be inferred by tangible monetary exchanges, there will always be a disconnect between the two. Tourism revenue in South Florida might well increase in a given year, but we cannot be certain that happiness and contentment have gone up with it. Money spent could actually be in response to a rainy season, which may have caused vacationers to spend more time indoors and thus harmed happiness and contentment—a rise in GDP would be a reduction in well-being.

Emphasis placed on the GDP, CPI, PPI, and other measures is indicative of the stress we place on monetary well-being in general. It is rather assumed that a positive change in annual GDP from one year to the next, which is simply a positive change in the velocity of money, means prosperity, an increase in the standard of living and well-being altogether—whence politicians' nearly involuntary promotion of economic growth and spending as a way to increase

> What governs the world is neither a dogma, nor a faith, nor a tradition. It is not the Gospel, nor the Koran, nor Aristotle, nor Voltaire; no more is it the Constitution of 1852 or that of 1793. It is the Great Ledger whose pages carry only two words in large letters: on one side Debit, on the other, Credit.
>
> —PIERRE-JOSEPH PROUDHON,
> *GUERRE ET PAIX* (1864)

well-being. It is reasoned that policies which increase growth are necessarily good and policies which slow the rate of growth are necessarily bad, quite as if there is no limit to the utility of the increased production measured by the stats and no unintended consequences whatever.

When the exchange of money is the central gauge for well-being, a new perspective is adopted by individuals and policymakers alike. Simply, all activities that require money are assumed to be not only valid enterprises, but also beneficial to the economy as a whole. The aim is to generate fiscal traffic no matter what non-monetary costs are incurred, the result of which is a rise in GDP and, presumably, a rise in well-being.

This is a core principle of Keynesian economic policy: to use government spending and saving to counter the fluctuations of the Trade Cycle. Keynes and his 'ism' will be addressed on a later page; here it is enough to point out how much the method relies on abstract measures such as the GDP. In order to make the right tweaks to the money supply and banking, whether through spending or regulations, Keynes thought it was necessary to keep on hand all the latest macroeconomic data—total output, price levels, unemployment, and so on. As a matter of fact, it was not until the 1930s, when Keynesianism was taking hold of the Western political mind, that the GDP and similar tracking mechanisms were developed. As it turns out, the dominant approach to economic policy in the twentieth century was heavily reliant on the abstraction of wealth.

In one sense, this rationale cannot be doubted. The purchase of goods and services is the way most people satisfy their wants and needs, so a greater volume in sales would imply a greater satisfaction of those needs and wants. More automobile sales means there's a good chance that more people are satisfying their desires to drive around in automobiles. At the same time, however, increased production means more energy is being used, more pollution will be produced, and the natural environment will be harmed to a greater degree. Far from satisfying needs, this unanticipated byproduct might even create new needs in that the pollution will have to be cleaned up. Until it is, it will likely diminish the quality of life around the factory. When seen through the abstraction of statistics, increased production is only good. Indeed, the pollution itself is even beneficial because it takes monetary transactions to clean up, and so it too increases GDP.

The Broken Window

On these grounds, nearly all activities can be seen as productive and thus instrumental to improving the standard of living as long as they come with some form of monetary exchange. Not only the production of automobiles, trains, airplanes, and so on, but also their byproducts—pollution, draining of natural resources, et cetera. In promoting trade for the sake of monetary exchanges, one must promote the unintentional drawbacks as well as the intended benefits. Ironically, even destruction and war can be seen as productive since of course these ventures require the expense of money just as creation and industry do. This was the frame of mind with which many economists of the 1940s and beyond welcomed World War II as an economic panacea that brought an end to the Great Depression. The statistics were clear: unemployment was zero, GDP had skyrocketed, and production ran at peak levels. Forget the fact that most of the civilization's resources were squandered on the battlefield and upwards of 50 to 70 million lives were lost in the conflict worldwide.

Reliance on monetary statistics to convey well-being renders one liable to accept and even encourage destruction in order to increase production. The paradox was pointed out by nineteenth-century French economist Frédéric Bastiat in his parable of the broken window. In the parable, Bastiat describes a scene in which a boy breaks the window of a town shop. The crowd that gathers naturally pities the shopkeeper and admonishes the vandal. But almost instantly the crowd has a change of heart. They realize that the broken glass means the shopkeeper must spend some six francs to have the window replaced. Six francs to the glazier means that business has been conducted where it would not have been otherwise. In short, the vandal, crude and thoughtless as he seems, has actually helped to generate trade and stimulate the economy.

Bastiat argues that this line of reasoning is acceptable to those who regard only that which is seen—the broken window, the fact that the shopkeeper must now pay the glazier six francs, newly circulating money, et cetera, all visible consequences of the vandalism. What is not seen is the fact that the shopkeeper cannot now spend six francs on something he would have preferred to spend it on—a pair of shoes from the cobbler, a new book for his library, or something else. Those who promote the broken window as the source of economic stimulus neglect the fact that the shopkeeper would likely have made use of the money in some capacity, and that the six francs to the glazier means six less francs to the cobbler or book publisher.

The broken window fallacy overlooks yet one more important point: Destruction is always unproductive because it removes a good that had at least some value. Breaking the window may stimulate the glazier's business, which is great for him, but the overall economy suffers from the destruction. Whereas the shopkeeper could have spent his money on shoes and thus been in possession of shoes and a window, now he must spend his money on the replacement of a window and thus is only in possession of a window. All such vandalism must be regarded as a net loss since the production that comes out of it is merely redundant and thus retrogressive.

Though the economy gains no real wealth, it appears to hold a great deal of wealth when viewing just monetary transactions. Herein lies the fallacy of the broken window as well as the fallacy of economic policy altogether: When attempting to bolster the economy by increasing monetary exchange, it is possible and rather probable to end up harming the economy and a people's well-being as a whole.

In Bastiat's day, a humorless case was made for the burning of Paris, which, it was assumed, would call for unprecedented cleaning and construction and so allow for unprecedented growth in the economy. The reasoning allowed World War II to be viewed in a positive light and has continued to resonate throughout economic thought for the last 150 years: Destruction leads to reconstruction, which grows the economy, so let us engage in destruction.

Western nations saw Keynesianism played out to its fullest in the 1950s and '60s, when high taxation, high government spending, high employment, and high sustained industrial growth were the ideal to be attained no matter what the costs. Only within the last few decades have we begun to recognize the fact that economic growth, measured by an increase in GDP, is not necessarily a good thing and can come with a slew of unintended consequences. Of course, the revelation did not come until well after the Keynesian spend-and-growth policy had become gospel in the governments of the West and made a reversal practically impossible.

The Pursuit of Wealth as a Zero-Sum Game

One last piece of evidence can be offered to show how complete the transformation of wealth has been. It rests in the fact that value has become objective, and in the competitive condition that arises when a single thing serves as a shared goal for an entire people. As an economy grows more and more interdependent, the medium of exchange used therein grows more and more important.

When the economy is closed, the medium of exchange eclipses all other forms of wealth and becomes the sole form, which everyone seeks for their own well-being. At this point, everyone is striving for the same thing, and the pursuit of wealth thus becomes a competition between all active players.

That ours has become a competitive system is hardly questionable. It is taken for granted these days that Western Capitalism is a 'dog-eat-dog world' of 'cut-throat competition' where 'only the strong survive'. The fact that these sentiments have become tired clichés alone proves their widespread sanction. A few points will suffice to illustrate.

On the workaday plane, one will notice the customary odium of the very rich in America. Over the course of the twentieth century, a great antipathy has built up against anyone who makes a lot of money or who at one point made a lot of money, to the extent that the mention of Sam Walton or Bill Gates causes involuntary convulsions. The thought is that, since there are very rich people in the world, everyone else must be that much poorer; the more money the retail and software tycoons control, the less there is for everyone else. The wealth of the world is seen as a pie from which everyone takes a slice, and, since Sam Walton's and Bill Gates' slices are larger, everyone else's slice must be that much smaller.

This gut reaction to the very rich has not always been so automatic. In the late nineteenth and early twentieth centuries, when the concept of a billionaire was first established, the common view of the rich was one of esteem and respect. Financial masters like John D. Rockefeller and Andrew Carnegie were seen as honorable men who had gotten rich by providing the country with what it wanted. It was almost as if the general public benefited from the tycoons' wealth as much as they did.

Not long into the twentieth century, that glossy view began to change. So called 'muckrakers' like Ida M. Tarbell and Upton Sinclair revealed the dark side of American industry and initiated a successful campaign to prove that the great nineteenth-century industrialists had exploited the working classes and made their fortunes at the expense of others. From that time on, wealth was considered a strictly competitive game that had losers as well as the obvious winners.

The transformation of wealth from real goods and services to money makes this competition the inevitable state. In our time, it is almost taken for granted that money is the only wealth worth mentioning, and that gain by one necessarily means loss for another. It is a 'zero-sum game', or so it has been called.

As noted American economist Paul Krugman has argued, the zero-sum condition of the American economy is but a "matter of arithmetic°". The math works as follows: If Bill Gates acquires $40 billion, that means the rest of us have in one form or another given him that $40 billion; thus we have $40 billion less. When money is the only thing people care about, this equation is clearly zero-sum, and we have necessarily lost what Bill Gates has won. The fact that we have gotten $40 billion worth of goods and services in return is not considered. All that is taken into account is the fact that Bill Gates has so much money and we do not.

Krugman's authority on this matter is backed by his status as a Nobel Prize winner, which only goes to show how dominant this viewpoint is in modern thought. It is to vindicate thinkers as early as Rousseau and Proudhon, who suggested that one man's ownership of property was necessarily the denial of property for others—that "Property is theft!", as Proudhon famously asserted. Given this money-driven economy, where goods are disposable and service is superfluous, where monetary transactions are the only kind of output that counts, and a person's worth is measured by a dollar amount, it is a viewpoint that is nearly impossible to avoid.

4. THE ZERO-SUM PROBLEM

ONE MIGHT SAY THAT the usefulness of money is the source of its disadvantages. The fact that money is so highly functional means that everyone wants it; but the fact that everyone wants it means that their pursuit of it becomes a highly competitive situation in which one party can only gain at the expense of others. As the close of the economic system made everyone dependent on money, the currency assumed the role of a singular shared aim, and the economy converted into a strictly competitive situation, what might be called a 'zero-sum game'.

Such is the inevitable condition when any single entity serves as the ultimate goal for a given number of parties. Just as in chess or tennis, for example, a single objective serves as the ultimate goal for both players involved. In the case of these games and nearly all others, the result sought is victory in one form or another. Since both parties are seeking that single goal, only one can be successful, and the other players must necessarily lose. It is for this reason among others that, beginning in the twentieth century, economists began to use the study of games as a way to understand and predict certain economic factors.

There had always been a sensible contingent of economists who saw their science as different from the physical sciences. Physics, biology, and chemistry, for example, all sought to explain and classify the properties and laws of a disinterested physical universe. To study the social sciences, on the other hand, one would have to take into account the changeable players involved. As in Keynes' Beauty Contest, the contestants played a role in the outcome.

By the mid-century, the confinement of the closed economy was increasingly evident, and the economy as a whole began to resemble a game in which each individual was a player among several hundreds of millions engaged in a contest to gain money. Every decision made within the economy was like a decision made in an ultra-complex game of chess or tennis.

With this view of the economy, mathematician John von Neumann and economist Oskar Morgenstern sought to devise a method which analyzed games in the hope of finding a more analogous approach to the science. According to Neumann and Morgenstern, the science of economics required an entirely new mathematics based on probability and rational decision-making. They developed this new mathematics and published it in their pathbreaking 1944 *Theory of Games and Economic Behavior*. Since then, economists have used Game Theory to explain actions and solve problems for all kinds of real economic conditions, ranging from business budgeting to the Cold War arms race.

Zero-Sum World

The premise for any game is the existence of two or more rational players who are striving for a given reward called a 'payoff'. That payoff can be anything—a win, a million dollars, a bag of Indiana kettle corn. As long as all the players involved are in pursuit of the same payoff and have the ability to act in effort to achieve the goal, they are participating in a game.

The concept of a zero-sum or fixed-sum game stems from the notion that the total payoff is limited or fixed, such that total gains and losses always equal the same fixed amount. For example, a game in which the winner gets $100 and the loser must pay $100 is a zero-sum game because the end tally equals zero. The fact that it is a fixed sum means that one player can only win at the expense of the other, and no matter who wins or who loses, the difference will always sum to zero.

The traditional metaphor for fixed-sum games is that of a pie from which everyone takes a slice. If one person takes a larger slice, that extra portion must necessarily come from someone else's slice, meaning that the other will have a smaller portion. Just as in a tennis match, where one player's winning a point means that the other player has lost a point, all fixed-sum games are based in strict competition.

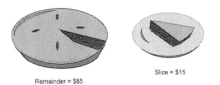

Whole pie = $100

Remainder = $85

Slice = $15

FIG. 11—Fixed Sum Pie.

Other games, called non-zero-sum or variable-sum games, have been referenced to in contrast to the competitive nature of the zero-sum game. In a non-zero-sum game, the total payoff can change so that any number of the participants can gain or lose based on the success of their strategies. For instance, one player might win $75 and the next might win $25 so that the total payoff is $100. If a single game could possibly produce payoffs of different amounts, then its payoff is variable and is considered a non-zero-sum game.

In fact, the distinction between zero-sum and non-zero-sum is superfluous. The important factor in all games, whether they are zero-sum or technically variable-sum, is not the total amount of winnings available, but the fact that the players are competing against one another for the same payoff—one player's gain must the others' loss whether or not the total payoff remains static. The underlying basis for any game is competition, not some fixed total payoff. We can see how even variable payoffs can be strictly competitive by simply converting the nominal sum to a percentage. The one who wins a greater percentage wins in relative comparison to the one who wins a lesser amount. In cases where the total payoff is not fixed, for example, the effect of competition is the same.

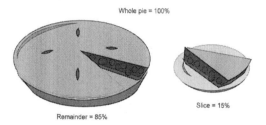

Whole pie = 100%

Slice = 15%

Remainder = 85%

FIG. 12—Variable Sum Pie.

Consider, for example, the difference between a technically zero-sum game and one that is supposedly non-zero-sum. In the first game, the winner receives $25 and the loser loses $25. This is the prototypical zero-sum game, in that the gains and losses from both players add up to zero. If Player A chooses a winning strategy, he wins $25 and Player B loses $25. Player A's gain and Player B's loss sum to zero.

In the second game, the winner receives $100, but the loser doesn't lose $100 and rather receives a consolation prize of $50. Here, the thought is that the game is non-zero-sum because the payoff equals more than zero (in this case, it equals $150). But even here, gain for one is loss for another since the players are striving for the same goal—the $100 win—and trying

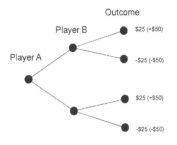

FIG. 13—Fixed Sum Game,
Extensive Game Form.

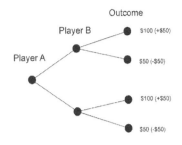
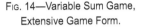

FIG. 14—Variable Sum Game,
Extensive Game Form.

This diagram presents a simple game in which the loser pays the winner $25. Player A goes first, choosing one of two options, then Player B goes, also choosing one of two options. Once both players have made their choices, one wins and the other loses as represented by the outcome column. The payoff listed is the monetary gain while the figure listed in parentheses is the differential over or under the opponent.

In this diagram, the same game is played, but the payoff is variable in that both players can win money, showed in the outcome column. But, while the monetary gain for both players is positive, the relative payoff is only positive for one.

to avoid the secondary prize. In both games, the difference between the two players' payoffs is $50—the winner advances beyond the loser in both games by the same amount. The players are in the same relative position in the non-zero-sum game as they were in the zero-sum game; in both cases, the winner gains the advantage.

Even if the payoff for a game is completely variable, as is the case when the winner's payoff equals a number of points scored (say, when a fantasy football owner wins a dollar amount equal to the number of points won in a match, which can theoretically be limitless), the effect is the same as it is with a zero-sum or any other fixed-sum game. Because the players are striving for the same payoff—in this case, the most money earned—the result must be that one player's ability to earn points is his opponent's inability to do so. One player's gain is his opponent's loss.

In this light, it could be argued that there is no such thing as a non-zero-sum game where all participants can win something. If there is a game at all, by definition, there must be a given payoff that all players are after, and so there must be a winner who gets the prize and a loser who doesn't. The amount by which the winner wins is necessarily equal to the amount by which the loser loses.

This is not to say that non-zero-sum situations are nonexistent, but rather that once a given activity takes the form of a non-zero-sum situation, it loses the qualities that make it a game. Likewise, as soon as a condition takes on the qualities of a game, it is by nature competitive and thus a zero or fixed-sum situation.

Three possibilities come to mind in which an activity could be non-zero-sum in its effect, where all parties could win or lose based on their own actions. And, in each of these scenarios, the qualities that make the activity a game would necessarily be absent. The first situation is when the participants all have differing goals.

Take, for example, one tennis player who wants to exercise while the other wants to get a tan. In this case, both players can play a match of tennis to achieve what they desire given the proper exertion and the right position of the sun. It can be called a non-zero-sum condition because both participants can gain during the activity and the rewards do not have to sum to zero. But, as such, it cannot be called a game in the proper sense; the players are not striving for the same payoff and are thus not competing against each other.

The second non-zero-sum scenario is when the goal is collective—when, for instance, the participants are working together to achieve a mutual goal. This is the case when the tennis players both want to achieve a well-played match, for example. To accomplish this mutual goal, they work together to provide a fair amount of action and sportsmanship. Here, too, both participants can win notwithstanding the fact that only one player can actually claim victory in the match. They cannot be said to be competing in the strict sense, and the game cannot be considered a true game.

Finally, another non-zero-sum situation may arise when the participants pursue a payoff that is in essence unlimited. To stick with the tennis theme, such a case could be conceivable if the players agreed to play, not for points won, but for hits made. This could theoretically last forever considering the willingness of each player to continue hitting the ball. In this scenario as well, both players will win as long as they take part in the event, and so it can be called a non-zero-sum condition. Again, however, the fact that it is non-zero-sum means that there is no competition and there is no game.

* * *

While non-zero-sum conditions are hard to find in games, they are easily found in the real world. It takes no far stretch of the imagination to see how two players in a given economic situation could desire two different things—an apple farmer wants oranges and an orange farmer wants apples, to take a basic example. Nor is it terribly outlandish to imagine a situation in which two or more work together to achieve a shared goal—a town's citizens working together to build a well, for instance. Given our world's finite resources, it is not as easy to imagine the third kind of non-zero-sum game, in which the payoff is unlimited, but even here it is possible considering a relatively abundant world and relatively limited needs. Two players might both want oranges, for example, and there is nothing necessarily stopping both of them from farming their own orange groves. The resources may technically be limited in a given economic scenario, such as the case in any finite realm, but as long as the players can all satisfy their needs, the resources seem unlimited for all practical purposes.

All of this changes when the economy becomes money-based. To begin, given a money-driven economy, all the players necessarily strive for the same payoff. It is thus impossible for any number of players to engage in the first kind of non-zero-sum situation, where each pursues his own interest without interfering with the pursuits of others. They all want the same thing and can only get more by taking it or withholding it from others. There is competition and therefore a zero-sum situation.

The second kind of non-zero-sum situation is also impossible in a money-based economy. Here, the fact of a single goal presupposes competition so that no two players can work together to attain their individual goals. Indeed, the players involved cannot share a goal at all because any amount of money that might be gained can only be possessed by one of them, and necessarily withheld from the others.

Lastly, the total possible payoff in a money-driven economy is inherently limited by the amount of money in circulation, and so the third kind of non-zero-sum game is also impossible to achieve in a real-world economy. Theoretically, the money supply could be expanded without limit—and indeed this concept has precedence in the era of paper money printed by government fiat—but, under such circumstances, that money would cease to be money in the sense that it was intended, and it would thus be disqualified as a currency for the economy. There is, after all, a reason why dirt is not used as money.

Regard Germany's marks after their hyperinflation in the 1920s, when at one point one trillion barely sufficed to buy a loaf of bread. Needless to say, the money had lost its usefulness as money, and many resorted to fueling their stoves with it as an alternative. In situations where a given money supply is limitless, some other form of money would naturally arise in its place to provide a more stable method of exchange. This is to say that only money with a limited supply has any use in an economy and, given an infinite supply, it will no longer serve its regulating purpose. By nature, then, a money-driven economy cannot be non-zero-sum in the third sense.

As we can see from this exercise, all money-based economies must be zero-sum in the broad sense if not in the technical sense. While a money-based economy might well have a fluctuating payoff, the fact is that gain for one implies loss for another, and so it is strictly competitive. This is the concept that is meant by most when they refer to the economy as a zero-sum game, and so it is this concept that should come to mind with its use.

The Prisoner's Dilemma

The terminology related to Game Theory is misleading on another front as well. The term 'solution' is used in Game Theory to describe the combination of strategies that will give any player his best result considering the other players' probable strategies. But this is not a solution in the sense of solving the zero-sum problem and finding a way for everyone to win. Rather, it is a solution in the sense of finding a compromise in which everyone gets the best he can with the limited choices he is given. In most scenarios, the so-called solution is a middle ground, neither particularly beneficial nor detrimental to any participant, where each is likely to end up given his advantages or disadvantages in the game.

A standard illustration in Game Theory known as the 'prisoner's dilemma' helps to show how a given solution might well end up with none of the players winning at all. The dilemma, formalized by mathematician Albert J. Tucker, can be summarized as follows: Two suspects are arrested on burglary charges and questioned by the police. Because the police have insufficient evidence for a conviction, the district attorney is hoping for confessions. The police can convict the suspects on a lesser charge of concealed weapons and will try to use this to persuade the suspects into squealing on each other.

Having separated the prisoners, the D.A. visits each to offer a deal. If neither prisoner confesses, they will both go to jail for one year on concealed weapons charges. If, however, one prisoner squeals on his partner and his partner says nothing, the first prisoner gets off without jail time and the accomplice gets a full five-year sentence. If they both squeal, they will both get three years.

The deal is laid out below in a game matrix (Figure 15). The choices Prisoner 1 has are shown in the rows while the choices Prisoner 2 has are shown in the columns. The length of jail time each prisoner gets for each outcome is listed by years in the corresponding cells, the first number representing the first prisoner's jail time and the second number representing the second prisoner's.

		Prisoner 2	
		Stay Silent	Squeal
Prisoner 1	Stay Silent	1 , 1	5 , 0
	Squeal	0 , 5	3 , 3

FIG. 15—The Prisoner's Dilemma Represented in a Game Matrix.

Thus the dilemma is set—squealing is certainly the best strategy for both players since they could get off the hook without jail time. But in this dilemma, each prisoner must take into consideration the play of the other to ensure the most favorable outcome. Doing this, the players will realize that squealing is the other's best option as well, and that they might also take that route. When both confess, they find, the outcome is worse than when both stay silent; they both get three years rather than just one. As such, they will both do better by choosing their second best option. The solution to the prisoner's dilemma, then, is for the players to compromise and stay silent.

This scenario is often identified as non-zero-sum because, depending on each player's actions, the results can vary. The total number of years spent in jail could be as few as two and as many as six. Strictly speaking, the prisoner's dilemma is not a game since it is assumed that the participants are not competing against each other and are rather cooperating with each other to receive the least amount of total jail time. As in the example of two tennis players trying to create a well-played match, the prisoners must work together to ensure the best outcome for both.

In the event that the prisoners are not allied in their attempt to minimize total jail time—if, for instance, each wants to get less jail time than the other—then the scenario necessarily becomes competitive. Let us say that the heist was a success and the money is buried where the police cannot find it. Each prisoner wants to get out of jail before the other so as to access the money before his accomplice gets a chance. In this case, the only beneficial strategy is to squeal while the other remains silent. That is the only approach in which one prisoner can gain a relative advantage over the other and thus win the game. The other options result in either the loss of the money (when the prisoner stays silent while his accomplice squeals) or a neutral outcome (when both prisoners do the same thing, are released from jail at the same time, and have to fight each other for the dough). In this contest, it is clear that the only strategy worth attempting is to squeal.

It is important to note the effect the introduction of money has on the dilemma. As soon as the goal is shifted from lower total jail time to money, the strategies become clear and a strict competition arises between the prisoners. Of course, the new goal needn't be money—it could be some other single objective such as a car, a stash of gold chains, or a one-year supply of ShamWows—but as long as some single goal is held by all parties involved, competition will result. Money is an easy mechanism for this since everyone knows its value and will justify competition for it.

With the help of this illustration, we find that there are two general possibilities for those involved in any competition. The first is the outcome in which one of the contenders wins and the other loses—in the prisoner's dilemma, this is what happens when one prisoner squeals and the other stays silent. The second possibility is more or less a compromise in which neither contender wins or loses—this happens when both prisoners do the same thing. These two possibilities, win/loss and compromise, make up the only potential outcomes for any given competition. Most games, especially sports, have only one potential outcome—the win/loss outcome. Soccer and American football can end in ties, but when they do, the outcome is typically accompanied by sincere disappointment on both sides. The win is the reason for the game.

> Winning isn't everything; it's the only thing.
>
> —Henry Russel Sanders,
> UCLA football coach

Two Sides of the Same Coin

The competitiveness of the modern economy is best exemplified with reference to its most characteristic facet, the stock market. There, players of the game are all engaged in one form or another in the buying and selling of company stocks, the aim of which is to make more money than everyone else. The stock market is a zero-sum game because in it a player can only win if another player loses. To win in the market, one must buy a stock at a low price and sell it at a high price, the difference being the capital gains. But, if a trader is able to pull off this deed, some other trader must necessarily do the opposite by buying high and selling low. The difference for him is the loss incurred. Altogether, the profit made by the winner is equal to the amount surrendered by the loser, and they add up to zero.

As the legendary investor and one of the world's wealthiest men, Warren Buffett, has said, "The market, like the Lord, helps those who help themselves. But unlike the Lord, the market does not forgive those who know not what they do°." Loss is as much a part of the market as gain, and not everyone can gain as much as Warren Buffett has. Indeed, the qualities that make the stock market competitive mean that gain for one must mean loss for others—$40 billion in Warren Buffett's pocket is $40 billion less in the rest of our pockets. Ultimately, Krugmanian arithmetic rules the day.

The predominance of money in modern economics means that the entire system is like the stock market in that every win is complemented by an equal and opposite loss. The various transactions between all the players are the several ways in which they can go about competing with one another, and the combination of total moves one can make is the player's 'strategy'. Buying and selling, whether they pertain to the purchase of a $3 stock or a $3 gallon of milk, comprise the wide-ranging suite of plays that competitors in the modern economy can make. Ultimately, all such transactions, from the grocery store counter sale to the boardroom mega-mergers, amount to varied degrees of the same process—an exchange in the interest of an all-encompassing pursuit of money.

Now, a reworking of perception is required to understand the strategy behind giving up an amount of money in a purchase for the ultimate purpose of making more money. Conventional wisdom says that if the goal is to make money, one should be disinclined to give it up. When the goal is money, one should be less willing, for instance, to buy goods and services and try his best to hold on to the money he has. Of course, one can still make use of the goods and services he buys with money in order to make more money. A graphic designer can use the computer he buys to build customer websites, and thus make more money. The outlay of money leads directly to the income of more money.

All economic purchases these days are based in the same tactic. By purchasing a company, for example, investment bankers can sell the goods attained—whether they are in the form of company stock or the firm's assets—at a later time or in a different market at a higher price. We can use Warren Buffett's purchase of Coca-Cola stock as a prime example of such arbitrage. When he bought the stock in 1988, the company was largely under-valued due to the crash of '87 and some turmoil in the executive ranks. Being the savvy businessman that he is, Buffett knew that the company was sound and would continue to produce a good return on equity under new management. Over the next several years, the stock price tripled. Buffett's strategy had paid off and in the process, multiplied his wealth.

The right allocation of one's goods and services, no matter what their price, could very well yield a greater return and thus make for a profitable investment. One must spend money to make money, as the saying goes. To take a more involved example, a Med student will readily put forth hundreds of thousands of dollars over the course of a seven-year period for a medical school diploma that will allow him to turn around and establish a medical practice that brings in hundreds of thousands of dollars each year. A few hundred thousand dollars turns into several hundred thousand dollars and most likely more. The initial outlay thus produces exponentially more money, and the exchange must be considered an overall gain for the individual.

What the diligent investigator will find is that all economic exchanges, from the simple buying and selling of stocks to the more complex medical school venture, amount to one brand or another of a strategy in the economic game to earn more money. And, with respect to every one of these strategies, there is always a winner and an equal and opposite loser. In the same transaction as Buffett's big win with Coca-Cola, for example, someone's wealth decreased by the same degree as Buffett's gain. Someone sold Coca-Cola stock to Buffett for the low price at which he bought it, and, likewise, someone bought it for the high price at which he sold it. In this way, the winning strategy was directly countered by a losing strategy of equal proportions.

In respect of property, as of all economic factors, harm and abuse cannot be dissevered from the good, any more than debit can from asset in double-entry book-keeping. The one necessarily spawns the other. To seek to do away with the abuses of property, is to destroy the thing itself; just as the striking of a debit from an account is tantamount to striking it from the credit record.

—PIERRE-JOSEPH PROUDHON, *CONFESSIONS D'UN REVOLUTIONNAIRE* (1849)

The poor could say that the employer's life is their death and therefore his death would be their life.

—JEAN CHARLES LÉONARD DE SISMONDI (1773-1842)

Of course, it is not necessarily the case that the same person sold Coca-Cola low and bought it high—most likely many different people were involved in both transactions. Yet, the principle still holds in that the stock was sold by some group at the low point and bought by another group at the high point. All who were included in those groups together lost the same amount that Buffett gained. Here, as in all such exchanges, the gains and losses summed to zero.

So too does the medical school example have losers to complement the winner. While the winner is obvious, the losers are much more dispersed and unidentifiable than even in the stock exchange scenario. Generally, though, one can say that as much as the Med student gained from the transaction, some person or group of persons lost an equal amount. Those losers could be classified as those who had to sell low and buy high—in the medical school example, those people who had to sell the information and diploma at a low cost and later buy the medical services at a higher price. All in all, the money that the doctor makes in the transaction must come from someone or some group.

Naturally, those who are involved in selling low and buying high are not going to be the same people in any exchange so complex and extended over time. And, indeed, those who are directly involved with each transaction may not be the real losers—the teachers and administrators who were directly responsible for the student's education are probably not economic losers in any meaningful way. The financial loss might be displaced two or three or more transactions beyond the pertinent ones—say, for instance, in the taxpayers who subsidize the school and the student's education through government grants without seeing any direct return on their investment, or the custodian who does his part to keep up the university grounds at a cheap rate. Similarly, the patient who receives medical treatment from the doctor might not really be the one paying for it—he might be enrolled in a convoluted insurance scheme that distributes the cost over several millions of people, or he might be receiving treatment completely free and letting the municipal government and taxpayers pick up the bill. Ultimately, the loss must take place somewhere and by someone who either sells his goods or services for less than they are worth or buys goods and services for more than they are worth.

The difference between winning and losing strategies can be summed up as the difference between these two types—those who buy low and sell high and those who do the opposite. The former makes money and the latter loses money no matter what form the transaction takes—buying and selling an education, financial instruments, employment, or other goods and services. If one can consistently buy low and sell high, he will end up ahead of the curve and successful in the game of life; if one cannot manage to do so, he will end up behind the curve and fail.

The Profit of Loss

Though competition can be aggressive and often ruthless these days, it is most commonly viewed in a positive light. Consider sports and the kind of entertainment a good basketball or football game brings; or the closeness that can result from rivalries between family members, friends, and colleagues. While it is true that all competition comes with struggle and defeat, the hardships endured in most competitive situations are easily seen as the necessary downsides that allow for the prominent upsides.

Sports offer the clearest example. Who would go to watch a baseball game if there was no chance of a team's failure? Who would watch a tennis match if the players were not able to lose points? Without the threat of loss, there would be no real purpose to the sport and no real joy in victory. The game would be meaningless—as a matter of fact, it would not be a game at all. And so we embrace loss, or perhaps just the threat of loss, in our games if only so that we may enjoy the thrill of victory.

On the economic plane, the typical view is also rather positive. The predominant notion, especially in America, is that, by providing a competitive framework in which economic players can succeed or fail, each participant is given motivation to overcome obstacles, innovate, and create new ways of doing things. It is suggested that competition spurred all American industrial and cultural achievements from the founding of colonial democracy to the invention of the telegraph, the electric light, and the airplane. Competition stimulates innovation, without which we would still be living in the Dark Ages.

Of course, failure in the economic arena is much harder to bear than in the arena of sports. Social and economic loss can mean starvation and homelessness—even death. One can shrug off the loss of a basketball game or a chess match; not so with the stock market or job market. There, wins and losses can mean life or death. Still, and in part because of the extreme nature of failure in the economic world, it is argued that the benefits of competition far outweigh the drawbacks. Because men are in competition for scarce resources, they are motivated to create and innovate in order to overcome the world's deficiencies. In this way, the loss inherent in economic competition actually brings forth a bounty of growth and progress. The hardships of economic loss are a part of what Schumpeter termed 'Creative Destruction', the indispensable clearing of the ground which encourages a new wave of growth to come afterward.

Competition has thus been championed by thinkers from as early as the mid-nineteenth century, and it found in English philosopher Herbert Spencer perhaps its most vocal proponent. In his *Principles of Biology*, Spencer ventured to claim that the competition produced by population growth was the proximate cause of progress in all of history. "It produced the original diffusion of the race," he argued. "It compelled men to abandon predatory habits and take to agriculture. It led to the clearing of the Earth's surface. It forced men into the social state; made social organization inevitable; and has developed the social sentiments. It has stimulated to progressive improvements in production and to increased skill and intelligence. It is daily thrusting us into closer contact and more mutually-dependent relationships°."

One recalls Toynbee's *Study of History*, which examines in detail how each of the great civilizations of the world formed, not in some pristine area of perfect harmony, but through a difficult series of natural challenges and responses. The Egyptians faced desiccation of the Lower Nile, the Greeks faced the Aegean, Western civilization faced new ground, and so on. The civilizations that were able to respond to their natural challenges and overcome imminent defeat—the Egyptians, the Babylonians, the Greeks, the Chinese, the Japanese, and the Occident, among an elite group of others—have been the great cultures of the world. Their stories of survival and triumph are the narratives of history.

Throughout the past, the same struggle can be found, quite as if it were an innate aspect of human nature, as if man actually required such limitations and challenges in order to produce and create to his greatest capacity. It was with this progressive effect of competition in mind that a branch of sociology arose in the late nineteenth century, later called 'Social Darwinism'. Equipped with the practically self-evident truths of evolution, thinkers and polemicists alike argued that the theory of natural selection could be applied not only to the biological world, but also to the economic and social sphere as well. They viewed competition as a natural and even predetermined mechanism for ridding the world of the weak, the incapable, and the feeble, leaving only the strongest and most competent to reign. It was Spencer who coined the term 'Survival of the Fittest' in his application of Darwin's *Origin of the Species* to the socioeconomic plane. The idea was that, through competition on the economic level, the best adapted would survive, thus weeding out the least intelligent and industrious.

To Spencer and others, the Survival of the Fittest was the necessary natural mechanism by which the human race progressed. Having been the victors, the great industrialists of the period were, of course, the greatest proponents of the concept. John D. Rockefeller compared the growth of a large business to the biological process by which plants grow. "The American Beauty rose," Rockefeller said, "can be produced in the splendor and fragrance which bring cheer to its beholder only by sacrificing the early buds which grow up around it. This is not an evil tendency in business. It is merely the working-out of a law of nature and a law of God." In his *Gospel of Wealth*, Andrew Carnegie likewise claimed that competition and the accumulation of wealth were laws of nature, going on to say that indeed they were "the highest results of human experience, the soil in which society so far has produced the best fruit."

And who can deny the magnificent accomplishments of the great industrialists of the time? Their creativity and innovation, along with the effervescent dynamism of the American people, led to what was perhaps the most productive and innovative age in the history of Man. As Nietzsche explained, all life is based on the use and consumption of other life; exploitation was not bad, but rather natural and thus a necessary process in the development of greater beings—Nietzsche's 'Übermensch', or 'Superman'. Big fishes eat little fishes, and that is the whole of the story°.

The twentieth century offers quintessential examples of the kind of progress generated by competition. Take for instance post-war Germany and Japan, countries that had been so ravaged by destruction that some commentators doubted whether recovery was possible. But because those countries were forced to compete in the industries dominated by the United States, they were forced to transcend their impediments and become powerhouse industrial nations. The rise of German and Japanese auto manufacturing from the 1950s through to the '80s is a testament to the countries' resiliency and the kind of creative force that competition brings about.

By contrast, the United States had become so dominant in the automotive industry during the same period that it did not need to compete with any foreign power. Without competition, the industry became bloated and full of itself, cutting innovation and ultimately producing goods that were not only uncompetitive but rather undesirable. The result was seen in the 1980s, when German and Japanese automobiles overtook American-made cars in market share and have dominated ever since. We are only now seeing the American automobile industry break out of a decades-long coma that left its 'Big Three' manufacturers bankrupt and ostracized.

One will note that the same coincidence took place with the other superpower of the century, the Soviet Union. There, competition was reduced to a bare minimum, and so domestic industry had no incentive to improve. Meanwhile, with the Cold War

> In Italy, for thirty years under the Borgias, they had warfare, terror, murder and bloodshed, but they produced Michelangelo, Leonardo da Vinci and the Renaissance. In Switzerland, they had brotherly love, they had five hundred years of democracy and peace, and what did that produce? The cuckoo clock.
>
> —HARRY LIME IN *THE THIRD MAN* (1949)

escalating, the Soviet military faced significant international competition and thus had great incentive to improve. This juxtaposition created a paradox in which Russian washing machines were backward and decrepit while Russian MiGs were advanced and powerful. The difference was that the washing machine manufacturers faced no competition and could survive without improving, while the MiG manufacturers were forced to innovate to stay in the game.

Across the board and throughout history, we see the same story of men and nations overcoming the competition for scarce resources by innovating and creating new methods and new products, Toynbee's response to the challenges that make Man great.

Yet, despite the tendency for competition to draw out the best in men, the objective critic must acknowledge its tendency to draw out the worst in men as well. Just as the threat of loss and the prospect of victory can encourage one to strive for higher aims, work harder, and create, so too can it encourage one to orchestrate base schemes, connive, and manipulate others. When the goal is to defeat the opponent, an individual, group, or nation will use any and all means to do so, even if those means are out of bounds, as it were. In trying to best the United States, for instance, the Russians were not limited to developing advanced aircraft and progressing tactical aviation; they incorporated a fair amount of espionage and terror to achieve their goal as well, not to mention an all-out imperial campaign to spread Communism around the world.

Indeed, the casual observer today might conclude that the less honorable strategies are used with more frequency than the principled. Everywhere one looks in our highly competitive society, there is someone trying to scheme someone else, trying to finagle a few simoleons here and there, and doing everything he can to make a buck, notwithstanding corruption and fraud. He goes about his business quite as if it is the accepted way to make a living, as if he has no compunction.

Of course, compunction is a luxury most cannot afford in a competitive situation. Given a closed system, one must either eat or be eaten; if one does not manipulate others, they will most certainly manipulate him. Ultimately, honor, principles, and even scruples become liabilities that merely hinder one's ability to survive. It is almost as if the competitive framework nullifies the potential for honor in all actions. Justice and appropriateness are not even considered; all that is left is beat or be beaten.

A change in mentality occurs when a system shifts from open to closed, from boundless as it had been before the 1890s to strictly competitive as it was after. The fact is that, in a competitive situation, to get what one wants, one need not do well, be virtuous, or even be productive; one need not even try to do well at all; the only thing one needs to focus on is doing better than his opposition. Improvement, innovation, and progress are unnecessary since one can win without doing any of these as long as his opponents somehow do worse.

To use an example from sports, a basketball team can win a game even if it shoots poorly, turns the ball over, and fouls out all of its players; as long as the other team does worse, the first team will win. And so one must conclude that it is just as profitable for one's opponents to do poorly as it is for one's own team to do well, regardless of whether they are honorable or moral. To be sure, without such responsibilities, one is free to focus more energy on the contest. Regard the Prisoner's Dilemma—the prisoner will do much better if he squeals on his accomplice, yet convinces his partner that he won't. The winner is the player who is able to trick his opponent most persuasively.

Such deception is the ever-present temptation in the competitive world. As even Spencer was sure to admit, the process of economic selection as seen in the business world teems with "illicit practices of every form and shade, from venial deception up to all but direct theft ... Tricks innumerable, lies acted or uttered, elaborately-devised frauds, are prevalent: many of them established as 'customs of the trade'; nay, not only established, but defended'". It is only natural to defend such deceit because the circumstances demand it. When the game is for survival, then any and all methods are suitable.

Whence the rise in the nineteenth century of the utilitarian style of Realpolitik. It is, after all, the most rational form of political economy in a closed system, not necessarily malicious or dastardly, as it might seem, but calculatingly cold—realistic—in accepting the notion that the utopian ideal cannot be attained and that some must lose in order for others to win. Realpolitik is Machiavellian in that it is a pragmatic approach that works in securing the most good for the most people, notwithstanding the few who lose out in the equation, which is regrettable but acceptable nonetheless.

> Any player unaware of the fool in the market probably is the fool in the market.
>
> —Warren Buffett (born 1930)

Now, it is not as though competition was invented in the 1890s. On the contrary, it was a part of the Western way of life from the very start and, with it, both the progressive benefits and counterproductive drawbacks. The change that occurred was in the necessity of competition. Whereas it had always been possible to decline struggle, now it was obligatory. The new obligation meant in large part a new outlook on that struggle. In a strictly competitive arena, when everyone is striving for the same goal and one must lose in order for another to win, manipulation is not only acceptable, but, as a function of limits, it becomes the only way to succeed. While trickery and fraud had always been a possible way of dealing with others in business, now, to no small degree, it had become the only way of doing business.

Since gain for one means loss for another, the reasonable inference is that making others lose is the necessary means to success. In the new paradigm, beating others in business, in the stock market, or even in the street on the way to work become essential elements of one's success. In the end, the exploitation noted in Spencer's time becomes the standard order of business in the twentieth century.

*   *   *

In an economy as complex and intricate as ours, the array of possible careers and opportunities is so vast that reason suggests anyone can find a way to employ a winning strategy in some capacity. Since we are all in the same position in the pursuit of money, it can be said that we have what is called an 'even playing field', or an equal opportunity to succeed in the world. It is assumed that anyone with a will to work should be able to find a job or in some way produce what people need and thus accumulate enough money to survive and thrive in the modern economy.

But, as we have seen, in a closed system there are as many instances of failure as there are of success. If a number of individuals employ winning strategies in their actions, a number of individuals will employ losing strategies equaling the former in scope. A closer look will reveal that there are those who are better postured to take advantage of such competition. Using certain leverage, an active player can better ensure a favorable outcome in any part of the game, and thus secure a favorable outcome in the game as a whole.

5. MONOPOLY

WHEN 'COMPETITION' IS MENTIONED these days, the first thing that comes to mind is not fewer options, but more; not people striving to take advantage of others, but people offering more choices; not control and exploitation, but opportunity and liberation. This is because the concept is used primarily in reference to industry and the competition between companies. It is assumed that competition implies the introduction of new competitors in a given market, which means more choices and greater leverage for the consumer. As in the case of a fare war between airlines or gas stations, two or more companies battle it out for the business of potential customers, doing anything and everything in their power to ensure greater market share. Ultimately, the customer gets his choice of products at the lowest price possible.

Of course, the same contest viewed from the perspective of the companies is rather negative. While the customers get to name their price, the companies are forced to take lower profits and possibly restructure their budgets in order to stay in the game. What is good for the customer is generally bad for the business and vice versa.

Viewed from yet another angle, one can see how competition can be negative for the individual as well. When a single company offers something that everyone in a given market needs—let's say jobs, for instance—the individuals that make up the market may be forced to compete in order to get those jobs. Competing workers are like competing companies, as they too must lower their prices to stay in the game. Instead of lowering fares or price tags on goods, they must lower the amount of wages they except to receive for their work in order to satisfy the demands of their prospective employers. Sweatshops in Southeast Asia and Western factories at the turn of the twentieth century come to mind. In both, laborers would work 12 to 16-hour shifts and risk injury and even death to maintain a job. Here we see that competition is rather negative and can be life-threatening under the worst circumstances.

And so, depending upon one's perspective, competition can be either good or bad—good for those who possess the commodity sought and bad for those competing for possession of that commodity. The trick, one might say, would be to always possess that which is highly sought and let everyone else compete for it.

Of course, in the modern economy, no one can be a true bystander; we have all been forced into competition because we are all engaged in the same pursuit of money. And yet, as one can see from daily experience, some are in a better position than others in this pursuit. The ability to employ a winning strategy is contingent on a player's ability to buy low and sell high, and, as we will see, one's ability to do this is not simply granted as a rule of the game but rather dependent upon the player's standing in the game. One must attain a certain level of power before he can manage a winning strategy, and power is based on the amount of money one controls. In short, one need not spend excessive time, effort, or resources to acquire money and thus employ a winning strategy; he just has to control large quantities of it.

The key to this strategy rests in a fundamental aspect of the money economy: Money is only valuable if people are willing to give something in return for it—bread, wheelbarrows, iPhones, one-hour massages, and so on. It just so happens that people are only willing to give things in return for money when they are in need of it. The more they need it, the more they are willing to give in return for it.

This leads to a stunning conclusion, perhaps even a paradox: A rich person is only rich if he can, in effect, sell his money to a very many others for goods and services. The more they need money, the more goods and services he can demand from them. Money becomes like the diamonds in the Diamond-Water Paradox; the diamonds are more valuable because they are scarcer—people are willing to pay more for them because there are fewer of them around. The more diamonds one holds to himself, then, and the more people that are without them, the more he can get in exchange for them. Similarly, a rich person is only rich if there are lots of people who are not rich. The point, then, is to get into a position in which one has money and lots of other people do not—the point is to monopolize money.

> Take now some hard-headed business man, who has no theories, but knows how to make money. Say to him: "Here is a little village; in ten years it will be a great city—in ten years the railroad will have taken the place of the stage coach, the electric light of the candle; it will abound with all the machinery and improvements that so enormously multiply the effective power of labor. Will in ten years, interest be any higher?" He will tell you, "No!" Will the wages of the common labor be any higher?" He will tell you, "No the wages of common labor will not be any higher." "What, then, will be higher?" "Rent, the value of land. Go, get yourself a piece of ground, and hold possession." And if, under such circumstances, you take his advice, you need do nothing more. You may sit down and smoke your pipe; you may lie around like the lazzaroni of Naples or the leperos of Mexico; you may go up in a balloon or down a hole in the ground; and without doing one stroke of work, without adding one iota of wealth to the community, in ten years you will be rich! In the new city you may have a luxurious mansion, but among its public buildings will be an alms-house.
>
> —HENRY GEORGE,
> *PROGRESS AND POVERTY* (1882)

The strategy is seen throughout the modern economy. Wealthy individuals or large companies seek to expand their holdings so that anyone who wishes to do business in a particular field must do it through them. In order to do so, they buy up smaller companies so that competition is squelched. Eventually, there is nowhere for small companies to grow. This process leads to the ever-expanding control of the means of production by the wealthy few. Ultimately, they end up controlling more than they need or can make use of, but, since other people need their resources, they can still benefit.

The Benefit of Leverage

The concept of monopoly only became relevant in the mid-to-late nineteenth century as the close of the economy grew imminent. Before the close, monopolies were not often considered and certainly not in the negative way they are today. That is because, in an open economy, where anyone has the option to pack up and reject the current system, no one else has the ability to control any particular resource, as there is always the potential to simply find more of it or produce it oneself. As such, nobody can monopolize goods and so nobody can demand excessive prices for those goods.

This is true even when a technical monopoly exists, in which there is only one seller for a particular good. Even then, it is always possible for a buyer to reject the seller's offer. As Menger showed in his *Principles of Economics*, monopoly conditions are not terribly different from those of pure competition, in which both buyers and sellers can take or leave the terms of the exchange. If, for example, a monopolist hoards a particular good and sets the price at a ridiculous level, the consumers interested in that good can simply reject the contract and do without the good. A consumer acting economically will do business with a seller only if he can secure the useful good at a price that is economically beneficial to him. Otherwise, he will reject the offer.

This is to say that, in an open economy, monopolists do not automatically have the power to dictate the terms of a given exchange. This fundamental aspect of trade applies to all such potential exchanges, even if there is but one seller, as in the case of a monopoly (or, as the case may be, a few large sellers, as in an oligopoly).

After the close, however, monopoly becomes a much more pertinent issue. Once alternatives are limited, the possession of any good, or the ability to produce it, becomes dependent upon other people. When a single seller hoards a particular good in a closed economy, buyers are not able to go elsewhere or produce the good themselves. They are thus more or less forced to buy at the seller's chosen price. Of course they also have the option of doing without the good, which is possible in the case of luxuries and frivolities. With necessities, such as food, shelter, and clothing, the consumer has no real choice. It is the seller's price or else.

In the modern economy, all goods and services fall into the latter category. In order to obtain any good or service these days, one must first obtain money; and so it is possible to monopolize all goods and services, essential or superfluous, necessity or luxury, by monopolizing money.

Thus we find that those who own large quantities of the currency are the ones who control its price. Put in another way, the rich dictate what money is worth and thus what can be bought and sold with it. The richer one is, the greater his power is in dictating the terms of contracts, and, by the same token, the poorer one is, the less influential he is.

The Rich Get Richer

We can see how this fact of economic nature can be exploited by those in power and thus used to grow power. Competition arises when more than one party desires something scarce, whether it is money or some other resource, such as water, apples, or petroleum. If all parties desire the scarce commodity equally, then the competition will be based on equal terms. In such cases, the amount each competitor is willing to provide in exchange for the commodity—the amount of effort, work, or goods he is willing to trade, for example—will be the same as the others. To regard an instance of barter, if two farmers need the same amount of water to irrigate their crops, they will be willing to offer the same amount of crops in exchange for a given amount of water.

If, however, different parties desire the scarce resource by differing degrees, the amount offered in exchange will also differ. If, for instance, one farmer needs twice as much water as the other, the first will be willing to offer some amount more than the second in exchange for the extra water. The amount more will not necessarily be proportional to his higher need, but we can assume that it will be a greater amount to some extent. In short, the more one wants a sought commodity, the more one will give in order to obtain it.

Now, the level of need one has for a given commodity is nothing intrinsic. As in the example above, one farmer could quite reasonably be satisfied with one unit of water while another farmer needs two. The two farmers share certain characteristics, but since they differ in other ways, their needs diverge. There are of course very basic needs that every human requires for survival, those being summed up by the triumvirate of food, shelter, and security, which are dictated less by whim and more by natural physiology; but even these can change over time and given different circumstances. For example, one person might require a 3,000-calorie diet to function properly every day, while another could be sustained by a mere 1,500 calories.

Generally, we can say that the less one has of a desired commodity, the more one needs it, which is especially true for the basics such as food, shelter, and security. If one lacks a consistent supply of food, one will generally want more of it; the same goes for shelter, security, and even other needs not considered basic. This generality, mixed with the drive to put forth effort, means that the condition one finds oneself in is likely to affect one's ability to maneuver in it. The less one has of a given commodity, the more he needs it and the more he will be willing to give for it; meanwhile, the more one has of a particular commodity, the less he needs it and the less he will be willing to give for more.

Applying this principle to the modern money-driven economy, in which one's inherent human needs are tied directly to the possession and application of money, we find that the less money one has, the more he needs it and the more he will be willing to give in order to obtain it. By the same token, the more money one has, the less he needs it and the less he will be willing to give in order to obtain more of it. Thus, the amount of labor, the quantity or quality of goods, and so on, that one will be willing to offer in exchange for money will be contingent on his overall level of wealth.

The upshot is that those who possess large quantities of money maintain greater power in a given economic situation and are thus in a position to take advantage of those who do not have much money. The wealthy in the equation can purchase at a discount the labor or goods that the poor are willing to offer, either making use of those goods and services or turning around and selling them for a profit. In this way, the possession of money becomes an asset in one's strategy to obtain more. Those who have little money will be willing to give more effort, work, goods, et cetera, in order to attain more of it than would those who have lots of money. The wealthy, meanwhile, could demand more work, goods, et cetera, for their money and thus capitalize on it.

And so we come to the conclusion that one has the ability to dictate the terms of a contract by his possession of wealth alone. By monopolizing wealth and thus creating a distinction between himself and his counterpart, he can skew the terms of the contract in his favor.

This is the principle behind some of the most perplexing and frustrating aspects of the modern economy. As evidenced throughout history, the rich tend to get richer and the poor tend to get poorer, a trend which only seems to intensify as the economy grows more complex and interdependent. As a matter of fact, one will note that this phenomenon gets more pronounced in economically bad times. The rich get richer to the greatest degree when everyone else is suffering the most, which is why we saw so many millionaires crop up in the 1930s during the Great Depression, when nearly a third of the workforce was unemployed. It was as if the very few benefited from the poverty of the multitudes. The more the multitudes needed money, the more the rich could get from them in exchange for money, and so the process continued.

The principle is illustrated succinctly in Frank Capra's *It's a Wonderful Life,* which seems to have resonated in the American Canon as a document of the Great Depression as well as a statement of spiritual and community well-being. When the crash hits and everyone comes screaming into the Building and Loan to get their money—which isn't there—one of the frenzied depositors claims that Mr. Potter, the town's fat millionaire, is willing to give everyone 50¢ on the dollar for every Bailey Building and Loan share. Someone yells that half is better than none, and the crowd begins to run over to Potter.

But George explains what Potter is trying to do: take over the Bailey Building and Loan so that he can control everything in Bedford Falls and charge anything he wants. "Don't you see what's happening?" he cries. "Potter isn't selling. Potter's buying. And why? Because we're panicking and he's not, that's why. He's picking up some bargains." In a closed economy, the very rich can afford to pick up bargains because they can afford not to panic. The lower classes—the workers that are financially dependent on everyone else—have no such luxury.

Observers of the recent financial crisis can see any number of equitable real-life examples. As the multibillion-dollar financial powerhouse firms were reeling in their losses, investors were watching their portfolios deflate by half, and workers were watching their retirement funds disappear, some very wealthy individuals were able to make excellent investments. Take for example the kinds of deals that Warren Buffett was wheeling. At one point before Lehman Brothers collapsed, the company was in negotiations with Buffett for a rescue loan. Since Lehman was in such trouble, Buffett was able to dictate the terms: $4 billion with a 9% dividend. That would mean a $360 million profit in a single year, a striking set of terms even by the standards of the so-called Oracle of Omaha. Lehman rejected the offer and subsequently went bankrupt.

As the crisis escalated and the financial firms fell deeper into their hole, Buffett's leverage grew that much more substantial. In negotiating a deal with Goldman Sachs, Buffett was able to secure a warrant that would deliver a return much greater than that proposed for the Lehman deal. At this writing, the return would amount to a $2.2 billion profit, one equal to 44% of the original investment. And so it would seem that, when you're rich, you can afford to get richer; when you're poor, the only thing you can afford is to get poorer.

> Every man is rich or poor according to the degree in which he can afford to endure the necessaries, conveniences, and amusements of human life.
>
> —Adam Smith,
> *The Wealth of Nations* (1776)

> A man is rich in proportion to the number of things he can afford to let alone.
>
> —Henry David Thoreau (1817-62)

The Poor Get Poorer

To examine how disparity in wealth affects exchanges in everyday life, let us consider a thought experiment in which two disparate individuals have possession of the same kind of good. Let us say that both the wealthy Mr. Money Bags and the impoverished Little Tramp are in possession of a 1982 Oldsmobile Delta 88. The car is run-down and requires a significant amount of work to be useful and quite a bit more to be presentable. Given this possession, each individual has two options: to (1) keep the car, use it for transportation, and do what it takes to maintain its functionality and appearance; or (2) sell the car and use the proceeds toward some other purchase, whether a car or something else.

Because of their monetary standings, Money Bags and the Tramp look at the same physical good and see two different things. To Money Bags, the Olds is nothing but a burden. In his mind, transportation should be more like a brand new Rolls Royce, not some run-down clunker. To the Tramp, on the other hand, the Olds looks like an opportunity. He has longed for a job but has always lacked the transportation to get there. The old piece of scrap metal in front of him is like a gold mine.

Mr. Money Bags needs little discernment before he sells the car and puts the profit toward the purchase of a new Rolls, which requires no maintenance and looks absolutely brilliant pulling up to his Park Avenue flat. The Little Tramp is of course faced with a tougher choice. He could sell the car, naturally, but would not be able to add the proceeds to additional capital because he doesn't have any. As such, he wouldn't be able to turn around and buy a much better car, much less a new Rolls Royce. He is ashamed by the appearance of the Olds and gets frustrated by the routine breakdowns, but, when faced with the option of selling or keeping the car, he really has no choice. He needs transportation to get to work, which is required to pay for his necessities, and the Oldsmobile is the only means at his disposal.

With an overview of the comparison, we see that Mr. Money Bags' wealth has not only allowed him to get rid of the clunker and ride in style, but has also freed him to be more productive because he doesn't have to worry about the monthly trip to the garage that the old car requires. Money Bags is able to spend his time making more money instead of spending it on the upkeep of his vehicle. Meanwhile, the Little Tramp must take the time to maintain the old car; he ends up being less productive and making less money in the long run.

This juxtaposition shows in one vignette how easily a rich person can use his wealth to get richer while the poor person must spend time and money and, as a result, will find it harder to pull himself out of poverty. The principle holds true for almost all such decisions, big or small, that can affect one's overall wealth.

To take a pertinent example, consider the kind of options given to the wealthy and impoverished when looking for a home. First, the wealthy person can and often does write a check to purchase his house, paying cash for the domicile even if it is a multimillion-dollar mansion with an infinity pool over an ocean view. In this way, the wealthy person instantly saves money on financing because he has no need for a mortgage. And, because he can turn over the money instantly, he can usually get some percentage knocked off the price tag by the brokers, who will skip a number of formalities and save money themselves. What's more is that the speed with which he can facilitate a deal means that he can sell the property at any time—when, for example, the value has appreciated by a significant amount and he can make a swift profit. Altogether, the home is more than just a living space for the millionaire; it is an investment that allows the owner to buy low and sell high.

By the same token, a home is usually more than just a living space for the poor person as well—it is a money trap. To begin, the poor person is most likely not able to buy a house at all but rather forced to rent someone else's house, and renting is a cost with a return that is likely to be less than the outlay. Shelter is important, of course—indeed, it is necessary for survival—but after a year's worth of renting, the tenant has nothing to show for his expenses. Unlike one who buys his house and thus gains some physical property in exchange, the renter obtains no property in the deal and is forced to expend money to simply survive.

Even if the individual has enough income to take out a mortgage and technically buy the house, the scenario is more or less the same. Instead of renting from the landlord, the resident must rent from the bank, paying his lease in the form of interest. It is true that the resident (in principle, a 'homeowner') will have a house at the end of the exchange, but over the course of a 30-year mortgage, he will have paid a substantial amount more than the value of the property. A typical estimate shows that a homeowner will have paid some $330,000 for a $100,000 house over 30 years. Having the property at the end of the deal is certainly worth something, and indeed the value might well rise in the interim such that it is worth $150,000 or $200,000 more.

Still, it is clear that the amount paid is a distorted figure, and the simple fact that the buyer cannot write a check to cover the total expense means that he will end up paying more over time. In other words, he is forced to buy high and sell low.

Open-eyed spectators will note that the same predicament faces anyone who lives in traditionally high-crime areas, where the cost of doing business is elevated due to the increased risks. A grocery store owner must contend not only with the typical expenses of stocking and reselling produce, but also with the expenses required to prevent and recover loss due to theft and vandalism. The store owner will logically charge more for the products he sells in order to make a profit, and the ultimate loser in the situation is the honest customer who must pay more for his groceries. Simply living in a poor neighborhood increases the cost of living because of the threat of crime.

Affluent neighborhoods without such threats attract businesses that can work under tighter margins and thus charge less for their products. It is for this reason that a pineapple will sell for $2.99 at a store in an affluent suburb and for $4.49 at a store in an urban ghetto. Again, a person's wealth influences his strategy in obtaining more.

If nothing else, the wealthy are at an advantage simply by their ability to take their time and research their investments. Just like large corporations which profit from economies of scale, doing business in large deals equals lower business costs. The fact that the wealthy are able to invest large sums of money in a given position means that the potential gain will be proportionately larger and thus worth spending more time on. One of Warren Buffett's investments might amount to a billion dollars or more, the return for which might reach three or four times as much. As such, he has the incentive to spend a proportionately larger amount of time researching the company, making sure the management's sound, investigating the financial history of the firm, and so on.

Meanwhile, a small-time investor cannot justify spending weeks reading up on a modest investment, which stands to return only a modest profit. His $2,000 might garner another $4,000, which is no doubt substantial, but it cannot justify spending weeks or months researching a single company. Of course, without doing the necessary research, the chances are higher that he will make a bad investment and lose a significant portion of his capital.

And so there is a natural impulse to save money for purposes beyond its use as investment capital. Its value grows as fewer people have access to it, so the more a single owner controls of it, the more valuable it becomes to him. Saving is thus akin to the basketball or football team that winds down the clock toward the end of the game in an effort to preserve a victory. They are winning and will stall on offense in order to withhold precious game time from their opponents. The winning team might even stall to the extent that they fail to run their offense properly and even turn the ball over. The thought is that even if their foes get possession of the ball, they will have to scramble to catch up and will most likely be unable to execute their plays to the best of their ability. By withholding resources, the winning team forces their opponents to panic. It is no wonder, then, that during these waning moments in a game, the score differential often expands and what may have been a fairly close game turns into a blowout.

Similarly, misers will withhold money even if it means failure in some straightforward economical sense. By ensuring that others do not have a lot of money, the miser ensures that his money will garner more in return, thus making him richer. Picture Scrooge in Charles Dickens' classic *A Christmas Carol*. He no more enjoys his wealth than makes use of it, but as long as he continues pinching pennies and paying Bob Cratchit a pittance, he can grow richer. Like the sportsman who monopolizes time, the financier who monopolizes money gains an advantage in the contest.

Time is the scarcest of all resources, especially in the modern economy. Not a few marketers have made use of this dearth by playing on the consumer's desire to take advantage of deals 'before time runs out' or 'before it's too late'. And who hasn't fallen for one of their tricks? The urge to buy impulsively, whether it is a plane fare that is rising, a stock that is ripe for the picking, or a plain old sale at a retail chain, is a compelling, almost maddening force in the consumer culture. When the buyer believes he is pressed for time, he is more likely to make a rash decision and be drawn into a deal that may or may not be all it appears on the surface.

Effective Monopolies

The conclusion drawn is that, in a money-driven system, one's power is equal to his share of total wealth. In this way, the modern economy can be viewed as a weighted electorate in which the power is divided by the amount of money each voter has. Those with more money have more votes, and those with less money have fewer votes.

As Game Theory has shown, this way of divvying up power has allowed the wealthy to accumulate a disproportionate amount of power at the expense of the impoverished in many situations. According to the theory behind the Banzhaf Power Index, a mathematical tool used to determine the power distribution in a given election, weighted voting systems can and often do give the powerful few near dictatorial reign over others, despite what appears to be a fair allotment of votes. The index is based on the fact that a party's true power lies not in the number of votes it is able to cast, but in the number of votes it has *relative* to those of others.

If, for instance, Teddy has 16 votes, 15 other people have one vote each, and a majority is necessary for a win, Teddy's power appears to be 16-to-1 as compared to each of the others, and 16-to-15 as compared to all of the others combined. One might say that Teddy has a slight advantage over all the others put together. But since Teddy has a majority of the votes, his allotment is necessary for a win in every election. As such, he is more or less a dictator and can do whatever he pleases.

In less extreme instances, those in power can still multiply their sway and effectively disenfranchise others who have less power. The real-life scenario in which John F. Banzhaf applied his model was similarly skewed, though it did not include any single majority-holder. Banzhaf, a New York state lawyer, set out to prove that his county's voting system was unfair in that it granted power to the few, highly populous communities that dominated the council. Though the allotment of votes based on population seemed fair, the power each voter had was skewed to the extent that only three of the communities exercised any real influence on the council and, at the same time, the other three were effectively disenfranchised.

The county included five communities in total, which were divided by population into six separate voting districts as follows:

FIG. 16—Banzhaf Community Vote Distribution.

Since the distribution was based on population, it seemed to be fair. The smaller communities should have fewer votes than the larger communities; votes should be proportional to the population. As can be seen, the system contained a total of 30 possible votes and required a simple majority of 16 to pass any bill. Banzhaf illustrated the scenario numerically by first noting the number of votes needed for a measure to pass, then noting the players in sequence by the number of votes each had, indicated by the notation below:

16; 9, 9, 7, 3, 1, 1

FIG. 17—Vote Distribution in Banzhaf Notation.

By analyzing every possible configuration of votes, Banzhaf identified each winning coalition of voters and then identified which voters

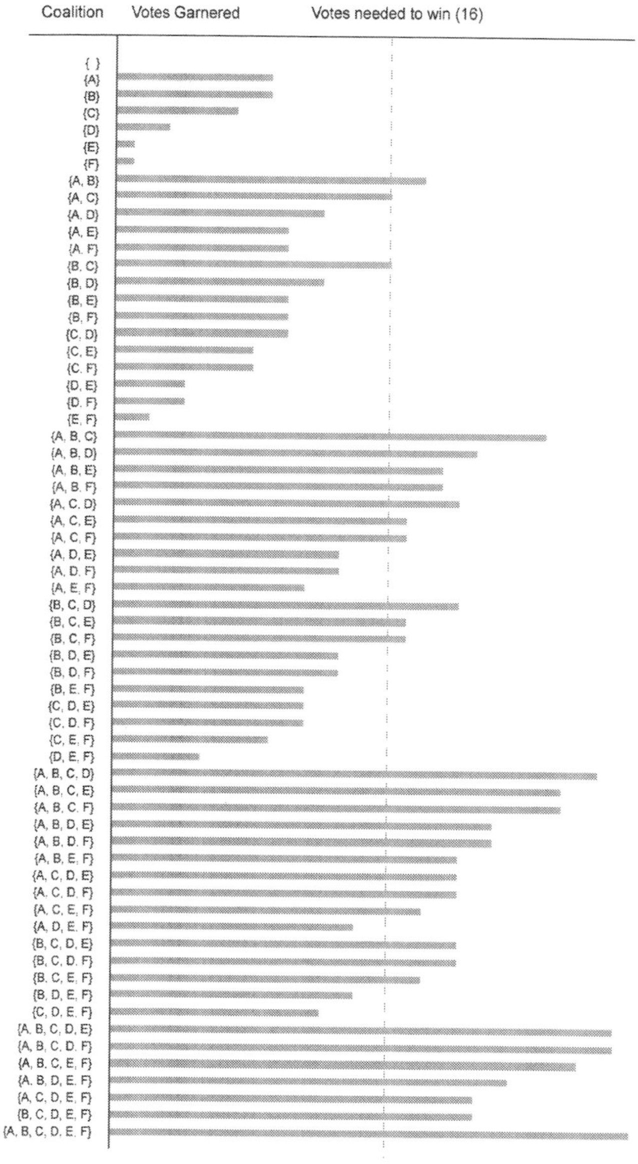

FIG. 18—Possible Coalitions in Banzhaf Vote System.

had power in each given coalition. His method for assigning power was to simply draw out each potential coalition and highlight which voter was necessary for the coalition to win. If a coalition would fail without a given voter, that voter had power in that coalition; if the coalition would still win without a given voter, that voter lacked power. The diagram was laid out in order of simplicity with no voters in the first coalition and all voters in agreement for the last possibility for a total of 64 potential coalitions.

By counting the number of instances in which each voter has sway, the total power each voter has can be identified. As can be seen in the diagram, the only voters with the power to sway the measures are A, B, and C. The other voters, D, E, and F, though maintaining their own votes, lack the ability to sway any measure one way or another and are thus rendered impotent. D, E, and F are what game theorists call 'dummies' because they hold no voice in their given situation, even when they form a coalition among themselves. The power of each voter in the county is shown in the power index:

(A:32 , B:32 , C:32 , D:0 , E:0 , F:0)

FIG. 19—Power Index In Community Vote System.

A simpler example of this scenario can be laid out using three voters. Take for example the voting members of a college administration. The dean is given two votes, and both the faculty and student body have one vote each. In Banzhaf notation, assuming a majority is needed for a measure to pass, the problem looks like this:

3; 2, 1, 1

FIG. 20—Academic Vote Distribution.

Here, the number of coalitions possible is eight:

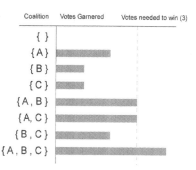

FIG. 21—Possible Coalitions In Academic Vote System.

In this example, it can be shown that, though the share of votes is divided in a 2-to-1 favor for the dean over the others, the dean actually holds a 3-to-1 advantage over the two other voters in terms of power, which is annotated (A:3, B:1, C:1).

The Banzhaf Power Index and similar tools have been used to identify imbalance in voting systems and, as in Banzhaf's case, to exact reform. In more complex systems, the imbalance is not quite as easily tabulated. For example, the United States Electoral College, which consists of 51 voters and 538 total votes, presents a significantly more complex problem with respect to the amount of computing needed to merely lay it out. Determining whether any one voter has more or less relative power has not even been possible until recent advances in computer technology have increased the capacity to run such enormous algorithms. For example, one technician who ran the data for the Electoral College found that there were 4.29 billion possible coalitions, a process that took a sophisticated computer more than twenty-four hours to run.

And yet, it is apparent that complex voting systems such as the U.S. Electoral College fall victim to the same kind of distortion. Witness the influence the biggest six or seven states have in every national election.

Once California, Texas, New York, Florida, Pennsylvania, Illinois, and Ohio have voted, the contest is practically decided. In the aughts, an outright victory could be secured with these and four other states—Michigan, Georgia, New Jersey, and North Carolina. The other thirty-nine states can be neglected completely.

One will find that this kind of power distribution works even when the system is not a confined electorate like that of the United States or Nassau County in New York, but that of an entire economy. The number of players is exponentially larger and the degree of variance is so great that it is practically impossible to determine the exact power that any given player maintains; but when the difference in wealth is substantial enough, even the economy as a whole can be distorted.

The key, as with voting systems, is to maintain a majority. As explained above, in a closed economy the goal is not to attain any particular amount of monetary wealth, but to attain a relative advantage. The bigger the relative disparity, the greater the power differential. And so, with the premise that an imbalance of command can lead to disproportionate power, we can see that even in a system as intricate as the modern economy—indeed, especially in a system as intricate—the imbalance can lead to disproportionate power distribution.

In striking illustration, a contemporary theorist has endeavored to illustrate the U.S. income distribution as a series of stacks of $100 bills across a football field. Taking for granted the width of the dollar bills was not accounted for—only the height of the stack was represented—the graph showed what appeared to be an 'L'-shaped curve, with the lowest income earners at one end and the highest at the other. The diagram is represented in Figure 22.

The U.S. population is drawn out person-by-person across the length of the football field in order of each individual's income. On the left, the income is essentially zero, and on the right, the income is hundreds of millions of dollars or more (the actual number is not specified since the income of the wealthiest Americans fluctuates with the market). The

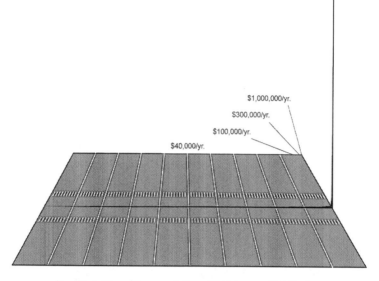

 is the figure described below:

FIG. 22—L-Curve Representation of U.S. Income Distribution.

median U.S. family income is represented at the 50-yard line by a stack of $100 bills about 1.6 inches high equaling about $40,000.

Five yards from the goal line, we find a family that earns about $100,000 per year, which is represented by a stack of $100 bills about 4 inches high. One yard from the goal line, we find a family that earns about $300,000 per year, which is represented by a stack of $100 bills about a foot high. One foot from the goal line, the income is at $1 million, represented by a stack of $100 bills about 40 inches high.

In a good year, the wealthiest Americans can make upwards of $1 billion or more in capital gains. In that case, the high end of the curve would reach about one kilometer high in relation to the football field (since $1 million = 40 inches and 40 inches = about 1 meter; $1 billion = $1 million x 1,000 and 1 meter x 1,000 = 1 kilometer). To offer some perspective as to the magnitude of this amount of money, the graph can be expanded to show the L-curve at 1 kilometer.

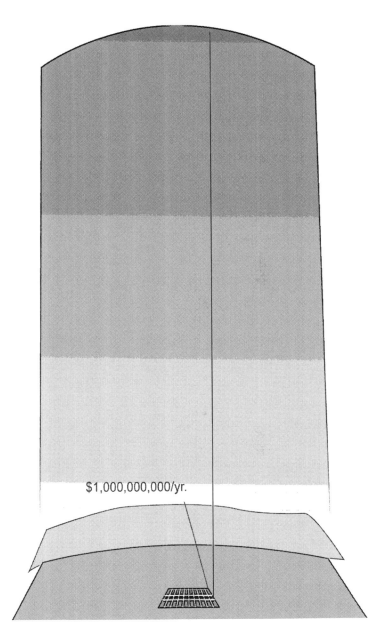

$1,000,000,000/yr.

Fɪɢ. 23—L-Curve at One Kilometer.

The designer of this illustration extended his graph to literally astronomical heights when he speculated the income of the absolute wealthiest Americans such as Bill Gates, who is believed to have seen his wealth increase $50 billion in one year at the height of the dot-com bubble. The graph would show the height of Bill Gates' income represented by a stack of $100 bills surpassing Mt. Everest some five times over (50 kilometers into the sky).

The exercise is of course purely theoretical and can only be accepted as a general understanding of the distribution of income. Any scientific employment of the application can only be made with significant qualifications. For example, the dimensions of the diagram are designed to reflect the disparity between the rich and the poor, but they have been set arbitrarily and so do not offer a precise glimpse at real wealth for either group. The different heights of various stacks of $100 bills might give us an idea of the disparity, but there is no accounting for the goods and services available at such levels. And again, the graph sets no width for each household on the horizontal axis. As such, it arbitrarily fits everyone into a football field, when the number of households represented is more than 100 million. As it is, the 'L' is more striking, but it underrepresents the total distributed power of the lower income bracket. One hundred million households earning $50,000 per year is $5 trillion—a substantial source of wealth by any standard.

Still, the graph does show how disproportionate income is in America and gives us an idea of the kind of imbalance of economic power that exists. To show the distribution in a more familiar form, we can use the statistics gathered on household wealth by the Federal Reserve Board in the 2004 Survey of Consumer Finances. There, we see that the top percentile of Americans hold some 34.3% of the entire wealth of the country. That means that alone, the top 1% of the country's population possesses more than a third of the total wealth. Expanding it to the top 5%, we find that the number is more than half the entire wealth at 58.9%. The diagram below shows the imbalance of wealth as a whole.

Percent of Population	Percent of Wealth	Cumulative Wealth
1	34.3	34.3
2-5	24.6	58.9
6-10	12.3	71.2
11-20	13.4	84.7
21-40	11.3	96
41-60	3.8	99.8
61-100	0.2	100

FIG. 24—U.S. Wealth Distribution.

While the power held by the wealthy does not equal the same kind of advantage held by the populace in weighted voting systems, comparisons can be made for the sake of perspective. If, for example, we were to integrate the distribution of American wealth into the Banzhaf Power Index format, using the Nassau County allotment of six voters, the disparity between the top and the bottom would become that much clearer.

Converting the distribution of U.S. wealth into six sections based on average income for the given sectors of the population, we find that the distribution of wealth looks far more disproportionate than that represented in other voting systems, as the top wage earners in America maintain a dominating 5-to-1 advantage over the next highest player and more than a 25-to-1 advantage over the lowest ranking player. Laying out the scenario in Banzhaf notation with a majority needed to sway the vote would look like this:

19; 25, 5, 3, 2, 1, 1

FIG. 25—U.S. Wealth Distribution and
Power Index in Banzhaf Notation.

As we can plainly see, only the top voter holds the ability to influence a given measure, and thus he maintains what is more or less a monopoly of power. Even if all the other players formed a coalition, it wouldn't be strong enough to counteract the vote of the top player.

Naturally, the wealthiest Americans do not all work together and vote the same way, as the illustration suggests. Again, this exercise is only for general perspective. Still, it can be said that the wealthiest Americans do all work toward a similar aim—the accumulation and monopolization of wealth. Even if we were to divide the number of votes into individual households, the data would show the same kind of disparity. With the estimate that total U.S. household wealth equals $50 trillion, and considering that there are about 100 million households therein, we can say that the median household has one vote (about $50,000 net worth) and the top household has around one million votes (about $50 billion net worth).

A monopoly of money in the truest sense (= 'one seller') is impossible. If any one party held a true monopoly of a given currency, it would cease to be useful as money and an alternative would crop up to take its place. As we have seen, money is only useful if a large contingent of people agree that it is to be used as money and employ it as such. At the same time, a quasi-monopoly of money is possible, where a relative few control the majority of the currency. This is exactly what we have seen over the course of the twentieth century and still see today in America and throughout the West. We have also seen that such a quasi-monopoly can and will act as a true monopoly in the power it wields under the right circumstances. Given the disproportionate strength that any advantage can offer, those players with the advantages can control the game as if they held a true monopoly.

Anatomy of Monopoly

The concept of a monopoly is best seen in the story of John D. Rockefeller's Standard Oil Company. The historic corporation was and, it could be argued, still is one of the greatest private companies in the history of the world. By the same token, and in large part because of its dominant place in the market, it is also one of the most reviled companies to have ever conducted a trade. With a brief survey, the objective spectator can see just why the names Rockefeller and Standard Oil have become synonymous with both masterful business practices and detestable corruption—the quintessential monopoly.

By 1860, the petroleum industry had become rather lucrative. Not only did the resource possess highly useful qualities that made it ideal for lubrication, illumination, medication, and fuel, so too had E. L. Drake's artesian well made large-scale oil extraction a relatively safe and reliable procedure. With a promising upstart refinery based in Cleveland, Rockefeller, alongside his brother and a number of other partners, set out to seize the potential in this latent business.

Rockefeller, the real engine behind the business, led Standard Oil like all great industrialists of the age—with a congenital knack for hard work, saving, and deal-making. Proof can be found in nearly every move he made. Instead of investing in the saturated drilling market, Rockefeller focused on refining and distribution. This allowed him to carve out a place in a fertile market and grow his business as other drilling companies competed with one another. Similarly, Rockefeller sought to make full use of the dynamic resource. While kerosene was petroleum's primary salable good, Rockefeller sought to make use of the elements that other petroleum companies wasted. He used extra oil to fuel and lubricate his machines and founded a company to sell a synthetic beeswax, Vaseline, using a byproduct of the refining process. Every aspect of the business was attended to and streamlined to ensure the greatest return. When the company saw profit enough to expand, Rockefeller and his associates did so with gusto, buying up competition, keeping the companies that had been organized efficiently, and dismantling the less well-organized firms. Standard Oil was, in short, a model of the distribution of labor and economies of scale.

But only when the company had grown to dominate a large portion of the market did Rockefeller's business acumen come to true fruition. Once the business was a sufficient size, the born strategist was able to use that size to grow even further. Rockefeller had two main instruments in his arsenal, which both made use of Standard's high volume of sales. First, since the company was so large, it could guarantee a consistent flow of shipments via railroads and so could make use of its extra leverage in negotiating contracts. In a prototypical deal with Lake Shore Railroad in 1868, Standard Oil agreed to ship a certain amount of petroleum, ensuring the railroad consistent business, in exchange for a large discount on that shipping (an astounding 71% off the normal price). Whereas other oil companies had to pay regular prices on their irregular consignments, Standard Oil could ship for practically nothing. Turning the savings around to his customers, Rockefeller could reduce his prices and so guarantee more sales. In this way, Rockefeller was able to use the size of his company to gain leverage in the market and ultimately grow his business.

Likewise, Rockefeller was also able to use his high volume to drive prices further down and oust smaller competitors from the market. If there was a market controlled by some other oil company, Rockefeller would introduce Standard's products at prices far below the going rate, sometimes at a loss to Standard Oil. Sales would flow over to Standard Oil, and the smaller competitors would be starved of business. They would eventually be unable to compete and would leave the market. The larger and more dominant that Standard became, the better equipped it was to handle short-term losses, and so the more power it could wield in driving out competition.

As a part of his strategy to crowd out competitors, Rockefeller was known to make tactical purchases and investments that left his rivals without the means to conduct their business. At the height of Standard's growth, the company reserved unused train cars so that other refiners could not ship their products. At times, Rockefeller bought up all available chemicals and barrels to prevent competitors from processing the raw resources and storing their goods. Standard was able to make such purchases because it had already amassed a great deal of capital. Even if the company was unable to use the excess material, it would profit from being able to dictate its own prices without the threat of competition.

Standard Oil's sway in the industry was so dominant that, in 1890, it was estimated to control some 90% of the market—this, even before locomotive power and the automobile became essential components of the American way of life. The more powerful Standard became, the more the railroads and consumers depended on the behemoth. It came to a point where the railroads were willing to aid in Rockefeller's strategy just so that they could continue to receive his business. One report tells of a Standard Oil competitor that attempted to ship its oil underground across one railroad's property, and, by Rockefeller's request, was prohibited from building an underground connection. In order to transport its oil, then, the company was forced to bring the shipment up to the railroad property, transport the oil to individual containers to cross the rail, and then reassemble the cargo on the other side to continue the delivery. When Rockefeller heard about this, he urged the railroad to block the line with unused cars and thus disable all possible transport at the junction.

One can see how rival companies could easily grow frustrated and vengeful at such practices. It is no wonder, for instance, that the impetus behind Ida M. Tarbell's exposé on Standard Oil lay in the very fact that her father had been an oil man who was beaten by Rockefeller's cunning, just like so many others. Standard Oil was the most powerful petroleum company in the country, and it successfully used that power to hold down others and gain more control.

When state officials began to learn of the company's anti-competitive practices, they put laws in place aimed at breaking the monopoly up. Yet Standard Oil devised ways of maintaining its lofty position. When, for instance, Ohio changed its rules to keep companies from doing business in other states, Standard Oil simply separated its Ohio branch and controlled it from a new headquarters in New York. To better disburse their holdings, Rockefeller and his associates invented the business model of a trust, which appeared to comprise many disparate companies with their own stockholders but was in reality a single company in which all stock was conveyed to a small group of directors 'in trust'. The concept was quickly adopted by many large firms and became the bugbear of populists throughout the 1890s and 1900s.

Eventually, officials turned to the federal government and the Sherman Antitrust Act in an effort to bring down the great company. And, to some degree, the break-up that resulted was a success. In 1911, the Supreme Court ordered Standard Oil to separate into 34 different companies with their own directors, essentially ending the dominant monopoly. Of course, when one traces the mergers and acquisitions of the 'baby Standard' companies throughout the twentieth century, it is clear that the Rockefeller legacy lives on. Just as surely as John D. bought up competition to control some 90% of the market, so too have the various splinter companies merged to create one dominant firm, Exxon Mobil, which is no less a monopoly than the Standard Oil Company was in 1911.

In the twenty-first century, it seems as though the large, monopolistic corporation is the natural destination for all good businesses. By use of the same strategies employed by Rockefeller and Standard Oil, all companies seek to expand, acquire, push out, and dominate the market so that they alone control it, or do so with a few others as in an oligopoly. Whether one considers Walmart, Microsoft, Apple, Starbucks, the phone companies, grocery stores, or other outlets, one can see how the framework in the modern economy supports and perhaps compels monopolistic expansion. If a company does not grow large enough to control and consume other companies, it cannot compete and will therefore become prey to those other companies. The pattern is recognizable in all large corporations— buy up competition, dismantle inefficient portions, maintain efficient ones, lower prices, make deals with distributors, and crowd out rivals.

If there is a modern version of Standard Oil, it might well be found in the expansive retail chain Walmart. Similarly despised in a modern, insouciant way, Walmart has followed a comparable business model and dominated the retail market just like Standard dominated the oil market a century ago. Everyone knows the story—Walmart executives identify a virgin market and introduce a new store; with highly efficient distribution and a warehouse-style inventory system, the branch offers a wide variety of goods at bargain prices. Without similar leverage, local mom-and-pop stores are forced to go out of business, thus leaving Walmart the only retailer in a given region.

As we have seen, a true monopoly in the sense of one seller is practically impossible these days. Walmart and the others are considered monopolies, not because they are technically the sole sellers, but because they hold large enough market shares to influence the flow of money. The effect is the same. If a company is so dominant that it becomes unprofitable for a competitor to enter the market, it is thought that the leader holds a monopoly in that market. Interestingly, the same charges have been made against Amazon and other large Internet retailers for running local independents out of business. The way the market is viewed, there could be no limit to the number of monopolies out there.

The fact that it is unprofitable for a competitor to enter the market means that the so-called monopoly is conducting business so efficiently that no one else can do it better. Walmart can control the market as it does because no other retail outlet can offer prices that are as low, plain and simple. Essentially, that is the end goal of modern economics—to produce and make available products at the most efficient rate to offer the customer the best products at the lowest prices. The economies of scale provided by large corporations make such low prices and high standards of living possible. In a way, Walmart, Exxon Mobil, Amazon, Microsoft, Apple, Starbucks, and others are the ultimate fulfillment of Adam Smith's vision.

The Hands of a Few Men

The kind of monopoly and consolidation of wealth we see these days has been the norm since the turn of the twentieth century. Just as Frederick

Jackson Turner had predicted in 1903, the companies that made up the railroad, shipping, steel, and refining industries were all reduced to a handful of conglomerates˚. By merger, formation of trusts, or mere competitive attrition, the major companies in the United States had dwindled in number and exploded in scope. The kind of wealth amassed by the great nineteenth-century industrialists—Rockefeller, Carnegie, Vanderbilt, Astor, and the others—alone attests to the kind of consolidation taking place.

A recent estimation found that between the years 1897 and 1904, some 4,227 American companies fused into 257 conglomerates. The same study found that by 1904 some 318 trusts had gained control of nearly 40% of the nation's manufacturing assets. In rapid succession, it would seem, the wealth of the nation was being concentrated into a very select corner of the economy. The process was perhaps best seen in the banking industry, in which the formation of trusts had become a science. In his scathing attack on monopolistic power, *Other People's Money*, future Supreme Court Justice Louis Brandeis showed that the bankers of the early twentieth century, such as the great J. P. Morgan, had interests in a wide assortment of industrial companies, often sitting on the board of directors for many of them and, in effect, consolidating all of the various industries into one.

At the height of the so-called 'Money Trust' prior to World War I, congressional investigator Samuel Untermeyer estimated that J. P. Morgan and his partners were directors, trustees, and shareholders of corporations that were capitalized at around $30 billion, which was roughly 40% of all industrial, commercial, and financial capital in the United States at the time. Today's equivalent would be around $7.5 trillion, or nearly four times the value of the financier's namesake, JPMorgan Chase & Co., which held assets of around $2 trillion in 2010.

It was with this emergent threat of monopoly in mind that John Maynard Keynes later grew so critical of excessive saving, which he defined as holding onto an amount of money that exceeds what is needed for planned investment. Whenever someone saved beyond the amount needed to purchase a necessary good—food, clothes, a washing machine, a car, or a house, for instance—Keynes argued that it robbed the economy of its lifeblood. All the money that was stored in the vaults of some rich man's bank account was currency that was not being used in trade, investments, and employment. The ultimate result of saving was a loss of liquidity, a fall in effective demand, and a drop in overall production. By hoarding money, the rich harmed the economy, turning growth into recessions and even turning recessions into depressions.

Keynes' analysis gave formal backing to a growing concern that, in the United States, industry and wealth had become far too consolidated for the good of the nation. As governor of New York in 1911, the soon-to-be president Woodrow Wilson declared, "The great monopoly in this country is the money monopoly. So long as that exists, our old variety and freedom and individual energy of development are out of the question." Wilson's speech came at the crest of a wave of fervor to do something about the recurrent bank crises and the increasing power of a very few investment bankers on Wall Street.

Like Keynes after him, Wilson realized that the highly interdependent economy brought about by 400 years of development hinged on its flow of money. Modern industry needed capital, and capital, as he and a number of others were beginning to make known, was largely being absorbed by a relative few. "The growth of our nation," he said, "and all of our activities are in the hands of a few men, who, even if their actions be honest and intended for the public interest, are necessarily concentrated upon the great undertakings in which their own money is involved and who, necessarily, by every reason of their own limitations, chill and check and destroy genuine economic freedom." To be sure, as Wilson would have said, the monopolization of wealth by the very rich hindered the economic freedom of everyone else and was a liability rather than a boon to prosperity.

6. EXPLOITATION

THE CONCERN THAT WOODROW WILSON, Louis Brandeis, and others had about the supposed monopolies was clear: With the kind of power that the very rich wielded, they could influence a great portion of the economy and thus sway the economic decisions of the populace. Their economic power eclipsed everyone else's political power and rendered Capitalism vulnerable to corruption and exploitation. With their effective money monopolies, they could more or less do anything they wanted, especially when it came at the expense of others.

This condition was a radical departure from that which the West had grown accustomed to. From the time of the Spanish Scholastics, individuals, families, and groups had gotten used to the freedom of choice, whether it came in the form of their residence, their religion, or even their Saturday night feast. No one person, business, or king could tell them what to do. As a result, an aspiring businessman, company, or nation could only profit from others if those others profited as well. Capitalism worked because success was mutually inclusive. As in Adam Smith's Invisible Hand, the natural drive to improve one's own lot led directly and conclusively to helping others and improving their lots as well.

In a closed system, this foundation is undermined. When one cannot supply his own necessary goods, he is reliant on others and so places his livelihood and well-being at least to some extent in their hands. Without the freedom of choice, one is forced to accept anything that is offered, whether it is good or bad, useful or not. Of course, in a big enough economy, choices may seem plentiful, but they will always lack the only real choice that can truly provide fair trade—the choice to say 'No' to the system altogether and be completely self-sufficient.

And so it remains up to those in power—the owners, the possessors of the means of production—to dictate what the workers and consumers get and for how much. They might offer beneficial and useful goods, but, then again, they may not. Indeed, there is added incentive to push bad products because of the competitive spirit inherent in an interdependent society. Interdependency between people naturally brings about a higher demand for the means of exchange, and money thus becomes the central aim in all economic transactions. As such, wealth is objective and competition is inevitable. Since all are striving for the same end, the only way one can succeed is by making others fail, and, ultimately, the pursuit of wealth becomes an effort to undermine the pursuits of others.

> A power over a man's subsistence amounts to a power over his will.
>
> —ALEXANDER HAMILTON, "FEDERALIST No. 79" (1788)

> Independence of mind or strength of character is rarely found among those who cannot be confident that they will make their way by their own effort.
>
> —FRIEDRICH A. HAYEK, THE ROAD TO SERFDOM (1944)

> Necessitous men are not free men.
>
> —FRANKLIN D. ROOSEVELT, 1944 STATE OF THE UNION ADDRESS

Here we see the reverse of the Invisible Hand. Whereas it used to be that the natural drive to improve one's lot led to helping others, in a competitive situation, the natural drive to improve one's lot leads directly and conclusively to harming others and preventing them from improving their own lots. The result is not free trade, as it is in a truly capitalist economy, but rather manipulation and control; not cooperation and harmony, but exploitation. In a closed economy, it is the only recourse.

This is to say that a market system in a closed economy is not really a market system at all. Without the free choice of individuals, the economy cannot be one of Capitalism, but rather what might be called 'Vulgar Capitalism', or an economy which appears to be made of men negotiating and making free trades with one another but which is in reality made up of a strict hierarchy of masters over servants, as it was in feudal times.

Like Marx's concept of Vulgar Economics, Vulgar Capitalism can be said to focus merely on the superficial aspects of the system—that which is seen and not that which is unseen. This is why so many mistake this bastard version of Capitalism for its legitimate parent. At the turn of the twentieth century, Westerners enjoyed perhaps the highest level of political freedom that any people in the history of the world had ever enjoyed. And yet at the same time, due to a closing frontier, they were slowly assuming the shackles of an invisible and devastating confinement that promised to plunge them into the deepest nadir of slavery that any people had ever endured.

Workers were of course free to take this or that job, and consumers were free to buy this or that product, and indeed they were free to not work or to refrain from buying any products at all; but, as Belloc said, these free contracts were leonine in nature. Workers and consumers were like hyenas or antelopes in the economic jungle, supposedly equipped with their own motives and actions yet well under the control of the king of the domain. True, they could negotiate with the lord, but if they failed to come to terms, they would face starvation or even death—no real alternative at all. And so they were compelled to come to terms no matter how degrading or deflating those terms were.

Plan of the Man

The premise behind exploitation is simple, and not as malicious as it is commonly understood to be. The word 'exploit' means 'to take advantage of'—not 'maliciously harm' but simply 'make use of'. It just so happens that some are in a position to make use of others in a way that profits the former and harms the latter, and so it seems malicious.

This situation arises in society when a relative few people own the large majority of the wealth and thus control the means of production. Since everyone needs the means of production for sustenance, the dispossessed masses must rely on the relative few. Given such an advantage, the owners of the means of production are at leisure to demand whatever they want in exchange for sustenance, whether it is considered a fair amount or not and, in the end, it is up to them. In Pareto's Law, it is a natural occurrence throughout history that reliably 20% of the population owns 80% of the wealth. At the same time, a relative many (80% of the population) lack wealth (owning a mere 20%) and thus lack the means of production. Since 100% of the population needs sustenance, the few are in a position to exploit the many.

As the owners dictate the terms, all contracts will be designed in their favor. Belloc explained the phenomenon as a necessary inference "that there will be under Capitalism a conscious, direct, and planned exploitation of the majority, the free citizens who do not own by the minority who are owners. For wealth must be produced: the whole of that community must live: and the possessors can make such terms with the non-possessors as shall make it certain that a portion of what the non-possessors have pro-duced shall go to the possessors°."

Exploitation occurs in one general way—owners raise the prices on the goods that the dispossessed consumers and workers need. This single method manifests into two different kinds of exploitation depending on the kind of relationship between the owner and dispossessed. When the owner is a seller of goods, exploitation takes the form of higher prices—the consumer is exploited by the seller by having to pay more for necessary goods than they are worth. When the owner is an employer, on the other hand, exploitation takes the form of lower wages—the laborer is exploited by the businessman by having to accept lower pay than his work is worth. Viewed together, they are the same kind of manipulation as both feature a party compelled to give more than he receives and another party who is willing to take more than he gives in a particular exchange.

We recognize the second form of exploitation more readily perhaps because it is more striking than the first. A seller who exploits his customers might rip them off by a few dollars here and there, which can be easily overlooked in a busy economy. Meanwhile, an owner who exploits his worker might swindle thousands of dollars in wages. Likewise, the consumer might be better equipped to negotiate with the monopolistic company since he is only dealing with one product, which he is more likely to find elsewhere or for some time do without. On the other hand, the worker and his family rely almost entirely on his salary for their well-being, have a much lower chance of finding it elsewhere, and cannot do without it in the least.

This is not to say that exploitation in the form of exorbitant prices does not occur in the modern economy, just that it is less noticeable and less capable of sparking indignation. However, in some cases price exploitation garners attention to a much more widespread degree than wage exploitation. The price of gas is perhaps the most prominent instance of exploitative selling because it is such a fundamental component of the daily lives of all Westerners, and because the oil companies earn such high profits from their sales.

But the price of gas is not the only instance of exploitative prices. Cell phone services, cable services, banking and investment services, and, as some would have it, the price of coffee are all exploitative of their customers, costing up to 10 or 20 times what the product could be bought for in another venue or at another time. Since the customer is unwilling or unable to search for alternatives, much less to compare values, he will agree to the exorbitant expenses.

With many of these services, the customer realizes that the base rate—the rate he agrees to pay when signing up—is just the start of the outlay, and subsequent charges, fees, and add-ons amount to as much if not more than the original figure. Phone service, for instance, might cost $35 a month, but by the time the necessary add-ons of text messaging, voice mail, picture mail, Internet, and e-mail are included, the monthly bill might reach upward of $100. The sense is that the customer is getting 'nickle-and-dimed', charged for little things here and there, that all add up in the end.

In a consumerist economy, rising prices are easily recognizable and heavily frowned upon. For this reason, companies will try their best to keep prices minimal and steady. When companies exploit their customers, then, they usually do so by putting out shoddy products or by diluting their goods with lower-quality, higher-yielding materials rather than by raising prices. Dilution can be passed over without notice, but rising prices won't go unnoticed by any economically conscious consumer. Significant examples are found throughout the food industry in the replacement of high-quality, natural ingredients with artificial, processed substitutes: butter for easy-to-make and cost-effective vegetable shortening or margarine, sugar for corn syrup, and salt for monosodium glutamate, among others. It is no coincidence that the use of these additives and preservatives saw a sharp increase in the decades around 1900 to the extent that, in the early twentieth century, they were found in every corner of the Western diet.

Ever since the turn of the century, the strategy has been to cut corners, sneak poor quality goods by the customer, and reduce the frills. When customers are habituated to certain patterns, this kind of exploitation is easily employed. While the price remains the same, the cost of producing and selling the goods falls, and so the company can turn small changes in their product into large profits.

By and large, however, the most hated companies in the world have attained their distinction, not because they exploit their customers with high prices or inferior products, but because they exploit their workers with low wages. Indeed, the Standard Oils of the past and Walmarts of today are known for giving customers the best deals in the business by selling reliable products at bargain basement prices. Their exploitation is said to come in the form of paying their workers low wages, withholding benefits, and skewing schedules to limit profitable work strategies.

It is here that we find the standard concept of exploitation made popular by Marx: The workers are the ones actually producing the goods, but since they have no means of production, they can only work under the terms of those who do—the owners. Recognizing this, the owners arrange contracts that oblige laborers to work longer than their pay compensates. While the workers' pay is equivalent to the output of, say, five hours of labor, they agree to work for twelve hours. All output created beyond five hours of work is 'surplus value' collected by the owners at the expense of the workers.

In most cases, it is the relentless pursuit of efficiency and low costs that drives major corporations to exploit their workers to greater degrees and to seek out new, cheaper sources of labor. Around the turn of the twentieth century, it became a prevalent strategy for manufacturing companies to employ immigrant workers, women, and even children to do the work that established American men would charge much more to do. In order to get the most of the workers, companies were said to thrust their employees onto assembly lines with little or no training, keep them for twelve, four-

All methods for the production of surplus value are at the same time methods of accumulation; and every extension of accumulation becomes again a means for the development of these methods. It follows therefore that in proportion as capital accumulates, the lot of the labourer, be his payment high or low, must grow worse. Accumulation of wealth at one pole is, therefore, at the same time, accumulation of misery, agony of toil, slavery, ignorance, brutality, mental degradation, at the opposite pole. i.e., on the side of the class that produces its own product in the form of capital.

—KARL MARX, *Das Kapital* (1867)

teen, and even sixteen-hour shifts, and, according to some reports, lock them in their work stations to ensure focus.

Skeptics need not look beyond the muckraking journalism of the turn of the century to glimpse the sort of inhuman conditions that the working poor endured. Jacob Riis' 1890 photo essay titled *How the Other Half Lives* featured a series of images detailing conditions of New York's immigrant workers. One glimpse tells the story: cramped quarters with five or six dirtied men and women, piled in between makeshift beds and dressers, their clothes tattered and their belongings stacked in ratty boxes like trash receptacles. The stark indigence was nearly impossible to believe, much less accept, and yet there it was. In a similar fashion, Upton Sinclair brought to light equally disturbing conditions in Chicago with his 1906 novel *The Jungle*, which fictionalized extensive abuses and unsanitary practices in the city's meatpacking industry. Throughout the West, it seemed, the story was the same of innocent persons living in the worst squalor imaginable.

Despite President Roosevelt's shrugging off such commentary as fantastic, concerned spectators knew that these dismal circumstances were real enough and that they harmed the well-being of everyone involved. A 1911 fire at the Triangle Shirtwaist Factory in New York City validated the fear in tragic fashion. One hundred forty-six of the five hundred workers died in the disaster, mostly because of inadequate fire prevention mechanisms; overcrowded quarters, elevators, and fire escapes; and inexperienced, panicky workers. Some of the seamstresses were only thirteen years old. When the owners of the factory were brought to trial for manslaughter, they were found not guilty.

While regulations, union efforts, and better technology put pressure on businesses to improve working conditions throughout the twentieth century, the parallel rise in the cost of labor forced companies to search for cheap labor abroad. The result was the extensive colonization of undeveloped countries and subsequent utilization of foreign labor forces. In a pattern similar to the European colonialism of the sixteenth and seventeenth centuries, Western nations again expanded into all corners of the globe, bringing their industry and business practices with them. The upshot was the same kind of exploitation experienced domestically, just with an international flair. The kind of conditions seen in New York, Chicago, and San Francisco were reproduced en masse across Southeast Asia, China, India, Central and South America, and Africa. Without considerable economic growth in these countries, and restrictive local governments, the disparity in wealth has remained rather consistent in the undeveloped nations and has thus provided Western companies a steady source of cheap labor.

Even today we still hear reports of sweatshops and so-called 'slave labor' being perpetrated in Southeast Asian countries, largely by apparel companies. The businesses that benefit from such exploitation are regularly vilified but rarely prosecuted. To eliminate the companies guilty of such practices would be to eliminate all the great manufacturers and retailers in the modern economy—Nike, Coca-Cola, Calvin Klein, Jones Apparel, American Apparel, American Eagle, Liz Claiborne, OshKosh B'gosh, Sears, Tommy Hilfiger, Gap, Levi Strauss, Carrefour, Dickies, Disney, Guess, Hanes, Speedo, Toys 'R' Us, and, of course, Walmart. All have used cheap foreign labor to some extent, and all have been able to convert their products into high-value retail goods at home.

The Blight of Nature

There is another form of exploitation that is quite unlike either raising prices or reducing wages, though it is yet another situation in which the owner gets more than he deserves while everyone else gets less. This form of exploitation is the tendency for powerful businessmen and companies to recklessly use up natural resources and pollute the environment.

With the rise of machine industry in the nineteenth century, pollution in the form of fossil fuel emissions and chemical contamination became a major concern for communities throughout the West. By 1900, it was clear that the new manufacturing practices came with many disagreeable aspects. In an effort to produce mechanical goods and new, synthetic products, manufacturers were obliged to burn great amounts of wood, coal, and petroleum, to output large amounts of waste, and to deal with many unfamiliar chemicals with questionable byproducts that proved harmful to the health of workers, consumers, and bystanders alike.

Indeed, pollution and environmental damage could well be the most maddening kind of exploitation because it can affect many more people than either high prices or low wages—even if they are displaced from the production and sale of the goods or completely unrelated to it. The sense of injustice is multiplied when the victim can assume little or no liability.

Audience reaction to Sinclair's *Jungle* reflects this inclination. Readers were most unsettled not by the harsh labor conditions that the immigrant workers suffered through, but rather by the unsanitary conditions and the threat of contamination inherent under those circumstances. They were appalled not by the hardships that Jurgis and his family went through but by the thought that their own food supply could be affected by the same dirty practices as in the book. As the author put it, "I aimed for the people's hearts and hit them in the stomach."

Monopolistic owners can get away with pollution and environmental damage for the same reason that they can dictate the terms of labor contracts and the price of goods. In short, there is no alternative, so the people are forced to accept whatever the towering corporations will give. Just as with the Banzhaf town council example, in which the larger towns could do whatever they pleased even if it came at the expense of the smaller towns, an effective monopoly could allow wealthy industrialists to build a power plant in a poor area, let the pollution spew into the surrounding environment, and escape to some far-off haven miles away from the contamination.

The large-scale use of chemicals in farming is one of the best known and, at the same time, least disputed practices in the modern economy. The powerful synthetic pesticide DDT was introduced during World War II to kill malaria and typhus-transmitting mosquitoes in areas around military and civilian quarters. Its success led directly to its use in agriculture after the war, but it was not until 1962, with the publication of Rachel Carson's *Silent Spring*, that the public grew aware of the pesticide's potential toxicity in larger animals and humans. In the book, Carson raised the question of indiscriminating use of chemicals when their effects, both short term and long, were not readily known. She noticed that animal life in her neighborhood, most notably songbirds, had diminished with the increased use of the pesticide. Later studies found that the chemical could last up to 30 years in the soil, disrupt the reproduction patterns of amphibians and birds, and prove moderately toxic to humans and other animals.

Though DDT has been banned, chemical companies continue to produce pesticides, farmers continue to use them to protect crops, and no one can be quite sure what effects they have on human health. This threat extends into nearly all corners of modern industrial life. Everywhere in the modern economy, chemicals and compounds are used as preservatives, sealants, and thinners, and practically all are hazardous when humans are exposed to them in significant quantities. At one point in the early 1900s, it was sound practice to use the highly poisonous element lead in paint, automobile gasoline, and even baby food containers; by the mid-twentieth century, the highly toxic mineral asbestos was being used throughout North America for insulation, fire-retardant coatings, concrete, bricks, gaskets, drywall, roofing, and furniture. Only after fatal lessons did the public learn of the hazards in dealing with such substances.

Most readers will be familiar with the recent instance of contamination from Pacific Gas and Electric in California because of the movie based on the prominent litigator for the case Erin Brockovich. There, as in the Silent Spring, a chemical used in the maintenance of the company's equipment found its way into the groundwater and thus into the nearby community's drinking water. The case drew public attention, and the plaintiffs in the direct-action suit were awarded a record $333 million for the incident.

No one can be quite sure how harmful pesticides and other contaminants are or what levels can be found in the average American's food, water, and air supplies. Claims of illness, death, and an effect on the earth's overall climate rightly raise suspicion°. Sensational charges brought by global warming alarmists ought to be metered with a healthy dose of common sense. And yet there can be no doubt that the presence of pollution is unnatural and undesirable, and that, if one were given the choice, he would eradicate it altogether. Pollution in any form is abnormal, unclean, and repulsive to any human being with eyes to see, a nose to smell, and a tongue to taste. In 2010, the BP oil rig catastrophe has shown to what extent corporate dealings and unchecked industry can blight the natural world. Even if no human deaths result, the leak must be considered one of the greatest disasters in all of man's history for the unsightliness of oil-covered beaches alone.

Sympathy for the Devil

Now, it is easy to regard these kinds of exploitation as intentional malice committed by immoral or altogether evil people. It is a natural reaction to shudder at the obvious injustice of poverty amid plenty and to look for someone to blame. And, in even the most level-headed analyses, anyone seeking a culprit comes predictably to the owners, the capitalists, the bourgeois class as a whole—they must be the ones guilty in this matter since, after all, it is they who benefit from the injustice.

They frolic on their 40-acre estates with sprawling lawns and magnificent mansions while the rest of us struggle for room in broken-down tenement homes; they are rich enough to buy the highest quality goods on the market while the rest of us are forced to buy inferior and even harmful goods in order to economize; they spend their days on lush golf courses at country clubs free of pollutants while the rest of us trudge along beside sewers and smoke-emitting factories. Surely those capitalists, those millionaires on the hill, are guilty of this injustice. It has become a cliché to say that the rich are greedy, ruthless, and insatiable in their quest to exploit the working class, and that the poor are helpless, generous, and noble in their wretched, guiltless condition.

And certainly, there is validity in this conjecture. It is only reasonable to assume that, when one group takes advantage of another, the first group is to blame. No one will doubt that the exploiters have striven to achieve the great wealth that they possess. But it is another thing to suggest that because they have gained so much wealth they are in some way more greedy or ruthless than the next person, who has not gained as much wealth. There is no reason to assume that the successful capitalists are inherently more avaricious or less humane than anyone in the working class struggling to make ends meet. The successful people in this economy—the owners, the CEOs, the capitalists—are just like the average worker or consumer. They are human like the rest of us, with the same needs and wants as anyone else; they have just been in a better position to satisfy those needs and wants than the rest of us.

Like a star sportsman, the successful businessman is just better at the game than his fellow competitors. Peyton Manning, Alex Rodriguez, and Roger Federer strive to win just as much as some of their less successful opponents, and they want to defeat others no more than their adversaries want to defeat them. They simply play the game to the best of their ability, and it just so happens that the best of their ability is better than most others'. Their success, then, is no more a sign of their evil nature than the failure of others is a sign of the others' virtue. All parties are engaged in the same game, and using one's skills to get the better of another is just a part of it.

Similarly, one cannot admonish the investor who is able to buy a stock at a low price any more than he can scold the investor who sells it to him. Why should he be looked down upon for spotting a good investment and capitalizing on it just because someone else loses out by selling the stock at a low price? The first is surely gaining at the expense of the other and is perhaps even exploiting the other, but can he be faulted for it?

Doubtless, there is a contingent of owners, CEOs, and capitalists who have from the start set out to take advantage of others. Some perhaps even take satisfaction in their abuse of the lower classes. These exploiters certainly deserve the ire of the moralist and the political economist. Yet, to blame exploitation on the avarice and malevolence of a few people, as did Marx and a number of followers, is both insufficient and misleading. Avarice and malevolence have existed from time immemorial and everywhere around the world, though it can be determined that exploitation has been so ubiquitous. With an objective view, one can see that exploitation comes only when there is a competitive condition—when one scarce resource is sought by many, and a struggle ensues for the possession of that resource. The exploiters are no more culpable for the condition than are the exploited; all the players simply find themselves in the game as a matter of course. Ultimately, if a worker, businessman, or financier does not take advantage of others, he will certainly be taken advantage of by others, and so one cannot reproach those who take advantage first.

For this reason, exploitation cannot be blamed on evil people. Even when the exploitation degrades into criminal action, as with the trusts of the early twentieth century and most recently in the form of Enron, World-Com, Tyco, and Adelphia, it can be said that those involved are no more evil than the middle-class worker struggling to grow his 401k. Academic Michael C. Jensen's view is apt. With reference to the kind of corruption and exploitation witnessed with Enron and the others, he said, "This doesn't come about because of crooks. It wasn't as if the mafia had taken over corporate America. We are too quick to say, and the media feeds it, that if a bad thing happens, a bad person did it and that person had evil intentions. It is much more likely that there were some bad systems in place°." Everyone takes part in the great contest; it just so happens that the ones on top have the advantage over the ones below, and they make use of it.

This is to say that exploitation is the logical and even justifiable course of action for anyone in position to take advantage of others. The possessors, by nature and without any intentional cruelty toward the non-possessors, are simply playing the game as best they can. Just because they are in a position to play it better than everyone else doesn't change the fundamental reason in it.

Exploitation, as harsh as it might sound, is as natural as the lion's dominion over the zebras and antelope in the Serengeti and ought not to be regarded as some conspiracy of any particular class over another. In a competitive economy, all have the same end goal and all have incentive to exploit those who are in a position to be exploited. One could speculate that the majority of those non-possessors currently being exploited would administer the same exploitative practices on others if they were at some point to become possessors.

In the end, exploitation can be seen as a mere consequence of rational economic thinking, a truth that is shown throughout the history of business whether one considers Standard Oil, J. P. Morgan, Walmart, or Microsoft. All along, the story is one of sound business decisions being made from start to finish. When John D. Rockefeller engineered a deal with the railroads to get rebates on his transportation, it was good business; when J. P. Morgan used client funds to sway stock prices in his favor, it was good business; and when Walmart lowers its prices to oust smaller competitors, it is just good business. Nothing malevolent animates these decisions; they're just practical business sense. Michael Corleone's dictum in *The Godfather* rings true: "It's not personal, it's just business." And when exploitation is looked at as a sound business strategy, who can deny its validity?

Defending exploitation is no easy task, yet it is possible to show that exploitation is as a reasonable and rather understandable course of action. To take a basic example, regard the kind of choices a manufacturer has when the price of a necessary component of his production process rises. Assuming he is unable to find the part anywhere else for a lower cost, the manufacturer has a few options. First, he can keep his business unchanged and thus incur a loss to the extent of the increased costs. This would mean a lower profit and a lower income for the principle stakeholder—the owner himself.

Upon consideration, however, he realizes that there are ways around taking a loss and that these other options might be more economically sound. The manufacturer might well increase his prices to offset the higher cost, in which case the loss is redirected from the owner to the customers. Given a flexible market with few competitors, this might be an easy choice to make. Otherwise, if the manufacturer could not afford to charge more for his product—if, for example, he was in a crowded market in which competitors would encroach on his business—he could reduce expenses in other ways by organizing a more efficient plant, doing away with excess expenditures, reducing waste, and so on. More likely than not, this last option will include reducing labor costs, either by letting workers go, shortening their hours, or cutting their wages.

Of all his options, the first one—keeping his business the way it is—will have the most noticeable impact because it is the option that concerns the fewest people. A $100,000 cost would mean a $100,000 loss in profit and therefore a $100,000 loss in income. With the other options, the higher costs are distributed over several people, possibly thousands or millions depending on the size of the market. If the manufacturer sells a million units per month, he could offset a $100,000 cost by increasing the price of each unit by ten cents—a comparative bargain.

Likewise, if the manufacturer is forced to reorganize his factory expenses, the costs could also be dispersed. With 1,000 employees, the manufacturer could offset a $100,000 cost by reducing wages $100 each. This is certainly a burden for the employees, but it is a far cry from the $100,000 that the manufacturer would have to incur with the first option.

The situation might come down to a choice between taking a $100,000 loss or firing someone who makes $100,000. Any reasonable businessman would see this as an obvious choice. Unless the employee is so integral to the success of the company that his absence would mean a loss of $100,000 or more per year, the choice is already made.

It is wrong to suggest, as Marx did, that all profits gained by capitalists are unjust and that the only value added to a business comes from manipulated workers. This belief, stemmed from Marx's Labor Theory of Value, says that all of the value in a product, whether it is a rack of lamb, a kerosene lantern, or a Model T, comes from the labor put into it. According to

Marx, capitalist owners put no labor into these products, and so they add no value to them. All of their profit comes from exploitative surplus value.

But even the ardent communist must concede that capitalists provide something to the equation, if only by amassing and maintaining the capital goods that laborers use to perform their tasks. Production of every good or service in the modern economy depends upon a great mass of machines, buildings, and infrastructure necessary for output and distribution, and all of this requires large sums of capital, which the capitalist provides.

Upon reflection, the role that capitalists play these days is so much more far-reaching than the amount of work of any single laborer that it is ridiculous to suggest that the capitalists bring nothing to the equation. One might argue that the lion's share of work is accomplished in a modern company, not through the workers, but by the capitalist's materials, the machines, and the systems themselves—the business infrastructure. How can all profit be exploitation in a manufacturing plant comprised solely of machine robots as found in modern computer factories? The more complex a business becomes, the more capable and productive the infrastructure must be, and so the more integral the capitalist owner becomes.

Marx saw this, naturally, and reconciled the fact with the notion that all of the capitalist's machinery and tools are only valuable because of the labor that was put into them during their creation; and, again, the capital implements that helped to create those only obtained value by the labor put into them. According to Marx, the value of any such capital can be traced back to the labor put into it and therefore is not to be in any way credited to the capitalist.

But this is to neglect the sheer ability of capitalists to amass wealth in the first place, an ability that is by no means easy or simply the result of chance. Owners and executives also offer management and organization that is essential to the complex intricacies of modern businesses.

By whatever measure one uses, it must be said that the owners do provide some value to the end product and therefore do not derive their profits solely from exploitation. There is simply no clear way to gauge what percent of the profit is derived from the capitalist and what is derived from the laborers. Once the labor is mixed with the capital, the end product is wholly the outcome of both. Without one or the other, it would not exist.

Who is to say what percentage of a company's total profit should be allotted to an unskilled laborer, a salesman, or a CFO? And would fair terms mean that every unskilled laborer or executive is allotted the same wages or different based on productivity? In the nineteenth century, the growth of industry began to make the distribution of worth a very complicated task. Now, with value chains that extend well into dozens and even hundreds of levels, the practice is rather impossible.

A diligent mathematician might be obliged to dissect a given good or service to determine what percentage of its worth is provided by the capitalist and what is provided by each laborer; but in the end the effort would amount to a value judgment. And, in a closed society, the only value judgment that holds any weight is that of the owner, an advantage that, despite the exploitation that may arise, comes innocently from the arrangement of persons and property.

The Only Game In Town

The key in all exploitation is that the dispossessed, the exploited laborers and consumers, must all go along with the exploitation for it to work. Granted their hand is rather forced, yet they must still acquiesce for the owners to exploit them. It is as Loria, Pareto, and Belloc all claimed: The workers are the ones who actually do the labor, and the consumers who do the buying; and so they are the driving force of exploitation.

And, inasmuch as they are voluntarily taking part in the exploitation, their role is a motivated one. They see their work and their purchases as a way to get something they want—a paycheck, food on the table, an income with which to pay the rent. In pushing for the things they want, the working class serves as an engine of the trade as much as the upper class. One of the greatest secrets in all of modern economics is that the members of the proletariat all want money as much as, if not more than, the bourgeoisie. Since the proletariat's needs are more urgent, it could be argued that they want it more than the allegedly money-grubbing bourgeoisie do. Everyone is greedy in that they want money and see no limit to its use; the upper classes are just in a position to use that impulse to their benefit.

This fact calls to mind the Jacobins in the French Revolution, illustrated most expertly by Charles Dickens in *A Tale of Two Cities* with the character of Madame Defarge. As a member of the proletariat class, she views the bourgeoisie as evil and oppressive. Yet, when she gains power over them during the upheaval, she perpetrates just as much, if not more, evil and oppression as the hated aristos. In a closed system, everyone wants power and will use it to their benefit if given the opportunity.

In this light, we see how the possessors of the means of production can use the dispossessed to fuel their efforts. By offering what the proletariat want, capitalists can get the laborers to work hard and long hours, thus driving their machine of industry. The harder the proletariat work, the more money they get; but the more the capitalists profit off of them as well. In the

Question 10: In what way does the proletarian differ from the slave?

Answer: The slave is sold once and for all, the proletarian has to sell himself by the day and by the hour. The slave is the property of one master and for that very reason has a guaranteed subsistence, however wretched it may be. The proletarian is, so to speak, the slave of the entire bourgeois class, not of one master, and therefore has no guaranteed subsistence, since nobody buys his labour if he does not need it. The slave is accounted a thing and not a member of civil society. The proletarian is recognised as a person, as a member of civil society. The slave may, therefore, have a better subsistence than the proletarian but the latter stands at a higher stage of development. The slave frees himself by becoming a proletarian, abolishing from the totality of property relationships only the relationship of slavery. The proletarian can free himself only by abolishing property in general.

—FRIEDRICH ENGELS, *DRAFT OF A COMMUNIST CONFESSION OF FAITH* (1847)

closed economy, the worker can only benefit if the capitalist benefits more. So the harder the working class struggles to earn money to escape their condition, the more the capitalist profits and the more entrenched the workers become.

The open-eyed spectator might wonder why the working classes continue to struggle the way they do knowing that they are ultimately only making their superiors richer and thereby making their own lot more impossible to break free from. Thomas Malthus lamented the fact that the working classes found their escape in the pleasures of the bottle and the bed, which only seemed to multiply their numbers, thus making them poorer and giving the owners an even greater advantage over them. The answer rests in the motives inherent in the capitalist system. As Schumpeter pointed out in *Capitalism, Socialism, and Democracy*, the free market promises rewards so alluring that one cannot hope to resist it. Mansions, fine luxury cars, top-notch restaurants every night—everyone in sight of the spectacular prizes of the rich is willing to do everything it takes to meet the same end, even if they know that only a select few can be so rich and that their chances of being one of those few are slim to none. The prize remains in vulgar capitalist economies as much as it does in authentic capitalist economies. In Vulgar Capitalism, exploitation only drives up the rewards of success and therefore makes the prize that much more captivating.

And so the dispossessed workers and consumers are stuck in something of a trap. Like any red-blooded humans, they want to be rich and succeed in the world. But in order to increase his wealth, the worker or consumer must first increase the wealth of his employer, his landlord, or the seller. By doing this, the owner gains in relative wealth and leaves the worker or consumer essentially poorer. Though the worker or consumer makes money and adds goods to his collection, he loses in contrast to the very wealthy and so actually loses ground in the game. Like the basketball team that manages only to score a single basket for every two scored by its opponent, the impression of advance is overshadowed by the relative retrogression.

By the outset of the twentieth century, there was an overwhelming sense that everyone in the economy was engaged in a sort of zero-sum game, in which the gains of one would necessarily mean a loss for others. Like one enormous poker game, the economy was made up of individual players trying to outwit one another in the hope of outdoing or at least out-bluffing them. Competition was rife, and the best one could hope for was to take advantage of the next person before the next person took advantage of him. Amid this brutal competition, an increasing number were beginning to realize that not everyone had the same luck. The deck was stacked in the favor of a few while the rest were faced with nearly impossible odds.

Just like the hopeless gambler who cannot resist another bet, those with the cards stacked against them were not about to give up. On the contrary, a gambler is adamant in proportion to his losses, and the higher the stakes, the more tempting the wager. He continues to bet—double or nothing, double or nothing—and continues to lose. Each loss makes the next bet that much more necessary, and so he continues to sink into a deeper and deeper hole. Finally, if it is ever brought to an end and he is removed from the heat of the contest, he might realize the damage he has done. At that point, it is too late; he is finished.

Likewise, the worker is also motivated in his quest for redemption, constantly pushing for a lucky break or some sort of a winning streak. Even if he cannot find it, he continues to struggle, which benefits his employer more and thus leaves him in a deeper hole. Any loss in business or debt incurred only makes the next venture or the next investment that much more important. Gradually, he finds himself in a hole from which it is almost impossible to escape.

The ease of modern living is like an irresistible beacon. The people want cheap goods, comfortable living arrangements, high-tech electronics—everything that the modern economy makes so abundant. But in demanding these goods and services, the people necessarily entrench themselves further in a hole of bondage and servitude. The more they demand the easy life, the more ensconced they become in a life of toil; the harder they struggle to escape, the further they fall.

Former Treasury Secretary Donald Regan commented in 1988, after the stock market chaos of the previous year, that "The public has every reason to believe the present game is rigged. It is. Many would be better off in the casinos, since, there, people expect to lose but have a good meal and a good time while doing it." And yet, everyone seems to gravitate toward the market and high finance like moths to flame. The average worker or consumer is in a trap from which he cannot fathom escaping, and so he continues to feed it without let-up. He cannot help but to admit, like the hopeless gambler, that 'Everyone knows the game is rigged, but it's the only game in town.'

III
GOVERNMENT

1. THE GREAT SWITCH

As WE HAVE SEEN SO FAR in this study, the modern economy tends toward a system of interdependency, in which each individual is only able to satisfy his needs through cooperation with millions and perhaps billions of others. Unable to prosper or even survive on his own, the modern individual can only get the goods and services he needs from society, and, to do that, he needs to obtain and make use of society's agreed mechanism for exchange—money. With economic activity distilled down to money, the economy becomes a closed system in which that single commodity serves as the goal for everyone.

Given a single goal, the economy becomes strictly competitive, or what might be called a zero-sum game. Though various strategies for gaining wealth are employed independently, in all cases an economic player can only gain if someone else loses. This competition gives incentive for the monopolization of wealth and ultimately the exploitation of those who lack it. As we have seen, the free market system that gives rise to higher productivity and standards of living tends toward the very interdependency that brings forth hegemony and control.

The capitalist system was built on the idea of self-rule. From the discovery of the New World on, the thought was that granting people political freedom to pursue wealth as they pleased would lead to an abundance of economic wealth and an ever-increasing quality of life for everyone. At the turn of the twentieth century, however, it was becoming abundantly clear that this laissez-faire thinking had led to unforeseen consequences. By World War I, a new form of aristocracy had taken hold of society and could control it with as much or more effectiveness than the old princes had. The members of this financial oligarchy, as Louis Brandeis called it, did not necessarily break the rules to attain their status; indeed, for the most part everything they did was legal, and the vast majority of the men involved were reputable members of the community. But the power they wielded was so extreme as to threaten the very concept of equal rights.

America had arrived, so it seemed, at a new age where political freedom could no longer be depended upon to provide equal footing in economic arrangements. It was liberty in the old political sense that had led to concentration of power, to corruption, and, ultimately, to a new form of slavery of the proletariat by the business owners. The fact that most of this exploitation was perfectly legal on the political plane made it all the more alarming to onlookers. The belief was that something had to be done to ensure the freedom that had been granted to the people upon the founding of the United States.

But what else could be done? All possible measures to prevent exploitation and slavery had been taken at the founding with the granting of political freedoms and the Bill of Rights, or so it was supposed. Was this form of liberal democracy not enough? A growing number of reformers in the first decades of the twentieth century arrived at the shocking conclusion that, indeed, it was not adequate after all.

Not only was this liberal democracy not enough, but, as many concluded, it was largely the culprit. Freedom, in the sense of political autonomy, had been responsible for the kind of ruthless competition that culminated in the great monopolies of the 1880s and '90s, and political freedom had allowed the great industrialists and Wall Street lions of the Gilded Age to take advantage of average citizens. In the words of the prominent Baptist minister and leader of the Social Gospel movement, Walter Rauschenbusch, "Individualism means tyranny°."

To combat the monopolies and protect against the exploitation they engendered, it had been decided that a new set of rules must be constructed. Reformers of the period like Wilson, Brandeis, Rauschenbusch, William Jennings Bryan, and later John Maynard Keynes convinced the public of the absolute necessity of controlling the economy so as to ensure material well-being for all. Along with demand, a people must also have effective demand—and thus a steady flow of income—in order to survive. The ultimate aim stayed the same—freedom—but now, it had been determined, to be truly free one must have economic and material freedom as well as basic political freedom.

The shift in the kind of freedom sought for America encompassed a wide-ranging change in politico-economic thought during the double decade from 1890 to the early 1910s. Just as the close of the frontier flipped the pursuit of wealth from a subjective, personal endeavor to an objective, social endeavor, thus rendering the system a competitive zero-sum condition, so too did the concept of freedom undergo a revolution equal in scope and significance.

This shift was so monumental because it affected the very core of the American and, by extension, Western mode of life. Simply, to control the economy and provide material freedom for the people, the government was required to step in. No longer was the state able to rest disinterested on the sidelines, officiating the contest; now it was necessary for the government to join in the actual play of the game, to manipulate its course of action. The transition from a society largely independent of government intervention to one largely dependent upon it would be the narrative of the age.

This was the time of the Great Switch, as Barzun identified it, a period when the concept of 'Liberalism' performed a reversal and became its opposite. Up to the late nineteenth century, Liberalism had always been based in the notion that the government which governs best is the one which governs least. In the new economy, however, free enterprise was seen as unstable, corruptible, and harmful to the average citizen. Accordingly, it was considered necessary for some outside entity to come in and ensure fairness, equality, and thus liberty. That entity was the federal government. And it was a switch that was dependent on the changing society in which it was lodged. As society would grow more and more complex, government's role would grow in proportion.

Based as it was on a single concept that had a firm set of language reserved for it, the Great Switch was marked by a radical shift in terminology. In the twentieth century, the ideas 'Freedom', 'Liberty', and 'Liberalism' began to take on new meanings, the extent to which could be seen in the difficulty one faced in using the words. No longer was it sufficient to talk of freedom just by itself—freedom could mean two or three different concepts. Stipulations had to be made to clarify whether one was referring to the old form of political freedom or a new form of freedom that encompassed economic and material freedom as well.

Titles given to the period's political and economic documents reflect the disorderly atmosphere by their use of the word 'new'. Herbert Croly and Walter Lippmann's political magazine, for instance, first published in 1914, was titled *The New Republic* to echo the great changes brought on by Industrialization and the novel form of nation-state needed to preside over it. Teddy Roosevelt gave the country 'New Nationalism' and Woodrow Wilson's economic plan was called plainly 'New Freedom', advanced presumably because everyone realized the old kind of freedom had grown obsolete. All ventures indicated redefinition with one form or another of novel approach. The underlying theme stressed movement and progress, which was shown in the term granted to the period's reformers, 'Progressive'. What exactly they were progressing toward was not readily known—the important thing was that it was something *new*.

Altogether, the verbal gymnastics underscored the politico-economic shift occurring beneath. In one swift turn of events, the people of the

United States saw words that had promoted Laissez-Faire Capitalism now promoting government intervention, even Socialism, and vice versa. In 1900, the term 'liberal' meant free from government intervention; in 1920, it meant with as much government intervention as possible, all without so much as a formal announcement. As a result, all things old and classic naturally took on a negative connotation. The term 'conservative', long used to denote one who resisted Liberalism by means of 'conserving' the old monarchies, grew to mean simply 'reactionary' and 'stuffy'. Just as 'liberal' switched meanings to represent one who favored government intervention, 'conservative' also switched meanings to represent someone who favored Laissez-Faire Capitalism.

Schumpeter summarized the phenomenon as one of accidental tribute: "As a supreme, if unintended, compliment, the enemies of private enterprise have thought it wise to appropriate its label." Wise, indeed. As might be expected, a torrent of confusion has resulted from the verbal hijinks, the aftermath from which our political discourse has not quite recovered. Who is to say what policy provides freedom these days when the concepts of Liberty and Liberalism are so confounded?

The inquisitive will find that the state of freedom is much more complicated than it may seem on the surface, and both classical and modern liberals have justifiable claims to the designation. In one sense, freedom can be rightly seen as being without restrictions in some regard—to be free from debt, from the

> Here are two, not only different, but incompatible things, called by the same name—liberty.
>
> And it follows that each of the things is, by the respective parties, called by two different and incompatible names—liberty and tyranny.
>
> —ABRAHAM LINCOLN, ADDRESS AT SANITARY FAIR, BALTIMORE (1864)

threat of drought or deluge, or from the burden of shackles. In another sense, freedom can rightly be seen as having the ability to do something—the freedom to travel, to enjoy a long hike through the desert, or to eat a fine dinner at a restaurant on the Mediterranean coast. Which is true freedom if indeed it is either?

The ambiguity leads one to recall the distinction made by Nietzsche, who cared not about the restrictions one is freed from, but rather the abilities that he is freed to attain. "You call yourself free?" he asks through his mouthpiece in *Thus Spoke Zarathustra*, "Free from what? What does Zarathustra care! But brightly your eyes should signal to me: free *for* what?" To Nietzsche, freedom is not real unless it is directed toward some positive aim.

Distinction between the two kinds of freedom is the difference between what twentieth-century theorists called 'negative freedom' and 'positive freedom'. In his 1941 *Fear of Freedom*, Marxist humanist Erich Fromm described the two kinds of freedom respectively as the 'freedom *from*' something or other and the 'freedom *to do*' something or other. Political freedom is considered a negative freedom because government provides it in the absence of restrictions—by limiting its regulations, tariffs, and other coercive acts. In a word, political liberty is the freedom from oppression by the state. Material freedom, on the other hand, is called a positive freedom since it exists only in the presence of material and economic abilities—one can ensure it by providing an abundance of food and shelter, education, suffrage, and so on. To take a basic example, positive freedom would be the freedom to buy a house while negative freedom would be the ability to own the house without someone vandalizing or damaging it.

Focused as they were on the role of government in the people's lives, liberals throughout the history of the West always focused on the negative kind of freedom, the kind of freedom offered in the absence of restrictions. After all, it is always easier to list in a book of laws the things that a government cannot do to its people rather than the things it would allow. It is easier, for instance, to say that a government cannot censor speech than it is to list everything a person could possibly say. While the former brand of freedom is limited and confined to a certain number of basic principles, the latter is rather infinite in scope and would be cumbersome to recount.

This is doubtless why the rule of law, dating back to its early sketches in Plato and Aristotle, and later in Magna Carta, has traditionally been a rule of negative freedoms, or what the state cannot do to its people, rather than a rule of positive freedoms, or what the people should be able to do. Though it has always aimed at positive freedoms in the sense that its people would garner higher productivity and wealth and spiritual contentment, the actual law was designed as a framework for limiting the government's restrictions on its people. This is why the U.S. Constitution, and particularly its Bill of Rights, has become the modern legal document par excellence, comprised as it is almost entirely of negative freedoms.

To list positive freedoms in any capacity would amount to an encyclopedia of rights and certainly would not be suitable for a constitution accessible to every citizen. Eighteenth-century French philosopher Claude Adrien Helvétius put it well by saying, "The free man is the man who is not in irons, nor imprisoned in a gaol, nor terrorized like a slave by the fear of punishment." According to Helvétius, it was an absurdity to say that "to not fly like an eagle or swim like a whale" was lack of freedom.

> The powers not delegated to the United States by the Constitution, nor prohibited by it to the States, are reserved to the States respectively, or to the people.
>
> —THE TENTH AMENDMENT OF THE CONSTITUTION OF THE UNITED STATES OF AMERICA (1789)

In the twentieth century, however, academics, economists, and politicians alike began to grow increasingly concerned that the negative kind of freedom was not enough to ensure the promises of a liberal society. Simply limiting government was not enough to ensure that everyone could be afforded life, liberty, and the pursuit of property; a more direct provision had become necessary. As such, the succession was clear: Positive freedom, not negative freedom, would be the rule of the new century. It took less than fifty years for intellectuals to arrive at the conclusion that indeed positive freedom—that is, the ability to buy a house, enjoy a hike through the desert, and eat at a restaurant on the Mediterranean coast—is one's being altogether. "Positive freedom," as Fromm states, "is identical with the full realization of the individual's potentialities, together with his ability to live actively and spontaneously." Only by identifying and supplying the necessities of every human could we finally achieve the objective of Western Civilization.

The Birth of the Third Way

Inasmuch as the new goal of society was to provide positive rather than negative freedom, the federal government was the natural means. To begin, it was the only organization that could possibly be big and powerful enough to accomplish all that the Great Switch liberals aimed for. Only a state government that encompassed the entire nation and held jurisdiction throughout could manage such a sprawling enterprise as the economy. More importantly, the government was a voice of the people, which meant that it was the only real institution that could hold the implicit backing of the public. Corporations were private institutions, all with their own self-interests, which, as seen in the kinds of exploitation perpetrated throughout the business world, often conflicted with the public interest. Combined with its extensiveness, its assumed status as the emblem of the entire nation made the federal government the ideal candidate for Progressive reforms.

The rationale was simple and understandable: The economy—and thus the well-being of the citizens—was controlled by a few bankers and industrialists. Though Capitalism naturally led to this structure, and was so condemned for it, everyone saw the great efficiency and productivity of the modern economic system, and so there was no real push to dismantle the whole thing as Marx would have done. But the thought was that, as long as some small clique of elites was going to run the show, it might as well be a small clique of elites that was beholden to the people. Through democratic elections, the government was that clique.

The close of the frontier had left the people with few options. As exploitation was clearly unacceptable, the people either had to revolt and destroy the modern economy or work with it and seek protection through the law. Some certainly favored the former, but all levelheaded reformers saw the folly in such destructiveness and gravitated toward the latter. Frederick Jackson Turner conveyed this logic with his typical eloquence: "As the western settler began to face the problem of magnitude in the areas he was occupying; as he began to adjust his life to the modern forces of capital and to complex productive processes; as he began to see that, go where he would, the question of credit and currency, of transportation and distribution in general conditioned his success, he sought relief by legislation. He began to lose his primitive attitude of individualism, government began to look less like a necessary evil and more like an instrument for the perpetuation of his democratic ideals. In brief, the defenses of the pioneer democrat began to shift from free land to legislation, from the ideal of individualism to the ideal of social control through regulation by law°."

Turner recognized that the American of the early twentieth century was not an extreme socialist looking to overturn all capitalist institutions. As he explained, "He had no sympathy with a radical reconstruction of society by the revolution of socialism; even his alliances with the movement of organized labor, which paralleled that of organized capital in the East, were only half-hearted. But he was becoming alarmed over the future of the free democratic ideal. The essential point is that his conception of the right of government to control social process had undergone a change. He was coming to regard legislation as an instrument of social construction. The individualism of the Kentucky pioneer of 1796 was giving way to the Populism of the Kansas pioneer of 1896."

Populism and Progressivism were corollary movements with a single DNA, founded on the government of wealth in favor of the people. Just as the robber barons controlled the money supply in the late 1800s, the government would do so in the 1900s. And, instead of controlling it to the benefit of only the few owners, the government would control it to the benefit of the public. Instead of making deals and cornering markets to draw wealth further into the hands of the very rich, the government would write laws and police the economy to spread money out to the lower classes.

Not only would this prevent exploitation and thus alleviate the bitter struggle of the working poor, so too would it make the individuals of that class productive members of society, a development that would increase total wealth and thus improve the economy as a whole. The impoverished worker, hungry and perhaps homeless, can produce only so much as his plight allows. Give him sustenance, a stable home, and a steady income, and he will convert that energy into production. Give him effective demand to match his natural demands, and he will be able to make use of the country's abundant supply.

At its very core, Modern Liberalism was designed to provide the masses with economic security. The foundations could be seen in a set of reforms instituted by German Ministerpräsident Otto von Bismarck beginning in the 1880s. Part far-seeing initiative and part political handiwork, Bismarck was responsible for bringing about the first major social welfare programs in the modern world. His accomplishments included worker health insurance, accident insurance, and disability and old-age pensions, among other groundbreaking reforms. In adumbrating what would later become the Welfare State, Bismarck stole the socialists' thunder by developing a way for the workers to be taken care of without going to the extremes advocated by contemporary socialists. The solution was not wholly capitalist or wholly communist, but another breed of socio-political organization, a 'third way' as it would later be called.

However convenient the new appellation seemed, it could not be denied that the third way meant compromise and large-scale government intervention. The people would have freedom, but not complete freedom; the state would have power, but not complete power. Ultimately, the reforms introduced meant an altogether statist standard—that is, removing responsibility from individuals and placing it in the hands of a central authority—to take from the wealthy few through taxation and regulation, and give to the impoverished many through subsidies and provisions. After Bismarck, progressives of all stripes agreed that it was the only fair course to take.

By the first decade of the twentieth century, the welfare vogue had grown incontrovertible, even to the extent of capturing the birthplace of freedom, Great Britain, and her heir, the United States. In London, Lloyd George introduced the 'People's Budget', which was more or less made up of heavy taxes on luxuries aimed at bringing in revenue for increased welfare programs. George's 'liberal reforms' set the groundwork for what ultimately became the British Welfare State, and for years taking part in welfare programs was called 'going on the Lloyd George'.

In America, Wilson's New Freedom sought to do the same. It took three paths: taxation, regulation, and the institution of a national bank for the purpose of controlling the money supply. The casual observer is shocked to see how rapidly the plan was implemented.

In a tidal wave of legislation, years of protests and activism culminated in four major national policies in 1913 and '14: (1) the Revenue Act, which followed the ratification of the Sixteenth Amendment with a federal income tax beginning at 1% and rising to 7% for those with incomes in excess of $500,000; (2) the Federal Reserve Act, which instituted the Federal Reserve Bank aimed at regulating banks and the money supply; (3) the Clayton Anti-Trust Act, which was designed to inhibit the formation of monopolies; and (4) the Federal Trade Commission Act, which established the FTC with the object of preventing unfair business practices. These landmark laws, among several other key bills, defined Wilson's young presidency and essentially redefined the role of government in the economy. In two swift years, the president had signed into law a complete reversal of American Liberalism.

While there had been income taxes and central banks in the U.S. prior to 1913, and certainly Roosevelt and Taft had used the bully pulpit to break up trusts and cut anti-competitive business activities before Wilson, no state action had ever been so thorough or so sudden. Similar initiatives in the past had been brought about in response to specific events—the War of 1812, the American Civil War—and attracted so much resistance that they were repealed once the immediate threat had passed. In 1895, for example, a federal income tax was passed into law, but it was immediately challenged in court and found to be unconstitutional. Before the 1910s, no social welfare initiatives could stick.

Wilson's moves were so convincing and backed by such adamant zeal that even the vocal opposition could not conjure up an adequate resistance. And, as attention was being shifted to the Great War in Europe, the resolve of statists only stiffened. All wars tend to nationalize the public spirit and militarize institutions. This was especially true of the Great War, which was above all a war of imperialism, jingoism, and national racism. As the United States was drawn into the conflagration in 1917, a slew of measures were implemented that all but sealed the fate of Classical Liberalism and secured a long future for the modern brand—price controls, various new taxes, government nationalization of railroads, a War Industries Board, the War Revenue Act, the War Finance Corporation, so-called 'Liberty Loans', and publicly-issued debt in the form of treasury bonds designed to pay for the war, were all implemented in the fervor. It was a great switch in more ways than one.

When the Treaty of Versailles was signed in November 1919 and tentative peace returned to Europe, Westerners faced a politico-economic world that had been completely recast. From generally capitalist economies made of competing individuals, companies, and classes, every country in the West, not to mention Japan and China in the East, had produced a socialist framework in which the wealthy few were taxed heavily, if not being persecuted outright, and the impoverished masses received assistance and insurance and gained political power.

In three notable realms, the transition was taken to its natural extreme. Russia underwent revolution in 1917, the tsars were deposed, and the Marxist Bolsheviks seized control with Lenin as their leader and Stalin as a rising star; Mussolini reformed the Milano 'fascio' to inaugurate Italian Fascism and was himself rising in national power; and reparations were put in place in the Weimar Republic that would stir unrest and lead the way for Hitler's rise to power. Each of these major quakes caused far-reaching ripples, and, it could be said, the undercurrents that caused the first war continued on social and political fronts despite the armistice. The dominant call in these three venues—nation above persons, society above the individual—reverberated throughout the West and could be heard everywhere.

At home, the response to the war was much more negative in tone. A general isolationist strain had always run through the country's veins, and it remained despite the jingo nationalism of the pre-war period. Wilson won re-election in 1916 on the slogan 'He kept us out of war', then plunged the country into war, making the episode all the more objectionable. The economy was suffering a recession, the public had grown weary of reform, and it was all seen as related to Wilson's Progressivism.

Ultimately, in 1920, Warren G. Harding won a landslide election on the promise to reverse Wilson's failures and bring about a 'Return to Normalcy', id est, a return to the Laissez-Faire Capitalism on which the country had been founded. But the steps that Wilson and other Progressives had taken to correct and regulate the free market were already in place, and the resulting institutions had been firmly grounded by the militarization of the war. It would take a monumental effort to undo the reforms, and no one had the energy for it. Indeed, Harding's laissez-faire style meant that he set out to 'do nothing' with the government he inherited; and, in fact, the 'Do-Nothing President' actually became his derisive nickname.

Of course, Harding didn't do nothing; on the contrary, he signed into law a number of regulatory acts born of Wilson's legacy. Doing nothing simply meant that the newly established status quo—the regulations, the taxes, the general economic control—would continue unhampered. Harding lacked the reform fervor of his predecessor, and so everyone assumed that normalcy had returned after all.

The Triumph of the Central Bank

Perhaps the most important feature of the new status quo was the Federal Reserve. As a chief component of Wilson's barrage of reforms, the Federal Reserve was the product of a century-old debate on the constitutionality of a central bank and whether the federal government had the authority to regulate the money supply. From as early as the founding, this debate had raged, with notable proponents including George Washington, Alexander Hamilton, and Henry Clay on one side, and notable detractors including Thomas Jefferson and Andrew Jackson on the other.

With the ups and downs of the largely capitalist nineteenth-century economy, the demand for a central bank also went through a series of peaks and troughs. When times were good, the bank was seen as superfluous and unconstitutional; when times were bad, it was a necessary evil or even a plain necessity. Everyone could see the significant role such an institution could have. By increasing or decreasing the money supply through any number of mechanisms, the central bank could change the value of money and thus the value of all goods and services. With a set of refined tools—the ability to change interest rates, buy and sell securities on the open market, and change the reserve requirement of commercial banks—the central bank could encourage or discourage investment; it could limit or direct that investment to particular sectors; and it could grant the government near unlimited access to funds to be used in whatever capacity it saw fit, which would of course come in handy during times of national crisis like a world war or a banking panic. It was, in short, the ultimate weapon for the newly minted Welfare State.

The Federal Reserve's power in this capacity was the central ambition of most proponents. When times were bad, for instance, as when runs on banks threatened to dry up liquidity and diminish investment, the bank could provide needed funds to quell panic and return the economy to an even keel. As the banking system grew more and more complex in the early twentieth century, the business cycle became more and more severe. The Money Multiplier was expanding and contracting the money supply to unprecedented degrees, and the extension of credit in all areas of the economy meant that almost everyone was affected by the booms and busts.

In 1907, this economic instability was brought to a head when a run on the Knickerbocker Trust Company set off a panic that took its toll on stocks, the banking system, railroads, industrial metals, and steel companies. Previous bank panics had never reached the frenetic level reached by the one in 1907, and the resulting financial carnage reflected the chaos, as industrial production dropped further than any previous bank run and the second highest number of bankruptcies was filed as a result. In one year, overall production fell 11%, imports fell by 26%, and unemployment more than doubled from 3% to 8%.

Frantic officials scurried to create the National Monetary Commission, a congressional group designed to investigate the crash and propose legislative solutions. The proposal came in the form of the Aldrich Plan, which, at its root was a call for a new central bank, called the 'Federal Reserve' because it would control the economy's money flow by use of a large reserve of capital. Whereas financier J. P. Morgan had shored up reserves to support the banks during the Panic of 1907, public officials wanted an enterprise that was solely intended for this purpose and had no natural restrictions.

> Picture a party of the nation's greatest bankers stealing out of New York on a private railroad car under cover of darkness, stealthily riding hundreds of miles South, embarking on a mysterious launch, sneaking onto an island deserted by all but a few servants, living there a full week under such rigid secrecy that the names of not one of them was once mentioned, lest the servants learn the identity and disclose to the world this strangest, most secret expedition in the history of American finance. I am giving to the world, for the first time, the real story of how the famous Aldrich currency report, the foundation of our new currency system, was written.
>
> —B. C. FORBES ON THE JEKYLL ISLAND RETREAT, *MEN WHO ARE MAKING AMERICA* (1916)

Given such a power, the central bank could relieve troubled banks and curb any panic before it went too far or created an economic slump.

The Fed's 1923 Annual Report explains its purpose in stark terms: "The Federal Reserve banks are ... the source to which the member banks turn when the demands of the business community have outrun their own unaided resources. The Federal Reserve supplies the needed additions to credit in times of business expansion and takes up the slack in times of business recession°." As historian Paul Johnson described it, this agenda of the Federal Reserve was Keynesianism before Keynes formally expressed it.

At its inception, the Fed's power was limited to some extent by the gold standard. Since all money printed and distributed by the United States was backed by gold, the bank could only print money in proportion to the amount of gold it possessed. A fairly steady supply of gold meant that the supply of paper money had to be relatively stable as well.

At the same time, however, one of the Fed's powers was to change the ratio at which its paper notes were backed, which allowed the bank to change the money supply as if there were no real gold standard anyway. In addition to its other tools, the flexible gold standard allowed the Federal Reserve to manipulate the economy like no other institution had before it. And so, despite Harding's Return to Normalcy, the effects of the Fed's presence could not be mistaken. The base money supply actually fell slightly between 1921 and '29, but the total money in circulation rose by almost 62%. Thanks to eager lending policies, lowered reserve requirements, and low interest rates, the currency expanded at an unprecedented rate. Expansion of currency naturally led to expansion of investment, commerce, and consumerism. It was, in large part, why the twenties roared as they did.

When the inevitable correction came in 1929 and investors watched stock prices plummet, banks watched borrowers default on their loans, and depositors watched those banks vanish into thin air, the typical response echoed the Progressives' claim that Capitalism was inherently unstable, benefited the rich, and harmed the needy. Almost no one, save a few obscure economists, recognized the role that the central bank had played in the boom and bust, and almost everyone chalked it up to the failure of free-market Capitalism. *Business Week*'s invidious headline on June 24, 1931 summed up the general scorn when it mockingly asked, "Do You Still Believe in Lazy-Fairies?" The assumption was that Laissez Faire was make-believe. To a rising chorus of the time, those invisible fairies had gotten the world into what had become the Great Depression, just as so many early reformers had predicted, and Marx, Engels, Lenin, and Trotsky had prophesied.

If the crises of 1893, 1896, and 1907 hadn't done so, the crash of 1929 and the Great Depression vindicated the socialist reformers, proving once and for all that Capitalism was flawed. It did not matter that the Progressives' initiatives had been active for decades at that point or that Capitalism itself had suffered from a paralyzing confinement due to the close of the frontier. The irrefutable evidence was in the bread lines, the Hoovervilles set up around city parks, and the look of emaciated workers begging for jobs. These images argued that a laissez-faire system was bound to failure, and now some other system was needed to pull the people out of hardship.

Total Welfare

The concept of the Welfare State didn't win the hearts and minds of the public, at least in America, until the Great Depression supposedly proved that Capitalism was broken. If the new vision of government had a spokesman, it was Franklin D. Roosevelt, who swept up the presidency after the noticeable failure of his predecessor to combat the persistent depression. Roosevelt's aim was simple and based in large part on the foundations laid by his fifth cousin, Theodore.

In his speech to the 1932 Democratic Convention, with a nod to Teddy's 'Square Deal', Franklin presented what he called a 'New Deal' for the American people, a plan that sought to implement an army of economic programs that would flood the economy with capital and help pull the country out of the depression.

Anyone who remembers elementary school Social Studies knows that FDR's New Deal produced programs aimed at the three 'R's—relief, recovery, and reform—and supplied an alphabet soup of new organizations to accomplish just that: the Works Progress Administration (WPA) encouraged economic growth through construction projects, the Social Security Act (SSA) brought about a large-scale national pension program, the Federal Deposit Insurance Corporation (FDIC) guaranteed customer deposits in banks to stave off runs, the Tennessee Valley Authority (TVA) constructed a massive reservoir and power plant system, the Federal Housing Administration (FHA) provided a financing system for home buyers, and the Securities and Exchange Commission (SEC) was laid out to regulate and enforce the troubled securities industry.

Altogether, the goal was economic and material freedom, just as it had been with Bismarck, George, Wilson, and, it could be argued, Lenin, Stalin, Mussolini, and Hitler. The United States was only the last to join the group of European nations that had already implemented a comprehensive system that endeavored to provide its people with universal material well-being.

Now, the comparison between Roosevelt and the twentieth-century totalitarian dictators may seem harsh to the modern reader. But, while there are distinct differences, the ideological similarities cannot be denied. For instance, Benito Mussolini used the term 'totalitario' to describe his regime's goal of providing for the people totally—"Everything within the state, nothing without the state, nothing against the state." One might rightly wonder how this is substantively different from a president who sought to provide all necessities for his people from cradle to grave—protection against child labor exploitation, free public education, work, housing, insurance, and, ultimately, pensions until death. In Roosevelt's regime, what could possibly exist outside of the state? Although Roosevelt took a more diplomatic approach to arrive at and maintain his power, his promise to the people was the very same as that of Mussolini and the others. He was, after all, the only president to ever run for the office more than twice—indeed, a very Mussolini or Hitler-esque, consul-for-life sort of reign.

The point of comparing Roosevelt with totalitarian dictators is not to align the American president with obviously evil authoritarians but rather to stress the prevalence of the dominant zeitgeist of the age—the idea that the state was necessary for everything. Can one reasonably question the totalitarianism of a leader who, in one of his later speeches, called for a 'Second Bill of Rights', which explicitly implored the government to provide all necessities for all citizens? According to Roosevelt, the inalienable political rights acknowledged at the nation's founding "proved inadequate to assure us equality in the pursuit of happiness. We have come to a clear realization of the fact," he said, "that true individual freedom cannot exist without economic security and independence." And so he proposed that all citizens had the right to a bevy of material things: a useful and remunerative job; salary enough to pay for food, clothing, and recreation; a decent home; adequate medical care and the opportunity to achieve and enjoy good health; protection from the economic fears of old age, sickness, accident, and unemployment; and a good education.

And so, despite the apparent contrast in tactics, it must be concluded that the essence of the New Deal was one and the same as that of any statist plan emanating from Europe at the time. The discerning investigator is bound to find that the similar goals actually meant that the tactics used would have to be similar as well. Even though FDR never used militaristic devices in his rise to power or held down his political opponents with force, the promises he made to the public could only be made through comparable means because the central purpose of the New Deal was to provide material well-being to every citizen of the country, and, as we will see, the only way for the government to provide material well-being is through force.

Material well-being can only come with wealth. But the state, by nature, cannot produce wealth itself; it can only provide wealth by moving it around from one sector to another. In order to move wealth around, it must first take it from someone or some group, which means coercion. In a Welfare State, this coercion takes the form of taxes and regulation, enforced by the threat of imprisonment or death. It is a fundamental component of state intervention which cannot be denied by any objective onlooker, which means that, in its very essence, the Welfare State is a scheme based on violence and coercion. It aims to provide material freedom but, in order to do so, it must diminish political freedom first; to supply work, housing, and insurance to a group of laborers, the government must control, police, and coerce companies, construction, and social organizations. Indeed, in an egalitarian Welfare State, the government coerces everyone; all must be directed and controlled, including the laborers and consumers. In order for a planned economy to operate fully, the state must have its hands in all aspects of the economy. No one is exempt.

One might argue that in a Western Welfare State, the people are not coerced into paying the taxes, they do so voluntarily because they believe that it is the best way to organize a civil society. It may be socialist in nature, but it is *Democratic* Socialism because the people all vote for it and live in the system under their own free will. But this is to assume that everyone who pays taxes does so out of the kindness of their hearts. How much free will does the average citizen have when it comes to paying taxes after all? If he were so inclined, could he opt out of the welfare system? Could he decide not to pay the taxes and not to receive the alleged benefits? The prospect

Senator Reid: "I don't accept your phraseology. I don't think we force people."

Interviewer: "Taxation is not forceful?"

Senator Reid: "Well, no. In fact, quite the contrary."

Interviewer: "It's voluntary?"

Senator Reid: "Our system of government has a voluntary tax system."

Interviewer: "If you don't want to pay your taxes, you don't have to?"

Senator Reid: "Oh, of course you have to pay your taxes."

—Jan Helfeld interview with U.S. Senator Harry Reid (March, 2008)

seems rather absurd to the modern American. Of course he cannot opt out—if he did, the system wouldn't work.

If they are honest, even the most compassionate modern liberals will admit that the Welfare State framework is based on coercion. In order to provide material freedoms, the government must provide the people with wealth, and that wealth must come from somewhere. The only place it can come from is the people themselves.

Of course, early Great Switch liberals did not want to grant everyone the ability to fly like an eagle and swim like a whale; their goals were modest and quite reasonable—daily rations, affordable housing, protection from economic strain when ill, and so on. Certainly the country had enough wealth to provide these material freedoms to everyone. Reasonable as they may have been, however, these new forms of freedom would still require force. In order to regulate business, the government would have to control the activities of businesses and businessmen; in order to provide sustenance for the disadvantaged, the government would have to take sustenance from those who were not disadvantaged; and so on.

And this presented reformers with something of a dilemma. To provide economic freedom, the positive form of freedom now focused on, the government had to control the country's wealth, which meant taxes, regulations, et cetera. These necessary consequences were forms of restrictions and thus deleterious to the people's political freedoms. Ultimately, to provide material freedom, we would have to do away with political freedom; the Second Bill of Rights would terminate the first.

The great irony of Wilson's New Freedom and Roosevelt's New Deal is that they were really just new sets of rules and restrictions, and the freedoms they proposed to secure (sustenance, cheap credit, and equality), came only at the expense of other freedoms (such as privacy, free enterprise, and economic free will).

> We need a robust market economy that is truly as free as possible everywhere but with appropriate and effective regulation everywhere.
>
> —U.S. SECRETARY OF STATE HILARY CLINTON (MAY, 2010)

Government intervention proposed by the new welfare programs meant the paradoxical condition of providing freedom through restrictions, liberty by means of coercion.

A Faustian Bargain

In a lecture given at Oxford in 1958 titled *Two Concepts of Liberty*, British philosopher Isaiah Berlin argued that the notion of positive freedom was something of a chimera employed to cover up abuse of a people's negative freedoms 'for their own sake'. Totalitarians laid out a set of positive needs that their people could hardly deny, and then assumed authority in doing all that was necessary to provide for those needs. Berlin claimed that, since this gave the government the right to shackle political freedoms, it more or less gave government the right to coerce its people for any end it so desired, even if that end was contradictory to the goal of material freedom. In short, the promotion of positive freedom served merely as a license to diminish negative freedom.

Berlin's line of reasoning suggests that, as a matter of practical application, the distinction between the two kinds of freedom is an illusion. Positive and negative freedoms are really but two sides of the same coin that are both present wherever free-

> **The worst sufferer in this respect is, of course, the word "liberty." It is a word used as freely in totalitarian states as elsewhere. Indeed, it could almost be said—and it should serve as a warning to us to be on our guard against all the tempters who promise us New Liberties for Old—that wherever liberty as we understand it has been destroyed, this has almost always been done in the name of some new freedom promised to the people.**
>
> **—FRIEDRICH A. HAYEK,**
> *THE ROAD TO SERFDOM* (1944)

dom exists. Take for example the positive freedom of education or knowledge. That same positive freedom can also be seen negatively as well: Freedom is the absence of ignorance. Here we find two different perspectives on one single freedom. This goes for any supposed positive or negative freedom—wealth and the lack of poverty, space and the lack of encroachments, an abundance of food and the absence of hunger—all freedoms can be either positive or negative depending on the angle from which one looks at them.

To a large degree, political freedom is seen with respect to the entity that is thought to pose the greatest threat to it. Classical Liberals viewed freedom with respect to the state, since the greatest threat to freedom was the use of force and the greatest physical power was the state. As such, freedom was based largely on the absence of government restrictions, and so it was manifest as a negative. On the other hand, material freedom is viewed with respect to the ultimate goal. As such, freedom is based in the presence of things, and so it seems positive. But this is not to suggest that political freedoms lack ends or that material freedoms lack threats to their fulfillment. Both kinds of freedom have intended ends and potential threats; the difference is just which of these is more pragmatic to talk about.

In shifting the discourse from negative to positive freedoms, Modern Liberals only shifted the subject of talk from government to the people. Attention was paid to what material things the people should and would get, what kind of benefits they would receive, and what kind of life they would maintain. What was lost was focus on how those material things would be produced and where those benefits would come from. While the free citizen of the nineteenth century generally knew how and where his wealth would come from, since of course he was responsible for generating it, the free citizen of the twentieth did not care. He was too desperate, too hungry, to be able to accommodate such concerns, and so he was willing to trade political freedom for material freedom, liberty for security and comfort. Such was the extent of the impoverished worker's distress.

American philosopher Eric Hoffer explained the tendency well when he said, "To the frustrated, freedom from responsibility is more attractive than freedom from restraint. They are eager to barter their independence for relief from the burdens of willing, deciding and being responsible for inevitable failure. They willingly abdicate the directing of their lives to those who want to plan, command and shoulder all responsibility°." The bargain that Western societies have made to secure material freedom by means of state intervention is, as Indiana University political science scholar Vincent Ostrom eloquently put it, rather Faustian in nature. It is as if the society must give up its soul, its very means of self-sufficiency in the form of political freedom, in order to eat its fill, have money for quality clothes, and fly among the stars. In a time of severe confinement and stress, there may well seem no real alternative.

In the end, however, anyone able to take a step back and judge the dilemma will come to the same conclusion that Benjamin Franklin arrived at: "They who can give up essential liberty to obtain a little temporary safety, deserve neither liberty nor safety." As we will see, they who are willing to give up liberty for security receive neither as well.

2. NEW FEUDALISM

AFTER THE GREAT SWITCH had redefined freedom and the state mechanism designed to provide it, Western Civilization was looking at an entirely new way of life. The new paradigm was based on the notion that competition and exploitation were inefficient and destructive by themselves, and that the free market had to be reigned in somehow. Extensive state government, which had long been thought of as the malefactor in the politico-economic sphere, was now seen as the only device capable of such a task, and so had become the last hope for mankind. During the 1930s, in a world reeling from economic strife and conflict, large-scale state intervention appeared to be the only solution.

To replace Laissez-Faire Capitalism, Western nations tried out an assortment of brands of statist government, each with its own unique characteristics and impulses: Welfare Statism, Socialism, Democratic Socialism, National Socialism, Scientific Socialism, Market Socialism, Utopian Socialism, Revolutionary Socialism, Guild Socialism, Agrarian Socialism, Syndicalism, Mutualism, Marxism, Fourierism, Communism, Maoism, Fascism, and Totalitarianism. In general, all brands of the new government were socialist or collectivist in that they sought to redistribute wealth and control nearly all aspects of the economy through central planning. Ultimately, the new government types were uniform in their aim of countering the dominant characteristics of Capitalism, free enterprise and economic classes.

By the mid-1930s, it appeared that the various forms of statist government would succeed in toppling the capitalist status quo. While free-market Capitalism had largely been discredited by the Great War and the Great Depression, fascist states like Germany and Italy, as well as communist states like Russia and China, appeared to be operating harmoniously and peacefully. While France, Spain, Britain, and the United States were embroiled in the greatest economic hardship in recent history, collectivist states appeared to have solved the riddle of the Business Cycle and were prospering quite as if no crash had ever occurred.

Germany offers a brilliant example. After overcoming the reparations dictated by the Treaty of Versailles, Germany was able to regroup under Hitler's National Socialist Party and begin a period of economic growth that would last until the end of the Third Reich in 1945. From the early 1920s, in the wake of the devastating peace accord, to the late 1930s and the buildup to another world war, the country went through an astonishing transformation. In 1921, a loaf of bread was said to cost millions of marks in Berlin; in 1937, a resident of Berlin could buy anything and everything he wanted. In the early '20s, German industry had taken a tremendous hit and lay helpless against neighboring countries; in the late '30s, German technology and innovation was the most advanced in the history of the world.

Throughout the West and the East, collectivist states flourished like no modern nation had before. All optimistic onlookers celebrated the coming of an age of plenty and of social justice brought about by the overhaul in political economy. One recalls muckraker Lincoln Steffens' remark after having visited the Soviet Union in 1921: "I have been over to the future, and it works°."

But, despite the early mania for collectivist planning, more cautious onlookers knew that the benefits of the redistribution of wealth could come only with new and unforeseen costs that would necessarily render socialist states worse off in the long run. Though the new governments seemed to provide the twin promises of Socialism—equality and cooperation—wholly, to do so they would have had to engage in organizational methods that not only failed to hedge the concentration of wealth and power but actually further centralized wealth and afforded power to those who were most ambitious in their drive to control others. Rather than putting an end to class warfare and competition, Socialism and central planning only intensified the zero-sum condition and thus made it altogether more damaging. Contrary to all good intentions, socialist governments not only failed to slay the Juggernaut, but necessarily propelled it forward.

The Concentration of Power

To be sure, no one will deny that concentration of wealth and power is an essential first step to a socialized state. Redistribution of wealth is only possible when that wealth is collected and controlled by the state in a central place. As such, the overt plan of socialist government begins with the monopolization of wealth for which Capitalism is so reviled. And so we come to the ironic conclusion that, in order to solve the problem, we must first make it worse.

Recall Marx's promotion of the factory reform legislation of his day. While he encouraged it for its ability to give laborers better hours and thus alleviate some of their more urgent strains, he was most enthusiastic for it because he knew that it would precipitate revolution by giving larger businesses an advantage over smaller ones. By making the powerful owners even more powerful and allowing them to crowd out competition, the legislation hastened the concentration of power into one place, which, according to Marx, intensified unrest. The social reforms were beneficial because they made the situation worse and thus created a more urgent demand for revolution.

From as early as Sismondi, it had been suggested that the economy as a whole could be viewed as a large corporation that, if organized properly, could be run in a similar hierarchical fashion. If all the departments and systems of a single company could work together to achieve a mutually beneficial end of success, it was thought, then so too could the entire economy. Whole industries could act like divisions within the overarching firm; the financial sector could be like the finance department; the manufacturing sector could be the operations department; and so on. In this format, the government would be the executive offices.

The idea stemmed no doubt from Adam Smith and the basics of modern economics. Through specialism and the division of labor, cooperative individuals can work more efficiently and increase productivity significantly. The thought occurred that if this format worked for a single company, why not apply it to the entire economy? Sismondi and later Marx simply took the Smithian principles and extended them. The more comprehensive specialism and division of labor were, the theory went, the more effective the system as a whole would become. Moreover, directing everything from the top down would eliminate wasteful competition, and so the 'company' could achieve the utmost possible efficiency and profitability.

And who can deny the efficacy of modern industry? Only through the large-scale cooperation found in modern corporations could great structures such as the Empire State Building be erected, transcontinental railways be laid out, and great worldwide mining expeditions be undertaken. It stands to reason that the bigger and more comprehensive the system, the greater and more impressive its accomplishments. If the system could extend to encompass an entire economy, its accomplishments would be many times greater than those of solitary companies.

The résumé of the New Deal's Public Works Administration alone is sufficient to show the kind of facilities that can be produced when a countrywide system is enacted. The Hoover Dam in Nevada, the Triborough Bridge in New York, the River Walk in San Antonio, and Lake Shore Drive in Chicago, among many others, could only have been made possible, it is argued, by the cooperation of the nation as a whole. When the entire economy is molded into a single, corporatized entity, as it is with a large socialized state, the goals sought can be that much more extensive and wide-ranging. Wasteful competition is eliminated and everything functions seamlessly. In the first part of the twentieth century, the call was to make this extension a complete reality, and some of the best minds and workers endeavored to make it so.

To socialists, the extension was only reasonable. Marx thought it absurd that anyone could promote specialism and the division of labor for a single company and then shun the prospect of extending the practices to the entire economy. If it worked for one part, why should it not be applied to the whole? The logic was nearly irresistible.

But to accept the logic would be to make two questionable assumptions: first, that there is no limit to the extent to which productivity can improve from an organization's growth, and, second, that there is no substantive difference between a single company among many and a sovereign nation that comprises an entire economy.

The Black Hole of Bureaucracy

To begin, it is a leap to think that, just because productivity can improve by expanding the scope of production, this improvement can continue indefinitely. While specialism and the division of labor can and have been demonstrated to increase productivity in nearly every industry, it is false to assume that there are no limits to this increase and that simply adding workers will aid in the process. As we saw on an earlier page, the time saved by specialism can be very significant for a small operation, but less so as more workers are added. In most models, the learning curve is steep and affords little or no benefit after a certain point.

Indeed, with respect to industrial labor division, there is a point for every process when the amount of time saved per task by adding more specialized workers becomes negligible. This is when limitations on the physical constitution of workers and machines make it impossible to divide labor any further. As nineteenth-century economist Amasa Walker put it, beyond this point, "there is no division, but only repetition. Any attempt to refine the process so far as to give the workman less than one naturally complete motion of the body, will only embarrass and delay industry." This is the point at which growth may increase production, but not productivity; it may increase profits, but it cannot increase profits per item produced.

Nor is it guaranteed that production will increase at all. There is always the risk that an organization will grow large enough, and the tasks given to each worker grow so minimalist and thoughtless, that the workers lose focus and become less productive as a result. This is the risk identified by Adam Smith nearly 250 years ago concerning any specialized task that is removed from the ultimate purpose of the end product. The mind grows numb during specialized work, and one's attention to detail slips. In cases of extreme specialism, such as those in the modern factory or office, productivity might actually decrease as the size of the company increases. What modern factory laborer can stay focused enough through a 10-hour day to maintain the highest level of output throughout? What modern office worker can say that productivity is unaffected by the fact that he is just one of a thousand people doing the same seemingly insignificant task?

There is in industry, as Malthus and Ricardo among other economists discovered, a Law of Diminishing Returns, where the increase in proceeds slows down as investment increases. Viewed graphically, the output creates a curve from the initial boost in productivity toward an apex, where the investment ceases to produce the same amount of returns and eventually begins to cost the producer more.

To use a simplified illustration, consider the farmer who looks to optimize his output of crops. Initially, he plants one kilogram of seed on an acre of land for an output of one ton of crop. Since the land is fixed and the crops each require a certain amount of land to flourish, the amount of crops will never exceed a given amount despite the use of extra seed. Thus, adding another kilogram of seed will increase his produce by half a ton, adding another kilogram of seed will increase produce by a quarter ton, and

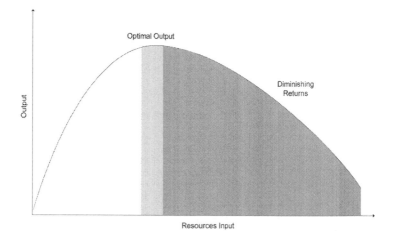

FIG. 26—Diminishing Returns.

so on up to the point where adding more seed will not produce any more crops at all. At the apex of the curve, the number of crops competing for water, soil, and sunlight will begin to hinder the growth of others and harm total output, after which added investment will only decrease returns.

The concept applies to human labor just as it does to material goods such as seeds and land. Indeed, human labor is particularly liable to this law because of the almost natural tendency toward bureaucracy. Anyone within sight of a growing company recognizes the typical transformation: Tasks that used to be done with a quick, personal interaction must now be done with a series of meetings and deployments. In a small company, resources are allocated on the fly, with split decisions being made regularly. In a large company, all tasks must be recorded by an extensive 'paper trail' of documents and forms so that nothing falls through the cracks. The larger the company, the more potential cracks, and the more need for bureaucracy to bridge them. In a large company, decisions are waylaid by countless meetings and committees and hardly ever make it through unscathed by compromise.

Anyone familiar with the modern office recognizes the frustration. If only one could just do the task himself, there wouldn't need to be an elaborate infrastructure or checking process—it would all be up to the individual. The modern consumer is all too aware of the Law of Diminishing Returns when he is faced with the service department in a large corporation. Rarely does one actually get the needed assistance on the first try; it is always 'May I put you on hold?' or 'Please wait while I transfer you to another customer representative'. Meanwhile, the customer ends up wasting hours trying to keep up with the rigmarole. When the right hand doesn't know what the left hand is doing, it is quite likely that they will contradict one another. It is a matter of nature in economies of scale; in the modern corporation, repetition and contradiction are just part of the game.

It is as though organizational growth is the loam from which bureaucracy naturally mushrooms. In 1976, British physician Max Gammon formulated a theory which stated that an organization's bureaucracy grows in proportion to its overall size. The larger an organization becomes, the more its useful work is readily and consciously supplanted by useless work, paperwork, administrative tasks, and so

Let me explain. The group running AA.com consists of at least 200 people spread out amongst many different groups, including, for example, QA, product planning, business analysis, code development, site operations, project planning, and user experience. Anyway, I guess what I'm saying is that AA.com is a huge corporate undertaking with a lot of tentacles that reach into a lot of interests. It's not small, by any means.

Oh how I wish we were, though! We could turn on a dime. We could just say 'No' to new feature requests. We could eliminate 'stovepiped' positions. We could cut out a lot of the friction created when so many organizations interact with each other. We could even redesign the AA.com home page without having to slog through endless review and approval cycles with their requisite revisions and re-reviews.

—FROM A CORRESPONDENCE ABOUT THE
DESIGN OF A POPULAR WEBSITE

Any sufficiently advanced bureaucracy is indistinguishable from molasses.

—ANONYMOUS WIT (CIRCA 1980)

on. As a matter of course, the new work may seem necessary, but it is directed toward management, formalities, and often toward simply filling up time rather than real productive work. The Theory of Bureaucratic Displacement, as Gammon called it, says that highly bureaucratic systems "will act rather like 'black holes' in the economic universe, simultaneously sucking in resources, and shrinking in terms of 'emitted' production." After a week on the job, the typical office worker these days might readily wonder if his time hasn't been eaten up by such an irrefutable cosmic force.

Being a physician, Gammon applied the theory to newly nationalized hospital services in Britain from 1965 to '73°. The study showed that during this time the institution grew significantly while its actual output, measured by the number of hospital beds occupied daily, actually declined. While hospital staff increased by 28%, administrative staff increased by 51%, and hospital output declined by 11%. According to Gammon, bureaucracy displaced the productive capacity of the hospital, ultimately subduing efficiency and output in general. In his report, Gammon was quick to point out that the wait list for hospital beds stayed around 600,000 patients throughout the study, indicating that the reduction in output was not due to a lower demand—it must have been due to the black hole effect of bureaucracy.

The Theory of Bureaucratic Displacement is akin to C. Northcote Parkinson's Law, which says that work tends to expand to fill the time available for its completion. In a November 1955 article published in *The Economist*, Parkinson showed that the decrease in British imperial control over the previous decades was contrasted by an increase in administration. According to Parkinson, colonial control diminished from 1935 to '43 and was almost non-existent by 1954; still, the number of officials continued to rise, from 372 in 1935 to 1,661 in 1954. Just as in Gammon's study of hospitals, the growing department meant more bureaucracy and in fact a drop in productivity.

Granted, an increase in international administration was bound to occur during and around the Second World War, yet there is no justification for the nearly 6% increase in officials during peacetime. Parkinson argues that work—and especially paper work—can be very elastic in its demands on time. Given a sufficient demand for work (id est, people who need something to do), an entire staff could be occupied for a whole day by the amount of tasks that a single worker could complete in a few hours.

The United States offers its own versions of the phenomenon. One study showed the same trend of diminishing production and increasing bureaucracy throughout the twentieth century in agriculture. In 1900, the United States was still a highly agricultural nation with six million farms across the country. At the time, there were no more than 3,000 workers in the Department of Agriculture. In the year 2000, the number of farms had dropped to two million, though the number of employees in the Department of Agriculture had exploded to over 100,000 people.

One cannot be sure as to what caused the boom in bureaucracy, whether it had anything to do with the number of farms at all, or if it was based on the technical facets of farming or something else. The amount of food put out by farms is much higher today than it was in 1900, and so it is reasonable to assume that more administration would be necessary. But it must also be acknowledged that the rules and regulations of the industry are much more abundant as well. One can be sure that the amount of administrative work dedicated to each farm has grown exponentially over the last hundred years, and that bureaucracy takes time that could otherwise be used productively.

This phenomenon is present just about everywhere and can be seen in the assumptions made with the typical 9-to-5 work day. Does every job in America really require 40 hours of work per week? It stands in the face of reason to think that it does, but the modern construct wouldn't have it any other way. Some jobs would be much more effectively accomplished if they were done in 20 hours or 10. To the modern manager or worker, the thought is inconceivable.

What Parkinson's Law and the Theory of Bureaucratic Displacement show is that there is a limit to the extent to which a given organization can expand and make use of Adam Smith's specialism and division of labor.

Indeed, upon reaching that limit and going beyond it, Smith's principles are turned upside down and thus reversed in effect.

In this way, the extension of corporatism to the entire economy is more or less the extension of both the pros and cons of the distribution of labor. While there are obvious benefits to the practice, there are certain drawbacks that must be acknowledged. It may well amplify the potential for higher production and greater efficiency, but, if so, it might also amplify the potential for lower productivity, waste, and corruption.

Just as the climate at any modern corporation encourages redundancy and misuse of time and resources, the same would be true of an economy-wide system under the government, and to an even greater degree given the enlarged scope. While bureaucracy in a single company displaces tasks and rewards by office space or perhaps the space between adjacent buildings, bureaucracy between companies and industries in the case of an economy-wide system would displace tasks and rewards by cities and even continents. The tendency for apathy in one's work, the likelihood of mistakes and miscues, and a sense of uselessness would multiply as the size of the bureaucracy grew; ultimately, so would the tendency for waste, corruption, and misallocation of resources.

The Difficulties of Archism

Now, it is possible that the single-firm economy would simply expand the benefits and drawbacks of the modern corporation to the entire economy, and that alone would be cause for concern considering the Law of Diminishing Returns. Though it is practically impossible to quantify the increase in benefits and drawbacks either way, we can assume that increasing the scope of a bureaucracy to the extent of the entire American economy would lead to greater waste and corruption. But a single-firm economy would have another distinguishing effect, one that is quantifiable in its absolute nature: the elimination of alternatives.

By design, an economy-wide system, directed by a central government, eliminates the potential for alternatives, whether competition between workers, consumers, or producers of the output. Companies competing in a free market are driven by the threat of rival firms and thus design their businesses based on the mere potential for their customers and workers to jump to an alternative. The company can only succeed if their customers and workers succeed. By contrast, an economy-wide company extinguishes competition and will thus design its business based on the guarantee of allegiance from its customers and workers.

The first thing that comes to mind is that an economy-wide system as envisioned by Marx and others differs little from the supposed free-market economy of the late nineteenth century, in which a few concentrated owners, the financial oligarchy, controlled a vast majority of the country's wealth, and the vast majority of workers and consumers were forced to do what the owners wanted just to get by. This monopolization was the main concern of Great Switch liberals and the primary reason for introducing government interference in the economy. Similarly, a centrally planned economy would eliminate the potential for alternatives and control the country's wealth. And, not only would it intensify the domination of wealth by a few elites by further centralizing the money supply into a single organization, it would add the authority of law to the diktat. The fact is that, unlike the power wielded by investment bankers and industrialists, the state's power to monopolize wealth would be backed by force and the threat of fines, imprisonment, or death. This raises the question: If monopolization of wealth leads to exploitation in the free market, what is to stop this new form of monopolization from leading to exploitation in a socialist state, especially considering the exploitation could be backed legally by force?

The answer reformers gave was that the government was the voice of the people, and so it would work in the interest of the people. It would only pursue policies that would benefit the people as a whole and not some privileged few. In short, the government would use its monopolized power to counter the effects of monopolization and thus provide equality.

Such a rationale rests on two premises, both of which are found to be rather precarious under scrutiny. The first is that the governing body can know the people's wishes at all times and can thus make the best choices with regard to the economy; the second is that, assuming the governing body has access to this information, it will be able to obey the orders of the public even to the neglect of its own selfish intentions. The first lofty assumption suggests that the governing body is virtually omniscient; the second suggests that the governing body will be made only of good-intentioned, self-sacrificing people—that it will be made of saints.

To examine the first: In order to know exactly what the people want at all times and for every action, a governing body would need a very sophisticated system of communication, which would prompt the people for their input for every possible desire and wish and transmit that information to a central repository. Now, one might well assume that even in this technically advanced age such a mechanism would be hard to generate. We can be certain that state governments do not employ anything of the sort. The best mode of communication they have at their service is a voting system which is administered once or twice a year and allows the people to choose elected representatives who might best convey their desires to the government. In some instances, this polling system allows the citizens to vote on specific measures that will affect them directly, though these make up a small minority of legislation passed.

Granted each country has its own form of election process, it can still be said that nearly all fail to convey the information needed for the government to act as the voice of the people in a sizeable proportion of its actions. The fact is that, in most voting systems, the electorate depends on elected representatives to speak for it, even when it is quite likely that no representative agrees with the voter on all relevant issues. To begin, there are just too many constituents for every possible representative to have the slightest inkling of what each citizen wants and needs°. Simply, it is impossible for any representative to take into account the needs of all his constituents. As a result, nowadays the voter is forced to choose between two or more candidates who share perhaps a handful of main concerns with the voter, and, beyond that, may well differ on everything else.

And yet, to vote for a politician would be to vote for his entire package, good and bad, even if one does not want the bad. In effect, one votes for five bills he doesn't want to get the two that he does want; for instance, he must accept the war to get the welfare. The modern cliché that a voter in a modern election must choose the lesser of two evils rings true; he doesn't vote on what he believes in, but rather on what he believes will hinder him the least. It can be no wonder that voter turnout is traditionally low in Western elections—voting is just not a viable way to communicate the citizen's beliefs and desires.

Moreover, the system that most governments have employed is based on some form or another of majority rule, so that the party who receives the most votes is the one that wins complete control, and the policy that gets the majority of votes is the one that all citizens must follow. Everyone else who voted for the losing parties must accept the rule of the winner despite the likely fact that they may well oppose the victors' every belief and desire.

Though everyone has a say in the election, once it has passed only those in the majority keep their voice and those in the minority are necessarily silenced. Medicare and Social Security represent perhaps the best examples of this in practice. These are programs which comprise the largest component of the federal budget, with Medicare taking up around 13% and Social Security taking up around 21% of the budget, and they are designed for everyone despite the fact that only 5 to perhaps 10% of the population is unable to plan and prepare for their own retirement. These programs may well be helpful to a handful of Americans, but, since we live in an all-or-nothing society, everyone is forced to comply. As Milton Friedman put it, government produces conformity even when there is no unanimity, a fact that Medicare and Social Security are only the primary examples of. In effect, all government action forces the will of the majority on the population as a whole.

This is to suggest that even the most direct government in existence today—the democratic-republic that America is supposedly framed upon—does not represent the people to the greatest extent possible. At best, such government embodies the voice of a certain majority of the voting public (if one can be assembled) as heard at some point in the recent past and on very broad issues. The minority's voice is not heard at all and is doubtless contradicted by the actions urged by the majority.

Alexis de Tocqueville's classic analysis of what he called the 'tyranny of the majority' suffices to illustrate the extent to which the majority in democratic nations control total wealth and subdue the needs of the minority. "The majority," he states in *Democracy in America*, "exercises a prodigious actual authority, and a moral influence which is scarcely less preponderant; no obstacles exist which can impede or so much as retard its progress, or which can induce it to heed the complaints of those whom it crushes upon its path." Like a true Juggernaut, a political majority is inclined to the same exploitative tendencies as a financial one.

There is a feasible system of communication that could be used to convey the beliefs and desires of the people, but it is one that collectivist governments flatly reject—the price system. Organized spontaneously with its swift adjustments and fluctuations, the price system is the only reliable reflection of the needs and wants of the individuals in a given society. In contrast to government action, the price system provides unanimity without conformity, allowing individuals to think and act without forcing others to do the same. Of course, the price system is not a perfect reflection of the people's needs and wants, by any means—Keynes for one proved that prices reflected effective demand and not, as it may have been assumed, real demand. Still, it is much more robust an indication of beliefs and desires, and much easier for the people to control than the voting system. A consumer can vote for or against a company or ruling party by purchasing or not purchasing this good or that service. By doing so, the consumer translates his intents in a very clear, quantifiable manner, thus adjusting the supply and demand for those goods and services. Altogether, the price system is a form of organic direct democracy that is exponentially more comprehensive and timely than any artificial voting system could possibly be.

Noting the deficiencies of the price system, however, and the effective demand problem that Keynes identified, socialist reformers concluded that the state could provide a better solution. Planned economies not only fail to use the price system to its greatest potential, but rather distort it by forcing certain kinds of production, hindering others, keeping prices high or low, and manipulating the buying power of the consumers. In order to accomplish their redistribution of wealth, centrally planned economies, and really all central governments, must necessarily abandon the best tool at their disposal for judging how their people can and should want to redistribute that wealth.

As Ludwig von Mises pointed out, there is in socialist nations a 'problem of calculation'. How, Mises asks, does a socialist government decide what should be produced or consumed? As he found, it can only do so arbitrarily, based on the bureaucrats' best guesses, because both the production and consumption processes are based on subjective value, which can change and shift depending on a number of unknown factors and cannot possibly be gauged by a few elites at the top of the organization. With regard to business executives and their employees or politicians and their constituents, the talk is of being 'out of touch', unable to relate to the needs and wants of the people far below them. In a socialist framework, it is the inevitable condition.

For example, how does a socialist government decide how much corn or beef or laundry detergent is enough to satisfy its people? It can determine a rough guideline based on what the administrators think, but what if a group in one part of the country suddenly craves more hamburgers? Or what if a new hybrid soap is developed? These shifts in beliefs and desires almost certainly cause wrinkles in demand, wrinkles that cannot possibly be distinguished by planners in an efficient or timely way. The upshot is, necessarily, delayed and ineffective governance.

The Realities of Public Choice

The second premise on which the voice-of-the-people rationale rests is that, assuming the officials in charge of ruling the country are able to track what it is the people want at all times, they are also able to conduct their actions in accordance with those desires and without distraction or corruption; it relies, in other words, on the officials being saints to no small degree. At first glance, one might be willing to afford such faith. It is true that there are plenty of government officials who get into politics in order to help the world, and there are certainly those who are diligent enough to see their aims followed through to the end. One cannot assume that government officials want to harm the people, though it may seem that way at times.

But whether they can achieve their good intentions is another question altogether. Just like the so-called robber barons of the nineteenth century, who presumably had no malevolent intentions, government officials are human beings with the same tendencies and faults as the best of us. And, if the robber barons operated in their own self-interest as opposed to that of the economy as a whole, mightn't government officials who have no malevolent intentions also operate in the interest of themselves instead of others?

It is true that government officials' jobs depend on their ability to secure well-being for others, and so their jobs depend on their ability to deny selfish interests. This is in contrast to, say, an investment banker, whose job is dependent upon his ability to secure well-being for himself and actually emphasize his selfish interests. Yet the barrier posed by the professional code of ethics of politicians and government officials is a thin screen that lets through most of the self-interest that is not otherwise accessed around back. Proofs derived in the Public Choice school of thought, developed by a number of twentieth-century American scholars including Kenneth Arrow, Duncan Black, James Buchanan, and Gordon Tullock, show that all public officials are economic actors, just like the rest of us, and that their actions are liable to be influenced by the same forces as the rest of us.

Politicians have self-interest at least with regard to getting elected and holding a post, and that process alone makes the prospect of complete self-lessness practically impossible. And experience shows that this self-interest extends to pretty much all of a politician's actions. In order to get elected and maintain his post, the politician must make promises to his constitu-ents and to his financial supporters. In order to come through on those promises, the politician must engineer his dealings in favor of the people who voted for him and funded his campaign. Just like the 'gifts' distributed by J. P. Morgan financiers in and around the crash of 1929, government officials might also issue various prizes for those who are close to them both personally and professionally. In short, there is no reason to believe that government officials are any more saintly than the rest of us when it comes to the distribution of other people's money. Who would deny Lord Acton's maxim that "Power tends to corrupt, and absolute power corrupts absolutely"?

Public Choice Theory is, as one of its founders, James Buchanan, called it, "politics without romance", that is, an analysis of policymakers' actions without the fanciful belief that they are saintly creatures capable of doing no harm. It is a curious fact of Modern Liberalism that so many able-mind-ed politicians and theorists once held and still hold firmly the romantic view that government administrators will, by virtue of their post, somehow be rid of the natural tendencies that lead industrialists and investment bank-ers to self-preserving and exploitative practices. One wonders, as Frédéric Bastiat did in his timeless work, *The Law*, how government officials could possibly be exempt from such inclinations. "If the natural tendencies of mankind are so bad," Bastiat posed, "that it is not safe to permit people to be free, how is it that the tendencies of these organizers are always good? Do not the legislators and their appointed agents also belong to the human race? Or do they believe that they themselves are made of a finer clay than the rest of mankind?°"

Amid a late twentieth-century revival of Classical Liberal thought, U.S. President Ronald Reagan echoed Bastiat's sentiments, saying, "We have been tempted to believe that society has become too complex to be managed by self-rule, that government by an elite group is superior to government for, by, and of the people. Well, if no one among us is capable of governing himself, then who among us has the capacity to govern someone else?°'" The stark questions show how absurd the notion really is.

Granted no governing body could be made of saints, we find that their decisions can be no sounder than those the rest of us make. And, considering the way the system is set up, with the decision-makers in control of large amounts of other people's money and charged with distributing it to still others, the likelihood is that those decisions will tend toward the uneconomic and unsound.

To roughly evaluate the decision-making process when it comes to economic exchanges, we can take a look at a set of possible variations that any given exchange might comprise based on the source and destination of the money and goods. In their pro-capitalist tome, *Free to Choose*, Milton and Rose Friedman describe four such possibilities: (1) you spend your own money on goods for yourself, as when you go shopping at the grocery store or mall; (2) you spend your own money on goods for someone else, as when you shop for Christmas or birthday presents; (3) you spend someone else's money on goods for yourself, as when you go for lunch on an expense account; and, (4) you spend someone else's money on goods for someone else, as when you buy the client's lunch on an expense account. All possible monetary exchanges can fall into one of these simple classifications, which can be laid out in tabular form as can be seen in Figure 27.

	Source of Funds	Recipient of Goods	Oversight
Self-Spending	You	You	High
Gift-Giving	You	Someone Else	Medium-High
Gift-Receiving	Someone Else	You	Medium-Low
Self-Less Spending	Someone Else	Someone Else	Low

Fig. 27—Relational Aegis Matrix.

From these simple classes, we can derive the relative level of soundness a decision would tend to have based on the decision-maker's proximity to the source of funds and the ultimate recipient of goods. The closer one is to the source of funds and to their recipient—when one is shopping for one's groceries, for example—the more attention he will pay to the value of the goods purchased and the price he pays for them. On the other hand, the more displaced he is from the source and the recipient—when one is buying a client's lunch on an expense account, for example—the less incentive he has to get a good deal.

Obviously, the degree to which this variance occurs will be different depending on the decision-maker's ability to adhere to specified guidelines, whether they are set personally or by command. One might well be able to disburse other people's money with as much interest and intensity as he would expend while shopping for himself. There is no reason to suppose this cannot possibly happen.

Still, experience proves that it is unlikely. For evidence, simply regard the kind of lavish expenditures sales associates and other executives make when attempting to entice potential clients. Entertaining is an enormous expense in nearly all industries these days, and has to no small degree become an industry itself, with restaurants and hotels thriving solely on the generous outlays of huge corporations attempting to attract clients. Simply, buyers and sellers dealing with money that is not theirs are like buyers and sellers dealing without prices at all, and it can therefore be no surprise when the prices that exist underneath all the flare begin to explode.

This phenomenon is, to a large degree, the basis for the Law of Diminishing Returns with respect to social endeavors. In a modern corporation, for instance, employees tend to slack off or at least grow increasingly ambivalent to their work the further that work is from the final reward. As compared with the first and second categories, in which the decision-maker's own funds are at stake, those engaged in the third and fourth categories of exchanges will be more willing to let irrelevant factors cloud their judgments, to settle for a subpar deal, and thus they will be more susceptible to fraud and other forms of corruption.

Government action lies almost wholly in the fourth category, and, as can be expected, one need not look far for evidence of government waste and ineptitude. Anyone who has been to the Post Office or Department of Motor Vehicles recently knows how inefficient government agencies can be—and these are just the service-oriented facets of the agencies, the ones visible to the suspecting public. The average taxpayer can only imagine how inefficient these agencies are beyond the public's scrutinizing eye.

Independent watchdog groups attempt to track the mismanagement of government agencies, but even the most diligent will fail to capture the extent of the fantastically overpriced items bought regularly, the outright waste, and 'missing money'. In a recent report, consumer advocate John Stossel attempted to convey the financial mismanagement that goes on at the Pentagon, where he says accounting discrepancies have totaled $2 trillion. When he asked David Walker, the head of the general accounting office at the time, how the agency could lose that much money, the bureaucrat chalked it up to size. "If you saw the number of systems that the Department of Defense had, with the lines of code, you would know the answer to that question. It is mind-boggling°."

Walker admitted that redundancy and waste occurred almost as a matter of fact. "If they have it, and don't know they have it, they may buy it again," he said. When Stossel finally suggested that no privately owned company would be able to get away with such waste before the shareholders would revolt, Walker's response was shockingly direct: "We're not a private company."

Of, By, and For the Special Interests

Not only does the system allow for mistakes and oversight, so too does it leave the door open to fraud and corruption. Given the abstracted method of representation in the voting system, public officials are to a great degree at leisure to dictate government action on their own terms, notwithstanding their constituents' wishes and not uncommonly directly against them.

In general, this is because a politician's constituents have only a small influence on his actions. It is true that the constituents are the ones that vote for or against the politician, and so it is they who decide whether he can keep his job. Beyond that, the constituents mean very little to the man or woman in office. Their sway comes only every once in a while in the form of an election, and then only inasmuch as the individual is a part of a large contingent of voters—the majority.

The lone activist who sends a letter to his representatives in order to persuade them on an issue, and receives an impersonal reply stating that they will have to just 'agree to disagree', knows all too well how little influence he has.

Nor is the lone constituent very motivated to try to influence his representatives. To check up on each congressman, city council member, and other representatives on up to the president, for every action they make, would amount to a full-time job in itself given the pure volume of political matters each official deals with. It is so difficult and time-consuming to sway government officials one way or another that it is almost impossible for a single person to find enough resources to ensure that any process will go his way. Checking up would defeat the purpose of a representative government anyway. The congressmen, city council members, and executives are all voted into office so that the people do not have to spend time worrying about every measure put up before the community.

Perhaps the most important factor in the relationship between the constituents and their representatives, however, is the fact that government action is just not designed to benefit individual citizens. Government action is so broad and comprehensive that, even if the lone constituent were successful in convincing his representatives on a particular measure, it would almost assuredly not benefit him in any justifiable way. He might see a few dollars in benefits or easier access to a particular destination, but the overarching lesson will be that the effort required to see a lobby through to its fruition simply does not pay.

Upon close examination, it becomes clear that public offices are just not geared toward individual constituents. Politicians try to act as though individuals matter, telling stories of individuals at campaign speeches and of how they are the intended beneficiaries of every policy made, but those stories only serve to promote the broader policy changes the politicians aims for. Ultimately, it is just not very practical for politicians to pay attention to individuals and families.

In order for constituents to become visible enough to the politicians, then, they have to band together, organize, and assemble some sort of unified front; they have to cease being individual citizens and become part of a large group, company, or union; they have to become, in other words, a 'special interest'.

The key lies in the structure of the system. If one looks at the representative process objectively, one will note that it has two salient features: highly concentrated amounts of money and a highly complex method of legislation necessary to disburse it. Given the first characteristic, the only party that is built to make use of government action is a group or company that is able to absorb large amounts of money in the interest of many people—a large corporation, for instance, that employs a great number of workers and has a large number of customers. The second characteristic of government means that the only parties that will be able to sway its actions are those that have a good base of resources in the first place and can devote time and effort to pushing for their legislation. In summary, government is almost wholly designed to be influenced by and thus give support to large, organized special interests.

To examine further, let us look at the kind of benefits that government can offer. With highly concentrated amounts of money and a complex method of legislation necessary to disburse it, beneficiaries must be able to justify receiving large quantities of funds, and they must have the necessary infrastructure in place to do so. The party must be organized and designed in such a way that it can manipulate the system and make use of the rewards. While individuals and families are in no way fit for such efforts, organized lobbyists, corporations, and unions have both the need for such large sums of money and the means to invest similarly large sums of resources to obtain it.

In the end, the parties that benefit from government action are exactly the kind of large, organized behemoths that the action is aimed at reigning in. A concrete example will drive the point home. In the late 1800s, the railroad industry was perhaps the greatest industry in America. Constantly expanding lines were making inter-city travel a regular event, and connecting the dominant East Coast with the Middlewest and South in an increasingly efficient manner. But, by the 1870s, as railroads had grown to become a principal means of travel for the thriving country, inconsistencies arose in the prices of passenger tickets. While long-distance travel between cities like New York and Chicago was relatively cheap due to numerous alternatives and competing railroads driving prices down, travel between close cities like Sandusky and Fort Wayne was relatively expensive because few carriers offered such routes, and prices were driven up due to lack of competition. Commercial shippers experienced similar rate differentials, and everyone experienced the same unfairness—low prices for the long haul and high prices for the short haul. It did not take long for a large contingent of these grieved travelers and shippers to vocalize a uniform complaint about 'discriminatory pricing'.

Combined with its wildcat tendencies and notorious cut-throat competition, the apparent discrimination made railroad companies easy targets for moralists and reformers across the country. To many, the industry had to be regulated and reformed. Some in the Populist movement demanded not only regulation, but nationalization of the railroads, presumably because they were too important to the economy to leave to their own devices in any way.

As a result of the protests, the Interstate Commerce Commission was formed in 1887 and finally began to take action around the turn of the century. By the time it had started chugging, however, the agitation that surrounded the industry was quelled partly by the ICC's establishment and partly because attention was redirected to other, more pressing concerns. In the meantime, the commission had been infiltrated by administrators who could hardly be described as consumer advocates; they were either railroad men themselves or at least worked with and depended on railroad men for their future incomes. And so, once the commission was up and running, it was clear to anyone within sight what direction it would take—it would benefit the railroads at the expense of the passengers and shippers.

The direction could be seen in the appointment of the ICC's first commissioner, Thomas Cooley, who had been a long-time lawyer for the railroads, and in some of the institution's first actions. To solve the long haul/short haul problem, for example, the commission simply raised prices on the long haul so that there would be no more 'discrimination'. Though it may have left prices at more proportionate levels, the result of the regulation, in essence, left the consumers worse off.

And so the kind of self-interested behavior that the commission was formed to diminish was neatly ingrained in the system from the start. As was captured in a letter by President James Garfield's Attorney General Richard J. Olney to railroad tycoon Charles E. Perkins, the ICC was nicely positioned to actually help the railroads, not restrict them. "The Commission," Olney said, "as its functions have now been limited by the courts, is, or can be made, of great use to the railroads. It satisfies the popular clamor for a Government supervision of the railroads, at the same time that the supervision is almost entirely nominal. Further, the older such a commission gets to be, the more inclined it will be found to take the business and railroad view of things. It thus becomes a sort of barrier between the railroad corporations and the people and a sort of protection against hasty and crude legislation hostile to railroad interests." Olney summed up the ruse by saying, "The part of wisdom is not to destroy the Commission, but to utilize it."

As soon as railroad executives saw the function in the commission, they began to devote a healthy portion of their budget to lobbying and public relations in effort to sway the regulation in their favor. They saw that they could use the central authority to engender legal grounds for higher rates, as they had with the long haul/short haul compromise, and they could engineer ways to limit competition so as to further monopolize the market for long-distance travel. One of the chief functions of the ICC was to organize railroads by cartels and assign routes so that each railroad could operate under the threat of less opposition. Naturally, less competition meant that the railroads could run more efficiently and so could hand the savings on to their customers. But, in the new arrangement, the customers had fewer options and so were bound to even stricter monopolization than they had been before.

In the 1920s and '30s, when automobile transportation exploded onto the scene, railroads naturally began to see their control diminish. Trucking presented the railroads with exactly the kind of competition that they had subdued for decades via the ICC. Trucking was inexpensive, faster, and just about anyone who could afford the cost of a truck could start a business. Of course, it didn't take long for the railroad interests to lobby for control of this burgeoning industry as well. In 1935, the Motor Carrier Act was passed, supposedly in the interest of the trucking companies, to bring automotive shippers under the jurisdiction of the ICC.

Included in the new regulation was the requirement that all truckers had to obtain a 'certificate of public convenience and necessity' to conduct business. Though all existing trucking companies were granted one at the onset of the act, proof required to qualify as an existing trucking company is said to have been rather fastidious and largely based upon the judgment of others. As a result, from 1940 to 1980, it was practically impossible for new companies to get into the business, and the same cartelization and monopolization that had occurred with the railroads also occurred with the trucking industry. The Reed-Bullwinkle Act of 1948 actually authorized truckers to fix rates by exempting them from antitrust laws.

Licensure and certification in general are ways to further the interests of those in power. Whereas the concepts of organizing a licensing bureau and establishing minimum criteria for entry in the market are logical and perhaps legitimate in their aim of ensuring that large companies do not crowd out competition or exploit their customers, these very disagreeable occurrences are almost always the result. Practitioners in most occupations have instituted some sort of association and licensing process to help regulate who may conduct business in the field, and almost all that do organize under licensure end up limiting competition and thus raising prices.

Engineers, surveyors, teachers, doctors and nurses, lawyers, psychologists, social workers, and accountants all have well-known and hard-to-achieve licensure programs that keep supply low and demand high. With the 2002 introduction of Sarbanes-Oxley in response to the Enron, Tyco, and WorldCom scandals, and the financial reform bill of 2010, it is as though a license has been placed on industry and business in general, making practically all new endeavors restrictive, burdensome, and thus unappealing. The result is not a decrease in corruption or malpractice, but rather a decrease in competition and an increase in consolidation which can only encourage more corruption and malpractice.

Everywhere one looks in the government, the story is the same. At first, some distressed group of reformers demand that an industry, large corporation, or cartel be dragged under the control of the government and heavily regulated so as to prevent exploitation; a commission, board, or department is formed and filled with the

The closer you look at Sarbanes-Oxley the more you realize it is almost perfectly designed to crush new business creation. The latest estimate for the annual cost of implementing Sarbox in a public corporation is $3.5 million. Pocket change for a Fortune 500 company; the entire annual profit of a newly public firm. Is it really any wonder that smart entrepreneurs look for a corporate sugar daddy instead of an IPO?

—EDITORIAL, *THE WALL STREET JOURNAL*, DECEMBER 6, 2008

most knowledgeable and experienced candidates for the task, naturally those who are closest allied with the hated industry or corporation; they sweep through regulation after regulation, which on the surface appears beneficial to the consumers or workers formerly being exploited but, in the end, only serves to further concentrate control and empower the exploitative companies. Ultimately, government serves as a more powerful tool in conducting the exploitation, not hindering it.

When the state is willing and able to provide large sums of money or regulatory power to particular causes and benefits, the almost inevitable response is that people will try as best they can to secure that money and power for themselves. It just so happens that the people who are best outfitted for such a lobby are the ones whom the reforms are aimed at restricting. Large companies, grandiose labor organizations, and sprawling associations all devote large swaths of their budget—sometimes all of it—to this new pursuit. The companies that can spend that kind of money will be the ones to benefit; those that cannot—the small startup company, the average sole proprietor—will lose out.

Special interests come in many forms and are as natural as the American dream. To the companies engaged in lobbying, it is just another way to make a profit. Just like the private companies who naturally exploit their workers and customers because they are doing all they can in a zero-sum game, so too does the federally subsidized or regulatory power naturally exploit its workers and customers. There is little substantive difference. Before government intervention, a company had to at least produce a desirable good; after government intervention, a company could just focus its efforts on navigating government regulation and the great storehouse of subsidies made available through welfare programs.

To take a more recent example, regard the agriculture industry, where around $20 billion a year in subsidies are dished out to farmers across the country. Special interests work every angle they can when money and power are to be gained, and the agriculture industry is no different. Archer Daniels Midland is a publicly traded food processing company with a market capitalization of $18.7 billion. Since it doesn't produce any retail-level goods, most shoppers do not recognize the name, but ADM's products are most likely in half of the groceries they buy.

ADM is also a major contributor to government bureaucracy. As a top producer of corn sweetener, for example, ADM has financed lobbyists and made contributions to politicians in a push for sugar quotas (aimed at making sugar more expensive and thus less marketable) and subsidies (to make corn sweeteners cheaper and thus more marketable). The idea is that these supports keep sugar prices high in the U.S. and thus make corn sweetener—and ADM—a profitable alternative. According to a *New Republic* article, the entire corn sweetener industry produced 1.7 million metric tons in 1979; and, after sugar quotas were reinstated in 1982, production grew to 5.5 million metric tons, more than 80% of which was generated by ADM°. The cost per consumer has been estimated at about $60 every year, which certainly won't break the bank, especially when it is divided up among thousands of products bought over the course of the year. But it adds up to around $3 billion per year for Americans together, and ADM takes the lion's share.

Another golden egg ADM has stumbled upon is the fuel additive ethanol, of which ADM is the largest producer in America. Ethanol—corn distilled into grain alcohol—is used to fortify alcoholic beverages like MD 20/20 and gin. It can also be used as a fuel additive. This second function has been seen as a boon for an energy-thirsty and security-threatened world. As such, ethanol is said to offer legitimate benefits despite the fact that policy analysts have claimed that the fuel itself is a subpar replacement for straight gasoline. The U.S. Department of Agriculture estimated that the cost of producing ethanol is double that of gasoline. As John Stossel put it, ethanol is like Hamburger Helper for gasoline, except it's more expensive.

Given its higher costs and lower effectiveness, ethanol is not a competitive product by itself. Still, we see it everywhere because of a number of subsidies given to ethanol producers from federal and state governments, the largest of which is an exemption from federal fuel taxes that amounts to 54¢ per gallon of ethanol sold. Estimates claim this tax break costs the U.S. Treasury more than $1 billion a year, making ethanol a viable product in the market and making ADM that much richer. Meanwhile, the taxpayers end up footing the bill.

In his concise *Economics in One Lesson*, journalist Henry Hazlitt granted that some public policies would end up helping the people in the long run, but that the system is designed so as to make these kinds of policies the exception rather than the rule. For most laws, subsidies, and regulations, the result is to help special interests at the expense of everyone else. "The group that would benefit by such policies," wrote Hazlitt, "having such a direct interest in them, will argue for them plausibly and persistently. It will hire the best buyable minds to devote their whole time to presenting its case. And it will finally either convince the general public that its case is sound, or so befuddle it that clear thinking on the subject becomes next to impossible."

Special interests invent all kinds of ways to influence government to help their companies, and often the rationale is a valid concern—national security, scientific research, protection of the food supply, protection of the environment, or job creation. No one can argue against the ultimate goal in any of these interests, but the means usually fall short of the aims. To increase exports, for instance, sound companies have been given subsidies in the hopes that they can market share abroad. While it certainly helps American workers when American companies grow overseas, an argument could be made that taxpayer dollars

> When plunder becomes a way of life for a group of men living together in society, they create for themselves in the course of time a legal system that authorizes it and a moral code that glorifies it.
>
> —FRÉDÉRIC BASTIAT (1801-50)

> It is even more apparent in our own day, when the régimes in many 'democratic' countries might be defined as a sort of feudalism that is primarily economic and in which the principal instrument of governing is the manipulation of political followings, whereas the military feudalism of the Middle Ages used force primarily as embodied in vassalage.
>
> —VILFREDO PARETO, *THE MIND AND SOCIETY, VOL. IV* (1916)

used to subsidize these efforts could be employed more effectively by the taxpayers themselves.

In 2008, for example, the National Endowment for the Humanities spent $4.2 million to conduct a 'National Conversation on Pluralism and Identity'; the Pentagon and Central Intelligence Agency devoted some $11 million to psychics who might provide special insights about various foreign threats; and the Department of Education spent $34 million supposedly helping Americans become better shoppers and homemakers°. I know of at least one taxpayer who could have come up with better ways to use his share of that money, however small that fraction may have been.

But a single taxpayer cannot compete with the various influences concentrated so heavily in Washington. With federal outlays estimated at nearly $4 trillion (and growing), it is understandable that whole industries would arise to figure out ways to get a hold of whatever bits and pieces of the total pie they can. Each one employs dozens or hundreds of workers to fine-tune lobbies and bills that help secure them more of the taxpayers' money. The upshot is an ever-sprawling complexity of convoluted systems and paperwork that no citizen can possibly take in or understand. Even the legislators themselves, who are allegedly responsible for the content of the bills, can have no concept of all the information that goes into law on a regular basis. To an increasing degree, only the special interests can control the system as it stands, and everyone else must pay the price.

3. THE COSTS OF TRANSFERRING WEALTH

GRANTING THE FACT THAT governments tend to be filled with inefficient and often corrupt officials, it is not necessary to assume that all governments fall under such inept control. It is possible, for instance, for the most principled and capable people in a society to get elected and carry out their tasks in an unselfish and dispassionate way. And it is right to assume that even states that do fall prey to the temptations of special interests and the encumbrances of bureaucracy can remain focused enough to accomplish what they set out to achieve. Assuming this is entirely possible, the question, then, becomes: What exactly do state governments set out to achieve, and by what means do they approach their goals?

Although the specific functions of the state are numerous and varied, it might be said that all state actions are related to a single aim—transferring wealth. In short, governments are wealth-transferring mechanisms, no more, no less. Governments may hope to attain all kinds of noble aims by their actions—the protection of persons and property, national defense, fulfillment of rights, and so on—but the way that they accomplish all of these is by transferring wealth from one sector to another.

The process goes like this: In general, an economy is made up of various sectors of private citizens who produce goods and services for other private citizens in exchange for more goods and services. The government comes in when administrators believe that some sector is not effective enough in providing for the general welfare and takes action to move resources toward or away from that sector. For instance, in times of international turmoil, the government may conclude that national defense must be reinforced, and so will allocate more resources to bolster the military. But the government can only send resources to military contractors, engineers, and manufacturers if it somehow takes those resources from other sectors. The money that the military uses to buy tanks and jets and bombs must come from some place, and the only place it can come from is other people, civilians, taxpayers.

Likewise, when government administrators find that a group of people lives in persistent hunger and homelessness, they may conclude that welfare institutions should be augmented and thus build more homeless shelters, provide more soup kitchens, and hand out more food stamps. In order to do this, however, resources must be taken from other sectors and sent to welfare organizations. Welfare, like military buildup and all other government action, is in essence a transfer of wealth.

There are three main tools the government uses to transfer wealth: fiscal policy, regulation, and monetary policy. In effect, all three are the same since their goals are all the same—control of the economy by moving wealth around—they just accomplish those goals in three different ways. Fiscal policy does so by taking in money through taxes and disbursing it through expenditures, regulations limit what can be done with wealth, and monetary policy changes the amount and value of money in the economy.

To see how all three tools are similar, let us look at each individually. Fiscal policy is a mechanism by which the state pulls in money, usually through taxes, and spends it on the various industries, companies, and individuals it views as potentially beneficial to the economy. In a sense, all economic policy can be viewed as a part of fiscal policy because all aspects of the government are reflected in the budget, whether it is building or improving municipal facilities such as roads, schools, or hospitals, or administering the military, the Post Office, the Department of Motor Vehicles, the Securities and Exchange Commission, or any number of other government agencies that fill the political sphere. Since all government action requires expenditures, and expenditures must have their start in some form of revenue, the whole enterprise is based in fiscal policy.

In the same way, taxes and expenditures can be viewed in a more general light as a means for the state to impose its will on the people. In this way, taxes and expenditures are forms of regulations and vice versa. For instance, a regulation that requires a business to install a handicapped access ramp to its tennis courts could be viewed as a kind of tax on that business and an expenditure to the construction company and handicapped patrons. Like all taxes, the business is forced to pay a certain amount more than it might have otherwise paid so that the construction company and handicapped patrons receive what the government views as beneficial. Regulation is a different kind of tax and expenditure where the wealth is moved around more directly between theoretically free parties. Consequently, all government action is regulatory in nature since regulation can be seen as a legal framework for economic activity, and all government action requires some form of legal framework to be established and maintained.

Lastly, monetary policy is based in the central bank and takes on a similar and yet more obscured approach. The idea is that, by changing the money supply, the government can control the amount of currency being circulated and thus control the amount of investment and, theoretically, the amount of production that the economy endeavors in. As such, monetary policy is a means by which the government can control the price of just about everything.

Monetary policy is also a form of regulation, or taxation and expenditure, in that it transfers resources from some groups of persons to others. True, the Federal Reserve can print money and so technically does not extract wealth from any party other than thin air, but the way money works means that a change in its overall supply can affect its value for everyone. As we have seen, money is only worth something if people are willing to trade real goods for it. Since the amount they are willing to exchange for it differs based on its availability, the mere process of printing money, though immediately increasing the wealth of whoever first obtains the currency, actually decreases the value of the money for everyone else. For this reason, it can be said that money printed by the central bank is a form of wealth transfer, as it takes wealth from savers and anyone far displaced from government action, giving it to spenders and those closely related to the state.

Zero-Sum Politics

The original intent behind wealth transferring was, of course, public welfare—to move an economy's resources around so that no citizens within the economy would have to go without the necessities. During the Great Depression and after, the ideas heard echoing above all others belonged to Keynes. He and other twentieth-century economists saw what Sismondi and Malthus had seen before them—that poverty in the midst of plenty was caused not by lack of production but by the dearth of money. People wanted goods, and goods were available if only the consumers had enough liquidity to facilitate the exchanges.

It was no far leap to arrive at the solution: Through various means, the state would take unused money from the upper classes and send it to the lower classes, who could use it for food, shelter, clothing, and so on. At its root, the philosophy suggests that by increasing taxes and regulations on the rich and the large corporations, government can create jobs, housing facilities, and welfare for the poor, thereby helping them onto their own two feet. Ultimately, the economy would even out so that everyone was on a level playing field.

But, ever since the Keynesians took center stage in the 1930s, wealth transferring became seen as something that provided much more than just economic equality. Indeed, it became stylish to fancy government as a sort of wealth generator, a magic producer of prosperity which could somehow do what private companies were economically incapable of doing. Government, by virtue of its ability to move money around, could push funds where they could be more productive, restrict them from where they were unproductive, and in the end create more total wealth. The impoverished citizens that the government would help could now be productive and thus add to society whereas they could not before. Indeed, beyond the notion of simply helping those in need, the more zealous Keynesians inferred that, if a government could spur investment, it was wholly creative.

The belief that government is actually a creative force is implied more often than it is argued directly. Still, the idea has permeated the popular consciousness throughout the twentieth century and continues to do so even today. Whenever the government perpetrates some economic maneuver, the effects are almost always saluted as wealth-generating. When the state sends millions of dollars to a contractor, for instance, who can then hire hundreds of employees to fulfill a contract, the government hails the creation of hundreds of jobs; when the Census hires hundreds of thousands of part-time workers to survey the population, government officials stick their chests out at the economic growth they have encouraged.

Advertisements for the 2010 U.S. Census reveal the mentality boldfaced. In its television campaign, the process of filling out the Census form is portrayed as a way to help everyone in a community with their various needs in order to create a better society. As the commercial's main character says, "I'm helping to build a better school for Pete . . . and Jen . . . And improving our roads for Mr. Grippo's carpool. I'm making health care better for— breathe, Risa, breathe!" Amid a triumphant march, the common man hero leads the charge: "My Census answers help our voices to be heard in Washington, so we can get our fair share of funding!" Just by filling out the Census, this everyman in his pajamas is building a community.

Such is the perception of all government endeavors. Just by pulling levers and flipping switches, government administrators are thought to be able to make use of resources to an extent unimaginable in the free market. The state is like the Wizard of Oz behind a curtain making everyone's wishes come true.

Of course, the skeptic wonders exactly how this wizard can help some individual or group if it is not through the means of transferring wealth. And, if it is through wealth transferring, is there not at least some group in the community that fails to benefit from the action? Indeed, is there not some group that must actually pay for the transfer? If Pete and Jen get more funding for their school, the skeptic asks, doesn't that mean that Ricky and Krissy get less funding for theirs? If Mr. Grippo's roads get more funds, doesn't that mean that Mrs. Lottie's roads will be attended to less? The skeptic gets no answers; he is just left to believe that somehow the government improves the lives of its citizens without necessarily harming the lives of anyone else, and that filling out the Census form is the miracle that accomplishes it all.

Ultimately, the conclusion that the honest viewer must come to is that there is no way for a citizen to benefit from government action without another citizen necessarily losing. In order for one sector to gain from government spending or regulations, another sector must necessarily lose in taxes or regulatory burdens. It is the way of any wealth-transferring institution. The Welfare State is, like the quasi-capitalist system of the 1890s and 1900s, a zero-sum game, in which one can only win if someone else is defeated. And so any benefit that is derived from the state for one must come in the form of a loss for another.

If an economy is a zero-sum game under free enterprise, then it is even more so under government control. If people compete and fight for money in a capitalist system, then they do so to an even greater degree in a statist system. And, just as the most aggressive, most coercive forces tend to rise to the top in the former, so too do they rise to the top in the latter. Transferring wealth has its costs, and, as might be anticipated, the costs are often unintended and counter to the original purpose.

The Burden of the Productive

The first major cost of wealth transferring is the most direct one: the loss to the individuals or groups from whom the wealth is taken. As we can see from the Census commercials, this cost is not as obvious as it might seem. Everyone sees the benefits of government action—the roads, the schools, the hospitals—but few if any pay attention to the costs born by the taxpayers, and that is where the burden lies. Because they must fund the government action, those taxpayers can no longer pay for maintenance for their cars, books for their own libraries, healthy food for their own diets, or some other endeavor they might like to pursue. Since these lost opportunities do not come into play, no one considers them.

This cost is the hidden opportunity cost identified by Bastiat in his Broken Window analogy. Everyone sees the shopkeeper's broken window, the need for a replacement, and the glazier's new work, so on the surface the vandalism is regarded as productive. The glazier will have a new amount of money with which he will be able to buy clothes, food, theater tickets, and so on. We do not see the shopkeeper's lost opportunity to buy a pair of shoes or something else, and so the cost in the equation is easily neglected.

Since the cobbler does not enter the picture, no one thinks about him. He is what William Graham Sumner called 'the Forgotten Man', the one whom no one cares about but who must pay the price for the action nonetheless. "The characteristic of all social doctors," Sumner says, "is that they fix their minds on some man or group of men whose case appeals to the sympathies and the imagination, and they plan remedies addressed to the particular trouble; they do not understand that all the parts of society hold together, and that forces which are set in action act and react throughout the whole organism, until an equilibrium is produced by a re-adjustment of all interests and rights. They therefore ignore entirely the source from which they must draw all the energy which they employ in their remedies, and they ignore all the effects on other members of society than the ones they have in view°."

Since the Forgotten Man is neither poor nor weak, the philanthropic do-gooders hardly notice him. He is not in need, so they need not concern themselves with him. The result is almost always that they end up taking advantage of him. "He will be found to be worthy, industrious, independent, and self-supporting. He minds his own business, and makes no complaint. Consequently," Sumner adds, "the philanthropists never think of him, and trample on him."

It is always easier to focus on what people receive in a certain exchange and neglect what other people necessarily miss out on because of it. As with Bastiat's Broken Window, government officials focus on that which is seen—improvements to schools, roads, and hospitals—and not that which is unseen. The Census commercial, for example, promotes state action as a way to get something new while neglecting all that could be obtained in lieu of the wealth distribution, and so it seems like a win-win situation.

> Bear in mind that towards the payment of debts there must be revenue; that to have revenue there must be taxes; and that no taxes can be devised which are not more or less inconvenient and unpleasant.
>
> —George Washington,
> Farewell Address (1796)

But it must be acknowledged that, in its essence, a state government is just not built to create wealth, only to take it from some and give it to others. It is not in any meaningful way a manufacturing plant or a farm; it is an office, a bureaucracy. No matter what the wealth is used for, whether it is used efficiently or effectively, someone always pays for it.

Now, most Collectivists will freely admit this cost of wealth transferring, and, as a matter of fact, promote it as the only fair thing to do. The belief is that the ones who bear the burden of taxes and regulations are very rich individuals and corporations, that they can and should want to shoulder the weight required to even out the playing field. And, it would seem, most bystanders in the country will agree—the very rich are to blame for our problems anyway, and so it is all right if they have to pay the costs of fixing those problems.

But the open-eyed spectator will note that the costs placed on the very rich might not be, and often are not, paid by them but rather deferred to the rest of the population. It is true that rich persons and corporations incur the actual taxes and regulations, but they are also in a position to be able to translate those costs into higher prices for the goods and services they sell, so that the people who end up paying for them are the consumers and workers, not the owners and rich capitalists. Just as in all forms of exploitation, the very rich, the owners of the means of production, are the ones who control the sundry exchanges in which the rest of us engage. And that goes for regulated exchanges as much as unregulated ones. If the rich are somehow required to pay more for a given exchange because of a new tax or regulation, they will find a way to raise their prices so that they can make the same profits as before.

> A government in which it is permitted for a certain class of men to say, 'Let those pay taxes who work, we should not pay because we do not work,' is no better than a government of Hottentots.
>
> —VOLTAIRE (1694-1778)

For instance, if a plastics manufacturer is forced to pay a new tax on carbon emissions, the owners will certainly incur some sort of additional costs, whether by paying for the tax directly or by adjusting their operations to reduce their carbon emissions and avoid the tax. Either way, the owners will just add that expense to the cost of doing business. And, just as it is with any other expense, they will attempt to offset it with greater revenue somewhere else. They will raise prices, or, in some cases, lower other costs, such as labor wages. One way or another, the costs will be deferred to the consumer or worker.

To bring it to the workaday plane, regard the common complaint that the very rich pay less in taxes than do the working classes. Warren Buffett, for example, the great investor ranked as one of the richest persons in the world, has admitted that he pays a lower percentage in taxes than his secretary, who is apparently not one of the richest persons in the world. How is it, one might wonder, that a system designed to extract wealth from the rich and give it to the poor allows this inequality? Simply, the very rich, by their ability to manipulate the system and configure a way around various tax liabilities and regulations, have been able to secure a more cost-effective way to make money. They can arrange their wealth so that their income is earned in tax-free endeavors such as real estate deals or low-tax endeavors such as securities; meanwhile, the average office clerk or machine technician has no such luxury since he must earn his income the old-fashioned, taxable way.

To be sure, the very rich and the owners of the means of production are in as much control with government regulations as they were without. The only difference is that they have more bureaucracy to wade through, more fine print to scour, and more interests to satisfy in the process. That only leads to more costs that they must incur and then transfer on to consumers and workers. Such a system doesn't hinder the rich and powerful; it gives them a practically infinite maze in which to hide and keep secret their endeavors so that their wealth is less obvious and more difficult to trap.

*   *   *

Of course, it is one thing for wealth-transferring to cost those who must supply the government with the wealth in the first place. But, whether or not that comes from the rich, it must be acknowledged that the costs of wealth transferring are not limited to these formal penalties. Ensconced in the process of government action are a number of other expenses that are no easier to pinpoint and calculate than they are to round up and get rid of. To begin, there is no doubt that the transfer of wealth, like any bureaucratic process, has administrative costs. Taking an amount of money from one sector and putting it into another necessarily requires someone to carry that money, the facilities to extract the money, and the means to disburse it. Altogether, the infrastructure needed to transfer the funds might well be more elaborate than the infrastructure designed to create or use the money in the first place.

A fundamental tenet of economics says that any exchange comes with transaction costs. When looking at David Ricardo's Law of Comparative Advantage, we saw that a simple exchange of goods required the traders to allocate some resources to the process itself—bringing the goods to market, advertising them, and fulfilling the sale. Likewise, government wealth-transferring must also bring goods to the table, advertise (paradoxically), and allot resources to the fulfillment of the exchange. This is why Washington, D.C., the hub of government action in the United States, has transformed from a boggy marsh in the eighteenth-century to a thriving metropolis in the twenty-first, with millions of people living and working within, all engaged in the intricate dealings associated with moving wealth.

Each of these activities presents a cost. The army of bureaucrats must be paid, the sprawling government buildings that house the army of bureaucrats must be erected, and all the administrative costs needed for such an enterprise must be accounted for like in any other business. The cost of administration might be best gauged by the size of the industry in relation to sectors in the rest of the economy. A study conducted by the Manufacturers Alliance found that, in the mid-aughts, government accounted for the same percentage of GDP (12.7%) as the entire manufacturing sector[*]. While manufacturing has steadily declined throughout the last century, government has grown to become a formidable player to the extent that, during the recent recession, the government was the only sector of the economy that was growing. And it was exploding—with use of its nearly limitless supply of newly invented money, the government was eager to get the economy back on track by adding as many jobs as it could, the Census being a major contributor.

It is for this reason that Keynes, when putting together his model for aggregate demand, made sure to acknowledge the government's role. By the 1930s, it was no longer sufficient to speak merely of consumption ('c') and investment ('i'); so too must government spending ('g') be added to the equation. In the neo-Keynesian world of the twenty-first century, 'g' is viewed to an increasing degree as a determinant of overall economic health. Today, no major politician or businessman can speak of private industry without mentioning what role government has had in shaping it.

But, again, it is not as though the government has just conjured up this sector out of thin air. All of the wealth created by the government must have come from somewhere. When the state creates jobs, businesses, and even whole industries, it can only pay for them through one form or another of taxation, which must come from the people. That means that one job created by the government, then, is a job that the private sector is deprived of; one thriving firm supported by the state is a company that cannot thrive in the free market. As such, the 'g' in the c-i-g model should be considered diversionary and not original by any means.

And this cost includes a much wider expanse than just that which is visible in the jobs and industries of the public sector. Since government can shift so much money around, it becomes profitable for private businesses to direct their efforts toward influencing exactly where that money is moved. And so, the mere presence of 'g' alters the composition of 'c' and 'i'. The efforts of private sector individuals, companies, and industries end up being directed toward the wealth transferring process, and, ultimately, everything becomes a factor of 'g'.

For instance, when the government puts aside some several billions of dollars to develop the solar power industry, the real cost is not just in the billions transferred to that arena, but all of the money that private firms must now divert to try to attain those funds. Companies give up what may or may not be a profitable and efficient business in order to get their hands on some large chunk of the money that the state is handing out so freely.

When so much money is available through a single channel, it is only natural that all businesses in sight of that prize will rearrange themselves for a chance to obtain those funds. Companies need to produce goods and carry on some semblance of normal business, but their output is demoted to only one component of their success—the other is their ability to prove their worthiness to the central government. By doing that, they can really strike gold.

And so resources are diverted not only in the government but in the private sector as well. It is a theme summarized precisely by writer Jonathan Rauch in his theory on 'Demosclorosis', or what he says is the paralyzing condition of the modern Welfare State. "By definition," says Rauch, "the power of government to solve problems comes from its ability to reassign resources, whether by taxing, spending, regulating, or simply passing laws. But that very ability energizes countless investors and entrepreneurs and ordinary Americans to go digging for gold by lobbying government." This is the natural consequence of a redistributive government in which large sums of money are available for those companies that can best finagle the legislative system. Rauch goes on to show that the ultimate effect is an entirely distorted economy. "In time, a whole industry—large, sophisticated, professional, and to a considerable extent self-serving—emerges and then assumes a life of its own."

Indeed, the complete power that government wealth transferring wields over the economy is not at all measured by the figures in the budget. To gauge its real scope, one must take into account the resources businesses and individuals allocate toward lobbying and persuading the policymakers, the time and effort spent writing grant proposals, the energy spent on meeting countless regulations, and all the resources they put forth to getting around the ones they cannot meet. All of these resources, which might have otherwise been directed toward productive or cumulative endeavors, now must be devoted to gaming the system and seeking the wealth that government is busy transferring. While the old strategy of producing desirable goods for consumers implies being productive and helpful to society as a whole, the new strategy of lobbying government can be rather unproductive and harmful. It does not matter to a company if there is an overall loss in the wealth transfer process, as long as they make a profit on it. If a company can make a million dollars in subsidies, for example, it is profitable to spend $999,999 in lobbying to obtain those subsidies. Formerly, that $999,999 would be spent trying to create goods or services that consumers could benefit from; now it is dedicated to unproductive ends. The company does not care since it has made a profit.

Wealth transferring acts like an enormous weight at the center of a sheet of rubber, toward which all the objects revolving about it involuntarily gravitate. The bigger and more massive the central government, the more the economic plane is warped by its presence, and the greater the inclination for all the orbiting objects to convene in the center. As in Gammon's Law of Bureaucratic Displacement, the state is the ultimate bureaucratic black hole, sucking in whole galaxies of industries and businesses, and emitting less and less light as it grows.

Skewing Supply and Demand

The effect of this massive presence can be seen perhaps most vividly in an economy's prices. One of the fundamental forms of regulation in the modern government is price controls, or limits on what goods or services can be bought and sold for. With the assumption that some prices are set too high and some prices are set too low for everyone to have the same opportunity, state governments have sought to impose regulations on them so as to provide a fairer market for the goods or services.

Of course, what this tends to do is simply alter the supply and demand for those goods and thus disrupt the market further. To see the effects, we can recall the simple Diamond-Water Paradox touched on earlier. In a free market, prices are allowed to fluctuate freely as supply and demand rise and fall. When supply is low and demand is high, as with diamonds for instance, the price will be high. When supply is high and demand is low, as with water, the price will be relatively low. If the supply of diamonds suddenly skyrocketed, ceteris paribus, their price would plummet. Similarly, as the supply of water diminishes, its price will rise.

In reflecting the current supply and demand of given goods or services, prices communicate information to both potential producers and consumers. This information is crucial for the producers and consumers because it tells them whether the good or service is worth producing or consuming. As such, a change in the price of a good or service can affect its supply and demand. If, for example, the price for diamonds rises, a miner may well see it as profitable to seek out more diamonds and bring them to market, and the supply will go up. If the price drops, the miner won't see his job as profitable and will seek out some other form of employment, and the supply of diamonds will stay the same or go down. By the same token, higher prices mean that fewer consumers will want to buy the diamonds, and demand will go down. Lower prices mean that more consumers will want to buy the precious gems, making the demand go up.

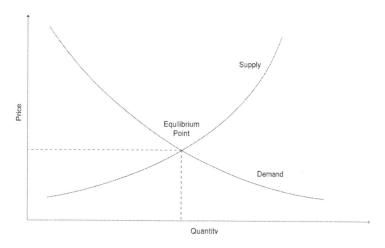

Fig. 28—Supply and Demand with Equilibrium Point.

This system is the natural result of all free-market conditions. Buyers and sellers are guided by the Invisible Hand toward a place where the most profitable amount of goods and services are exchanged and everyone gets what he sees as beneficial. The ultimate effect is that supply and demand of a good or service will meet at a certain point in the middle to provide an equilibrium price, the price at which an equal number of units would be offered by producers and wanted by consumers.

Transferring wealth undermines all of that. Setting the price for a good or service well above its natural equilibrium would increase its supply, as more producers would look to get in on the profitable enterprise, and diminish its demand, as potential buyers would be dissuaded by the steeper charges (see Figure 29). At the same time, setting a price well below its natural equilibrium would decrease its supply and bolster its demand, as producers would find less incentive to offer the good or service and consumers would find greater value in it. The upshot of such price controls is invariably either a surplus or a shortage. When the price is set above the natural equilibrium, supply goes up and demand goes down, resulting in a surplus; when the price is set below the natural equilibrium, supply goes down and demand goes up, resulting in a shortage.

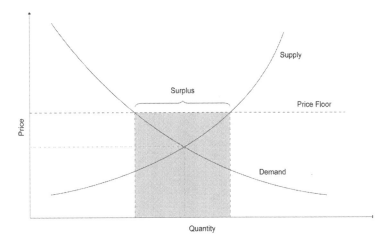

FIG. 29—Supply and Demand with Price Floor.

Evidence of this phenomenon can be seen throughout the twentieth century as price controls have been implemented and withdrawn by turns of various government initiatives. In every case, the short-term effect has always been either surplus or shortage as the economy adjusted to the altered state of affairs.

Perhaps one of the most illustrative examples of this is found in the gas shortages seen across America in the 1970s. In both 1974, after an OPEC oil embargo, and 1979, after the revolution in Iran, price controls were placed on gasoline to prevent gouging by the stations. As soon as the controls were in place, like clockwork, the supply went down and demand went up. It was the only foreseeable outcome, as the price controls gave less incentive for gas stations to conduct business and at the same time gave consumers added incentive to seek it out. The result was a shortage and the long lines at the pump that we have become so familiar with thanks to the accounts of the irate consumers who had to deal with them.

It is true that the disturbances in the Middle East affected the supply of oil, and prices would naturally have gone up in the absence of the controls, but, as Milton and Rose Friedman pointed out in their study of the matter, the disruption did not lead to shortages around the world, only where price controls were instated. For instance, Germany and Japan avoided shortages and long lines because they did not instate price controls. Certainly, state-side consumers benefited from lower prices—they could buy a tank of gas for as much or less than they could a decade before—but as much as drivers saved in gasoline expenses, they surely lost when considering all the time and resources wasted searching for open stations and waiting for hours in line to obtain the cheap gas.

In contrast to the experience of the 1970s, consider the price of gasoline in the last few years as an example of what happens when controls are not put in place. In 2008, prices at gas stations reached more than $5 a gallon in some cities across the U.S., due in large part to the oil-producing nations' decision to limit output and raise the price of crude petroleum. Widespread outrage swept across the country in response to the skyrocketing prices and, during the presidential election, calls were heard for tax relief and regulations on the gas companies.

In the fall of that year, something shocking happened—prices fell on their own. Without government regulation or tax relief, gas prices suddenly began to drop and continued dropping until people were paying 1990s prices at some gas stations. In June 2008, this driver spent $5.03 a gallon; in November, he recalls paying $1.80—all without the government stepping in and without shortages or long lines at the pump.

What happened is that people stopped driving as much; they traded their SUVs for hybrids and simply kept off the roads. With less gas being used, the demand for gas dropped and, as is the case whenever demand drops, retailers adjusted prices to encourage more business. It is the natural course of events that bring supply and demand together at equilibrium. When the prices are allowed to move where they will, inequality and displacement are avoided, and business flows like normal.

It must be admitted that people ended up paying more during 2008 for gas than they were accustomed to paying. This ended up hurting those who could not pay such exorbitant prices and hindered them from conducting business to the extent they may have wished. Price controls are aimed at helping those disadvantaged and impoverished by allowing them to carry on as they had before.

But the ultimate effect of controls is to skew the supply and demand such that the entire system falls off-kilter. All are punished from the resultant inefficient and contradictory system, and no one can be said to gain from wasted time, especially the impoverished.

Programs specifically directed at providing assistance to the underprivileged are perhaps the most disruptive and thus the most harmful. Price controls instituted for housing provide the most striking example. During and after World War II, rent controls were established across America to meet growing housing needs spurred by the influx of returning GIs. But, rather than helping the GIs find good, affordable housing, the controls backfired. The result, as could have been expected, was lower supply of housing and higher demand. Economist Thomas Sowell showed that there was no inherent cause for the shortage, as the country's population and its housing stock both increased by about 10% during the war. A shortage developed, however, because price controls altered the market.

The logic is easy to follow. Suppliers were less inclined to rent out their housing at the lower prices, so they withheld units; and, at the same time, consumers were more inclined to acquire space due to the more affordable rates. While fewer apartments were put on the market, more individuals and families looked to occupy places of their own, housing they couldn't afford before the war. Sowell gave a personal account of this phenomenon in his *Basic Economics*.

He explained that his own family had been confined to a two-bedroom dwelling before the war, but with cheaper prices afterward, they were able to occupy two apartments with a total of four bedrooms by the end of the war. Like other Americans with comfortable living arrangements at the time, he and his relatives were baffled as to why so many could not find housing.

Shortages persisted throughout the 1940s despite rent control laws and only evaporated with the repeal of large-scale controls in the 1950s. In cities where rent controls were fixed, such as San Francisco and New York, supplies continued to remain lower than demand and shortages persist to this day. Demographics of the rent-controlled units in these areas clearly illustrate the correlation—rent controls skew prices and thus give renters incentives to spread out and occupy more space. The 2002 San Francisco Affordable Housing Study found that residents of rent-controlled units were fewer in number and less likely to have children than those in market-priced units. While the national average is around 26%, some 49% of San Francisco's housing units are occupied by single residents. Likewise, Census reports show that 48% of households in Manhattan are occupied by only one person.

A 1997 *New York Times* article summed up the predicament of cities under rent control, where frivolous tenants soak up prime real estate while needy families sit by waiting. "There are plenty of cheap subsidized and rent-regulated apartments around," the author states, "but these rarely become available, and to get one you generally have to know someone or spend years on a waiting list." Examples helped to demonstrate. "A building rehabilitated with money from the city has $600-a-month one-bedroom apartments set aside for artists. A subsidized two-bedroom apartment rents for $44 a month. A $93-a-month one-bedroom rent-controlled apartment has been empty in recent months because its tenant has been at his Florida home, but he's not about to give up the lease°." The reasonable observer wonders why he would. It would be a financial blunder to give up such a gold mine.

Just as demand goes up under rent controls, supply goes down. One study showed that, within three years of the imposition of rent controls in Toronto, 23% of rental units in owner-occupied structures such as duplexes were pulled from the market. If it is not profitable, then desertion is the only reasonable course of action.

The extreme can be seen in the housing units that have been simply abandoned by their owners, who left the structures vacant and boarded-up to avoid the utility and maintenance costs they could no longer afford. During the 1980s, it was even fashionable to 'burn out' the residences in order to collect the insurance payments on the buildings before abandoning them. Filmmakers documented the scenes in the Bronx and Queens amid what appeared to be apocalyptic wastelands of towering trash piles accumulated in the middle of empty, smoke-stained brick buildings. At one point, estimates claimed that there were at least four times the number of abandoned units in New York as there were homeless people.

* * *

Like shortages, surpluses occur based on the same artificial levels of supply and demand, though they appear because of price floors rather than price ceilings. Regard a hypothetical example using the sale of bottled water. Say the going price for water is $2 a unit. Then, let us say that, for some reason, government decides to set a minimum price for bottled water higher than the natural equilibrium, say at $4. Here too the result would be a predictable shift in the supply and demand, though in the opposite direction. Supply would rise because those who procure and bottle the water would be enticed by the higher profit potential, but the demand would fall due to the higher prices. Ultimately, fewer exchanges would be made and a surplus would accumulate.

This can be seen in the case of one of the most pervasive price floors in the United States, the minimum wage. In this form of control, the government sets the price of labor—wages—such that it can go no lower than a given hourly rate. The idea is that no one can be exploited and everyone will be able to earn a 'living wage'.

The minimum wage is used as a way to lift up the underprivileged, to ensure that the working classes can survive and thrive in the competitive world. It is a commendable aim without a doubt, but has unintended consequences that tend to nullify its benefits. When minimum wage laws are enacted, for instance, some degree of a surplus of labor inevitably arises. Just as the surplus of bottled water appears when its supply increases and demand decreases, the surplus of labor can also be witnessed by an increase in supply and a decrease in demand. Since wages are set artificially high, more people want to work and fewer employers want to hire them, a condition that is also called unemployment.

In effect, minimum wage laws mean that less qualified workers who would have accepted lower rates cannot be employed. It is for this reason that critics of minimum wage laws have argued that the controls force employers to discriminate against those less qualified workers. True, employers must increase wages for the workers they keep, but, given enough constraints on profit, they might well be forced to reduce the number of employees being paid those higher salaries. Total work would then be redistributed among the employees still working so that their output would equal their newly increased wages. Thus, minimum wage laws give employers incentive to hire only the most productive workers and discriminate against the least productive workers. Whereas the latter might have found some employment at half the minimum wage and thus been given a chance to bring in some earnings and possibly learn skills on the job, they are now relegated to unemployment, and thus have less of a chance to learn the skills necessary to improve.

In fact, as Chicago School economist George Stigler found in his *Economics of Minimum Wage Legislation*, this redistribution of labor can be so effective that a rise in minimum wages might cause employment to fall to a greater degree than wages rise, thereby reducing earnings in the aggregate, an effect that is worse for the workers as a whole. Minimum wage laws are naturally geared toward helping the lower classes, but can it be said that higher wages for fewer workers is a better deal than lower wages for more?

The correlation between a rise in minimum wages and unemployment is not always the clearest connection to make. The complexities of any labor market presuppose a number of variables, all of which play a significant role in both wage rates and unemployment. Still, most empirical studies show that minimum wage laws increase unemployment, especially among the lowest-skilled workers. One such study focused on the correlation between the rise in minimum wages and unemployment among minority teens. In 1948, the minimum wage was 40¢ per hour, unemployment was about 3.8% overall, and about 10% for teenagers, both white and black. The discrepancy between older and younger workers was attributed to the inexperience of a group first entering the labor market. In 1950, the minimum wage was nearly doubled to 75¢, and, in 1956, it was increased again to $1.00. While unemployment fell overall after the boost in minimum wages, unemployment among teenagers shot up, and a gap appeared between white and black teenagers. By the late 1970s, unemployment for white teens was 15 to 20% and 35 to 45% for black teens[*].

Cui Bono?

In most cases of surpluses and shortages caused by government action, the state takes on the liability of the excess or dearth of goods and services. This is only reasonable considering that the state is the cause of the disequilibrium. It only makes sense that, if government is causing a good to be produced at a higher volume than it normally would, government should buy up the unused goods. The same rule applies when government causes less of a good to be produced, in which case the state would provide consumers with their unmet needs. In the instance of rent control, where the result has been a housing shortage and homelessness, the government has assumed the task of subsidizing housing projects as well as building and maintaining homeless shelters to compensate. In the case of minimum wage laws, where unemployment has been the result, government has instituted unemployment insurance and other welfare programs.

On the large scale, the overall effect of government intervention might well be the same as it was before—workers, employed or unemployed, might be getting the same earnings; families may have the same housing available, more or less. But, since the government assumes the extra burden and a significant chunk of those funds goes to facilitating the programs, the taxpayers end up paying a higher price and the economy as a whole suffers because of the added bureaucracy. It may seem as though we are paying someone to dig a hole and then fill it back up again. The ground remains level, and no real economic gain can be found, but it has cost the economy in time lost and resources used. The end result is waste and wealth frittered away.

Agricultural price controls have been a part of the system as long as any other, perhaps because of the importance of farming and food products in the economy. Everyone needs to eat, and so it is thought that we need farmers to succeed and prosper. And so government programs and controls have been relied upon to ensure farmers' success.

During the Great Depression, this principle was underscored by a series of programs. Prices of farm products dropped so severely that many farmers' incomes were not high enough to pay for their expenses. As a result, many were forced out of business. This was, of course, no different than the state of other sectors in the economy, but, since agriculture was so essential to the health of the people, it was argued that farm prices should

be propped up so that farmers could stay in business and in turn support
the entire economy.

The solution proposed was to return the prices of farm goods to 'parity'
with prices of goods from a previous time. Lobbyists used the period from
1909 to 1914 to set the parity, partly because prices were more consistent during that period but also because farmers flourished then in what
amounted to a golden age for agriculture.

Two main methods were employed to attain parity prices. First, some
farmers, such as those farming citrus fruits and nuts, were given mandates
to restrict the amount of goods brought to market. The lower supply would
thus encourage higher demand and higher prices for the goods. To ensure
the limited supply, the Secretary of Agriculture regulated local cartels and
prosecuted farmers who sold more than they were authorized to put on
the market. Second, other farmers, such as those farming corn, rice, wheat,
and tobacco, were granted freedom to produce as much as they wanted,
after which the government would simply buy up large quantities of the
goods and take them off the market. Estimates show that during some
years of the Great Depression the government bought as much as 25% of
the wheat grown domestically so that supply would remain low, demand
would remain high, and prices would rise.

The inquisitive will wonder what the government did with the food it
bought. Did it eat the supply literally? Or did it eat the loss figuratively? To
a large degree, it was the latter. The government was unable to make use
of the crops without putting them on the market and thus increasing the
supply. As a result, it was forced to destroy the food in order to keep prices
high. In one of the great ironies of the Great Depression, at a time when
hunger ran rampant throughout the country, the United States government
was responsible for wasting vast amounts of agricultural products to maintain its price controls. Reports tell of the federal government buying six
million hogs in one year alone simply to destroy them, of produce plowed
under, and of milk being poured down sewers, all to prop up prices so that
a supposedly essential component of the economy could survive.

The waste displayed by government programs during the Great Depression shows in full detail the paradox of government intervention. The purpose is naturally to help those in economic need and to prop up the economy as a whole. In order to do that, administrators have formulated a number of abstractions that indicate where wealth must be transferred and to what degree. But, by focusing on the abstract process of transferring wealth, the persons involved neglect the overall effect on the economy such that real wealth is destroyed. Government will argue for all kinds of taxes and expenditures, regulations and controls, all with the people's best interest in mind and a storehouse of seemingly logical data to support the actions, when, in the end, the thing that matters—the well-being of the people—deteriorates silently.

Not unlike the bystanders in Bastiat's Broken Window, public officials and private interests alike voice sound arguments for nearly all kinds of government initiatives, no matter how counterproductive, wasteful, or even utterly destructive they may be. Programs that seek to 'make work' for various individuals whether or not that work is beneficial to the economy, 'spread-the-work' projects that aim to ensure an increased amount of laborers are employed to do what fewer have done in the past, as well as anti-machinery movements that aim to limit the productivity of workers so as to ensure more secure jobs, are all part of a broad scheme to reduce overall effectiveness in the economy in hopes of increasing total wealth. The point is to shuffle money around to the greatest extent possible, and it doesn't matter if that money goes to any productive end or if it is simply frittered away; as long as money is circulated, the Keynesian assumption goes, well-being will rise.

As a ludicrous, though hardly surprising, consequence of the various wealth-transferring schemes maintained by the federal government, special interests that feed from the trough often secure their grants or subsidies in direct conflict with other special interests that are getting funds for the opposite purpose. Milton and Rose Friedman gave a striking account of this self-defeating activity: "In one massive building in Washington some government employees are working full-time trying to devise and implement plans to spend our money to discourage us from smoking cigarettes. In another massive building, perhaps miles away from the first, other employees, equally dedicated, equally hard-working, are working full-time spending our money to subsidize farmers to grow tobacco."

The Friedmans show how this occurs throughout Washington in every industry and for every kind of good or service—energy, agriculture, environment, security, and so on. When they do clash, the effects of these endeavors on society cancel out. Again, the government is paying someone to dig a hole and fill it back up. Meanwhile, the special interests receive their profits and the taxpayer is the one who must sign the check. This occurs almost without second thought, as if it is just part of the whole game.

Perhaps the most egregious yet still disregarded aspect of this paradox is the promotion of war as a creative enterprise. During the buildup to the Second World War, for example, compelling arguments were made that suggested entering the war would be good for the economy—unemployment would drop, production would boom, and the economy as a whole would grow to unprecedented levels. And indeed, all of the above occurred in the years after Pearl Harbor. After a decade of economic struggle, the war did bring the United States out of depression, unemployment was zero, industrial production skyrocketed, and there was tremendous growth across the board. But all of this was of course the abstract kind of growth that we have been conditioned to regard in a money-driven, government-run economy.

What is not accounted for is that all of the growth was geared toward destructive ends, not unlike in the Broken Window. Unemployment was so low because so many men were enlisted to fight and possibly die for their country; production was high, but the output was to be wasted on the battlefield; everyone was gainfully employed but limited in the goods they could buy and the services they could enjoy. Altogether, wealth was diminished during the war, but that wasn't the case according to the economists of the day.

Of course, it must be admitted, money was paid for the tanks and jets and bombs used in the war, just as money is paid for engineers to build bridges to nowhere or for farmers to grow crops that will be destroyed by the state. And, just as it is with all other monetary transactions, the bearer of that money can then go on to spend it on groceries, furniture, movies, and so on. And so, it is argued by Keynesians, the economy benefits from these kinds of government expenditures just as it benefits from private sector transactions—they encourage economic growth where there would otherwise be none. But this is to mistake abstract wealth for real, to assume that just because we have money we have well-being. Meanwhile, that real wealth is being destroyed and well-being as a whole is diminished.

The Unintended Consequences of Monetary Policy

The most significant way governments control prices is by controlling the supply of money. Ever since paper money became the dominant form of currency throughout world economies around 100 years ago, and especially since that paper money was removed from a gold standard in the United States in 1971, the amount of money in the system has been under the sole control of state governments, which can print or destroy billions of dollars whenever it sees fit. Laws restricting alternative currencies bolster this command and, ultimately, the money supplies of all major countries have become a matter of government fiat.

Like other controls, adjustments to the money supply have been urged to accomplish very specific and often rather logical goals. Mostly, they have been aimed at countering fluctuations in the Business Cycle. As was explored on an earlier page, the Business Cycle has long been seen by prominent economists as naturally unsteady, responsible for creating an unpredictable sequence of booms and recessions. Neither are particularly healthy for the economy. The booms cause gluts in output, and the recessions create deficiencies in effective demand. Thus, when a free-market economy is growing, it tends to swell into bubbles and, when it is shrinking, it tends to collapse into crashes and panics.

It has been argued that the free market gets out of control because of its self-perpetuating nature. When things go well, people have more money to invest, and so more business is done and people continue to improve their condition. On the other hand, when things are going poorly, people have less money to invest, and so less business is conducted and the condition continues to worsen.

This self-perpetuating nature is based in large part on the way money multiplies in a modern economy. As we saw in the chapter on Complexity, the fractional reserve banking system actually multiplies the amount of money in an economy by using and reusing it in layers of investment. A $100 base, for example, can turn into some $500 in active exchanges throughout the economy given a reasonable reserve requirement of 20%.

Of course, just as the fractional reserve system multiples the money stock in good times, it shrinks the money supply when things turn sour. A $100 withdrawal from a bank means that some $500 must be withdrawn from the system as a whole. Investments diminish as a result, which means fewer new enterprises, fewer jobs, and ultimately fewer consumers buying things on a retail level. With lower consumption, businesses struggle and have to cut back hours, and the effect is a self-perpetuating loss of liquidity.

As early twentieth-century economists concluded, the swings in the economy are caused, not by any inherent change in supply or demand—which would take much longer to be realized than the relatively short-lived booms and busts—but rather by severe fluctuations in the money supply. Heated financial bubbles, it has been deduced, are caused by too much liquidity; long-lasting recessions are caused by less liquidity.

By infusing more paper money into the economy during down times, and withdrawing money during booms, the government can turn an inherently unstable situation into a reliable, steady condition. The result is an even keel and an end to the booms and busts that have plagued free markets for centuries.

Fairly reasonable on the surface, the plan has two fatal oversights. The first is that officials who are in charge of running the countercyclical policies have to answer to forces of governmental bureaucracy, which always tend in the direction of spending and away from higher taxes. This means that monetary policy almost always seeks to increase the money supply and rarely to decrease it. As such, half of the essential strategy is neglected. And while it may seem nice to watch money grow as if it were from trees, this one-sided tendency necessarily defeats the original purpose of monetary policy, which was to maintain an even keel. Indeed, if too much liquidity is ever a problem, then the monetary policy of strict augmentation is explicitly harmful because it never attempts to counterbalance that growth.

This flaw is based in human nature and can be avoided given the right personnel, though it is not conceivable that, in a large, modern economy such as the United States, vote-hungry politicians will seek to deprive their electorates of liquidity. All politicians depend on making promises, and it is infinitely easier to follow through on those promises if they can tap into a limitless supply of funds. The politician who does not tap into those resources is not able to follow through and thus does not get elected or reelected.

But modern monetary policy is flawed in another, more fundamental way as well. Its second fatal flaw concerns the basic consequence of price controls in distorting supply and demand. As we saw on previous pages, price controls of any kind skew supply and demand such that the inevitable result is either a surplus or a shortage. This also goes for controls of the money stock because money, like any other commodity, is not only a measure of the price of the good or service it buys; it is a good itself with a price of its own. And, like any other commodity, the price of money is dependent upon its supply and demand; when its supply and demand change, so too does its price. Just as with diamonds and water, the more money that is available, the less value it will have; the less money there is, the more valuable it will be.

Furthermore, since money is involved in nearly all exchanges in the modern economy, its price affects the price of every other good and service in the system. The consequence of shifts in the price of money is a corresponding shift in the price of real goods and services. When money is worth more, the goods and services one buys with that money are worth less, and vice versa. The Spanish Scholastics learned this lesson well with the influx of precious metals from the Americas in the sixteenth century. They knew that an increase in the money supply causes price inflation and that, conversely, a decrease in the money supply causes price deflation. To deny this fact of political economy is to deny the Scholastics' advances and revert to mercantilist doctrine, a return that takes us back to the sixteenth century or before.

To examine this consequence more closely, we can take another look at prices in general. A price represents the amount buyers will pay for a certain good or service. As the supply and demand of that good or service change, so too does the amount one will be willing to pay for it. Say a fur goes for $3,000 in the free market. A sudden increase in the supply of furs will invariably cause the price to go down. Fur retailers will have a harder time selling their goods, and so will lower their prices to entice more customers. Instead of $3,000, for instance, one might offer $2,000. Because of the shift in supply and demand, the furrier must accept less for his product.

With this simple example, we see how changes in supply and demand can alter the price of a good or service. But the example does not only show a change in the price of furs; one will note that it also indicates a change in the price of the other commodity exchanged as well—in this case, money. Just as a fur went from being worth $3,000 to $2,000, a dollar went from being worth $1/3,000^{th}$ of a fur to being worth $1/2,000^{th}$. As the fur became less expensive in terms of dollars, the dollar became more expensive in terms of furs.

Ultimately, all economic exchanges show the price for both items being traded. It's not just that an iPhone is worth $399, but that a dollar is worth $1/399^{th}$ of an iPhone; a flight to Greece is not just worth $787, but a dollar is worth $1/787^{th}$ of a flight to Greece; and so on. And when the supply or demand of any of the goods in an exchange shifts, the price of both items will change.

The more abundant the currency, the more of it will be required to purchase a good or service. To mirror the hypothetical above, if the furrier had all the money he wanted—if money grew on trees, for example, or was dropped out of helicopters into his backyard—the price of that money would go down in terms of furs. Instead of valuing a dollar at $1/3,000^{th}$ of a fur, the furrier might value it at $1/4,000^{th}$. If, on the other hand, money became scarcer, its price would go up in terms of furs. If the furrier's money supply diminished by some amount, he might want dollars more, and so value them at $1/2,000^{th}$ of a fur instead of $1/3,000^{th}$.

Extending the principle, we find that, in general, the more money there is in an economy, the less valuable it is and the less each individual participant can get in exchange for it. When the money supply increases, the consumer of groceries can get fewer apples or peaches or boxes of cereal for his money, just as the consumer of furs can get a smaller fraction of that luxury item with each dollar. Whereas the consumer used to be able to buy two apples for a dollar, he can now buy only one. This kind of price inflation is ingrained in the mentality of any modern Westerner. The assumption is that prices rise as a part of their nature—that the price of a movie or the cost of an automobile will go up every year, and that, to counter the trend, our wages must go up as well. The reason for this is because the government, with the help of the Federal Reserve, has set a policy of positive monetary growth. As the money supply increases, it is only natural for prices to increase with it. And so we can see that, though it may appear to be a natural occurrence, inflation is a wholly artificial phenomenon, conjured up by economists and perpetrated by the Federal Reserve.

Of course, most people don't look to see how much money is in the economy and therefore cannot know how much the money they have or don't have is worth. In fact, the bureau that is in charge of the money supply in the United States does not publish the figures showing how much money is in the economy for fear that such figures would distress the public.

Still, the amount of money in a given economy can be perceived by the average citizen and so can affect the prices of everyday goods and services. Because the price of those everyday goods and services are usually based on the price of supplies and overhead costs, and supplies and overhead costs are based on industrial and manufacturing prices, and so on, a change in one affects all corners of the economy. To sum up: When there is more money in the economy, people tend to spend it more freely; when money is spent more freely, producers tend to raise their prices to keep up with demand; rising prices cause a domino effect, and eventually the entire economy undergoes a price inflation.

This process has its origin at the very source of the increased money supply—the government. Let us consider the typical process whereby the government increases the money stock. Congress signs into law a bill that will direct $70 billion to the construction of a bridge. In order to raise the funds needed to pay for the project, the government might issue debt in the form of bonds by selling T-bills on the open market. The government can then hire a construction company with the newly acquired money. Just like that, $70 billion is generated and thrust into the economy.

But, as this money is introduced, the supply and demand begin to alter. The new contract increases demand for the construction company's work. As with any product that experiences an increase in demand, the construction company's price—the amount for which it is willing and able to conduct new work—will rise. This is the spark that ignites the inflation. Price levels will continue to rise on two fronts—by those customers who require the contractor's services and must bolster income to cover costs, and by those companies and individuals who are on the receiving end of the contractor's increased expenditures. If the government contractor and its employees are labeled Group A, the second wave of price increases will occur for goods and services offered by Group B. Similarly, Group B will cause price increases in Group C, and so on.

The number of companies and individuals in each group will grow as the inflation carries on, and, eventually, the process will expand to include every person in the economy. Ultimately, the prices for every good and service will be raised to meet the new volume of currency. This finishing point is not reached by a direct path nor, given the number of variables, is it reached without delay; but the result is inflation across the board.

Now, it must be said that the amount of money is not the only factor involved in the price of goods. As illustrated above, the supply and demand of goods and services also affect prices. Still, the money supply is the most important factor because its rate of change can be so much greater than that of goods and services. Output of goods and services is generally slow to increase or decrease, especially in the aggregate, given its natural dependence on multiple gears of industry. When it does increase or decrease, it does so based on widespread technical advances that the economy as a whole absorbs gradually and can usually accommodate so that prices remain fairly steady.

Meanwhile, the money supply can be adjusted speedily by simply printing or destroying bank notes. This can be done as quickly as the presses can turn. And, theoretically, since the numbers on the face of the money can be as high as the officials want them to be, the notional value could be infinite. The difference between the two kinds of economic adjustments can be seen in extreme examples of both. To look at the variance in the output of real goods, we can turn to two different countries during completely different times. At the height of Japanese economic growth after World War II, output increased at an annual rate of 10%; and, from peak to trough during the Great Depression in America, from 1929 to 1932, output fell by about 40%. These extremes illustrate the extent to which output can increase or decrease over finite periods. The average change in output over the course of the twentieth century for the United States was about a 3% increase every year.

By contrast, at the height of German hyperinflation after the first World War the money supply increased 300% per month. Such a rapid expansion can only be attributed to the efficiency with which paper money can be produced. With a strictly fiat currency, there is no real barrier to its growth. This is why the preeminent monetarist of our age, Milton Friedman, stated that price inflation is strictly a monetary phenomenon without a disclaimer on the effect of output.

Altogether, it must be said that monetary policy manifestly works against its intent. The original goal of monetary policy was to alleviate the severity of the Business Cycle by increasing the money supply during times of economic trouble and decreasing it during times of economic growth. But, if this tactic were successful, consumers would actually have lower purchasing power during down times and higher purchasing power during boom times.

By increasing the money supply, the government makes dollars worth less and so further hinders the people it intends to help. At the same time, decreasing the money supply makes dollars worth more and so reinforces the people it intends to check.

In the Carboniferous Epoch we were promised abundance for all,

By robbing selected Peter to pay for collective Paul;

But, though we had plenty of money, there was nothing our money could buy,

And the Gods of the Copybook Headings said: "If you don't work you die."

—RUDYARD KIPLING, "THE GODS OF THE COPYBOOK HEADINGS" (1919)

What's more is that monetary policy, however egalitarian its intentions, is designed in such a way that it affects different people at different times, placing a disproportionate burden of the inflation or deflation on a fraction of the population while allowing others to enjoy the benefits without much in the way of costs. With regard to the illustration above, we can see how those in Group A benefit from the boost in money supply because their incomes increase before prices do. In effect, their purchasing power rises at first while everyone else's falls to some extent.

Group B also benefits because their incomes rise before any widespread inflation occurs, though they have to pay higher prices for some of the goods and services provided by Group A. The same goes for Group C to a lesser extent, and so on down the line. The latter groups in the process, however—Groups X, Y, and Z, for instance—find that the prices for most of the goods and services they buy have increased before they see any increase in their incomes. These latter groups—the largest, most independent groups—are the ones upon whom the real burden of inflation rests, because theirs is the purchasing power that is diminished to the greatest degree by the time they can enjoy a boost in prices.

Milton Friedman's famous helicopter fable, recounted in his financial history *Money Mischief*, demonstrates the kind of trouble that adjustments to the money supply can cause. In the tale, Friedman describes an isolated society that suddenly encounters a mysterious helicopter that drops bags of money in everyone's backyard.

The exercise is supposed to reflect to some degree what happens when the government increases the money supply. Using the fictitious citizens' rationales, Friedman shows that the event inevitably leads to price inflation, and that, the earlier one picks up the money and uses it, the more he will benefit.

Monetary policy, then, like practically all state action, disproportionately rewards those closest to government—contractors, banks, lobbies, legislators, lawyers, and so on—and penalizes those who are displaced from it—sole proprietors, unorganized laborers, moms and pops, and so on. Just as the good intentions of minimum wage laws, rent controls, and farm subsidies often end up hurting those they propose to protect, adjusting the money supply actually harms the average citizen it is aimed at helping by lowering his purchasing power and raising that of the elite.

Monetary policy has become, in short, just another way for the upper class to exploit the underprivileged. In a way, as Henry Hazlitt put it, the inflation that arises from monetary policy is nothing more than a kind of tax, taken from the independent workers and underprivileged in the economy and given to the well-connected and well-established. It is a mere extension of the practices that jeopardize the free choice necessary for markets to work and threaten the well-being of the economy as a whole.

4. IN PERPETUUM

THE MORE GOVERNMENT DOES to skew economic factors, such as the supply and demand for goods and services and for money in general, the more important it becomes. As more programs are added to the repository, and more of the economy is affected by government fiat, it grows increasingly important for the individuals affected by that growth to play some role in the process by investing in lobbying, litigating, and politicking to get a share of the expanding sums; and, similarly, it becomes more and more costly to stand by and do nothing.

The fact is that government has become too immense to disregard. Throughout the nineteenth century and even until the Great Depression, with the exception of wartime, state and federal spending was no more than 12% of national income, with around two-thirds directed to the state and local levels. During FDR's New Deal, federal spending alone increased so that it took up around 10% of national income. Now, government spending is around 43% of national income, and two-thirds of that is dedicated to the federal level. Estimates predict that spending will continue to increase so that by 2019 some 60% of the national income will be absorbed by the government. The national debt, which currently stands at about 80% of the GDP, is estimated to exceed income in a few years[*].

Clearly, the government is an industry that no individual acting economically can afford to neglect. Washington correspondent Jeffrey Birnbaum once quoted a lobbyist who spoke for the consensus: "The modern government is huge, pervasive, intrusive into everybody's life. If you just let things take their course and don't get in the game, you get trampled on. You ignore it at your peril."

The recession of 2009 showed just how significant the government has become. News headlines claimed that the only growing industries were in the public sector. While real estate, finance, and technology were all retreating, government was advancing, just like the savvy monopolist of the late nineteenth century. As it was with Mr. Potter in *It's a Wonderful Life*, the government wasn't selling, it was buying. And every aspect of government action was gaining as a result.

One article dealing with the extravagant pensions that state employees have garnered in recent years envisaged a country with a new aristocracy made up entirely of opportunistic retired government workers living off the toil of private sector laborers˚. It is not too far of a stretch to think that we are all bound at some point to work for a branch of the government, whether by paying exorbitant taxes and submitting to cumbersome regulations, or by receiving subsidies, welfare, and government contracts directly.

As a result of such swelling power, more and more people flood into the system to take advantage of it. Individuals act economically no matter what circumstances they are in. If the citrus fruit industry is booming, then people will rush into the industry to get in on the action; if the solar panel business is booming, so too will people pour in to take advantage of the profits. We see it whenever a new technology or innovation sweeps through the economy and scores of businesses pop up to meet the emerging market's demand. Similarly, when government produces artificial demand for an industry, individuals and businesses will flock toward it. The more demand it creates, the more interest it generates. In short, government intervention spurs higher interest in the government.

What this means, then, is a sort of self-perpetuating cycle. As special interests and rights groups increase their share of the outlay, so other interests must lobby and apply pressure in the opposite direction in order to keep pace. Government action causes special interest reaction, and the process begins again with larger sums of money and even more comprehensive intervention at stake.

One ironic aspect of the modern social condition is the fact that the welfare state operates in a closed economy, no different than that which arose at the turn of the century. The economy is a zero-sum condition now as much as it was before the Fed and the Welfare State were established to defy it. As such, the benefits one individual or group receives thanks to tax breaks, subsidies, or other political maneuvering are actually losses for others, who must now invest their time and effort to lobby for their own tax breaks, subsidies, and other benefits. It is a gigantic tug-of-war with hundreds of thousands, if not millions, of participants all grasping for more and more rope.

As the focus on the bureaucratic behemoth in Washington increases, its sway grows that much more dominant and thus forces even more interest in it. "The more actively and ambitiously government moves resources around," says Jonathan Rauch, "the more can be gained by forming a group and lobbying for a bigger share, and so the stronger the incentive to do it." To counter the actions, more groups form to lobby against them, and a self-perpetuating cycle forms. "A built-in side effect of new government programs is their tendency to summon into being new constituencies—which, in turn, often lobby for yet other new programs, keeping the whole cycle going." The cycle flows naturally. People go where the money is; government has the power to shift money around and distort markets, so people tend to go where the government is taking action; the more action is taken, the more others must join in to secure their share; the more people involved, the more action government takes; and so on, in perpetuum. The bulging bureaucracy feeds off itself as the people simply dive in to provide more fodder.

Canker State

At the root of this chain reaction is modern government's position as both ruler and benefactor. Not only does the state dictate what must be done and how, it also plays a primary role in the doing. It diagnoses the problem and serves as the medicine. Indeed, the welfare state is the quintessential example of a business straddled with a conflict of interest. Just like any major profession nowadays—doctors, dentists, lawyers, mechanics, graphic designers—the more the client needs the services, the more the professional will get paid. So the professionals have an interest in making the client need (or at least convincing the client that he is in great need of) the services. We find the same predicament in government. The more the people need the government's help, the bigger and more powerful the government becomes. So public officials and lobbyists alike all have an interest in making the people need (or at least convincing the people that they are in great need of) the Welfare State.

Take for example the fact that price controls create surpluses and shortages. These

And ye shall understand, that when there be great feasts and solemnities of that idol, as the dedication of the church and the throning of the idol, all the country about meet there together. And they set this idol upon a car with great reverence, well arrayed with cloths of gold, of rich cloths of Tartary, of Camaka, and other precious cloths. And they lead him about the city with great solemnity. And before the car go first in the procession all the maidens of the country, two and two together full ordinatly. And after those maidens go the pilgrims. And some of them fall down under the wheels of the car, and let the car go over them, so that they be dead anon. And some have their arms or their limbs all to-broken, and some the sides. And all this do they for love of their god, in great devotion. And them thinketh that the more pain, and the more tribulation that they suffer for love of their god, the more joy they shall have in another world.

—SIR JOHN MANDEVILLE'S ACCOUNT OF
THE PROCESSION OF THE JUGGERNAUT,
TRAVELS (1357-71)

surpluses and shortages can only be remedied by some form of subsidies or credits. By taking action, the state necessarily creates a greater need for more action. It supports a system that continues to thrive as though there is nothing wrong, and yet, in order to do so, it requires the enormous apparatus below it to even survive. It is like a doctor that keeps prescribing medications to counter the side effects of other, previously prescribed medicines. There is seemingly no end to the process.

This is why the government is the beneficiary of nearly unlimited credence by the public body with respect to its authority. A government agency might be wasteful, unproductive, or wholly destructive, but, with the way the system is designed, it will garner funds nonetheless. Most government agencies are actually positioned to take in more money when they don't reach their goals or achieve what they intended. The notion is that their failure was the result of lacking funds; so more funds are asked for and granted, and the whole process begins again.

Most agencies are allotted a certain amount of funds over the course of a fiscal year. If they are for some reason able to accomplish what they sought to do without going over budget, to do their work at a discount, then their funds

Taken case by case, many of these policy choices are perfectly defensible. Taken as a whole, they suggest a system that only knows how to move in one direction. If consolidation creates a crisis, the answer is further consolidation. If economic centralization has unintended consequences, then you need political centralization to clean up the mess. If a government conspicuously fails to prevent a terrorist attack or a real estate bubble, then obviously it needs to be given more powers to prevent the next one, or the one after that.

—Ross Douthat, *The New York Times*
(May 18, 2010)

No visible means of support and you have not seen nothin' yet.

Everything's stuck together.

I don't know what you expect staring into the TV set.

Fighting fire with fire.

—David Byrne,
Burning Down the House (1983)

are cut for the next year. In other words, if they are efficient and productive, they are punished. Quite reasonably, then, the agencies attempt all kinds of tricks to spend the money they are allotted, not limited to repetitious or wasteful purchases, frivolous expenses, and ineptness. If the climate does not encourage corruption by itself, it will at least serve as a distraction for the administrators hoping to actually do something positive with the power they have been granted.

A case could certainly be made that an increase in the size of government is in part due to a larger, denser population and more powerful techne, forces that intensify complexity and aggravate the Business Cycle without doubt. But the most compelling forces in the equation are the internal motives, since they are the most direct. Money is readily available for any group or cause that can figure out some grievance or extraordinary need; they just have to expand the government to take advantage of the opportunity. It is the logical and most economically sound measure to take in the modern system.

Consider one piece of legislation that, on the surface, appeared like a landmark of equal rights and justice for all in a rapidly changing world—the Americans With Disabilities Act of 1990. Hailed as a breakthrough for civil liberties, it has also been the source of a great amount of government-driven action that has naturally resulted in a lot of money changing hands, a fact that escaped the attention of no savvy politician or lobbyist in Washington, nor lawyer or contractor around the country.

The underlying premise of the act was to expand access for handicapped persons at buildings, transit terminals, and other municipal structures. Terms of the law included vague statements that demanded "readily achievable" functions and "reasonable accommodations" for the disabled. In other words, it was up to a public official or local bureaucrat to decide what needed to be done to comply with the new legislation and who would be punished for violation. *The Washington Post* documented the response of the bill's passing into law with a summary from a lawyer's perspective. "Most major law firms are well aware that the law . . . will open up a vast new area of discrimination law and, potentially, a lot of business." At the time, seminars were held for law firms, disability rights advocates, and businesses that all became instantaneously interested in answers to such questions like "How does a ski resort get a paraplegic up a mountain?"

Present in the Americans with Disabilities Act, as in nearly all government action, are the unintended consequences of shifting resources and distorting the economy. Certainly, disabled persons, lawyers and contractors, and politicians are better off, but what of the businesses that had to pay construction companies to add ramps and elevators? The problem that the law sought to solve most likely resided in an established institution, and thus the source of livelihood for some other group or large contingent of people. The solution presented a new problem—how could these companies and groups get back the money they lost to the regulation? It is a problem that can only be solved with more government.

Passing laws and shifting resources are practices that in themselves bolster government. They are endeavored in large part these days for the sake of the officials and administrators and with no real end in mind. This is why so few government programs ever end, even if they are scheduled to expire after an

> **Health Care for America Now, the progressive coalition formed in the summer of 2008 to lay the groundwork for passing reform legislation, has decided not to pack up its tent and go home just yet. With health reform now law, the group will join a long line of interest groups that hang around Washington after their original reason for forming has passed.**
>
> **—NEWS ITEM, APR. 13, 2010**

allotted amount of time, and why the legislation process can be so painfully arduous even for the most straightforward laws. Even so-called reform bills end up taking the shape of so many convoluted and self-gratifying bills that can only be said to amplify the size of government. *The Congressional Quarterly*, reporting on the reform bill of 1985, quoted a Democrat sponsor who suggested holding up the passage of the bill so that it could "remain in limbo for a few more months. 'Why kill the goose that laid the golden egg?'

he asked." To many of the officials involved, the law-making and govern-ing process is a goose of golden eggs, to be cared for and indulged lest it disappear with all its fruits.

Adding to the Problem to Solve It

Seen in this light, the entire government works as a single, cooperative whole with the unified aim of growth. While citizens are led to believe that there are two parties working against one another to accomplish this or that unique goal, the upshot is that they are both working together to attain their mutual goal of ever-expanding bureaucracy. When government cre-ates action, the whole system gets bigger and more complex, allowing both major parties to cash in. When one side of the modern political leviathan wins a battle, both sides benefit. I am reminded of a Republican friend who had been a part of local politics for years before the 2006 changing of the guard, when some 30% of all elected officials switched from Republican to Democrat. On election night, as the fate of the party was clearly deter-mined, I expected her to be down and out, but there was no gloom about her. When I expressed my condolences, she shook her head, saying, "It's the same game, we just have to play it differently now."

As I have since learned, major losses in modern politics aren't the major disappointments they seem to be on the surface because the point is not really to win. The point of all the campaigning and stumping isn't to pro-mote and establish a workable system that lasts according to a given party's major tenets, as the rhetoric suggests; rather the point is to push one side or the other for the time being until the other can gain momentum enough to take back the lead.

The point is to generate competition between the parties so that the voters see that something worthwhile is at stake and are thus encouraged to put more money and resources into the pot.

Indeed, a big loss might well turn out to be the best thing a political party can endure since it will energize the base and get the interest and donations churning. One eminent Washington lobbyist from the Clinton years demonstrated the point clearly. "This congress and the promises that Clinton made," he said, "means an almost automatic defensiveness from the corporate community on most issues it faces." That meant more money for the opposition, business lobbyists, and, naturally, Republicans.

The point isn't necessarily to win, but rather to battle back and forth, to create an engaging crusade for both sides, and meanwhile soak up all kinds of funds and resources in the process. It is a concept familiar to anyone eager to keep large audiences entertained. Bookies ensure the greatest interest by altering the line as they take in bets. To them, as to politicians, it does not matter who wins as long as there are lots of people gambling. In fact, all major sports have implemented a salary cap to achieve the same ends. The MLB, NFL, and NBA all have an interest in making their games as competitive as possible so that fans stay loyal, watch the contests regularly, and buy the merchandise. Similarly, the government has interest in making its games as competitive as possible so that voters stay engaged, watch C-SPAN, and buy into all the legislative drama.

Contemporary politicking does not alleviate the zero-sum competitiveness, it only better defines it and makes it official. This is not to say that true problems are nonexistent outside of government intervention—they certainly do exist everywhere one looks in modern society—but rather that government intervention is a tricky mode of solving those problems, one that complicates matters and ends up creating new problems in the process. For this reason, it is reasonable to argue that fixing problems is itself part of the problem these days. Sure, problems abound, but to fix them, the government shifts around resources and distorts the economy, thus creating more problems in the process. The solution only adds to the problem, making it worse, and there seems to be no way out.

This self-perpetuating cycle is manifest in the careers of the most talented and ambitious figures in American politics over the last few decades, from Ronald Reagan and Newt Gingrich to Bill Clinton and Barack Obama, not to mention countless other bright young go-getters all determined to break through the convoluted mess of Washington, D.C. and finally make real progress. Despite their most capable faculties and, one can only assume, a most sincere belief in their ideals, each one has met with nearly unexplainable resistance and watched as Washington has grown bigger, more convoluted, and more intrusive during their terms.

The reason is the very nature of Washington. To step in and shake things up, to get things done, these high-minded public servants had to build pressure groups, lobby, and shift resources around; to make any real progress, they had to revert to the established tactics, which could only make the process more convoluted and intrusive. To solve the problems, they had to add to them and thus make them worse. Their only tools had handcuffed them; their methods defeated their purpose.

Take Ronald Reagan as the example par excellence of a youthful (despite his age), idealistic reformer bound to finally shake things up and diminish the towering behemoth once and for all. His speeches alone conveyed a person who understood the malfunctioning bureaucracy and who had the courage and savoir-faire to actually do something about it. Reagan assumed the presidency with a head full of steam and the momentum to finally fix the system, and there can be no doubt that by many measures the size of government did take a substantial hit during Reagan's presidency. The number of lobbyists, laws, and regulations, as well as taxes in general, all fell during the Reagan years. Still, due in large part to escalating defense costs, deficits ballooned as the federal budget continued its ascent, and the national debt became a much more sizeable burden as a result. Even the vigor of one of the most charismatic and idealistic presidents the United States has known could not reverse the seemingly unstoppable monster.

A decade later, Americans saw the same kind of high expectations dashed to the ground once again, this time under a different party and another captivating personality. Bill Clinton trotted into Washington with a slew of high-minded, post-partisan ambitions, but he too watched as his campaign promises fell victim to the ever-suffocating bureaucracy. Clinton pledged to take the country back from special interests and break down the gridlock that had crippled Washington, D.C. with a plan rivaled by none. But, even from the dawn of his presidency, one could predict the outcome. *The Legal Times* foreshadowed his eventual futility: "The one thing everyone agrees on," a lawyer was quoted as saying, "is that the government will now be more interested in regulating business. We are all expecting about a 33% increase in fees." To break down the gridlock, in other words, Clinton would have to generate more, and the process would continue to spiral.

This is the essence of the Juggernaut. To be effective, we need to eliminate the special interests and break the gridlock, but the only way to do that is by generating more laws and, in the process, appeasing more special interests, lobbies, and lawyers. To stop it from growing and advancing further, we fling ourselves before its crushing wheels, which only makes it more gigantic and unstoppable.

We have recently seen perhaps the greatest push for an end to 'politics as usual' come through the political sphere in the form of one of the most gifted polemicists in modern times, Barack Obama. The more commanding the Juggernaut becomes, it can be assumed, the greater the compulsion to tear it apart. Of course, as we have seen, the feverish desire to tear down the Juggernaut has only led to even more laws, regulations, spending, deficits, and debt. While his presidency is still young, many of Obama's vocal supporters have already cast doubt on whether he can accomplish any of his campaign promises, which thus far have all been either sidetracked, deprecated, or overtly transformed to some unfamiliar new plan, doubtless casualties in the Juggernaut's ruinous path.

Talk surrounding politics has grown more and more disillusioned in spite of the wave of optimism that Obama generated in 2008. Partisans and independents alike have denounced the whole system. Said one independent, "I'm disgusted by everything. We couldn't be at a worse place in this country°." The exaggeration may well be warranted given the utter helplessness with which voters have been burdened. When the president acknowledges the out-of-control deficit and the dire condition it creates for our country, and the only course of action he can think to take is to form a commission to report on ways that the federal deficits can be brought under control, one senses that the problem has gotten out of hand.

Voters do all they can, they get involved in grassroots activities and think they are making a difference, but no matter what they do, the system seems to keep rolling on, oblivious to the people's needs and wants, and siphoning in everything in its path. "They're all a bunch of liars," said another disgruntled voter, who had been toying with the idea of sitting out the 2009 Virginia state election. "You don't know who the heck to vote for anymore." And how could you when voting doesn't seem to provide you with what you want anyway?

The bailouts and stimulus packages of 2008 and '09 provide the quintessential examples of an out-of-control government. In action of historic proportions, the system propelled through Congress two enormous bills that, in the span of a few months, expanded the money supply by untold trillions of dollars, handing most of it to a class of elite bankers and businessmen who, by any standard, had been largely responsible for the financial turmoil the country was facing. If any American citizen could fully understand the bills, let alone have the time and resources to make an educated judgment on them, he was nowhere to be found in all of 2008 and '09. The bills were pushed through so quickly—of course, the government had no time to delay—that it was rather impossible for the people to understand what they were for or what they would accomplish anyway.

Indeed, as part of the Fed's policy, the public was not to know what these bills were designed to do. If the people knew about the bills in detail, it was thought, then they would panic and create even more turmoil. In short, the people were not to be trusted with what could be considered their own property and had to be sheltered from making decisions according to their own will. Despite the apparent disregard for the voters' sovereignty, the bills were expedited, and with them a galaxy of debts and burdens that Americans will be sorting out for decades or more.

It need not be argued that the politicians and bankers are carrying out some sinister plot or that they are maliciously trying to destroy the country. In fact, there is no reason to believe that they have anything but the country's best interests in mind. But, given a system such as ours, solving problems only leads to more damage and, ultimately, a self-perpetuating juggernaut that is impossible to stop. The officials want to solve problems, but the only way they know how is by generating all kinds of action surrounding a given predicament. And the public well knows that the more action that takes place, the more trouble the government creates. "I know they mean well," says one concerned voter, "but the more they do, the more problems come about. I wish they could just stop."

Regard the push for so-called health care reform in 2009 and '10. Naturally, health care is of significant concern in the modern world, and all compassionate citizens want to ensure that the system works efficiently and effectively for everyone. With statistics floating around that claim some 30% of Americans are uninsured for health coverage, a movement was mounted to reform the system and provide free health care for anyone who wanted it.

Critics realized that, though the surface arguments were noble indeed, any activity the government could undertake would inevitably come with a flurry of bureaucracy, hidden costs, and unintended consequences that could undermine the endeavor and make things worse. The health care industry is a major factor in the economy, as some estimates place its total value at one-seventh the total GDP, or around $2 trillion per year. The large-scale measures needed to reform such an industry would be so extensive that estimates put its

Here is a health care plan written by a committee whose chairman says he doesn't understand it, passed by a Congress that hasn't read it but exempts themselves from it, signed by a Prez who smokes, with funding administered by a treasury chief who didn't pay his taxes, to be overseen by a surgeon general who's obese, financed by a country that's broke . . . what could possibly go wrong?

—FACEBOOK STATUS, APRIL 2010

price tag at $1 trillion over the course of a decade. And the weary critic knows that the monetary costs are just the tip of the iceberg—the real costs lie in the time and effort it would take to meet regulations, the redundant and pointless work needed to conform to an increasingly warped economy, and the escalating constraints on freedom that would deaden incentive and innovation.

For some reason, politicians thought it pertinent to hold town hall meetings to discuss with their constituents the prospect of health care reform, and they were surprised to encounter a consistent and very vocal backlash against the proposals, as if people were opposed to free health insurance. Everywhere one turned, the protests voiced the same concerns: the more government does, the more damage it leaves behind; and huge projects like health care reform would only make matters worse. Protestors knew that health care could never be free and that government-run health care would cost the people more than any privately run enterprise ever would. The argument was often made that the state of the contemporary health care system had in no way been isolated from government intervention in the first place. There were already some hundreds of regulations in place before talk of reform began. But, just as with all broken government initiatives, officials have seen it fit to simply put more time and resources into it.

The fierce reaction found at the town hall meetings was directed not only at health care but at all government action in recent years. It was a response to decades of ineffectual votes and exploding government intervention; it was a retort against a foreign policy that had extended resources beyond natural limits; and, more than anything, it was a rebellion against the bailout and stimulus bills that had handed trillions of dollars to the banks without a word from the people. After all of this, the voters, the taxpayers, were finally given the opportunity to speak, and they took it.

In retrospect, it is a mystery why the officials hosted the town hall meetings at all. The procedure hadn't been attempted on such a large scale in recent memory. And, despite the protests encountered there, the proponents of health care reform kept pushing their bill on through no matter what came of the town hall gatherings. It was as if government officials had been sent a memo encouraging them to engage their constituents about the issue and allow them to be heard. But no open-eyed spectator could be fooled by the show. Not only were the town hall meetings piteous gestures that paled in comparison to the blatant neglect of public opinion with regard to the bailout and stimulus bills, the wars in Asia, and health care reform, but the officials didn't even use the forums correctly, arguing with constituents and using the platform to tell the people what they would get instead of listening to what they wanted. In short, the town hall meetings were not geared toward communicating the people's will to the politicians; they were organized to

Obama's Speech to Congress Is Last-Ditch Effort for Health Care Bill

—*FoxNews*, Sep. 3, 2009

A Last-Ditch Attempt to Salvage Health Care Reform?

—*Economic Policies*, Jan. 21, 2010

Obama Puts Forward Last-Ditch Health Care Plan

—*Associated Press*, Feb. 22, 2010

Obama Targets GOP in Last-Ditch Pitch for Health Care Bill

—*FoxNews*, Mar. 3, 2010

President Obama's last-ditch effort for health care reform bill

—*New York Daily News*, Mar. 20, 2010

make the people feel like they had a voice even though they did not. In the end, the Juggernaut would have its way, and there would be nothing the people could do about it.

One such town hall meeting, held by Indiana congressman Baron Hill in September 2009, conveyed the point concisely. When a student rose to ask why she couldn't film the meeting, the congressman replied that it was his town hall meeting and that he made the rules. When the crowd rumbled concern in response to such disregard for the people's authority, the congressman clarified his stance. "Let me repeat that one more time," he said.

"This is my town hall meeting for you. And you're not going to tell me how to run my congressional office." In other words, the people shouldn't have a say in how their government is run or how decisions are made regarding policies they pay for and that control their lives. Such is the way of the Juggernaut.

The president pleads for more civil discussion about the issues, where "we can disagree without being disagreeable or making wild accusations about the other side", but in this world dominated by the corporate-government leviathan, disagreement with the people in power means that a citizen will be forced against his will to do something that he has no intention of doing and that might very well hurt him, economically, politically, and perhaps even psychologically and physically. These days, it's 'my rights versus yours', my liberty against yours, and no two people can come away from a disagreement unscathed.

Juggernaut Cometh

And so the Juggernaut rolls on. The bigger it gets, the more enticing it becomes and the more people throw themselves before it. The size of government might not startle the average citizen used to hearing about the trillions of dollars that go through Washington every year, the trillion-dollar deficits and multi-trillion-dollar debts. These numbers are casually thrown about in discourse these days, usually without much context. No one really knows what this debt even means—the number is so far removed from reality, it seems as though it is normal and doesn't really affect anyone directly.

To gain some perspective, one can compare the size of the state today to that of a hundred years ago using the government's budget as a percentage of national income. From the founding through the nineteenth century, government spending stayed around 3% of national income with spikes during times of war. In 1903, national GDP was $25.9 billion and the federal budget was $1.76 billion—or 6.8% of income. As late as 1929, the percentage was still lower than 12%. In 2010, by contrast, the percentage was estimated to be 42%, meaning that $4 out of every $10 made in the United States is absorbed and redirected by the federal government in some way.

Of course, it is not as though this money is lost completely. Much of this spending is returned to the people through subsidies, grants, welfare checks, and the like. These figures are merely designed to show the size of government interference in the average citizen's life today relative to 100 years ago. In 1903, the government was significant, but it didn't matter in the way that it does today. Sending some 3% to 7% of one's income to Washington might have been inconvenient, but one could easily disregard the annoyance or get around it somehow.

Today, such a thought is inconceivable. One must send some 40% of one's income to the government, a chunk of wealth that simply cannot be overlooked. Considering that income equals one's ability to buy the goods and services one wants, the fact that the government takes 40% of it means that one's ability to buy the goods and services one wants is inhibited, or at least altered, by 40% or more. Given the import of monetary income these days, this is like saying that the government controls some 40% of the average American's well-being. An argument could be made that we have arrived at a time and place that former British Prime Minister Benjamin Disraeli once presaged as the worst political predicament possible—the state in which "no avenue to wealth and honor would subsist save through the government° ".

And this is only half of the story. The other half is the economic disfiguration that the government generates by means of its wealth transferring. In a different yet equally disruptive manner, laws and regulations end up controlling one's wealth as well. And, as could be expected, the volume of laws and regulations has been growing at the same pace as governmental budgets.

Robert C. Clark, former Dean of Harvard Law School, noted the increase by pointing out the number of statutes enacted in the area of health and consumer safety during what he called the three phases of liberalism.

During the Progressive Era, at the dawn of the twentieth century, there were five new laws; during FDR's New Deal, there were 11; and during the so-called 'Third Wave' of liberalism from 1964 to '79, there were 62.

This disproportionate increase is the norm and not the exception. A glance at the page count for the Federal Register, the annual catalog of the nation's statutes, will suffice to illustrate. In 1947, the Register totaled fewer than 10,000 pages—a hefty set of books that would span three feet on a shelf. By 1970, it had doubled, resting at 20,000 pages and some six feet on a bookshelf. In the following decade, the Register more than quadrupled in size so that, by 1980, it was 88,000 pages and took up 24 feet on a shelf.

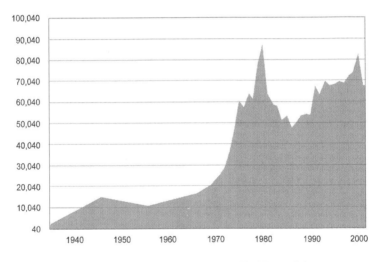

FIG. 30—Supply and Demand Chart with Equilibrium Point.

Given such considerable documentation, it is no wonder that those in charge of drafting and voting on the legislation often fail to read it themselves. One hears of 1,500-page bills that are scrapped and rewritten the night before passing. The fastest reader in the world is unable to absorb so much information, let alone busy politicians. Stories like these show why it is often impossible for the members of Congress to actually read the bills they sign into effect. Their employment of countless aides to assist in this kind of work does not help in their comprehension; instead, it only allows the bills to continue to explode in size.

The days when it was possible for the common citizen to have a fair grasp on the law have long since passed. The tax code alone, a law that every taxpaying citizen must presumably know and follow, has sprawled out of control such that it measures some 6,000 pages or close to it, as no one seems to know the total page count. Those citizens who are financially incapable of hiring legal assistants to advise them with endeavors like paying taxes run the risk of unknowingly breaking the law during their daily routines. As one political commentator put it, "In Washington, if you don't keep your eyes open you can wake up one morning and discover that your livelihood is illegal." Many have found such a circumstance to be true and spent time in jail as the consequence.

> "It will be of little avail to the people that the laws are made by men of their own choice, if the laws be so voluminous that they cannot be read, or so incoherent that they cannot be understood; if they be repealed or revised before they are promulgated, or undergo such incessant changes that no man who knows what the law is today can guess what it will be tomorrow."
>
> —JAMES MADISON, "FEDERALIST NO. 62", FEBRUARY 27, 1788

> I don't think you want me to waste my time to read every page of the health care bill. You know why? It's statutory language. We hire experts.
>
> —MAX BAUCUS (D-MT), AUGUST, 2010

America is still a relatively free country, but it is almost impossible to find a corner of one's life in which the government does not play at least some role. By its control of money and taxes alone, government rather dictates our behavior to a large degree. With the money we have left over from taxes, we are restricted and directed even further. Milton and Rose Friedman offer an excellent summary of the various infringements on freedom that our supposedly free country faces, though they stipulate that it is hardly comprehensive:

"We are not free to buy cyclamates or laetrile, and soon, perhaps, saccharin. Our physician is not free to prescribe many drugs for us that he may regard as most effective for our ailments, even though the drugs may be widely available abroad. We are not free to buy an automobile without seat belts, though, for the time being, we are still free to choose whether or not to buckle up." (This last has been made illegal since the book's publication.)

"Today, you are not free to offer your services as a lawyer, a dentist, a plumber, a barber, a mortician, or engage in a host of other occupations without first getting a permit or license from a government official. You are not free to work overtime at terms mutually agreeable to you and your employer unless the terms conform to rules and regulations laid down by a government official.

"You are not free to set up a bank, go into the taxicab business, or the business of selling electricity or telephone service, or running a railroad, bus line, or airline without first receiving permission from a government official.

"You are not free to raise funds on the capital markets unless you fill out the numerous forms the SEC requires and unless you satisfy the SEC that the prospectus you propose to issue presents such a bleak picture of your prospects that no investor in his right mind would invest in your project if he took the prospectus literally."

One might add a few other items to the list that have only recently made their way to the fore: You are not free to ride a motorcycle without a helmet, sell packaged food without displaying its nutritional value, sell fast food without warning customers of the hazards of trans fats, run a restaurant that allows smoking, run a hotel that allows smoking without displaying a warning sign, drive a car that gets fewer than 20 miles per gallon of gasoline, and, soon enough, surf the Internet without the approval of some government official.

The watchdog organization at Overcriminalized.com surveys federal laws that have made the most routine and innocent day-to-day activities illegal and, in some instances, made criminals out of normal citizens who are innocent by any standard of common sense. Case studies on the site regard a slew of unbelievable stories that would be comical if they hadn't actually happened in real life. One study tells of an orchid farmer whose house was stormed by armed marshals for fear that he was importing banned orchids—flowers that he never actually imported—and who was subsequently arrested and sent to jail for improper documentation. Other case studies tell of businessmen who were arrested for successfully investing funds in a growing company under the presumption of insider trading; of high schoolers being suspended from classes and banned from activities because they accidentally brought what might be considered weapons to school; and of a doctor who was accused of fraudulent reimbursements and declined paying a cash settlement, among others.

Altogether the story is one of an increasingly precarious situation in which just about anything can be viewed as a crime, and the arbitrary whim of a bureaucrat is the only thing between an honest citizen and fines, incarceration, and shame. This citizen knows first-hand how easily honest mistakes can turn into very expensive crimes given the convoluted and arbitrary modern legal system. It is not a stretch to estimate that everyone will commit some form of punishable infraction in the near future without malicious intent or even knowledge of the crime.

We have come to a point where the government has taken upon itself the duty of telling us how to use a ladder, how to organize office space, what food to eat and beverages to drink, how and what to teach our children, what we can and cannot do to earn money, how to invest our money once we've earned it, what remedies to take for ailments, and when and how to cross the street. Is there nothing we can do without the government's approval?

With state intrusion penetrating so far into our private lives, one is reminded of a slew of Nazi-period government programs that dealt with the day-to-day activities of German citizens. One such program, labeled 'Freizeitgestaltung', literally translates to 'The shaping of the use made of the people's free time', quite as if, as Friedrich A. Hayek posed, the time could possibly be free when the authority dictates how it is spent. The paradoxical conclusion is the characteristic sign of our age. Ours is a system of positive freedom, of liberty through coercion, and, as many are discovering, the greatest hindrance to this kind of freedom is individual sovereignty.

5. THE MORAL EFFECT
OF THE STATE

WHEN JOHN MAYNARD KEYNES' portrait appeared on the cover of *Time Magazine* in December 1965 with an article titled "We Are All Keynesians Now", it was as though the Welfare State had finally taken hold of the West and convinced its detractors that large-scale economic intervention was the only way of the future. After a series of crises in the '30s and '40s, Keynesian economics led the West to the longest period of growth that the world had ever seen in the '50s and '60s. To policymakers and the public in general, the plan seemed to be working.

But as Keynesianism grew in dominance and the government grew in scope, signs began to accumulate that the extensive controls put in place over the course of the twentieth century were eating away at the country's social fabric. Crime was rising at an alarming rate, widespread unrest began to plague major cities and college campuses, and a growing sense of alienation took hold of the culture as captured by the Harris Poll Alienation Index. While the West continued to experience vast improvements in material well-being throughout the twentieth century, the discriminating observer noted that, during the same period, the culture's intellectual and spiritual well-being deteriorated to an equal if not greater degree.

Perhaps the most salient example of spiritual poverty was seen in American cities, the centerpieces of New Liberalism and the crown of Industrialization. By the mid-1960s, American cities were falling apart. Partly due to a general migration to the South and West and into suburban communities, and partly due to highly disruptive government programs, city centers were rapidly falling into disrepair and unlawfulness. Housing projects displaced individuals and tore apart communities, and immense public works projects severed cities and decimated neighborhoods.

Not a few distressed commentators of the time documented the sense of injustice brought about by these changes. As writer John Cheever explained, "The uptown slums are being demolished, but the rectangular tenements that replace them have not a trace of invention. Their bleakness is absolute. No man has ever dreamed of a city of such monotonous severity, and there must be some bond between our houses and our dreams°."

The Keynesian belief was that putting enough money into public works and directing the right resources to the right places could totally eliminate poverty and increase production manifold. In the 1960s, notable Keynesian John Kenneth Galbraith was famously quoted as saying, "There is not a single problem in New York that could not be solved if the city's budget was doubled° ". Of course, soon after the quote, the budget trebled and then quadrupled, and the problems only got worse and more numerous.

It was becoming clear that the more money that was directed toward these initiatives, the worse the situation was becoming. In retaliation to New York City's vast public works Juggernaut of the '50s and '60s, activist Jane Jacobs encapsulated the ultimate consequences with her scathing essay, *The Death and Life of Great American Cities*: "Look what we have built with the first several billions: Low-income projects that become worse centers of delinquency, vandalism and general social hopelessness than the slums they were supposed to replace. Middle-income housing projects which are truly marvels of dullness and regimentation, sealed against any buoyancy or vitality of city life. Luxury housing projects that mitigate their inanity, or try to, with a vapid vulgarity. Cultural centers that are unable to support a good bookstore. Civic centers that are avoided by everyone but bums, who have fewer choices of loitering place than others. Commercial centers that are lackluster imitations of standardized suburban chain-store shopping. Promenades that go from no place to nowhere and have no promenaders. Expressways that eviscerate great cities. This is not the rebuilding of cities. This is the sacking of cities."

New York was perhaps the most notable instance of this sacking because it has always been the most characteristic of the great American metropolises. But the trend was seen across the country—Philadelphia, Boston, Washington, D.C., Miami, Pittsburgh, Cleveland, Detroit, Chicago, New Orleans, Houston, Dallas, San Antonio, Los Angeles, and San Francisco. Even the new cities of the South and West, such as Charlotte, Phoenix, San Diego, and Seattle, were all stamped with the mark of Liberalism run amuck. Everywhere the government intervened to a large degree, the result was the same—the draining of character, the depletion of initiative, and the exhaustion of industry.

What had happened to American cities was what was happening to the American character and what happens whenever reality is replaced with an abstraction—spirit is lost. Government's goal was the well-being of its people, but, in order to provide that, it had relied on statistics, indexes, growth charts, and numbers—pure data—to show where the people were and where they were going. Of course, no amount of facts and figures can truly relay the condition of a people, their wants and needs, or their greatest desires; that can only be found in the people themselves, their actions, their will. Government action based on the abstractions may have improved the figures, but it distorted the substance behind the surface. The numbers all look better on the façade, but the soul is in disarray.

Industry and virtue rest in an individual's will, in his volition and responsibility. When government interferes, volition is compromised, and industry and virtue die. Historian Craig Steven Wilder summarized the phenomenon well: "When traffic lanes and freeways and tall buildings and business districts become our priority, and we forget about people in neighborhoods;

we actually forget about what is the lifeblood of the city°.'" Forgetting about this lifeblood allows the authority to cut it off and, ultimately, causes the civilization to hemorrhage.

Granted, it is not wholly impossible to be industrious and virtuous under the control of some external authority, but it is much more difficult and comes about less organically. This is especially true for a culture that has been conditioned for centuries to the innate liberties of a free society. Its expectations and demands of freedom drive it toward greater potential than it will allow and, in the end, hinder its ability to overcome the restraints of the controlled society.

This eradication of responsibility is the ultimate effect of statism and, without question, the most devastating to the human condition. As the previous five hundred years had shown, personal responsibility provides mankind with Individualism and industry, and it was personal responsibility that ushered in the most productive and expansive era in history. With the close of the frontier during the 1890s and revival of statism during the Great Switch, the driving force behind that ingenuity was closed off and locked away. By relinquishing personal responsibility to governors, senators, congressmen, justices, presidents, CEOs, directors, celebrities—to the system as an integrated whole—men relinquished their very will. Without will, without volition or responsibility, men necessarily lose their conscience and, finally, their ability to be virtuous.

The acute effects of government intervention are, of course, subtler, but taken altogether, the moral effect of the state is inescapable. The reason rests in the very method of government action. In general, the state works by skewing the people's perceptions of economic resources, such as labor, housing, or stored capital. Of course, an individual's actions are based on his perception of the environment around him, and so a skewed perception will naturally distort his behavior in that environment, a distortion that leads to results such as inflated employment, lax housing loans, or frivolous investment. And here is where the government drains the people of their will. By shifting the field around and dictating the play of the game, the government effectively takes away the players' ability to strategize and perform by their own resolve. In order to succeed, they must simply give up their reason, their capacity to chose and make decisions, and just do as they are told.

In the end, this only makes the government that much more necessary. The less control people assume over their own thoughts and actions, the more reckless and dangerous they become to themselves, others, and society at large. Just as with interdependency in general, state control encourages thoughtlessness and thus recklessness. As such, the state ensures that the people are in further need of government care. By propping up the economy, supporting absent-minded endeavors, and regulating the minutiae of daily life, economic policy encourages irresponsibility and establishes a condition where government becomes indispensable.

> The old principle: who does not work shall not eat, has been replaced by a new one: who does not obey shall not eat.
>
> —LEON TROTSKY,
> *THE REVOLUTION BETRAYED* (1937)

> Until they become conscious, they will never rebel; and until after they have rebelled, they cannot become conscious.
>
> —GEORGE ORWELL,
> *NINETEEN EIGHTY-FOUR* (1949)

Minimum wage laws, for example, can create unemployment, which the state has taken upon itself to help alleviate with unemployment insurance and other welfare programs. These programs promote a sense of entitlement, which is lobbied for and then fulfilled through government by means of more labor laws and social safety nets. The first government program makes the people less capable of taking care of themselves such that they require more government programs, which make them even less capable, and so on, ad infinitum.

Here it must be argued that the moral effect of the state is nothing less than the amorality of the people. They are not necessarily immoral, but non-moral in that their actions are rendered involuntary, tractable; their actions are not driven by their will and so cannot have a moral value. As can be shown, this is the direct and necessary consequence of all coercive acts. When one is forced to do something against his will, he naturally puts his will aside and so becomes amoral in his actions. And, in the effort to compensate for the people's lack of morals, the state intervenes to a greater degree and thus grows more and more necessary.

This cannot be a criticism of the individual. Since he is being coerced, he has no choice in the matter and should not be censured. But that very condition will invariably lead to his depravity. It conditions him to a life without moral decisions and so renders him incapable of making decisions that are moral. In all of his actions, whether they are coerced or not, he will be unable to distinguish between good and bad. If and when it ever comes time to make a choice, he will be hindered in his ability to make the moral one—he will have to just go with the flow as he has done his entire life. Under the pressures of modern society, it is most likely that going with the flow will lead him in the way that best suits his urgent needs, and he will become animalistic and decadent.

The Amorality of a People

The path from coercion to immorality is not direct and it is not inevitable; the human conscience is a resilient blossom and powerful enough to overcome the greatest oppression. Still, it is a delicate plant, and the more severe its environment, the more likely is its complete wilting away.

One is reminded of the argument surrounding the emancipation of African slaves in the United States. A contingent rightly argued that the freed slaves would hardly be able to handle freedom if given it abruptly, that they would take advantage of their freedom by wandering around and wasting away. It was not their race that would prohibit moral behavior, but rather mere conditioning. No person born into and raised in servitude can instantaneously grow industrious and earn an income upon gaining freedom. That kind of willpower takes habituation and, at the very least, a thorough education. Freedmen who were able to rise above the oppression, such as Frederick Douglass, were among the greatest of nineteenth-century figures for this very rare characteristic.

The same is true for all oppressed peoples. In the West today, a fashionable claim says that the people of the Middle East are somehow naturally incapable of maintaining a democratic society, that they have always lived under despotic rule and always will no matter what construct the West tries to fit them in. The area's persistent sectarian violence becomes proof that the Middle Eastern peoples are incapable of liberty, quite as if all states in Southwest Asia are equally oppressive and immoral. And yet, one can speculate, if a Middle Eastern community prospered on its own for centuries without interference from its rivals or restraints from persistent tyrants, it would become a peaceful, flourishing democracy. Consider the Arab peoples of the medieval era for proof of their potential in free thought and dynamism.

In the Middle East, as it is around the world, the subservient character is born of tyranny and only fosters more tyranny. It is a self-perpetuating cycle begot of itself, not of some predetermined genetic configuration, that can only be broken by exiting the cycle and withdrawing from the tyranny, not by instating more controls or government intervention. This cycle of action and reaction can continue many times over in every instance of government interference so that the state's role grows with every program it installs. In short, the need for government intervention is government intervention itself.

This rather counterintuitive finding begins to gain credence when we consider the tendencies of state-run programs closer to home. To begin, new government action hardly ever corrects the problem it was designed to rectify. Indeed, of the major government-run enterprises dominant today, one can think of very few that actually accomplish their aims and then dissolve. The big ones—Social Security and Medicare—are organized quite like Ponzi schemes so that they naturally rely on future investments for current funding. The Department of Education, Agriculture, Veterans Affairs,

Homeland Security, Transportation, and a slew of others are all designed to remain indefinitely. Even the Department of Defense, which might be said to be the lone government agency that could exempt itself from perpetual endeavors seems set on a similar path as the others with the major conflicts it has engaged in over the twentieth century.

To be sure, government programs are simply not designed to cease, even when they are designed to put an end to some finite problem. Most programs fail or at least go well over budget, and all are reincarnated after the fact to continue on as some other form of intervention. On the contrary, failure in government programs is not a cause for withdrawal or termination, as one might suspect, but rather a justification for more funds and longer terms.

Evidence of the self-perpetuating nature of government programs can be seen in the persistence of the war on poverty or the fight for full employment. For eighty years, the U.S. government has been engaged in a full-scale battle to defeat the Business Cycle and end destitution, and for eighty years the Business Cycle and destitution have remained. Not only have they remained, but a case could be made that they have gotten worse. The rich continue to get richer while the poor continue to get poorer; the crash of 2008 proves that swings in the Business Cycle can be quite disastrous despite the careful supervision of the Fed; and unemployment and homelessness have peaked in recent years even though welfare programs are continuing to run in high gear. The reflex remedy for this ongoing problem? More government stimulus, intervention, and controls.

The fact is that there is only so much real wealth in a given economy, and that limit dictates how those in the society can behave. Pouring in additional money as the Fed might do, or forcing prices up or down for certain goods and services, may change the perception of the economy or the posture of certain sectors, but that perception is nothing more than an illusion created to spur certain behavior—most often investment and consumption. When that behavior takes place, it may feel natural for the investors or consumers to engage in, but in reality it is wholly based on a fiction.

Any resultant boom in investment and consumption is entirely dependent on the continued efforts of the government. If for any reason the artificial stimulus shifts or ceases, the inevitable result will be the recession that the policy intended to avoid in the first place. It is quite likely that the eventual bust will be worse because the government supports intensify the initial boom and thus the inevitable correction.

Austrian School economist Ludwig von Mises once likened the effect of monetary policy to that of a homebuilder who, under the false assumption of an endless supply of bricks, sets out to build an enormous mansion. Though he may only have enough bricks for a small abode, he maps out and begins to construct the great house, oblivious to his gaffe. As he nears the end of his supply, however, he realizes that he will not be able to finish the mansion and eventually has to undo what he has already spent so much time and effort on. To make use of his resources at all, he must destroy his half-finished mansion and rebuild the house, this time under more constrained guidelines.

In the real economy, as in the analogy, the skewed perception encourages skewed action and the eventual undoing of vast amounts of work. The thought is that the government can inject large doses of wealth into the economy in order to convey the notion that everything is great, that capital has been saved, and that it is a wonderful time to invest. But it is not real wealth, only artificial, abstract wealth in the form of money, which can only be gained by some at the loss of others. Eventually, prices will rise to catch up with the money stock, and investment and consumption will slow back down. The liquidity that flooded the system must eventually dry up and the recession will finally arrive.

Of course, as Keynes himself pointed out, there is no need for the monetary influx to cease at any point, and theoretically the injection of currency into the economy could continue forever, eternally propping up the economy whenever it begins to droop. In *The General Theory*, Keynes argued that "The right remedy for the trade cycle is not to be found in abolishing booms and thus keeping us permanently in a semi-slump; but in abolishing slumps and thus keeping us permanently in a quasi-boom." And so this argument has convinced policymakers over the remainder of the twentieth century and the first decade of this one—simply keep the economy going by infusing money and encouraging spending no matter what the real conditions of industry and well-being.

In our age of medicine and pervasive multi-colored pills, this interventionist policy may well seem like a viable solution. Whenever there is an ailment, the obvious solution is to inject some artificial tonic into the system to fix it. But, just like true medicinal treatments, economic policy typically gets rid of only the symptoms and covers up the problem without really fixing it. And, just as with medicine, economic policy also has its side effects, the most glaring being dependency. The inflationist nation is not unlike the partier who relies on two cups of coffee every morning to stay awake, or the crash victim who grows addicted to the morphine he takes to counter the pain. He must have the medicine or he will arrive at a condition worse than the one from which he started.

Milton Friedman's classic comparison of an inflationist nation to an alcoholic is precise. The drinker begins his romp to feel the physiological perks of a little buzz. After a few cocktails, he is riding high and doesn't think twice about drinking more and falling completely into drunkenness. The alcoholic feels great, people seem nicer, and his car runs much smoother. But slowly the effect of the toxin wears off and, once the alcohol begins to lose its effect, the drinker faces the pain of the inevitable hangover. At that point, he may well be uncontrollably tempted to take more drinks to alleviate the imminent headache. This works, of course, until the alcohol wears off again and he is obliged to continue the process with no end in sight. His body becomes conditioned for the high volume of alcohol and cannot function properly without it.

The inflationist nation too may begin its binge with the intent of getting a quick stimulus. The new liquidity acts very much like a shot of the hard stuff at happy hour, and the economy soon experiences a buzz as investors and consumers spend freely. As soon as the prices begin to rise and the boost of currency loses its effect, the government faces the peril of recession, whereupon the temptation of another increase in the money supply seems irresistible. And, just like the alcoholic, the inflationist nation must return to its poison again and again. It has conditioned itself for the constantly increasing volume of new liquidity and will break down without it.

By now, everyone will recognize how this mentality plays out in the real world and how it got us into the economic fix we currently face. The story is all too familiar: As the dot-com bubble began to burst in 2000, Fed Chairman Alan Greenspan took active measures to blow it back up again by reducing interest rates to encourage investment. In the course of 2001, the Fed cut the Prime Rate from its peak this decade of 9.50% to 5% and then cut it an additional .75% the next year. By that time, lax lending policies spurred by government initiatives and other factors in the real estate market made housing an enticing venture. This is when attention shifted from the frazzled dot-coms to the seemingly more staid real estate market.

It is also when we began to hear the clichés about home buying—house prices never go down, real estate is always a sound investment, flipping houses is a safe way to make money, and so on. With such fantastic tales being told about the housing market, far-fetched schemes were hatched to take advantage of it. One heard stories of college students taking out interest-only mortgages on houses that they would keep for four years and then sell at graduation with enough profit to pay their tuition. This was also the time when various financial boondoggles surrounding the housing market came into vogue—mortgage-backed securities, credit default swaps, interest-only mortgages, and the like. The financial industry was placing very risky bets on this escalating housing market, and everyone seemed to be riding high because of it.

It is true that housing, in any normal economy, is a much better investment than the over-priced stocks of August 2000, but the artificially low interest rates and other government policies geared specifically to home ownership made the housing market a goose of golden eggs that no investor could neglect. With such a mentality permeating the economy, it is no surprise that the dot-com bubble of the late 1990s swiftly transformed and became the housing bubble of the mid-aughts. One out-of-control mania was replaced by another, and, just as it was with the first, the second came crashing down in a spectacular collapse.

Nor can it be a surprise that the government sought as a remedy the same policies that helped create the bubbles in the first place. Since the crash of 2008, the government has tried everything imaginable to save us from recession and to jump-start the economy again. The most prominent aspect of this endeavor has been of course the bailout and stimulus packages that went into effect in November 2008 and April 2009. Other historic measures include lowering interest rates again and the initiation of programs aimed at getting consumers to spend more. One program offered first-time homebuyers an $8,000 credit, quite as if the government knew that housing wasn't a good enough investment on its own. The goal was to compel economic activity no matter what, even if it meant more risky lending and borrowing and the creation of yet another bubble.

> No one will know until this is actually in place how it works. But we believe we've done something that has been needed for a long time. It took a crisis to bring us to the point where we could actually get this job done.
>
> —SENATOR CHRISTOPHER DODD ON THE DODD-FRANK BILL FOR WALL STREET REFORM (JUNE 2010)

And so it has gone in the last few decades. Just like an alcoholic or morphine addict afraid of reality, the government habitually returns to the tonic that is at the root of its troubles. The more ardently it relies on economic policy, the more distorted the people's actions become, and the more the government is needed to uphold the warped economy. At this point, with so many layers of government intervention, it is practically impossible to tell the companies that are sound enough to stand on their own from those that are propped up by state intervention.

Historian and economist Thomas E. Woods' description of the recent wave of policy moves is apt: After trillions of dollars worth of bailouts and stimulus, all the government and banking industry have to show for them-selves is a *"Weekend at Bernie's* economy with sunglasses and Hawai'ian shirts on zombie companies supposed to give the impression of life and health." The best bet nowadays is to simply guess which zombies the government is going to prop up next and try to get in on the action.

Too Big to Fail

The argument has been made that, as soon as the bubble began to burst, the economy in general and several companies in particular were in dire need of assistance, and that without government intervention the crash would have been catastrophic. Of course, this begs the question, how did these companies and the economy as a whole get to a point where they were so precarious and could cause so much damage? Reports showed that almost all the major players in the economic world had leveraged them-selves around 32-to-1, which is to say that they had borrowed $32 for every dollar they had in capital. Homeowners, mortgage lenders, investment banks, and insurers were all borrowing astronomical amounts to make their investments. The standard for sound investments is around 10 or 12-to-1, and these companies were riding on three times that. What caused the companies to act so carelessly? What caused them to make financial moves that, in retrospect, were so precarious?

During the crisis, the popular explanation was that the primary actors in the debacle were simply too greedy and myopic in their various invest-ments, and their natural inclinations caused the bubble to expand and even-tually collapse. In a pure mania, like the dot-com bubble and the savings and loan bubble before it, the real estate bubble was fueled by a practically undetectable and uncontrollable fire of animalistic hunger for more.

Of course, the allure of such risky bets is obvious to anyone who understands financial markets. In short, it can pay to take risks. The inves-tor that gambles on an unknown stock can make five or ten times the amount initially invested; someone who invests $100,000 in a house could possibly gain $200,000 or $300,000 in the time he owns it. And, the more money invested, the greater the potential return, so borrowing to increase the initial investment makes the payoff that much more sizeable

In all such conceivable variations of investments, however, there are hazards. There is always the potential for a stock or home price to fall instead of rise as the investor had assumed it would. And, as with gains, the larger the initial investment, the larger the loss. As such, the borrower naturally wants to make sure that the investment is a good one; he will do his research, make sure the stock or house meets standards, and guarantee that the climate surrounding the investment is healthy, that the market is stable or the neighborhood prosperous. And so, just as there is incentive to invest as much as possible to increase the potential gain, there is also incentive to ensure the investment is sound and that it will not backfire. There is a natural balance of incentives when it comes to investments, where the motivation to take risks is metered by the danger of possibly losing out.

Under normal circumstances, all parties involved in a transaction have incentives to offset their greed with a rational assessment of the potential for success or failure. For this reason, one cannot simply blame the 2008 housing crisis or any other financial meltdown on greed or myopia. Both may be inherent in the situation, but they are also countered by a similarly inherent desire to avoid economic disaster. To blame the financial crisis on greed is, as some analysts have put it, like blaming a plane crash on gravity. Greed is an ever-present force that most individuals and institutions have learned to overcome in order to reach the heights of modern investment. To get to the real root of the problem, one must uncover exactly what it was that diminished the natural safeguards against recklessness and allowed the ever-present gravity to pull the system down.

Taking a step back, it becomes rather apparent that there is another player in the situation that has both the means and the motive to reduce those safeguards—the government. Since it became a significant player in the economy around the turn of the twentieth century, its aim has been to protect industries and trade in general from the vicissitudes of the Business Cycle. By implementing large-scale interventions, the government has made it somewhat unfeasible for individuals and businesses to use their rationality in the market, yet it has not barred them from letting their irrational, primeval impulses dictate their actions.

The result, as anyone can imagine, is the eager pursuit of gain without the fear of loss—in other words, excessive risk-taking without regard for potential downsides.

Economics professor Russ Roberts used the analogy of a poker game to describe the kinds of incentives in the modern world of government-influenced finance. To begin, the players make bets according to their own strategies while taking into consideration the potential risks and rewards of such bets. And, in normal games of poker, some win and some lose depending on the success of their strategies. But, in this game, there is another person in the room who has an interest in saving certain players from defeat—Uncle Sam. When Uncle Sam's favored players make poor decisions, lose more money than they have, and must leave the game, Uncle Sam steps in and gives them more money. He prohibits these players' failure to ensure their presence in the game and keep the bets flowing at a smooth pace.

As anyone can see from this analogy, the incentives are skewed in favor of risky action. The players who have Uncle Sam's backing have an incentive to bet their money on risky endeavors—the riskier the bet, the better, since more risk means greater potential gain. They know they will be bailed out in the event of failure, so they don't consider the possible downsides; all they see is the benefit they will receive. So too will others lend to them and invest in them, because they also know that the investment is a sure win, and they want a piece of the action as well.

Now, Uncle Sam's rationale might be reasonable. Some companies may well need propping up to survive. Such companies may have their hands in countless endeavors across the economy, in which case their failure would bring about a large-scale retraction of investments and liquidity in general.

It would be an utter catastrophe to let a player go bankrupt if, for instance, he had borrowed 32 times his own capital from other players to make his bets. Everyone at the table could potentially lose out. And so Uncle Sam does what he can to keep this player in the game, to guarantee his loans, and to prop him up so that he looks respectable.

This is the mentality behind the 'too big to fail' mantra that was so widely talked about during the 2008 crisis. Given our complex, interdependent system, it is a reasonable stance. Any single player in the economy affects several dozens, if not thousands, of others. And, when it comes to hundred-billion-dollar financial firms that facilitate the flow of money, the impact is that much more significant. Letting financial giants like Bear Sterns or AIG dissolve, for instance, would surely have had repercussions that extended beyond those firms and possibly to the entire economy.

But exempting them from failure can only lead the firms and individuals surrounding them in the direction of negligence. The player will act with less care, make riskier bets, and make due with inefficiency and corruption, all of which are guarded against naturally when the threat of failure exists. And so the self-perpetuating cycle continues: The more government steps in and regulates, the less capable private companies are at handling their own affairs, and the more government is needed to save them. Eventually, we have a scenario in which the state is responsible for an entire economy of semi-feeble institutions that increasingly extend their operations and take on risks that cannot possibly be prudently considered. When the state makes available large sources of cheap money, encourages risky loans and investments, and then insures the investors from any loss, it is a no-brainer for companies to lunge at the opportunity.

Financial analyst Peter Schiff describes these kinds of no-brainer decisions with the parable of a traveling circus. When the circus comes to town, a flood of new business comes with it, including vendors, performers, and spectators from all around. A local restaurant owner sees this upsurge in business as a chance to expand—he hires new employees and builds an extension on his restaurant to meet the new demands. Things are great while the circus is in town, as revenues are up and receipts are at an all-time high.

When the circus leaves, however, demand for his goods and services diminishes, and the restaurant owner realizes that he has overextended his resources in response to the fleeting event. Suddenly, he has too much supply for his demand and begins to see losses.

No one wants the restaurant owner to go out of business. We all like the food there and benefit greatly by its being around. But can it be reasoned that the government should send buckets of money to the restaurant owner so that he can maintain the high levels of business that he had grown dependent on while the circus was in town? We'd love for the restaurant to do well, but, if the owner made such poor decisions, then shouldn't he suffer the consequences when they turn sour? No reasonable citizen would suggest otherwise. Bailing out the restaurant would mean rewarding the owner for his poor decisions and most likely encouraging him to make more poor decisions when the circus comes to town again.

Similarly, banks and other financial giants that made reckless investments during the housing boom circus should pay the consequences of their poor decisions. When the too-big-to-fail defense is issued to let them off the hook, the entire outlook on investment is altered. No longer is the goal a matter of making the best choices with one's money and generating the most production while diminishing risk and losses; now the goal becomes growing big enough and having your hands in as many piles as possible so that you can be considered too big to fail, and thus effectively eliminate all risk of loss.

Moral Hazard

This is in effect the ultimate outcome of an economic policy that allows prices and incomes to rise as far as the air will allow, but then steps in and cuts off the losses when things begin to deflate. Everyone knows that there can't be gains without losses, and yet this is exactly what the government is trying to accomplish. Former Fed chairman Alan Greenspan actually earned a tribute thanks to his tendency of letting prices fly off the handle during bubbles and then intervening to bail out troubled firms during the subsequent downturns. The 'Greenspan put' was the name given to financial instruments specifically geared for large banks and insurers who wanted to invest recklessly and still have the option of selling at a set price if the investment went bad. In this way, companies will take on all the risk they dare because risk implies the potential for greater gains while the losses are all absorbed by the government and, ultimately, the taxpayers.

To investors, the Greenspan put and the too-big-to-fail mentality are more or less insurance policies that no one has to pay for. And, like all free insurance, these economic gadgets tend to encourage riskier behavior. Insurance in general has the effect of skewing behavior in the direction of recklessness, an effect that is redoubled when there is no premium put on the insurance policy, as is the case with government-backed insurance. Here we encounter the phenomenon known as the 'moral hazard', the tendency for a party sheltered from risk to behave in a different, more hazardous way than it would if fully exposed to the risks. The patient is willing to eat unhealthy foods when he has free health insurance, the driver is willing to park his car downtown when he knows his insurance will pay to repair any scratches, and so on. It is not necessarily malicious or even conscientious, but it is almost inevitable that one will act more recklessly given the proper insulation from loss.

Go ahead, eat the raw blowfish. We've got you covered. Health insurance for those who eat dangerously.

—AD COPY FOR A HEALTH INSURANCE COMPANY BESIDE A PICTURE OF AN INFLATED BLOWFISH (CIRCA MAY 2010)

Now, insurance is a part of the market as much as stocks, bonds, manufacturers, traders, and bankers are. Indeed, most insurance policies are embedded into the market prices of goods and services and not readily visible to the consumer. For example, the rate of interest that a bank offers potential depositors varies depending on the agreed duration of the deposit—it is higher if the money is deposited long-term and lower if the money is free to be withdrawn at any point. The higher interest rate is like an insurance premium that the bank pays its depositor to guarantee that he will not withdraw his funds.

Other, subtler forms of insurance are also ingrained in the price of doing all kinds of business. The cost of renting a store in a shabby neighborhood, for example, is relatively higher than renting space in a nice neighborhood because the risks of doing business in the bad area are higher. The building owner has to account for the extra costs associated with security and the removal of vandalism, for instance, and so must recoup those expenses through his prices. The higher the risk in any endeavor, the higher the price will be in reflection of the embedded insurance.

All endeavors have some level of risk. Any time a person puts his money into a stock, or even a bond, it could possibly be lost by the time he attempts to retrieve it. This is why it has always been prudent to research possible investments, even if one is only looking to deposit money in a bank for safekeeping. The fact that a bank will take your deposited money and most likely make its own investments with it means that there is great risk involved in merely making that deposit.

Of course, we hardly see it that way these days since the FDIC insures our money automatically up to a certain point. We simply deposit the cash and expect it to be there whenever we want it. We expect this no matter what the bank does with the money, and so we do not meter our depository actions with respect to the bank's investment plans. This laxity naturally extends to the banks, which receive deposits no matter what they do with them. Even if they fly off the handle and invest in highly risky endeavors, they will continue to receive capital. They are like late-90s dot-com companies floating on an endless supply of venture capital—they get it even if they spend it on lavish parties and 24-hour cereal buffets.

As can be evidenced by the kind of bank runs that occurred before the FDIC was instated in 1933, the security of one's money has always been a very real concern. The fact that so many elderly people still store their money at home—under their mattress, no doubt—is a remnant of a much more cautious age. Nowadays, that thought seems absurd and old-fashioned. But it brings to light the real risks involved in the modern banking system, risks that still exist (perhaps to a greater degree), even though they are easily neglected because of the supposedly free governmental protection.

The FDIC is insurance like any other form of insurance, and so we can see that there is no substantive difference in the way the banking system works now than it did before 1933. Indeed, since people freely put their money in banks without even thinking twice about what the bank will do with it, there is a much higher percentage of wealth stored in banks today than there was in the past. With more on deposit, banks have had more capital with which to invest and therefore more leverage in their various schemes.

It is not as though banks are less risky than they were before the FDIC; on the contrary, as we have seen with several banking fiascos in the last couple of decades, banks are still very precarious institutions. It's just that the average consumer does not think about the risk because he will not have to face the repercussions if the schemes go wrong. When he doesn't think about the risk, he can act more freely with his money.

This freedom is the ultimate aim of insurance and the too-big-to-fail mentality as a whole. It is to allow a depositor, investor, or trader the freedom to proceed without having to worry about the potential loss, which, it is assumed, will be covered by someone else. But, besides freeing the customer to do what he wants with his money, the fearlessness can easily turn to carelessness and recklessness. Indeed, in a market economy, where fear of loss is the very source of prudence, fearlessness *is* carelessness and recklessness.

Risk is a powerful force, even when it is applied to completely abstract sums of money. Its presence means that the least prudent ventures will be avoided even if those ventures promise higher possible returns. The higher chance of loss means that most will stay away from those endeavors.

Whenever that risk is removed, chances are that one will be more inclined to pursue the venture, especially if the perceived returns stay the same. The premium one pays for the insurance certainly reduces the value of the returns, but, if those returns are large enough, they can cover a significant premium and still make a profit. The moral hazard of a given insurance policy is amplified when there is no premium at all, or the customer at least believes there is no cost (as in the case with the FDIC or federal bailouts). The venture is thought to have little or no risk and yet all of the possible returns. Anyone who did not partake in such an endeavor would be foolish. Of course, all insurance claims must be paid for one way or another. Like any other form of insurance, the FDIC has costs, too; it requires premiums to be paid just like other insurance companies and often has to cover losses when bad investments fail. The premiums are paid in the form of taxes, and the coverage comes in the form of paying off insured moneys when banks fail to recoup their loans.

The overall effect of insurance is summed up by the question: What happens when a people's actions reflect the assumption that they can only win in a given situation, no matter how risky it is? The answer is that there will be more risky behavior. The more risk that is taken on, the greater the chance of failure, and the more need for coverage. Eventually, the risk will catch up to those involved and the result will be large-scale, perhaps catastrophic, loss. This decade's housing boom and bust is the imperative example of a seemingly no-loss scenario that ended up creating monumental damage.

The crash of 2008 showed us how insurance as a form of protection can be an insufficient safeguard and even exacerbate the problem. The instruments used in the various financial schemes were designed to help curb the loss in a given scenario, but, as could be expected, insurance contracts have themselves become ways for investors to try to multiply their money and even add risk to the whole scenario. Credit default swaps are a prime example. It must be admitted that those who sold these convoluted forms of insurance simply assumed they were a way to make extra money and not really to protect against someone else's loss. We know this because, in retrospect, the insurance companies—AIG, for instance—did not have funds to cover the losses when the loans did default. Of course, there was no overwhelming reason to believe the loans would default considering so many of them had been made through government-backed Fannie Mae and Freddie Mac, the parents of a whole brood of moral hazards.

The conclusion most took from the events of that year is that, in an interdependent world, even insurance can be insufficient to protect the average citizen. And to some degree, the conclusion is correct. The average citizen was not responsible for taking on the bad credit default swaps or even the bad mortgages, but when the companies and individuals that were involved failed, everyone paid the price. The capital was dried up, investment halted, businesses cut back hours, consumers began spending less, and so everything continued until retirement plans shriveled up, the stock market fell 40%, and unemployment jumped to double-digits. As Russ Roberts pointed out, "There is an old saying in poker: If you don't know who the sucker is at the table, it's probably you. We are the suckers. And most of us didn't even know we were sitting at the table."

Parasite Economy

In the wake of this decade's financial crisis, the conclusion that must be met with is that government intervention, while being aimed at providing support and indemnity for the economic system, rather debilitated firms and individuals from making sound decisions and thrust them into riskier behavior. Government welfare may accomplish what it intends, but in doing so it degrades the people's judgment and makes them more dependent on the state. Ultimately, the result is a populace which is less and less capable and intent on taking care of itself. All they can do or are willing to do is simply take what is given to them. The people become victims, parasites that have no trace of industry about them.

The upshot is what might be called a plague of parasitism. Self-sufficiency is no longer viable, and the only reasonable way to make a living is by mooching off the toil of others. As former lawyer and activist Roger Conner put it, "The temptation now is for people who have problems that they can cope with great effort be convinced to give in and wallow in their fate as a victim." No longer does one have to produce goods and services and assume responsibility to earn a living—as long as government is bailing businesses and people out, it is actually economically foolish to pursue the American Dream. The new American Dream is to live on the dole and strike it rich with a lucky grant or bailout. "It makes people think, 'I'd be a chump if I did otherwise'," Conner said. " 'If I take responsibility for what I do and what happens to me, I'm a fool.' "

In his *Logic of Collective Action*, American economist Mancur Olson showed that this parasitism is just the natural consequence of any condition in which individuals lose their sovereignty amid ever-expanding groups. Considering the difference between small groups, such as a family or community, and large groups, such as those that make up modern nation-states, Olson showed how the temptation to sit back and let others do essential work grows more prominent the bigger the group becomes. This is true even when the members of the group are of the same mindset and share common interests.

To use a basic illustration, regard two communities, one small and one large, which are both in need of a road to connect them to a highway. In the first community, of let's say five persons, all the individuals in the group have the same interest in building the road and, it can be assumed, will work with the others to construct it, whether by actually performing the labor or trading their share of that labor for other goods or services. They realize that if they do not participate, they will likely not be included in the benefits— either the road will not be built, or the others will somehow exclude them from its use. Since the population is so small, such exclusionary measures are feasible and quite reasonable. Thus, in a small group, it can be assumed that the members will be motivated to work together to reach shared aims.

Notice, however, when considering the larger hypothetical community of 100 individuals. Suddenly, the rationale shifts. First of all, the amount of work needed to organize and distribute the labor grows exponentially. Even if the road will be the same size and require the same amount of work to build, the overall work increases because there are more people involved. Moreover, the chances that one of the citizens could slip through the cracks without doing any work increases. If 5 or 10 of the 100 are adamant about building the road, they will build it even if the other 90 or 95 don't do anything, and most likely will have no problems sneaking on and using the road. In that case, those others end up getting a road for nothing. This incentive alone makes it economical to 'free ride' on the work of others.

At the same time, the motivation for proponents of the road diminishes for this same reason. The more free riders in a community there are, the more work the productive sector must put out, and, ultimately, the less return they will see on their investment. Their drive to construct the road also diminishes to the extent that the road is never truly considered.

This principle can be summed up by the dichotomy of concentrated benefits and diffuse costs—in large groups, benefits can be concentrated while costs can easily be spread out among everyone. It can be seen in everyday occurrences: A litterer benefits to some great extent by throwing trash on the ground because he can get rid of a cumbersome belonging; on the other hand, the typical citizen must pay only a small price since the litter takes up such a small portion of his panorama, and to have it cleaned costs each citizen a slight fraction of a janitor's salary. In this light, it would seem, it pays to litter and just let someone else pick up the trash—it pays to be a parasite.

When everyone thinks this way, of course, free riding becomes the standard and no one works for a living. As in Ayn Rand's *Atlas Shrugged*, in which the productive citizens go on strike to escape the looting of their wealth, all that is left are looters trying to loot from other looters. It cannot last. And so this mentality goes for all actions. Charity, good will, and prudent self-discipline are all put aside because society has assumed these responsibilities for its members. Helping out one's fellow man becomes irrational and especially uneconomic. As Albert J. Nock pointed out in his seminal 1935 essay, *Our Enemy, the State*, a passerby on the street is less likely to give the beggar a quarter because,

Nothing is more certain than that a general profligacy and corruption of manners make a people ripe for destruction. A good form of government may hold the rotten materials together for some time, but beyond a certain pitch, even the best constitution will be ineffectual, and slavery must ensue.

—JOHN WITHERSPOON, *THE DOMINION OF PROVIDENCE OVER THE PASSIONS OF MEN* (1776)

of course, the government has already taken the quarter from him with the intent of giving it to the homeless man. Helping out the beggar would amount to doubling one's burden, a decision which no economizing individual can justify.

With regard to the government and society at large, the Welfare State is a great mechanism for the very purpose of privatizing gain and socializing costs, for providing freedom to its citizens without responsibility. The government privatizes gains as in the case of unemployment insurance, subsidies, and bailouts, and socializes costs through taxes and regulations.

And so parasitism becomes the only economically sound course of action. Says Conner, "Where we're headed is the notion that 'I never have to insure myself, protect myself, take responsibility for myself, plan for myself, because there'll always be someone there to pick up the pieces.'"

Flies are buzzing around my head

Vultures circling the dead

Picking up every last crumb

Big fish eat the little ones

Big fish eat the little ones

Not my problem give me some

—RADIOHEAD, *OPTIMISTIC* (2000)

Whenever given the choice, one will always choose to exploit the public facility and preserve the personal. This is why we see public transportation, parks, and other infrastructure badly vandalized and permitted to fall into disrepair. It is also the reason why we see government programs running out of funds, going over budget, and still not getting the job done. Here we come back to the Tragedy of the Commons that has plagued civil society from time immemorial. When the benefits are realized on a personal plane and the risks are socialized, there is no incentive to conserve resources, to ensure the best deal, or otherwise act prudently—someone else will always pick up the tab.

Upon reflection of the parasite economy, it must be argued that Socialism, by nature, propagates the very culture it aims to remedy. Far from issuing a world of enlightened, benevolent citizens, Socialism creates a condition of opportunistic and grasping individuals, cold to the needs of others and focused entirely on their own material well-being. The state is more and more controlling, and the people are more and more needy. And so we arrive at the paradox that selflessness leads directly and absolutely to selfishness and greed.

In a parasitic economy, the only sound approach is to take advantage of the system and all that is handed out 'for free'. The competition for that loot is as aggressive as it can be, and so the members of the society are left with a residual antipathy that is no less strict or exacting than the class war of Vulgar Capitalism. The more socialized a society is, the greater this tension becomes.

The extent of the struggle can best be seen in the documents of a time and place where outright Communism existed as the rule for more than half a century. That is, of course, in Soviet Russia. In a correspondence with her cousin Boris Pasternak, Russian writer and scholar Olga Freidenberg described her homeland by what she called 'skloka', a searing condition apparently unique to the Soviet experience.

"Wherever you looked," she wrote, "in all our institutions, in all our homes, skloka was brewing. Skloka is a phenomenon born of our social order, an entirely new term and concept, not to be translated into any language of the civilized world. It's hard to define. It stands for base, trivial hostility, unconscionable spite, breeding petty intrigues, the vicious pitting of one clique against another. It thrives on calumny, informing, spying, scheming, slander, the igniting of base passions. Taut nerves and weakening morals allow one individual or group to rabidly hate another individual or group. Skloka is natural for people who have been incited to attack one another, who have been made bestial by desperation, who have been driven to the wall. Skloka is the Alpha and Omega of our politics. Skloka is our method."

It is a matter of pure speculation whether the United States could arrive at such a place described by Ms. Freidenberg. If Schumpeter's predictions are correct, the twenty-first century will see all Western nations follow Russia into entirely state-run juggernauts of their own. While we certainly face no Soviet brand of Socialism right now, the impulses that delivered Russia to those frightful circumstances are all present in our Western economy—they are, after all, ingrained in the roots of modern economics. Despite the recognized failure of Communism in the Soviet Union, the pressure remains, the mechanism which dominated the Soviets is more or less in place in Washington and other Western capitals, and the mentality which urged it has been gaining favor over the course of the past century.

Perhaps the most menacing trend in the modern state is the people's increasing reliance on the government and its various programs. The bigger government becomes, the more it seems its citizens are incapable of performing even the most basic daily activities—the more regulations government lays down on walking, talking, eating, playing, working, teaching, learning, and so on, the less capable we are at performing these basic life functions. As we have seen, the kind of freedom sought in the twentieth century—that is, the positive kind of freedom, the kind that grants us material well-being and all of our necessities—has come only at the expense of the power of choice and thus all of our responsibility in the matter. An individual in our modern Welfare State may finally get all that he needs, but he has lost his individuality in the process; he lives, but carries on lifelessly.

The Reign of Skloka

In his 1958 classic *The Affluent Society*, Harvard economist John Kenneth Galbraith fashioned the concept of the 'conventional wisdom' to explain what he saw as a great, immovable rock of standards and sentiments on which a given society bases its thoughts and actions. According to him, all great civilizations accumulate this storehouse of knowledge and turn to it whenever their beliefs are challenged. But, since it is so vast and all-encompassing, the conventional wisdom is hard to shift or replace and so can stay around long after its substance has been refuted by evidence or experience. It persists even when false.

In Galbraith's view, the conventional wisdom of his day was that of the classical economists, Smith, Ricardo, and Malthus. It said that markets could self-correct, that the business cycle would even out over time, and that people who suffered through economic troughs would later succeed in economic peaks. This argument said that people should be allowed to produce and consume whatever they desired, and, in the end, all would benefit from the rising tide of a laissez-faire system. This mentality had dominated Western civilization since the

> **What sphinx of cement and aluminium bashed open their skulls and ate up their brains and imagination?**
>
> **Moloch! Solitude! Filth! Ugliness! Ashcans and unobtainable dollars!**
>
> **Moloch the incomprehensible prison! Moloch the crossbone soulless jailhouse and Congress of sorrows! Moloch whose buildings are judgement! Moloch the vast stone war! Moloch the stunned governments!**
>
> **Moloch whose mind is pure machinery! Moloch whose blood is running money! Moloch whose fingers are ten armies! Moloch whose breast is a cannibal dynamo! Moloch whose ear is a smoking tomb!**
>
> **Moloch whose love is endless oil and stone! Moloch whose soul is electricity and banks! Moloch whose poverty is the specter of genius!**
>
> —ALLEN GINSBERG, "HOWL" (1956)

Enlightenment and was proved to a large degree valid by the immense improvement in technical abilities and the vast expanse of wealth that the West had accrued since Smith's time.

But, as Galbraith posited, there was a fatal flaw in this time-honored set of beliefs. With the rise of Industrialism, technical advances and increases in population had made Western economies highly volatile and interdependent, such that the Business Cycle loomed as a constant threat to the well-being of the impoverished and to the society as a whole. The Western people, granted a largely free market for nearly two hundred years, had proved it to be a rather precarious and perhaps dangerous mode of society. In the highly competitive free market, owners exploited workers and consumers, and everyone lost out because of the class conflict.

Twentieth-century experience proved that the idealized world of the classical economists was misguided or at least misinformed. Indeed, poverty persisted amid all the plenty, and, as Galbraith showed, the working poor seemed to be getting relatively poorer compared to the rich. According to Galbraith, the conventional wisdom had a flaw. There was no Invisible Hand, as Smith saw it, which directed men toward mutually beneficial aims in a free market. Rather, when given freedom, men would necessarily engage in a greedy, destructive pursuit of self-interests, which left a portion of the population destitute and struggling for survival. Far from some Smithian heaven, indeed, life better resembled a Hobbesian hell, "solitary, poor, nasty, brutish, and short," which could only culminate in an all-out "war of every man against every man".

Fortunately for Galbraith and other Keynesians, modern society also provided the answer to the problems of the age. To be sure, the Western world had become very affluent—miraculously, no doubt—with so much wealth as to exceed that of any civilization in history many times over. "Nearly all," Galbraith states, "throughout all history, have been poor. The exception, almost insignificant in the whole span of human existence, has been the last few generations in the comparatively small corner of the world populated by Europeans. Here, and especially in the United States, there has been great and quite unprecedented affluence." The answer, naturally, was to spread that wealth equitably, to ensure that everyone could benefit from it and that no one would ever go without.

To accomplish this simple feat, Galbraith turned to the state. By use of fiscal policy, regulations, and monetary policy, government could control the economy effectively, redistribute wealth, and eliminate suffering, accomplishments unthinkable in the eighteenth and even nineteenth centuries. In a concerted effort, Galbraith and other Keynesians undertook a campaign to overturn the prevailing classical school of thought and bring political economy up to date with comprehensive state intervention. To overcome the Hobbesian melee, the civilization would instate an all-powerful monarch, which would control the economy and lead the country like a leviathan.

Today, it must be admitted that Galbraith and the Keynesians have been rather successful in their crusade. In the twenty-first century, it is Galbraith's understanding of economics and not Smith's that most subscribe to. To a large degree, most believe the notion that free markets are inherently unstable, that the Business Cycle harms innocent bystanders, and that the government can and must play a role in the economy in order to ensure the most basic human freedoms. Smith, Ricardo, and Malthus have all retired from textbooks, being, like Newtonian Physics, good to a certain point and then no more. They have been replaced with Keynes, Samuelson, and Galbraith, the economists of a Quantum age.

The field has been trending this way throughout the twentieth century to the extent that Galbraith's model has now become the conventional wisdom and countless people recite it as an undeniable fact, not even in need of defending. President Obama summarized the consensus in his 2009 Inaugural Address, in which he stated that "The question we ask today is not whether our government is too big or too small, but whether it works, whether it helps families find jobs at a decent wage, care they can afford, a retirement that is dignified." The assumption is that no family or individual can find jobs at decent wages or health care or retirement on their own; they are helpless in the face of modern complexity and need government to provide for them from cradle to grave.

These days, the fact of ever-expanding government is just assumed. Everyone knows that government is necessary, having based their beliefs on experience. The government has always been a major player in our lives—when we want something done, we expect government to be there to do it. It is the provider of charity as in Albert J. Nock's parable, it is the supporter of the arts, the protector of health and safety, and countless other essentials, and so it is just assumed that it has always been there and must always be there in the future. We know of no other way in life.

The average modern might think of what would happen without a strong central power. Without government, it is presumed, there would be no police for discipline, no military for protection, no schools for education, no roads, libraries, museums, or parks. Without government, the people would be helpless and hapless; it would be mass hysteria and bedlam in the streets because no one would be able to conduct fair trades with others; conniving and treachery would run rampant. To be sure, the word for the absence of government, anarchy, has come to mean exactly that— 'utter chaos', 'no rule in a world of absolute lawlessness'.

But, before this survey of modern statism comes to a close, it would be prudent to re-evaluate the new conventional wisdom under the premise that it too, like the conventional wisdom of times past, might have flaws and has possibly grown outmoded in its dominance.

As a primary point of contention, the skeptic might call attention to the basis for the leviathan which Galbraith and other Keynesians propose. No matter what the purpose is seen to be, all can agree that the state has always been possible only when a strong, productive populace supports it. The state can only redistribute wealth when the people have first created the wealth it aims to redistribute. And there has been no method of wealth creation that has been more successful and reliable in all of history than the free-market capitalist system. Indeed, the welfare statist government, as envisaged by the Keynesians, depends on the very system that it aims to correct. The stronger they wish the state to be, the stronger the capitalist market must be.

What's more, the skeptic will find that not only does the interventionist state rely on the free-market system to survive and thrive, but so too does it naturally interfere with the lifeblood of that free-market system, made of individualism and responsibility, such that it can no longer provide the wealth that it would provide in a free system. Simply, the state is designed to reign in individualism and responsibility, and so neither the Free Market nor the Welfare State can flourish the way they were intended. By its very existence, the state cuts off its only supply of power and substance. Government requires the laissez-faire ethos, and yet destroys it at the same time. It is the Faustian dilemma played out across the entire civilization.

Many will argue that it is possible to maintain the various impulses that make free-market Capitalism successful while redirecting its production toward more socially acceptable ends, as it is in so-called 'democratic socialist' countries, for instance, such as those in Scandinavia. In such a system, the state dictates what is to be done with the wealth, but, it is thought, the people voluntarily choose who runs the state and what that state does. That way, both free markets and extensive government regulation work together to create a steady, sustainable economy.

Of course, if the people's choices are voluntary, then there is nothing wrong with the democratic socialist system—they, like any in a free market, will maintain individualism and assume responsibility to the extent that any voluntarily acting people would. As such, the economy will prosper and create wealth like all great civilizations. But the reality contradicts this happy vision. The premise behind all socialist, collectivist, or statist systems is that the people, when granted freedom of thought and action, will not do what's right; that voluntary action will necessarily lead to struggle and pain; and that the government is needed to ensure that the people do what they should, and to quell the war of all against all that would arise in a free system.

The fundamental question that must be asked with regard to the crisis of our age is the same question that has been asked throughout the past five hundred years by Victoria and Charles V, Locke and Hobbes, Jefferson and Hamilton, Pareto and Belloc, Mises and Keynes: Is man capable of self-rule?

To an increasing degree, the answer has come in the negative. Contemporary society is just too complex, too technically advanced, and too interdependent for any single citizen to possibly know what is best for himself, much less what is best for the people around him and those who he affects in some far-off place.

More importantly, man is weak, as he is described in *The Grand Inquisitor*, Ivan's poem as recited in Dostoevsky's philosophical and psychological masterpiece *The Brothers Karamazov*. Man, by nature, cannot meet Christ's expectations of him, and thus needs the help of the church—the state, as it has become—to survive and to do what is right. He requires protection from predatory corporations, the endless mazes of competition, and the relentless nadryvy of modern society. Man especially needs protection from himself, without which he will self-destruct in a rage of pitiful wantonness.

The poem is in itself a document on the moral effect of the state. It is set in Seville, Spain during the sixteenth century, at the height of the Inquisition (the date cannot have been pure coincidence). The poem's title character, the Grand Inquisitor, the bishop of Seville, has recently completed the auto da fé of burning several heretics at the stake and drawing the unwearied devotion of the people, when Christ appears. Everyone knows that it is Him—a blind man pleads to be healed and He heals him; He raises a girl from the dead—there is no question that it must be Him.

As abruptly as He appears, the Grand Inquisitor seizes Him and throws Him in jail. Immediately, the people turn from Christ to the Inquisitor and drop to kiss his feet. The Inquisitor's rationale is familiar: Christ has come to give His people freedom, the kind that He displayed in the desert when the "great spirit of negation" had enticed Him with three temptations. Christ did not throw Himself from the peak to display His miracle; instead He refused the temptation and entreated man to do the same.

But, as the Grand Inquisitor states, man is not capable of such strength. Christ could do it, but His praying that man too refuse such temptation is beyond the realm of possibilities. Man is weak; he needs the bread that the church can give him, and so will devote himself to the church to secure his rations. Christ granted them freedom and demanded responsibility, for man to make the bread himself, but that only showed that He did not love them at all, for freedom only brought conflict and responsibility only brought confusion. Only the Grand Inquisitor brought them happiness. And so the Grand Inquisitor had no choice but to jail the Savior and indeed burn him at the stake for coming to "hinder" what the church had been doing—His work all along.

Dostoevsky's description of the Grand Inquisitor's quest to provide the people with happiness foretold precisely the vital aims of all of Modern Liberalism. The goal is happiness—security, material freedom, the bread necessary for survival—which only the state is willing to provide. The people fall at the feet of the rulers, their 'archy', no matter which brand of state they represent, because it is thought that they are the only ones who love them. To the childlike people, it does not matter what the state must do to provide this happiness as long as it is provided reliably. This is so even if the state takes away their very humanity, the very reward that Christ offers for the willing. Indeed, the people will readily give it up, just to have security. As the Inquisitor states, "In the end, they will lay their freedom at our feet and say to us, 'Make us your slaves, but feed us!' "

And yet, the paradox that we have seen in the last hundred years is that, as the people willingly become slaves, as they sacrifice their responsibility and volition for the security of bread, they starve the system of its very means of feeding them; in doing so, they slay their Savior and destroy their only chance for redemption.

IV
AUTARCHY

1. REASSESSMENT

CULTURAL HISTORIAN JACQUES BARZUN noted in his great account
of Western Civilization that "An age is defined by its problems, not proposed solutions, which are many and thus divide." Everyone agrees on what
the problem is—one manifestation or other of the system, the humongous
Juggernaut that towers over all our beliefs and actions—but all are at odds
as to the real constitution of that problem and thus how to correct it. As
a result, attempts at solving it conflict with each other and stir up more
problems that must be countered in turn. The result is a self-perpetuating
process that can only lead in the direction of more problems.

In our age, it is safe to say that the solutions not only divide, but add to
the problems and thus make them worse. We have come to a point where,
no matter what one believes and hopes for in the world, he can only get
what he wants if it comes at the expense of someone else. And so he can
only solve the problem by creating new problems for others, problems that
can only be solved by creating yet more problems, and so on.

For example, one group would solve our problems by implementing
a slew of regulations, which would doubtless safeguard against a whole
host of threats posed by corporate America, polluting manufacturers, and
manipulative marketers. But doing so would harm another group's liveli-

hood, diminish their ability to conduct business, and raise the cost of their products so that consumers and workers end up worse off as a result. That group would solve the problems by cutting taxes and offering breaks for the same corporations, manufacturers, and marketers, which would doubtless mean greater freedoms to produce goods and make a profit, but also greater freedoms to connive their customers, pollute the environment, and make risky investments that end up hurting everyone in the end.

One group wants subsidies for its interests, which are entirely American and would surely help the economy as a whole. But another group claims that those subsidies harm the economy by distorting the supply and demand and rewarding inefficient business practices while punishing efficient ones. The latter group would get rid of all subsidies, unless, perhaps, the subsidies benefited them, in which case they would help American interests and the economy as a whole and should be salvaged.

One group wants higher taxes to help pay for schools, roads, bridges, and welfare; yet, at the same time, those in the group do all they can to finagle their tax returns so that they can stay in a lower tax bracket and thus pay less in taxes. The rich should pay more in taxes, they say, but only those who are richer than they are.

This same mentality can be seen throughout our culture and in every sector of the economy. The solution is easy—we must do this, this, and that in order to ensure sound business and free choice; but, of course, the only way to ensure this, this, and that is to take from others, hinder their production, and limit their freedoms. The only way to gain is for others to lose; the only way to solve problems is to create new ones.

To a large degree, this argument is rationalized in the context of a culture divide. There are two great ideological forces at play in the modern society, and only one is on the side of the just, the moral, and the economically sound, while the other is necessarily on the side of the unjust, the immoral, and the economically specious. Given this dichotomy, the dilemma any modern reformer faces is practically answered for him. It is okay that someone else must lose in this situation because, of course, they are evil and should lose. It's all right that our side can only win if the other side loses because the other side is wrong and therefore ignorant and backward, and so they should lose in order for us to win.

These forces, both of which have been granted a variety of appellations in recent decades, can be summed up by the terms 'Right' and 'Left', though any number of opposites have been used to describe them. 'Conservative' and 'Liberal', 'Classical Liberal' and 'Modern Liberal', 'Reactionary' and 'Progressive', 'Right-winger' and 'Leftist', 'Wing-nut' and 'Nutjob', 'Crackpot' and 'Loony-toon', and so on, have all been used to describe more or less the same two opposing sides of the great debate. No matter what they are called, the claim is the same: One contradicts the other and can only flourish—indeed, can only survive—if the other loses. And so both factions in the conflict battle it out, advancing and retreating in a giant tug-of-war, all the while coming up with a storehouse of creative names and insults to keep the struggle lively.

The divide is best characterized by the disparate perspectives that arose in discussions of the 2008 and '09 bailouts and stimulus packages. With regard to a single financial meltdown and subsequent government action, two different people could come up with two completely different diagnoses and suggested remedies. For instance, liberal filmmaker Michael Moore mocked the bailouts of 2008, calling them in his sarcastic manner the inevitable way of Capitalism; his solution was more regulation. Meanwhile, conservative talk show host Glenn Beck blasted the bailouts in a scathing attack on the socialist tendencies in the U.S. government; his solution was less regulation. One event, two vastly different views.

In reality, both were right, albeit shortsighted. The financial crisis was, as the modern liberal would have it, the result of greedy businessmen, grasping corporations, and reckless capitalists out to get all the money they could at the expense of others. At the same time, it was also the result, as the conservative would have it, of a government that had extended beyond its bounds, encouraging risky behavior and saving the reckless from ruin in order to keep the economy growing. But, it must be said that both parties were responsible for the turmoil. Pointing the finger at one group, one party, or one individual and putting all the blame on them is not only incomplete, it's a rather misleading tactic that actually adds to the problem. When the burden is put on one group of people, that group will only want to retaliate and return the burden to someone else.

What the open-eyed spectator will discover is that the two sides of this great debate, the Left and the Right, actually agree on at least one main aspect. Though they are engaged in an all-out battle of ideas (and perhaps more), participants on both sides fall more or less on opposing sides of the same boat. One side's solution would detract from the other side's livelihood and thus create a new problem to solve. That solution, in turn, would detract from the first side's livelihood and create another problem. And so the process continues, each side pushing and pulling back and forth until the boat capsizes and no one gets what he wants.

Taking a step back, a pattern begins to emerge. From an outside view, both contestants in the battle, as polar and antagonistic as they may seem, are actually engaged in the same action, fighting toward the same end. They might appear to be different and to have contradictory characteristics, but both the Left and the Right are in fact one and the same when it comes to their proposed solutions—basically, to beat the other side—and their strategies—by means of the tools inherent in the system. They may be diametrically opposed to one another, but they are analogous in their opposition; they are akin in their conflict. As G. K. Chesterton once pointed out, two nations that go to war are not in bitter disagreement, as it might seem; rather, they are very much in agreement in that they both think that war is the right course of action. In the great modern politico-economic conflict, the combatants are all in agreement that the only way to solve the problem is to defeat the other side. Since both parties approach the conflict from this tack, the only way they can win is if the other side loses, and so the result is a perpetual divergence that can only intensify with time.

Here, we come to the real problem. When solutions begin to make the problem worse, the deeper and more involved its contestants get, the harder they will try to escape, and the further entrapped they become. But, from a broader approach, we can see a way out. The fact that the proposed solutions all aim to detract from the other side's livelihood and well-being means that they are not really true solutions after all; they are but partial solutions, suited for one party or the other, for some finite period, not for everyone, not for all time. They rest on the premise that, to get what one wants, one must obtain it from others or withhold it from society at large; that one can only succeed at the expense of another.

This is the zero-sum problem examined earlier, and it is this predicament that stands as the true problem in our age. The problem is not that groups hold to certain ideologies, or even that they are actively trying to instate those ideologies; rather, the problem is that the system is so confined that one group can only assert its ideology by restricting the ideology of others. The problem is not that one group keeps getting tax breaks while others who are more in need assume a higher tax burden; nor is it that some businesses get subsidies while others do not; rather, the problem is that one group can only gain from a tax break if some other group loses, and that, in order for one company to get a subsidy, another company has to pay for it. To sum up, the problem is not that certain people win and other people lose; the problem is that people can only win at all if other people lose. It is the zero-sum problem.

> **Modern hostility is a base thing, and arises, not out of a generous difference, but out of a sort of bitter and sneering similarity. It is because we are all copying each other that we are all cursing each other.**
>
> —G.K. CHESTERTON, "ON WAR AND PEACE", *ILLUSTRATED LONDON NEWS*, APRIL 25, 1908

This central problem can be seen in the conflicts that arise throughout the modern culture. To get what one wants in politics, the opposition must lose; to assert one's stance on abortion, gay marriage, gun laws, and so on, everyone on the other side must be refuted. The notion that one person can only gain at the expense of others means that any kind of life he proposes to live will necessarily be problematic for others. In a closed economy, where one can only succeed if someone else fails, such 'solutions' are the only possible way. The Right complains that the government is coercive and forces its people to do things it wouldn't otherwise do; the Left complains that corporations are the coercive ones that force consumers to do things they wouldn't otherwise do. But neither the state nor the corporations could possibly be coercive if we lived in an open economy. Only when people have no real alternative in the matter can governments or corporations, or anyone else for that matter, do whatever they want to whomever they want. The closed condition is the deciding factor.

Toward an Open Economy

Now, if it can be agreed that the closed economy is the problem, then the solution is a matter of course: Open the economy. A real solution entails escaping from this restrictive condition, so that gain for one can mean gain for others as well. To achieve this, we must open the economy as it had been before the 1890s, when equal footing was possible, involuntary exploitation was rather impossible, and economic growth ran parallel to social conscience. Any other suggested solutions will only further entrench society in its zero-sum condition, making it more and more difficult to break free. To escape the zero-sum condition, to open up the economy, is the real solution and the only viable one for our current predicament.

Of course, this is much easier said than done. Given the modern system, an open economy is no more understandable than it is imaginable. What would it take to provide an open economy? Is it even possible?

To begin, we must look at what an open economy would entail, which starts with understanding exactly what 'openness' really is. So far in this study, 'openness' has referred to the ability to make choices. Thus, an open economy would be a place in which each participant was at liberty to think and act in accordance with his own volition, to engage in contracts voluntarily, and to rule his life in the competence of his own authority. On the other hand, a closed economy would be a place in which one must deal with others to obtain necessities and luxuries, where one must either cooperate or compete with others for resources. Whereas a closed economy means competition, an open economy includes alternatives to both cooperation and competition so that no such action would be necessary. In other words, an open economy would mean complete autarchy—self-rule for everyone.

As we have seen on an earlier page, the only true way to achieve autarchy is by first obtaining the ability to provide for one's needs and wants on one's own. To attain autarchy, one must first attain autarky, or self-sufficiency. Ultimately, to solve the zero-sum problem, each individual must be able to provide wholly for himself and to detach from the system entirely. Only when that fundamental freedom has been secured can a people truly be free to guard against exploitation and coercion, and to engage in contracts that are just and productive.

And so the simplest, roughest sketch of the solution would be this: self-sufficiency in order to provide self-rule. Right away, the alert reader will sense the difficulty in such an endeavor. Given our highly interdependent society, it would mean an entirely new way of doing things. Self-sufficiency is a foreign concept in our age, and there is little to suggest that it is achievable when considering all that would need to change.

The closed system as we know it is our system for better or worse, and almost everything we do or think is based in that system. The tools we would use to fix the government, the banks, or the market, for instance, are all based on those same institutions—we rely on one to repair another, but none can effect much change since they all rely upon the others. Reform is not unlike trying to move a rug that you're standing on—you can push and pull all you want, but you'll only end up falling over in the process.

There are three major dilemmas to be faced once the ultimate goal of opening up the economy is established. First, it cannot be taken for granted that opening the economy will be a pleasant process or that everyone in the system is willing to make the sacrifices necessary to move in such a direction. Reopening the economy would require becoming a culture of self-sufficiency, or at least a country capable of securing the potential to do so, and could mean immense, fundamental change that could very well shake our civilization to the ground. Many might not be up for such a venture despite the inconvenient circumstances they may currently find themselves in.

Though the average American may be hassled by taxation, inflation, exploitation, regulations, and other '-tions', he is nonetheless very comfortable in his contemporary system, and that is a benefit that cannot be underestimated when considering reform. His food, shelter, and security are all granted to him, and he has all the grande lattes, iGadgets, and mp3s he could want without leaving the coziness of his ergonomic lounge chair. From his perspective, it is quite reasonable to assume that anything that would disrupt his snug life would be at best unfavorable.

It is possible that most Westerners enjoy the perks of modern society so much that they are willing to put up with all its drawbacks just to maintain the status quo. One might well be content to deal with the closed economy, to compete ad infinitum for greater shares of the great pie of wealth, and to let some great bureaucracy dictate his livelihood because he realizes that, thus far, that great bureaucracy has been able to provide him with a largely satisfying existence. He is not free, but he is fat and happy. And so he gladly trades sovereignty for security and just floats on.

Second, even if we agree that opening the economy is a worthwhile endeavor that must be undertaken, it is not clear that such a plan would even be possible. It can be assumed that self-sufficiency would require at least some form of free land for the people to inhabit and claim for their own. But, of course, all free land has been taken up and the frontier has closed. After the 1890s, there was no longer a place that offered free land to anyone, especially in the way that it had been offered to Westerners over the previous few centuries. The world is finite after all, and the population is so vast as to make expansion—especially the brand of expansion experienced by the West from 1500 to 1900—untenable. As a result, we are bound to our neighbors in an increasingly intimate way, complexity and interdependency seem to be here to stay, and the dream of freedom is unthinkable. To many, society has grown too complex for anyone to live independently;

the closed-economy Juggernaut is the only way. This is the second dilemma facing reformers.

Finally, assuming that the problems we face are due to the closed economy, it is not clear how we could reopen it. The closed economy came in large part as the natural consequence of interdependency, which is the natural outcome of specialism, labor division, and trade. Questions arise: To open the economy, would we have to set in reverse these economic advances? Or would we have to find a new frontier to provide the liberties we seek? Might new and innovative techniques be all that is needed to overcome our obstacles? Since the theory is a relatively new one, the prospects are unknown and recourse may seem alien.

These concerns are decidedly important, and most provide an explanation as to why such a solution has not yet been presented in the popular discourse. It is for this reason that a careful assessment is required before any detailed survey of the solution is attempted.

The desirability of autarchy. The first dilemma is perhaps the most troubling. It rests on the notion that reform means change, and change is rather undesirable in such a plush society. This first dilemma is the most far-reaching and would be the most difficult to overcome since it involves base emotions and not just intellect. One might make an argument that appeals to those base emotions, but doing so would only displace the irrational stance. For example, one might argue that the comfortable life we have come to know is bound to end very soon because of the precariousness of our system. Because of our bad habits and greed, we have created a looming economic disaster that will completely wipe out civilization as we know it. The argument would then suggest that we might as well shake up the system ourselves before the system shakes us up.

But the levelheaded political economist cannot subscribe to the doomsday theories that are so popular these days. Though it is not very sensational, history proves that our current mode of governance—in a way, a kind of feudal mode of governance—could go on for centuries without much upheaval at all, just as it did during the Middle Ages. One is inclined to agree with Schumpeter that Socialism—and especially the quasi-capitalist brand of Socialism that the United States and Britain are most representative of—can persist for millennia if need be. Indeed, one form or another of Statism might well be the only system possible in a closed economy, which would explain the almost magnetic pull we have felt toward it over the last century.

The only real threat to a socialist economy is the promise of freedom, which undermines the system's inner workings and diverts its resources. But the promise of freedom can come only with an open economy, in which choices are available and no one is obligated to live for someone else. The dissolution of the U.S.S.R. is an apt example. It happened about a decade after the United States and Britain made significant moves to reduce the amount of bureaucracy in their governments and create freer states and was the result, one could say, of the reopening of the economy and the promise of freedom.

While neither Britain nor the United States had returned to the pinnacle of freedom they had demonstrated during the nineteenth century, the mere impression of greater freedom in the West meant that there was a new hope for the people in the East. That new hope translated into a widespread rejection of Soviet-style government and a move toward individual sovereignty.

Whenever there is an opportunity for freedom, the economy is open and the constructs that uphold Socialism necessarily dissipate. On the other hand, when there is no further opportunity for freedom, the economy is closed and the constructs that lead to Socialism necessarily take hold. That is the very predicament we face here in America in the new century. There is no further opportunity for freedom, no country to which we can flee to become freer, and no bastion of liberty on which we can focus our gaze, so Socialism will likely continue to gain strength.

One is reminded of the traditional story of the Russian lady gave a speech about losing her homeland twice, once in 1917 when she fled to Cuba to avoid the wrath of the Bolsheviks, and again in the 1950s when she fled to America to avoid Castro's regime. When a sensitive listener offered pity for the poor lady who had lived such a tumultuous life, the lady shook her head. "I, unlucky? Oh, no. I am one of the luckiest women in the world. Twice I have lost my country; twice I have had a country to which I could go. When you Americans lose your country, where will you go?"

The answer to the rhetorical question is, of course, nowhere. There is no place to go since America is the frontier. If it doesn't happen in America, as one academic put it, it won't happen. The upshot is that America can grow more and more socialist without the threat of breaking up. There is no natural limitation like there was for Russia and Cuba. The house of cards may eventually fall, and when it does it will be as calamitous as the most dire prophesies suggest. But it cannot happen unless alternatives to the system are presented, an event that will be prolonged as far as can be managed by those living comfortably on the system's luxuries.

Appeals to that distant future are reasonably shrugged off. If a person making a healthy income these days, going to work in a downtown high-rise and vacationing in the Gulf of Mexico, is given the choice to either continue doing what he's doing or to cut back, sacrifice, and wean off the system for the benefit of his great-great-grandchildren, there is no doubt which option he will select. Not only would the latter mean accepting a lower standard of living, but he would most likely be the only one to do so and would then be sacrificing for the benefit of others in the system. As he reasonably sees it, the Juggernaut will continue to roll on, so he might as well try to cash in as it does. There is no way he will choose the irrational, uneconomical alternative, and so he will be content to live off the system until forced to do otherwise.

Twentieth-century historian Will Durant proposed the notion that America would have its Renaissance whenever it learned to reverence liberty as well as wealth. That time will only come when liberty has become feasible again, when the economy is opened, and individuals can once again govern their actions with their own volition. Until then, it may be a cold, dark age.

And so it can be argued that only an intellectual argument and not an emotional plea can be successful in energizing true reform. And this leads us to our next dilemma, since all intellectual arguments hinge on a practical approach.

The feasibility of autarchy. With regard to the analysis above, one is led to believe that opening the economy is not as feasible as one might hope. If the opportunity for freedom were presented, then people would certainly take advantage of it. Since we see a formerly great and free people instead falling into a dichotomy of oppressors and servants, we might conclude that there is no opportunity for freedom available. The survey of the economic close explored on an earlier page explains why: An open economy requires self-sufficiency, which requires free land, and we have found in the last century that such a prospect is no longer available. The frontier is closed; the land is taken.

Even if we were to find some vast new world as we did five hundred years ago, continued expansion into that land would be viewed under a different light these days. We now know that the expansion of European powers into the New World caused irreparable devastation to the indigenous peoples of both Africa and America. This tragedy was underscored in the 1890s, when the close of the frontier was first recognized and thinkers all turned their gaze toward Southeast Asia, Polynesia, and Africa for an escape. It was reasoned that conquests in these other territories would expand the frontier to other lands and thus give Americans a continued sense of growth and development.

Despite the good intentions, the imperialism that resulted was the cause of much strife throughout the world and the leading contributor to a century filled with war. Whether it was manifest in the German aggression in Europe; Japanese invasions on mainland Asia; Portuguese, Spanish, French, and Dutch colonization in Africa and Southeast Asia; Russian expansion in Eastern Europe and Central Asia; or British and U.S. colonization pretty much everywhere, the expansionist ethos that drove Western nations into underdeveloped regions brought about widespread unrest and instability, the repercussions of which we are still dealing with today. One of the most violent and persistent conflicts in the world today—that between the Palestinians and Israelis—is essentially based in the colonization and incessant expansion of one group into another group's territory.

When viewing it this way, it is obvious that the expansion of the frontier is dangerous and often causes more harm than good. Add to it the notion that man has shown himself to be a wasteful, even rapacious user of resources, and the expansion into virgin lands becomes an environmental evil as well as a sociopolitical one.

But all of this is to mistake the true notion of expansion for a caricature based on the impact it has on others; it is to mistake advance for intrusion, extension for encroachment. Expansion, in itself, does not require the taking over of another people's lands or the subjugation of those people, though it often has. Expansion can and has occurred without harming others, and this is the brand of expansion that reformers should be interested in. Indeed, the only kind of expansion that can bring about a truly open economy is the kind that steers clear of the conquering of a foreign people, which merely broadens exploitation to a greater scope.

An open economy is our goal, not just expansion for the sake of expansion. Only if we can gain independence from the system through the practice will that goal truly be met. With that being said, such an expansion is still nearly unthinkable these days. In the sixteenth century, Europeans could expand to the New World with idealistic fervor since they had no idea of the devastation they would cause on the Amerind peoples. Today, we have no such luxury. Due to the repercussions of our previous expansion, our culture's self-conscious mindset is ever aware of the threats we pose to other peoples. No legitimate case can now be made for imperialism. It has come to the point, then, that any expansion we hope to undertake must progress in a way that does not harm others or the environment—a demanding prospect to be sure.

At the same time, expansion is not the only way to open the economy. Though expansion is certainly a powerful mechanism for the task, there are other equally potent tools at the disposal of any industrious and intentional people to open the economy. The work of Vincent Ostrom and Nobel Prize winner Elinor Ostrom has in both theoretical and empirical ways shown that cooperation and self-rule are possible given a limited expanse of land. Naturally, we live in a finite world with limited resources. Since it is quite likely for communities to overextend and exhaust the resources they have, the hasty reaction is to determine that some governmental force must come in and take command. But this would only solve the problem by making it worse. The Ostroms have shown that this mentality overlooks the many cases throughout history in which communities have established rules and sustainable production techniques themselves, without the intrusion of a coercive government—solving the problem by eliminating the zero-sum condition altogether.

> Apathy can be overcome by enthusiasm, and enthusiasm can only be aroused by two things: first, an ideal, which takes the imagination by storm, and second, a definite intelligible plan for carrying that ideal into practice.
>
> —ARNOLD J. TOYNBEE (1889-1975)

It is with an eye on this work and that of other notable political economists that we turn to the last dilemma: how exactly a solution to our problem can be accomplished.

The logistics of autarchy. Granting there might be a contingent willing to pursue this vast reconstruction, and that those in this contingent possess a reasonable understanding about the difficulties that will be involved in such a world-shattering endeavor, it is constructive to lay out a potential course of action that might serve as a guideline for the project. Naturally, with an effort that is so vast and complex, the plan would be monumental itself. A thorough analysis of the steps needed cannot be supplied here, but there is occasion to provide a theoretical summary of the effort. In lieu of a comprehensive design, I hope that the various books and studies pointed to throughout can provide the reader with a library of specifics necessary to make such a solution work.

In essence, the process involves taking a system that is based in complex, interdependent constructs and extracting from it a highly diversified assembly of individual, independent ideas. On a whole, the process takes us from large to small, far-reaching to local, centralized to polycentric, and hierarchic to autarchic. As can be imagined, the process is applicable to nearly all aspects of society—on the occupational plane, the social plane, and the political plane, to name only the most prominent. The closed economy resides in every aspect of a person's life, and so it is reasonable to employ the strategy of opening the economy in every aspect as well. As we will find, this process of going from big to small is universal in its application.

By way of summary, the process of opening the economy can be broken down into three phases, represented by the three terms: 'relief', 'reform', and 'renaissance'. The first phase—relief—comprises a variety of ways to use the system to help deflate it. For the most part, the system is organized to grow more and more oppressive with every action that we take, even when the actions are geared toward alleviating such strains. However, the system does provide several means by which we can increase individualism and efficiency. As citizens, we can vote, and, for the most part, we can choose how to spend our money. These two actions alone can provide relief from the Juggernaut and help direct us toward a freer economy. These are techniques that all Americans (and Westerners, for that matter) can take part in, no matter what their status or privilege. The next chapter will examine these techniques in detail.

The second phase—reform—involves changing the system and is largely focused on the system's currency. Reform requires extensive reorganization of institutions that are already in place, and it will take much more time, and a greater number of equally dedicated participants, to accomplish than the relief phase. While relief might come haphazardly and in segments, reform must come in a definite, concentrated effort.

Ultimately, the goal is to completely transcend the current system and provide a new one in a kind of renaissance, or a rebirth. This last phase, as can be deduced from its designation, is made of an entirely new approach to society in general and requires nothing less than a leap forward in technology, practice, and critical thought. While such leaps have taken place in the past without much advance notice, they could have been predicted given certain rationale and foresight. Just as Columbus could imagine a Western route to India, so too can we picture a new route to our standard activities; just as sixteenth-century thinker Giordano Bruno could envisage space travel, so too can we conceive of equally far-reaching possibilities. And so envisioning this new route will be the first task in the third phase of the solution.

In the end, each phase is necessary in establishing an open economy full of self-sufficient individuals. If reformers approach the process with determination, it is possible that the aims outlined here can be accomplished within a generation. Many of the proposed techniques can be accomplished within a year and will place the society on a direct path to the goal. After all, the kind of ingenuity and productivity that lies dormant within the human spirit is great. Imagine all the layers of bureaucracy piled on man's volition, the oppressive forces of monopoly and exploitation, and the state's relentless regulations and taxation, and note how much the people of the West still manage to produce. Now imagine a world without all of that weight. There is nothing beyond the reach of mankind. Everything is possible. And it is up to us to make it happen.

2. WORKING WITHIN
THE SYSTEM

AT ONE POINT IN 2009, when it seemed as though the Juggernaut was just steamrolling over the people's liberties and economic rights, an esteemed Republican congressman sent out an e-mail in attempt to give his constituents hope and at least some idea of the power they had in changing the system. The resounding response was, "What can I do?" People wanted to do something to effect change, but they didn't know what. The congressman's answer, as could have been expected, was to get active in the political process: "Stand up at every public meeting you can get to and speak out. Attend Town Hall Meetings. Call into talk shows. Write letters to the editor. Leave comments after every article that you read online. E-mail your friends. Link to information. Post on blogs, on Facebook and Twitter. Support candidates and causes."

Of course, the typical citizen disgusted by the rampaging Juggernaut wants to get as far away from the political process as possible. Getting involved in rallies and campaigns sounds a little like pulling your fingers apart to escape Chinese handcuffs—it only makes it worse. The more involved one becomes in the political process, the more powerful it becomes, and the more necessary it is for the sake of the whole society to work. The typical activist begins to see a pattern and cannot help but to become disillusioned by the prospects.

What's more, 'getting involved' might be too much work for most people, who rightly just want to earn a living and get by. Sure, going to town hall meetings and calling in to talk shows might help to sway public opinion and move the system in the right direction, but it takes a lot of time and effort. Attending a town hall meeting will occupy one's entire afternoon or evening, time that could be spent doing something that is actually productive, like washing the car, exercising, or writing the next great American novel. Why should one take time away from potentially productive activities to make his voice heard, especially if speaking out is not guaranteed to produce the desired results? Doing so will only put him behind in the great competition for wealth and give others an easy advantage.

While no one will question that getting involved is an admirable endeavor, it may not be the most practical or the most effective. If the point is to diminish the power of the Juggernaut, it could be argued that getting involved is one of the least effective methods. To that end, one should pull back from the system rather than devote time and energy to it. Only by starving it of its resources can we slow down the self-perpetuating spiral and regain at least some of our autonomy.

The most significant measures available in this regard are beyond the scope of an individual's action. True reform can only be accomplished by taking apart large blocks of infrastructure as they stand, and only large, organized groups can effect that kind of change. A single person is rather powerless in the face of such efforts. However, there are a number of things the average citizen can do to accomplish this subtle goal of pulling back from the system and deflating it to some degree. Day-to-day activities, lifestyle choices, habits, work arrangements, and investment techniques all play a role in the way the economy is formed, and so treating each one differently can have an effect on the Juggernaut. When a large contingent of the society alters its behavior in these regards, the outcome can be substantial.

Of course, none of these changes in behavior should inconvenience the individual or require him to give up other productive activities. Relief must be profitable in the economic sense as well as in the ethical and social sense for it to have any validity in the modern world. Otherwise, few will view it as viable and thus few will take part. The solution must benefit the individual first because it is in the individual that the goal rests.

Generally, the best way for an individual to help alleviate the swelling Juggernaut is to remove himself from it, take part in less activities that bolster it, buy fewer goods that come from it, and shift his attention away from it. While there is no single, straightforward way to do so, we can begin by identifying several things the Juggernaut requires most and that we, as citizens, can withhold from it.

Simplifying

To begin, the Juggernaut is based primarily on intricate, multifaceted schemes that involve countless numbers of people and interchangeable parts. How we got to that point is rather intuitive and summarizes the Juggernaut as a whole: First, man's natural desire to produce great quantities of wealth led Western technicians to devise increasingly efficient and effective modes of production centered around specialism, labor division, and trade. The more powerful production capacity became, the more complex the network of assemblies, companies, and industries that followed.

As a result, individuals grew more and more interconnected and ultimately more and more dependent on one another. The more complex a given business or technological good, the more it requires a great, convoluted system to support it, and the more that system begets oversight, misdirected resources, and waste. It occurs to the bystander that one easy way to help diminish the size of that system and thereby decrease the oversight and waste is for individuals to simply demand less complex schemes—to simplify one's life in manner and environment. The less often such complex systems are demanded, the less they will thrive, and the less the system as a whole will augment.

The idea of simplification is rather pervasive in our exceedingly complex age, primarily for the benefits it provides the individual. The modern world issues relentless deadlines, commitments, and superfluities, which all take their toll on the individual's sense of order and soundness. As a result, stress, headaches, and anxiety proliferate in the modern world, perhaps as much as capital does. The thought is that all the taxing appointments and obligations have overwhelmed the individual and displaced the basic joys in life—the sweetness of a good piece of fruit, the pleasure of a good conversation, a friendly smile. The modern economy, it seems, has flipped the importance of the basics and superfluities so that one is obliged to concentrate on the latter to a much greater degree than the former. The mantra of our age, as Oliver Wendell Holmes put it, is "Give us the luxuries of life and we will dispense with the necessities."

But, as many are discovering, the necessities are the real substance of life, they are what make life worthwhile, and, ironically, they are what we have assembled this towering Juggernaut to provide for in the first place. The goal, then, is to free oneself from the ties of modern complexity, to reduce the number of meetings and possessions, and to get back to the basics.

To some extent, simplification is not economically sound. The hard worker takes on many seemingly superfluous tasks and items because, in the end, they will give him a little bit of an edge when shopping or when on the job. Work obligations alone account for many if not most of one's total obligations and help to provide higher incomes and better working conditions. While it is not suggested to cut back on these types of obligations just to free up some time to relax, there may well be a number of appointments and possessions that can be eliminated at no economic cost, and doing so may even result in some economic gain.

Business consultant Richard Watson has made note of at least two distant cousins of the sarcastic interjection, 'Too Much Information' (TMI):

'Too Much Choice' (TMC) and 'Too Many Options' (TMO). The notion is that, in a modern world, time famine is one of the greatest challenges active people face, and the ballooning number of choices we have to make intensifies the famine.

This pressure is imposed on everyone, almost as an innate consequence of the highly specialized, consumerist society. Everywhere one turns, there is a new product, a new line of goods and services, a 'must have' for the collection. It is as if the consumer doesn't really have a choice after all, since he is more or less forced into making the choices whether he likes it or not.

Take for example the almost instinctive compulsion of consumers to collect particular goods. The human imagination is fertile and can turn almost anything that can be produced into a wonderful line of goods to accumulate, from coffee mugs and CDs to Elvis memorabilia and antique dolls. The enterprise starts out innocently enough: An individual has an interest, which turns into a hobby, which suddenly becomes an obsession that is impossible to overturn. One might like the style of a given doll or article of clothing and, soon enough, he finds himself searching everywhere for the like. Eventually, it becomes an obligation that he cannot neglect.

Friends and family add to the phenomenon because this collection presents a reliable gift idea for any thoughtful relation. Obligatory gift giving is in itself a revealing sign of a society that has grown too complex for its own good. One writer conveyed the plight she faced when she took up a seemingly reasonable collection of Fiestaware, a bright, Mexican-styled china popular in the last decade. As soon as friends knew that she was 'into Fiesta', she started receiving it on every occasion—birthdays, holidays, and 'just because'. The collection became too strenuous to bear, despite the fact that the collectibles were highly functional and durable. It had grown into a little self-perpetuating industry of its own, and managing the collection was suddenly

> That's all your house is—it's a place to keep your stuff while you go out and get more stuff.
>
> —GEORGE CARLIN (1937 – 2008)

a part-time job. Such collections are more practical than non-functional ones like Elvis paraphernalia, but even useful collections can be a burden.

Collections inadvertently grow beyond the original intent, however reasonable it had been. Note how the ardent technology buff cannot have enough gadgets, even when his collection seems to adequately meet his needs. To be sure, he does not collect gadgets to satisfy his physiological or even economic needs, but rather to satisfy his psychological and social needs, to be on top of the latest trends, or to demonstrate to everyone his undeniable coolness.

The social networking phenomenon is a current in this trend that everyone can relate to, even those who have managed to stay away from Myspace, Facebook, Twitter, and the rest. A person's usage starts small, adding friends here and there and posting a few photos. Before he knows it, he's got a full-fledged profile with flashing graphics, videos, virtual shots of whiskey, a mafia, and a booming virtual farm with digital goats and succotash.

It must be said that most engage in collections, bargain hunting, and social networking, not particularly because they need extraneous gadgets and activities, but because they want some form of justification. Specialism and bureaucracy have left most people spending the majority of their days in situations that are monotonous and devoid of any sense of accomplishment. Collections and hobbies give them a feeling of immediate and positive gratification that helps to alleviate any stress felt at work and provide the comforting justification that everyone needs.

Of course, this is a false sense of justification, fabricated specifically to counter the dull day-to-day. Eventually, as this activity becomes burdensome in itself, it begins to resemble the monotonous and unproductive workplace, whereupon one will try to find a new collection or hobby to satisfy one's urges. All the while, these occupations only further entrench the participants in the system, creating new needs and placing greater burdens on the individual. The only solution can be to eliminate these burdens to the best of one's ability.

The site to reference is Earth Easy, which offers ideas on simplifying with sustainable living as its core focus:
www.eartheasy.com/live_simplify.htm

The book to read is:
The Paradox of Choice by Barry Schwartz

Also read:
37Signals' book *Rework*, which contains several pertinent ideas on how to run a business simply and smoothly in the Internet age:
www.37signals.com/rework

Prioritizing

To help simplify one's life, it is essential to realize what the simple life consists in. One must determine exactly what is necessary and what is superfluous, what the basics are and what is just there to fabricate the sense of fulfillment. This process, as has been examined on earlier pages, is highly subjective since everyone has their own set of values and needs. No one can determine what is necessary in another person's life, and so there are no universal lists that everyone can follow to live a simple life. There are, however, general guidelines that can help people mold their own list of priorities.

With regard to an action, a potential event, or a purchase opportunity, it is necessary to realize exactly what benefit it provides. What is the purpose of watching TV, exercising, or chatting over coffee? What is the purpose of going to happy hour, to the mall, or to church? What is the goal in buying the new iMac, a new pair of jeans, or a used LP? Investigate the motives of all actions to get to their root and discover why they have been allotted so much time and effort.

Not surprisingly, many of one's actions will be found to have sound purposes based in one's fundamental needs and passions. Naturally, these should be maintained and possibly focused on to a greater extent. If a happy hour is designed to meet up with acquaintances with whom one would like to get in touch after being apart for some time, it is quite possible that catching up will provide a great deal of camaraderie and enjoyment, and thus be well worth the time and expenses required to make it happen. On the other hand, it is possible that a happy hour is scheduled just because that's what people do at 5:30 p.m. on Thursdays. Such rationale is dubious at best and will probably lead to less overall enjoyment, more burdens, and a more complicated life overall.

One should be careful not to do something or buy something as a result of habit or because 'it's just what people do'. Going with the flow in this way is the quickest route to piling up loads of unwanted obligations and unused possessions. It's basically allowing the Juggernaut to dictate one's actions. Consider the shopper who drives 20 miles out of the way just to purchase a sale item that he didn't realize he needed until he saw that it was on sale.

Going with the flow occurs in significant, long-term instances as much as in casual, everyday ones. It is easy to go with the flow and make it over to happy hour after work, but it is also quite easy, for example, to go to the doctor and schedule significant procedures because 'it's just what people do'. How many serious medical procedures does the average citizen take part in without fully understanding the consequences? For some time during the twentieth century, it was assumed that tonsils were no more than pesky hindrances that should be removed at the first opportunity, and thus having one's tonsils removed became something of a rite of passage. Only recently have we realized that tonsils are actually active components of the immune system and should be taken care of. How much time and effort was spent on tonsillectomies just because they had become the thing to do?

A person's life in the system is made up of a series of these kinds of involuntary actions that take one from infancy to old age without an ounce of intent, often using up time and energy for what is ultimately useless or, in some cases, harmful. The notion is simply to do what the Juggernaut requires whether or not that course of action is beneficial at all.

To see the extent of this mechanical process, regard the way high school, college, and even post-graduate study have become nearly essential in our society. It is just assumed that to live life properly, one must go to university, no matter what he studies or intends to do with his life. The fact that so many young adults plunge into college without really knowing its purpose is evident in the fact that so many end up changing majors several times in the four, five, or six year process. These days, it is understood that college graduates will have to spend a couple years after school deciding what they want to do with their lives as if they couldn't possibly have known before entering the 'real world'.

The site to browse is:

Becoming Minimalist, a blog which offers unique guides to living an 'intentional life':
www.becomingminimalist.com

Saying 'No' to Social Responsibility

Realizing the source of these impulses is the first step in preventing them. Once we appreciate that the motives stem from a paradoxical and counterproductive system, we can look to offset them or at least subdue them when they arise. It is much easier to say 'No' to a given opportunity when we realize that the urge to say 'Yes' is rather artificial and will only lead to further weight down the line.

One key ingredient in simplifying one's life is to acknowledge that one can appreciate something—a knickknack, an album, a velvet Elvis portrait—without possessing it or making it a part of his or her life. One doesn't need to buy something in order to regard or even esteem it; one can note its beauty, uniqueness, or flocculence and just let it be. The knowledge of its existence might be all that is necessary to gain the joy that it provides.

Of course, the compulsion to buy something or to fill up one's schedule with meaningless events is often compounded by a sense of social responsibility. Retailers and event planners naturally want buyers and attendees, and they will most likely be persuasive in their efforts to obtain them. Their techniques are often so subtle and effective that the target is hardly able to recognize the trap. A person might find it impossible to say 'No' because of the searing sense of guilt that mounts comes with doing so.

These days, consumers are urged to go out and buy things to help the economy, regardless of the consumer's need for goods or services—if they just buy and buy, everything will be better. The plea is Keynesianism at its most basic: The more money that changes hands, the richer we'll all be. Of course, the more money that changes hands, the more inflated the money supply becomes and the more dependent we become on the circulation of the currency for our own well-being. Buying goods or services that are not useful or productive may make the seller wealthier, but it doesn't necessarily make the economy stronger and is only wasteful for the buyer.

The sales techniques are all too familiar: 'Shop to help the economy!', 'Buy this product to keep the industry going!', and the like. The aim is to convince the consumer that his decision will affect not just himself but others as well. And, in the modern system, this is probably so—in order to survive, everyone needs others to participate in their activities and buy their products, even if those activities and products can't possibly benefit the potential buyer. Such manipulation is obvious when looked at objectively but not so clear in action. The target of the solicitation might not realize why he is agreeing to an event or a product that he knows is useless. Most likely it is because the solicitor has shifted the focus from the event or product at hand to a personal issue, such that saying 'No' to the event or product becomes saying 'No' to the person or idea.

To make it easier, one must return the focus back to the event or product at hand and away from the personal. One might note that the suggestion is a good idea, but that for whatever reason it is not going to happen. One might also minimize the absolute effect of the Yes/No answer by offering a percentage of one's likelihood of taking part. Instead of saying 'No, I don't want to go', one might say, 'I'm 43% likely to attend', thus indicating at least a portion of interest. At any rate, if the rationale is backed by a legitimate alternative, there should be no pressure in the matter. If the solicitor has his customer's best interest in mind, then there should not be hard feelings or guilt if the offer is declined. Only a malevolent solicitor would insist on holding a grudge.

Localizing

As soon as one has narrowed his list of essentials, it is worthwhile to figure out how to attain them most efficiently. The buy-local movement has flourished in recent months primarily in response to fears about global warming and efforts to reduce everyone's 'carbon footprint'. The argument acknowledges that a good produced at some far-away manufacturing plant might cost less monetarily at the checkout aisle but, because of the pollution that results from the highly complex mass production and distribution scheme needed to deliver that good, its true costs are much higher.

While the effort to reduce pollution is certainly a noble cause, another cost of the multilayered modern economy is its tendency to further entrench us in the ever-expanding system. The greater the distance between the location where a good is produced and where it is sold, the greater the number of employees and distribution channels are involved. An orange consumed in Indiana in February, for instance, must have been grown in California or Florida or some other temperate climate, and thus required at least several connections to reach its final destination. If one localizes one's fruit supply, buying mainly from the farmer's market down the street instead of at the large chain supermarket, the Juggernaut loses energy and necessarily decreases in size.

Of course, one need not grow everything in one's backyard in order to make an impact. Buying basics like eggs, milk, vegetables, and grains locally will go a long way in diminishing the power of the overarching system. Anyone who is energetic about the prospect will find that it is not terribly inconvenient to become what is known as a 'locavore' and eat only those products that have been produced within a local region.

Skeptics will note that oranges do not grow naturally in Indiana, and that for a Hoosier to obtain a homegrown orange in February would cost far too much to be worthwhile. The cost of the greenhouse facilities that would be needed to grow orange groves in wintry climates would alone account for a sizeable rise in retail price. After all, there is good reason why we have established the complex web of manufacture and distribution, which goes back to Ricardo's Law of Comparative Advantage. We want to embrace the system because it is so much more efficient and cost-effective.

That being as it may, it is not unthinkable for some local goods to cost the same or less than other goods produced at a distance. Farmers' markets in my town often sell locally-produced goods for less than the humongous chain groceries. Indeed, the convenience and quality of local goods and services might well be worth a few extra dollars, depending on the product. Often, produce that is harvested close to its point of sale requires fewer preservatives since it can be transported so quickly. All around, buying local can be a beneficial endeavor.

Clothing, manufactured items, handiwork, and other necessary goods and services can have as high a quality when provided by a small, local company as when provided by a towering, international corporation. Indeed, the small local upstart, in trying to gain customer loyalty, will often devote extra effort to its service while the huge conglomerates simply take their buyers for granted. Ultimately, when the retail price is the same, ceteris paribus, the local good reduces one's Juggernaut footprint, which, in the end, is as important to well-being as reducing the maligned carbon footprint.

The sites to browse are:

Eat Local, which offers a guide to localizing food production and
consumption:
www.sustainabletable.org/issues/eatlocal

A site dedicated to the community of locavores in the San Francisco area
with ideas that might be applied elsewhere:
www.locavores.com

Food Tree, which provides information about food with regard to quality
and origination:
www.foodtree.com

Buying Independent

Likewise, it is also strategic to buy from smaller, independent retailers
whenever possible. If a small retailer can offer a price that is competitive
with the large conglomerates—which, of course, is not very often—the
consumer should be eager to reward that smaller firm with the sale. Doing
so shifts resources away from the great behemoths riddled with bureaucracy and toward more concentrated and efficient businesses.

For good reason, large conglomerates are often able to provide better
quality goods at cheaper prices. Their ability to divide labor and compart-
mentalize tasks multiplies their efficiency to such an extent that it is almost
impossible for smaller companies to compete. As explained before, however, the same benefits lead directly to redundancy, bureaucracy, waste, and
pollution, which become a liability for most large corporations.

Walmart is the quintessential example. At least one consumer can con-
fidently say that no other retailer so consistently provides a line of adequate goods for cheaper prices than does the colossal Walmart chain. But
there is also no place that can so consistently provide a troop of apathetic,

incompetent, and disagreeable workers. And so, while the price tags may represent a good deal, customers who value service and decency in their shopping experience will likely avoid places like Walmart.

There is no replacement for cheap prices, to be sure, and one cannot recommend paying more for products just to avoid large, bureaucratic corporations. Still, there is merit in reassessing the entire shopping experience to realize that the end product is not the only, or even the most important, goal. It might be worth paying more for a product if it is accompanied by prompt, friendly service and a cozy atmosphere.

The sites to browse are:

Film Baby, which provides a database for independent filmmakers and audiences:
www.filmbaby.com

I Shop Indie, which offers an online retail store that contains only products by independent designers:
www.ishopindie.com

Indie Designer Labels:
www.indiedesignerlabels.com

Manufacturing Competition

Allied to the strategy of buying from local and independent producers is the notion that consumers have the power to sway the direction of the marketplace. After all, ours is still a somewhat free market, and, though the average citizen is limited to a large degree in what he can buy, he does have a number of choices available to him. With that choice comes leverage. By choosing one company over another, the consumer can effectively reject one kind of business and endorse another. Businesses still need consumer support in this day and age (despite the ever-growing influence of government subsidies and regulations), and so they will pay attention to consumers' demands at least to some extent. In this way, the consumer has a say in how the businesses are run and can change their ways by use of deliberate consumption.

If the buying public, for example, is opposed to the way British Petroleum has handled its oil leak catastrophe in the Gulf of Mexico, it can choose to buy from Shell or Exxon Mobil instead, the latter of which became all too familiar with the public's sway on business after its own disaster in Prince William Sound twenty years ago. Similarly, if a depositor does not like the risks his bank took before the recent financial crisis or is wary of the company that cannot seem to stay afloat without government bailout money, he can simply choose another bank.

The best way to find sound companies is via a third-party ratings agency. As we have found in recent years, not all ratings agencies are credible, which brings into question whether creating competition can be a wholly reliable endeavor. But there are a number of reliable options for the consumer who is willing to do a little groundwork. Recently, this consumer was able to turn a bad experience at an auto repair shop into a profitable situation by searching Yelp and finding a garage that not only treated its customers with respect but also had the best prices. Good companies are still out there and it is possible to find them with a little effort.

Again, it may not be economically advantageous for a consumer to buy a more reputable company's products. It is quite likely that the more corrupt business is the one that puts out less expensive goods. And, as explained on an earlier page, due to monopolies both public and private, these companies might well be in a position to continue their corrupt practices regardless of their effect on public opinion. In a closed system, demand is taken for granted, and so it is entirely possible that a consumer does not have the option to buy goods from a company that abstains from questionable behavior.

But, with the few last rays of Free-Market Capitalism we have, it might be possible for consumers to influence businesses with their purchases.

After all, no big business can survive without the tribute paid to it by its customers. And so, whenever possible, it is beneficial to withhold that tribute on principle if the company is found polluting, abusing its employees, putting out shabby products, or otherwise engaging in corrupt practices. By using one's purchases strategically, it is possible to affect the large corporations' bottom lines. If a large enough group can direct its purchases toward one company and away from a rival, the rival might change its practices to meet the demands of those customers.

The sites to browse are:

The Better Business Bureau, which aims at providing information about business practices based on customer feedback:
www.bbb.org

Yelp, which touts "Real people. Real reviews." for a way to rate companies and inform consumers of the practices that businesses perpetrate:
www.yelp.com

Consumer Search offers a user-friendly system that promises to 'simplify the complex' by collecting reviews, analyzing picks, and formulating recommendations:
www.consumersearch.com

Bauer Financial provides a database of 'very carefully' researched information and an easy-to-use rating system to gauge the strength of banks:
www.bauerfinancial.com

Saving

One of the old standbys of Keynesian economics is the notion that spending, no matter what it is for, is good for the economy. Whence we hear vocal arguments for the constant expansion of government debt and extravagant expenditures on public works and the like. Over the course of the twentieth century, this policy has seeped into the mindset of consumer economics as well, such that we are often bombarded by petitions to spend more on an individual basis.

The refrain is familiar to anyone within earshot of national politicians: 'Help save the economy—spend money!' 'Go out and buy furniture, groceries—anything—and everyone be better off!' Stimulus checks are divvied up and recipients are encouraged to use that money to go out and buy clothes, movies, and new cars. When that wave of stimulus floods the economy, it is thought, demand will go up, businesses will hire more employees, and the economy will resume its 'natural' climb upward.

Indeed, when the expendable income is not enough to get the economy jumping again, the recommendation is to go into debt to cover the necessary costs of consumption. The thought is to follow the government's lead and spend at all costs, even if it means spending money on goods that one does not need or spending more than one can afford. The effect of such consumption is thought to be so potent that it will generate enough wealth to cover the new economic growth as well as the debt accrued.

Of course, this policy neglects completely what wealth actually consists of and what it takes to make more. Buying and selling things no more produces wealth than digging a hole and filling it back up. As explored on an earlier page, monetary transactions produce the impression of creating wealth because we watch the numbers rise—money is spent, and we believe more wealth is suddenly produced.

But wealth is only redistributed in exchanges like this, not created. The only real way to create wealth is by actually producing something—by applying labor to land in order to obtain a useful good or service—and producing something means abstaining from consumption for a time in order to work on the useful good or service. In short, producing is saving with the aim of providing greater wealth in the future.

In a monetary economy, this is done by saving one's income and applying it as productive capital. Taking a step back from the hectic world of consumerism, one realizes that the recommended manner of constant buying and selling actually contradicts the fundamental method of wealth creation.

To generate wealth in the Keynesian sense is to reduce savings and thereby reduce one's capacity for producing wealth in the real sense. It appears to improve the economy as a whole—the GDP goes up, unemployment goes down, et cetera—while actually damaging individual well-being.

Thus, economic soundness would encourage the saving of money and capital, at least to the extent that the stored funds can generate new wealth down the road. One shouldn't aim to hoard money beyond its relevant use, and saving is not in itself a way to secure well-being. But, used wisely, it can be a helpful tool in the venture.

If saving is agreed to be a valid effort, the practices surrounding its use should reflect the precautions mentioned above. When determining where to save one's capital, for example, one should take care to store and invest it in local, independent institutions so as to reduce the Juggernaut footprint created. These days, as we have found, simply storing income in a bank can fuel extremely risky financial behavior that will ultimately end in disaster. As explored above, the moral hazard established by the FDIC and other governmental insurance programs means that people are inclined to freely stash their money in banks without doing any research to determine what those banks intend to do with their money. To the depositor, it doesn't matter what happens because he will get his money back regardless of whether the bank uses it to invest in collateralized debt obligations or in velvet Elvis wind chimes.

If, on the other hand, depositors were more discerning with their money, the banks would be as well. After some research, a prudent investor might still find his bank the safest and most reliable place to store his money. At the same time, another investor might discover new institutions that are safer and more reliable to invest in—for example, banks with 100% reserve requirements to ensure that a depositor's money is not used in subsequent, potentially risky, investments. Still others may choose to invest in sound, long-term commodities like gold or silver. In most cases, the prudent investor would presumably try to keep his wealth closer rather than frivolously spreading it across the economy as is most often done these days.

An individual or family should save their money just as they would save any other valuable, id est, in a way that will not allow it to be used in risky endeavors. A Bentley owner wouldn't let a friend borrow his car for a road trip to Tijuana, for instance, so neither should the owner of a few hundred thousand dollars let a bank borrow it for a sub-prime mortgage-backed security.

It is not easy to identify all the activities a bank engages in, and it is even more difficult to gauge the risk level involved in them. But there are certain banks that stand out above others as more cautious and responsible. Banks that needed the TARP money included in the financial bailout—Citibank, Chase, and Bank of America, to name a few—are good examples of high-risk institutions. Unless they have changed their ways, these banks should probably be avoided. On the other hand, banks that declined the TARP funds, such as regional institutions Frost (Texas), First Commonwealth (Pennsylvania), and Kearny Financial Corporation (Northeast), among others would be good places to store money.

Naturally, smaller, local banks have some drawbacks that might not be acceptable to the individual or family trying to make the most of their

The sites to browse are:

Independent Community Bankers of America
www.icba.org

Move Your Money, a campaign aimed at encouraging individuals and institutions to divest from large Wall Street banks and move funds to local financial institutions:
www.moveyourmoney.info

BB&T, a large bank which actually promotes the virtues of an "outstanding credit culture":
www.bbt.com

The website for this book contains a list of non-TARP banks and their various benefits at: *www.juggernautcometh.com*

money. Larger banks often provide their customers with a good variety of services including ATM access, high-yield savings accounts, online banking, and so on. BB&T, for instance, which is a large bank that was forced to accept TARP funds though it didn't need them, only serves the American Southeast and does not refund ATM charges collected by other banks. The smaller the bank, the less likely it will be able to afford such features. If a bank is not investing its deposits in securities, its savings program will probably not offer a return and may instead charge the depositor a monthly fee. Since the bank is not making money on its deposits, it needs additional income to cover its expenses.

And yet there are banks that do provide many of these services. The depositor willing to perform most of his banking in a local region should be able to find the right bank using resources that offer third-party analyses of bank strength and risk level.

Starting a Business

Perhaps the most elaborate technique involved in reducing dependence on the system comes in the form of starting one's own business. The idea is to do what one already does, whether it is web design, landscaping, physical therapy, or some other occupation, as an independent business or contractor instead of as an employee. While it may take some amount of paperwork to initially establish the company, the amount of additional work is comparable to that required in the hiring of an employee, and the long-term effects end up reducing the bureaucracy enough to compensate fully.

The major benefits of starting a business are twofold. First, by bringing responsibilities closer to the producer, running one's own business significantly reduces bureaucratic displacement. The decisions one makes as a business owner are localized, which leads to more direct accountability, better decision-making, and less waste. While long-term employee situations often rely more on office politics and hierarchies than on actual productivity, short-term contractual situations, by nature, are more focused on the work at hand.

Bringing responsibility closer to the producer reduces his dependence on others as well. Though the sole proprietor still relies on his customers for business, he no longer relies on coworkers and a hierarchy of managers to accomplish his tasks. The process is more succinct and transparent, and it is likely to be much more fluid as a result.

The second benefit of owning one's own business is based on the first. With fewer channels to pass through, independent business exchanges are subject to fewer taxes, and so the Juggernaut is starved of that much more fodder. In a business-to-employee situation, for example, the government makes sure to tax both the business paying the salary in the form of a payroll tax and the employee in the form of an income tax. In a business-to-business transaction, however, the government taxes just one time in the form of income tax. The payment can be written off as a business expense and thus avoid further taxation.

Overall, when switching to a direct customer-to-producer transaction, the amount of taxes paid is reduced from around 40-60% to around 10-35%. The work being done is the same, and the individual doing the work may receive the same payment for it, but the government gets paid less, and that means it has less fuel to burn.

While the money saved in taxes rests primarily on the side of the employer, the worker can also benefit. Making note of the money saved on payroll taxes, the worker can demand a higher pay rate. And, considering the greater freedom associated with running one's own business, the proprietor can justify the higher pay with more efficient service. Both parties benefit.

A few potential drawbacks are worth mentioning. First, some industries, such as the medical industry, simply don't lend themselves to the contractor style of operation. In general, however, the Internet and a more flexible office environment make it easier to bend the old rules of company policy. Compressed workweeks, telecommuting, and more product-based policies have nearly revolutionized the office environment and made the owner-contractor model very appealing to companies with foresight. At the same time, heightened regulations on employment have made the traditional method so economically burdensome that companies are compelled to search for alternatives.

Second, since the individual and the business are one and the same, the sole proprietor takes on greater liability, and incurring losses could lead to losing his personal savings, his home, and anything else in his possession. Thus, one will find that most sole proprietors work in low-liability industries—Internet advertising or financial advising as opposed to medical practice or restaurant management. To take advantage of the benefits of the owner-contractor model and avoid this added risk, one might set up an S corporation or limited liability company—businesses that operate like sole proprietorships without the risk inherent in the latter—instead of running a pure sole proprietorship or partnership.

Finally, the most apparent drawback is the added cost of running one's own business. In this situation, the individual is responsible not only for the costs of doing his work, but also for managing his business and securing his own benefits. A business owner cannot specialize as much as a large corporation can—he must take care of client relations, vendor relations, marketing, and operations in addition to his primary work. In addition, he must arrange for his own health insurance, retirement plan, and other benefits that are typically paid for by the employer these days.

While this certainly presents a significant new cost to the individual, it is quite possible to counterbalance that higher cost with a higher pay rate. Contract work almost always garners a higher pay rate than a salaried employee, sometimes by as much as 50 or 75%. For those willing and able to demand the higher pay, the contractor role is likely to bring in more money overall.

At any rate, bringing one's health insurance, retirement plan, and even client and vendor relations under one's own authority allows for much greater responsibility in the matter, just as with other aspects of the business. One can be better informed and thus make better decisions about these very important issues, which will make for greater success for the individual and a much more efficient system in the grand scheme.

> The site to browse is:
>
> Entrepreneur:
> *www.entrepreneur.com/bizstartups/index.html*
>
> The book to read is *How to Take Advantage of the People Who Are Trying to Take Advantage of You* by Joseph S.B. Morse.

Using the Franchise

While it cannot be denied that the Juggernaut feeds on the voting system and the great hodgepodge of lobbying and litigation that builds up around it, it must be said that the basic concept of a representative government has its merits and can work very well if it runs as it was designed. To reiterate Milton Friedman's point, the voting mechanism forces conformity and will only function smoothly and effectively if it is aimed at unanimous goals. The problem with elections these days is that they are aimed at producing results that cannot possibly be ordained by or even relevant to everyone. They are particular and exclusive and so must automatically cause conflict.

Nowadays, government is so complex that the average voter has no idea what to vote for or whether his input will have any effect at all. How can a resident of rural Nebraska possibly have worthwhile input in a debate about a proposed bridge in New York City? Unless that resident is Warren Buffett, it is almost certain that he cannot. But this is exactly what the system has evolved into—a way of determining who gets what and when despite the fact that no one voting for these disbursements has any knowledge of or interest in them at all.

Quite reasonably, this condition leaves the typical voter so disinterested that he wants absolutely nothing to do with it. So he turns away from his ability to vote, effectively abdicating his franchise and consequently granting more dominant power to the ones making the mess. California alone held some two or three major elections every year in the past decade, of which even the most ardent political hacks grew weary. All the while, the budget deficit grew out of control and the government teetered on bankruptcy. The more disgruntled the voters, the worse the condition became.

But the last thing jaded citizens should do is give up their chance to assign public officials through the vote. Voting is the most direct and, it could be argued, the most effective way to bring about change in a putrid political system. The key is knowing how to use the instrument. The principle to follow rests in the same principle that has driven the other solutions thus far: reduce the amount of bureaucracy, limit the scope and power of the government, and allow for more individual responsibility.

First, one must keep track of what one's representatives are doing. There is no sense in casting a vote if the voter is not informed. Of course, this initial step can be awfully cumbersome to one who just wants to get by and make a living. Ideally, in a representative government, there is no need to babysit the representatives—that's why we have representatives in the first place. Unfortunately, we cannot afford to stand by in our situation. One must track whether his representatives are reading the bills they vote on (a basic principle, but certainly not guaranteed these days), whether they are using their office in the proper capacity (id est, in the interest of their constituents and not special interests or their cronies), and whether the representatives are making sound choices in the way of cutting bureaucracy instead of building it up.

Once an individual has a firm grasp on the goings-on in Washington and his local seats of power, he can more effectively use his vote to support individuals and measures that intend to simplify and localize the system. After the vote has been cast, of course, the process starts over again. The voter is charged with the task of monitoring the newly elected officials and making sure they do what they were elected to do; if not, he should vote them out of office and replace them with people who are more capable of adhering to his principles.

The greatest problem with the voting mechanism is that it relies on choosing between available candidates. Someone must first run before he can be elected, and there is no assurance that those who run are worth voting for. Indeed, one cannot be surprised that public office is more enticing to those who want to grow the bureaucracy and the power of government as a whole; at the same time, it is unattractive to those who want to diminish the size and power of the state. As such, voters find their choices to be rather limited in scope, and there seems to be no proactive means available of overcoming the Juggernaut.

It is certainly possible for the right candidates to make their way through the system and prop themselves up for election. We have seen not a few public officials come to the fore recently who aim to reduce the amount of waste and inefficiency in government. One can assume, however, that

The sites to reference are:

Certified Constitutional Candidate, which issues certificates based on candidates' willingness (voiced and proven) to uphold the U.S. Constitution: *www.certifiedconstitutionalcandidate.com*

Citizens Against Government Waste, which offers a No Pork Pledge and Congressional Ratings among other features: *www.cagw.org*

The Prometheus Institute, which offers a Do-It-Yourself Democracy application for viewing pertinent laws, alerting authorities to local problems, and information on how to run for office, among other programs: *www.theprometheusinstitute.org*

The Center for Competitive Politics: *www.campaignfreedom.org*

these candidates are sacrificing more lucrative endeavors to engage in such a charitable venture. Simply put, public office is most profitable to those who want to expand government and least profitable for those who want to decrease the size of government. Using any basic economic understanding, candidates tend to be pro-leviathan.

Still, the more cumbersome the system becomes, the more profitable it will be to downsize it. As the system has grown exponentially in the last forty years, we have seen a countervailing surge in the Reagan-Thatcher approach of cutting regulation and privatizing industry. There is, of course, no way to predict the point at which the burden will become great enough to push voters and politicians toward downsizing. One will just have to rely on the inevitable pull and perhaps a little bit of luck.

* * *

All the techniques listed in this phase of the solution are vulnerable to the same limitations. Economizing individuals may very well prefer to neglect these techniques and simply go with the flow of a parasitic system. It is, after all, much more profitable for the CEO of a business to organize a lobby for government subsidies than it is for him to abstain from the brouhaha and vote for small-government Tea Partiers. It is much more profitable for a teacher to strive for a tenured position while earning a guaranteed salary than it is to start a charter school and work hard to educate children independently. Mancur Olson's Law of Collective Action has proven nearly impossible to overcome, even with the opportunities posed by these reasonably profitable techniques. It is for this reason that working within the system is likely insufficient to the task, and comprehensive reform will be necessary.

3. FIXING
THE SYSTEM

'REFORM' HAS BEEN A MAJOR catchword in Washington and other political centers for decades. It seems that everyone is eager to jump on one or another bandwagon of change to help correct what is clearly a failing system. Attentive citizens will be familiar with the various brands of change: campaign finance reform, immigration reform, tort reform, and, of course, the now notorious health care reform. The notion is that none of these institutions, which are undeniably crucial to the society as a whole, work properly, and that we must reorganize and reconstitute them so that they can work as intended. But, as can be seen with this latest flurry of proposed reforms, these ventures can and often do get muddled in the quagmire of modern politics such that they too become great bureaucracies that retard progress, hinder production, and eventually need to reform themselves.

Campaign finance reform was one of the hottest issues of the last decade or so. It has been important in large part because campaign expenses are seen as a key ingredient to fair elections, and everyone wants fair elections. Recent reports show, however, that new reform efforts have rarely led to lasting solutions and instead have led directly to more bureaucracy and ultimately to the restriction of fundamental American rights. According to the president of campaign finance think tank Center for Competitive Politics, Sean Parnell, reforms that simply rehash the system's methods rather than actually changing those methods naturally limit Americans' rights. "'Reforming' this system by over-regulating contributions to candidates and political committees is futile and tramples on citizens' First Amendment rights," Parnell said[.]

> We as a nation cannot resolve what have become deep and systemic structural imbalances in our economy simply by throwing more and more money and more and more regulations and more and more taxes at the problem.
>
> —GLENN HUBBARD AND PETER NAVARRO,
> *SEEDS OF DESTRUCTION* (2010)

This dilemma is the same one facing all good-intentioned activists these days: The only way to solve the problem is to add to it, thus making it worse. Reform efforts tend to focus on adding regulation because that is the only method people know of to effect change. But the regulation expands and takes on a life of its own until it becomes indistinguishable from the initial system it had been intended to correct. As with the recent health care reform, regulations are so elaborate that whole departments of administrators are needed to facilitate them once established.

Indeed, the reform mechanism in such a case is really designed as just a new branch of the ever-expanding federal government, complete with a troop of regulators throughout and a so-called Health Czar at the top. Any time czars are introduced, one can be certain that no true reform will take place.

As we have found, this attempt to provide freedom through restrictions is bound to contradiction; regulation cannot lead to liberty, only to counter-regulation and therefore a greater encroachment on overall liberty. If the goal of fixing the system is to provide more freedom and ultimately more well-being, then it must focus on eliminating regulation and getting out of the citizens' way, not restricting them further. In short, real reform would be to do away with anything that would need reform in the first place.

The argument will be made that regulation is designed to protect the people and thus provide them with freedom that they would otherwise be without in a strictly competitive arena. As they stand, for instance, institutions like immigration, tort litigation, health care, and high finance put the people in positions in which they can be taken advantage of by the powerful, rampaging corporate juggernauts. Regulations are imposed to limit what the corporations, banks, and insurance companies can do, and thus offer a shield for the people. Reform, in this sense, is intended to give the people, the consumers, the workers, and so on the freedom that they would otherwise not have.

But the method of a given reform is central to its end result. Only a measure that consists in breaking down barriers to freedom can truly be remedial or reformative; only when politicians speak of eliminating restrictions throughout society—even when they are designed to restrict corporations and banks to the benefit of workers and consumers—can they be taken seriously as reformers. All other initiatives are inevitably self-defeating.

For many reasons, the primary concern in reform efforts must rest in removing government interference in the economy. To begin, we cannot underestimate the importance of economic freedom. As we have seen, economic freedom leads to political freedom, and, inversely, economic oppression leads to political oppression. To recall Belloc's words, "To control the means of production is to control human life itself." Only when one controls his own means of production can he possibly attain political freedom.

Now, granted that economic freedom is essential, we must admit that the government is the chief hindrance in this arena. Simply, one cannot take part in any economic activity these days without being directly and appreciably affected by the government—working, shopping, producing, selling, investing, organizing, inventing. The Welfare State as we know it is, after all, primarily an economic body, built to control and transfer society's wealth. While there are aspects of the government that do not on the surface deal with the economy—military and foreign policy being notable examples—even these have become largely reliant on economic policy. In the modern Welfare State, shifting money around from one sector to another has become so pervasive that it is practically impossible to find a single industry—especially those involving military contractors and international relations—that is not completely distorted because of the redistribution of wealth by the government. In one way or another, all government action distorts the economy and thus restricts its natural flow.

Of course, there are other threats to economic freedom that have existed since the close of the economy and still persist today. The great bugbear of modern liberals, the corporation, with its own tendency toward bureaucratic displacement and its ability to command city life in all aspects, is unquestionably a threat to individual autonomy. One might call to mind the fact that threats posed by Gilded Age corporations, the financial oligarchy as Brandeis called it, served as the primary impetus for the creation of the Welfare State in the first place. And, it must be admitted, diminishing the state would only allow these other threats to regain their dominant influence. The rationale is that reform in the way of reducing government intervention will only eliminate the public monopoly and grant more power to private monopolists. Isn't at least some regulation necessary to prevent the private monopolists from being able to exploit their workers and customers?

This rationale is insufficient in one key aspect: The Welfare State as it stands does not prevent exploitation from private interests, and, as we saw in the last section, it rather encourages exploitation and exacerbates it in a way that private individuals and companies cannot. Through licensure and capitulation to special interests, the state has become one large corporation that only extends and intensifies the exploitation that smaller, mutually competitive corporations have attempted. Ultimately, with the authority of the law, the government enforces its exploitation by peril of imprisonment and even death, a last resort that even the most conniving corporate interests can only dream of. Only by using government can corporations reach the kind of dominance they are shown to hold in such popular diatribes as *Corporation* and Michael Moore's *Capitalism*. Getting rid of government interference in the economy, then, is the only way to get rid of a great majority of the supposed private exploitation that dominates the economy today.

Of course, government does not hold a monopoly on exploitation. It existed before the Welfare State and, it could be argued, would exist in the wake of true reform. As long as there are people willing to take more than they deserve and those willing to give more than they deserve—arguably, as long as men walk the earth—exploitation will be possible. This is not to say that it is inevitable or desirable in any way, just that there will always be the potential for it.

The only way to prevent exploitation is to provide a totally open economy, which at least requires alternatives to the predominant system. There is reason to be sanguine in the anticipation of such alternatives, and a number of them are presented in the following chapter on transcending the system. Here, we must first examine the process by which we can minimize the greatest barrier in the path to those alternatives—the state.

The intricacy of the modern economy suggests that reform must also be an intricate process. Like rearranging the pieces in a house of cards, taking out a support at random might bring the whole structure down. Many pieces will have to be worked on at the same time for the procedure to be successful. For this reason, a system of reforms cannot be absolutely chronological. The following actions will have to occur at times simultaneously and consecutively to ensure the least disruption. Generally, however, a reform strategy can follow a course beginning with the most general and basic reorganization and heading toward more specific and precise modifications.

Reform will also require the efforts of many people working together and is therefore beyond the scope of the writer or any individual reader. To bring to fruition the reforms outlined in this section requires no less than an organized concerted effort by like-minded reformers, which cannot be provided for or even laid out here. Granted readers are capable of forming such coalitions on their own, the following plan can serve as a guideline for action, beginning with the most immediate and minor procedures.

Thus, reform begins with the most fundamental aspect of the economy—money. The initial goal is to liberate the people's use of money so that further reforms can then fall into place.

Freeing Money

The most basic economic freedom is the ability to make exchanges by means individually chosen. Currently, there are a number of limitations to this freedom, the most direct being the criminalization of private currency. Though the Constitution does not forbid private coinage, the U.S. Mint has recently passed into law 18 U.S.C. § 486, a statute that expressly prohibits issuance of such currency. The statute reads:

> Whoever, except as authorized by law, makes or utters or passes, or attempts to utter or pass, any coins of gold or silver or other metal, or alloys of metals, intended for use as current money, whether in the resemblance of coins of the United States or of foreign countries, or of original design, shall be fined under this title or imprisoned not more than five years, or both.

The result of this law has been the seizure of large quantities of at least one notable alternative currency, the so-called 'Liberty Dollar°'. And, while the case against that currency is complex in itself and cannot be covered fully here, it must be asked why the government should confiscate any private coinage simply because it is not directly authorized by law. According to the verbiage of the statute, the only coins that can be made and circulated in the United States are those approved by the national mint—certainly a hindrance to economic freedom by any measure.

As such, the first step to freeing the economy is to repeal this law and any other such restriction on free currency. Of course, despite its directness, the prohibition of alternative coinage is a somewhat limited policy. The law only pertains to metallic coinage and not other forms such as paper or electronic currencies. In the modern world, paper and especially electronic currencies are a great deal more useful and certainly more efficient in their exchange, and no known regulations have been conjured to explicitly restrict the production of these forms of currency. Still, there is no viable reason why the establishment of alternative coins should be restricted, and, in the interest of free currency, the law should be eliminated.

At the same time, we should embrace the alternative currencies that are permitted by law and help to prevent future regulation on them. In its allowance of these means of exchange, the government permits a great deal of freedom in alternative currencies and gives citizens an excellent opportunity for greater dominion over their wealth.

To take just a few examples, we can see the varied success of alternative currencies already in use. Estimates place the number of active currencies in circulation in America to be in the hundreds, most of which are paper notes°. Many of these, such as Burlington Bread, which is circulated in Burlington, VT, and BerkShares, which are in use in Southern Massachusetts, are community-based moneys, established as a means to encourage localism and reduce carbon output. No government intervention against these currencies has been enacted thus far, at least to the extent that it has been publicly broadcast.

Internet-based currencies have also come to the fore in recent years. Reports on the Second Life project, in which real-life humans interact with each other in a virtual world through avatars, claim that millions trade hands daily°. Facebook money has also become a widely used mechanism for online exchanges made through the social networking giant. Given its detached environment, the Internet is the perfect place for alternative currencies to flourish.

The article to read is "Toward a Cashless Society" by Elizabeth Kolar, which can be found at The Freeman Online: *http://www.thefreemanonline.org/columns/toward-a-cashless-society/#*

The site to browse is The E. F. Schumacher Society, which promises to link people, land, and community by building local economies and also offers a list of alternative currencies now in use: *http://www.smallisbeautiful.org/local_currencies.html*

Denationalizing Currencies

Now, while the government permits these and other currencies, certain innate shortcomings make their widespread use and competition with government fiat currency practically impossible. To begin, these alternative currencies are designed for local use, whether in the spatial sense with a geographic local community or in the digital sense with a web-based community of like-minded individuals. Either way, the currencies cannot be used for exchanges beyond their given environments. One cannot use Facebook money, for instance, to buy a loaf of bread at the local supermarket, nor can a Berkshire resident use a few BerkShares to buy a margarita while on vacation in Key Largo. The currencies are not designed for such exchanges and are therefore not suitable in many cases.

Alternative currencies could be designed for widespread use and thus offer true competition for the fiat dollar. Internet-based moneys are but a few steps from achieving universal utility. Still, the very fact that government operates a fiat currency means that competition cannot be entirely fair. Government management of currency is necessarily based on fiat, which means that the value of the currency can be manipulated at the will of the officials controlling it. Whereas the purveyors of alternative currencies may alter their values at certain times, they are powerless against the market; the government, meanwhile, is not.

A competition between government-issued fiat currency and private alternatives is like the alleged competition in the health care industry generated by the introduction of a government-run health care provider. In the reform debate, the term used to describe government-run health care was 'public option', suggesting that it gave patients another option and thus more freedom in choosing their health care. The assumption completely neglected the fact that no government program is ever funded voluntarily, and that providing such an 'option' was the same as forcing taxpayers to fund a new state industry. The public option would be subsidized by the taxpayers, whether or not they wanted it, and so it made sense that it would be able to provide lower prices and 'compete' with traditional health care providers, which had to rely on their own marketing and product quality to solicit customers.

Similarly, the public money option is not really an option at all, but rather just an order to fund state operations. The U.S. dollar is more or less subsidized by taxpayers, whether or not they want to support it, and so it understandably dominates the market—who wouldn't want to use a currency backed by the biggest, most powerful company in the world? And so the technical ability for anyone to produce and distribute his own currency does not allow complete freedom in the matter. These alternative currencies can never be as valuable as the fiat money simply because they can never be forcibly backed by the American people. As a result, they will never grow to replace the dollar in any significant way.

Ultimately, the only way to truly free the economy is to do away with the government-run currency altogether, to "denationalize money", as Friedrich A. Hayek put it. The thought might strike the modern reader as absurd. How can a people even think to operate without a national currency? How is it even possible for an economy as complex as ours to function without a single, approved means of exchange such as the Federal Reserve note? Of course, these questions are valid considering the house of cards built up around us. It is an intricate system of infinitesimal parts, and government fiat money is interwoven between every one. But, in taking a step back, one can see that a system of competing private currencies is not too dissimilar from our current situation in form and function.

The primary concern associated with the denationalization of money is stability. Individuals and companies rely on the U.S. dollar in large part because it is backed by the most dominant government in the world and so, it is thought, maintains a strength and consistency that could not be matched by any other currency, especially a private one. The U.S. isn't going anywhere soon, so people can depend on its currency, or so the mentality goes.

This proposition is valid to a certain point, which is to say that the U.S. dollar is stable to some extent, though it is not as stable as it is thought to be. A look at the money supply over the past few decades reveals the fluctuations of the assumed stability of the American currency.

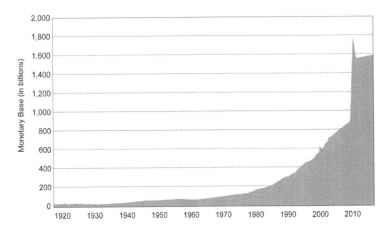

FIG. 32—Monetary Base of U.S. Dollars 1917-2010.

In the arena of international relations, a state is inclined to maintain a stable currency to attract investment. For other reasons, however, a government is inclined to engage in actions that weaken its currency and render it more volatile, actions touched on in the chapter on wealth transferring. In short, government is obliged to purchase goods and services without raising taxes. To do this, a government must print more money, thus diluting the supply and instigating price inflation. If the past decade is any indicator of the dollar's consistency, the bystander must be highly skeptical of the fiat currency's stability.

Other concerns rest in the mere efficacy of alternative currencies. The notion is that eliminating state fiat currency would cause multiple currencies to compete with each other for primacy in a confusing hodgepodge of exchange methods. This concern is built upon the fact that money works best when it is a consensus form of exchange—the more people using the money, the more one can acquire with it and the more powerful a tool it becomes. Multiple currencies would diminish the demand for money and thus diminish one's buying power.

And there can be no doubt that the introduction of multiple competing currencies would devalue each one to some degree. But there is no reason to believe that getting rid of a government fiat currency would necessarily lead to wide heterogeneity. Certainly, producers would be free to establish their own currency, just as they are today, but the competition that would result could very well lead to a single, dominant currency just like there is today. The difference would be that the currency would be dominant only because its owners believed it to be a strong investment, not because they were forced to use it or taxpayers were forced to support it. Such a currency would have the voluntary, not coerced, endorsement of the people who use it.

Nor is the prospect of multiple competing currencies terribly frightful. International financial markets offer a good example of multiple-currency exchanges that operate seamlessly on a daily basis. Exchange rates must be taken into account, as should brokerage fees, but for the most part, the transactions are no more complex than the average grocery store checkout.

Obstacles that do arise because of multiple currencies are becoming less challenging as a result of technical improvements. Credit card processing and Internet exchanges have allowed for swift, non-material transactions in nearly all corners of the economy. A retailer in Dublin, for example, can accept currency in the form of American Express, Visa, MasterCard, and even Discover, from consumers in Tokyo, Johannesburg, and São

Paulo in an instant via modern Internet stores. As the techne continues to improve, so too will affordability. One can even foresee the technical capabilities strengthening to the extent that competition forces transaction fees down and makes the medium altogether smooth and inexpensive. One gadget—the Square—is already forging the path toward this end by granting individuals the ability to swipe credit cards using their mobile device. It is not a stretch to imagine all transactions being made electronically; and from there, it is only a short step to personal, PayPal-esque transactions between unique private currencies all around the world.

> The article to read is "Let's Liberate Money" by Ernest G. Ross, which can be found on The Freeman Online:
> *www.thefreemanonline.org/columns/lets-liberate-money*
>
> The site to browse is the profile for Square:
> *www.squareup.com*

Ending the Fed

A key step in eliminating fiat currency and replacing it with privately established money is to get rid of the current central bank, the Federal Reserve. Since the house of cards has been built upon the foundations of the Fed, ending it will be a devastating and highly disruptive process. However, given the proper attention and a concerted effort from authorities and lay people alike, the process can run smoothly and painlessly.

In his treatise *Money, Bank Credit, and Economic Cycles*, Spanish economist Jesús Huerta de Soto provides a relatively straightforward approach to putting an end to the central bank and replacing it with what he calls complete banking freedom. His process consists in five logically progressing stages that take us from complete dependence on the central bank fiat currency to a situation of full banking freedom and independence from government control of the economy. To map the process of each stage, Huerta de Soto uses five criteria of measurement: (1) the level of freedom in banking, (2) the status of money with regard to national control, (3) the flexibility of exchange rates, (4) the rate of inflation, and (5) the observed and projected effects on economic cycles. With the goal of increasing each element to its highest potential, the process is designed to systematically and carefully wean the economy from its reliance on the central bank and into a situation in which all transactions are facilitated by means of private currencies.

Huerta de Soto's first stage resembles the United States' current system, with a central bank that is wholly dependent on the government, ad hoc management with no fixed monetary rule, a national currency, flexible exchange rates, substantial inflationary credit expansion, and the resultant stock market fluctuations, crises, and recessions. In the second stage, reform takes a few small steps toward the ultimate goal, first by making the central bank legally independent of the government, and second by establishing an intermediate fixed inflation rate that will set the monetary growth rate somewhere between 4 and 6%. The main purpose of this stage is to foster cooperation between international banks and encourage fixed exchange rates to ultimately reduce credit expansion and the fluctuations in the trade cycle. As Huerta de Soto explains, this second stage would bring the banking system to a position reflective of the current European banking system.

The third and most crucial stage would see two major reforms put in place: the establishment of 100% reserve requirements for all banks and a reduction in the monetary rule to around 2%. The impact of the first would be to limit the amount of credit banks can extend by legally requiring them to retain 100% of the deposits they take in. Since nearly all banks currently have a fractional reserve policy, this reform would bring about a transitional phase during which banks would reorganize to meet the new requirements. Banks would more or less split into two kinds of institutions: one that invests deposited money (and basically stands as a mutual fund) and another that maintains 100% of reserves (and becomes a bank in the legal sense).

At this point, depositors would be given the option to either take shares of the mutual fund or keep their demand deposits. Those who take the former would gain or lose value according to the fund's success or failure, just like with any mutual fund; those who choose the latter would receive newly printed cash for their deposits and the guarantee that the bank will not invest that money. Concerns about the mechanics of this process are centered on the issuance of the newly printed money. For the most part, they are more technical than this survey needs to be. Anyone who is interested in the various strategies proposed to issue this new money can be directed to Huerta de Soto's study. To sum up, however, the issuance of the new money is not inflationary since it only represents the amount of cash already assumed to exist in the form of demand deposits. With a strict 100% reserve policy put in place, artificial money created by lending out deposits would be eliminated altogether.

From there, the fourth stage would naturally proceed with the abolition of the central bank, the elimination of fiat currency, and the transition from nationalized currency to privately issued currency. Again, specifics in the process of converting to the private currency are examined in Huerta de Soto's study and need not concern us here. Since the currencies would be private, individuals and groups would be left to determine the most reliable and convenient form of currency to use.

The fifth and final stage would be marked by a completely private banking system which, according to the author of the survey, would consist in a single worldwide gold standard, 100% reserve ratio, fixed exchange rates, and a gradual deflation over time as the constant money supply is outpaced by reliable growth in production. The result, as Huerta de Soto asserts, will be zero expansionary credit, minimal speculation, a steady stock market and money supply, and, ultimately, the elimination of economic recession.

Critics will object to this plan's reliance on the 100% reserve requirement, suggesting that it is just extra regulation and therefore counter to its goal of absolutely free banking. While this criticism has merit, the ultimate aim of a system of banks with 100% reserve requirements is proper in its purpose.

Customers should have the option of depositing money in a bank without the risk of it being used for loans or investments. In principle, a free market for banking will make this kind of institution popular and most likely profitable. Currently, the easy lending practices of the Fed make storing money without investing it far too costly, and so institutions simply don't offer this as an option. Without the Fed, there will be no unnatural impetus to lend money, and the legal requirement for 100% reserves may be a short-lived regulation if a market for 100% reserve banks grows enough in the interim.

The book to read is De Soto's *Money, Bank Credit, and Economic Cycles*.

The chapter that deals with the process of establishing free banking is Chapter 9:
www.mises.org/resources/2745/Money-Bank-Credit-and-Economic-Cycles

Privatizing Regulation

The underlying aim in freeing currency is to grant citizens greater command over their wealth. With that command comes an increase in freedom—more choices of currency, for example—as well as an increase in responsibility. A greater burden is placed on the consumer when there is no government dictating the money supply and he must choose between competing currencies for his preferred means of exchange. Citizens will have to be more cognizant of the basis for their currency as well as its production, distribution, and storage.

Such an increase in awareness is both regrettable and welcomed. The time and effort it takes for each individual to make decisions related to buying and selling through independent currencies can be costly in very direct ways. For instance, the choice to use one currency over another, the discussion on whether a retailer will accept it, and confirmation of the price differential may add two or three minutes to any given purchase, not to mention the added calculations needed to account for exchange rates and the like. All end up costing both the consumer and the producer time, effort, and, ultimately, money.

But the additional costs may be worthwhile. Everyone benefits when consumers and producers are more mindful of the exchanges in which they are engaged. Prompting each citizen to pay attention to his own financial dealings is more or less like instituting a nationwide regulation program, one that employs hundreds of millions of administrators instead of just a few thousand. For this reason, society as a whole benefits from increased responsibility.

The critical effect of increased personal responsibility is the fact that government does not have to assume that responsibility, which ironically means freedom from government intervention. In the end, the result is that the government doesn't have to regulate the financial industry because the individuals are taking the burden of regulation upon themselves. No longer are fair credit reporting, secrecy, consumer complaints, management interlocks regulations, Sarbanes-Oxley, the SEC, FDIC, OTS, OCC, or any other lettered regulations necessary since the consumers will handle this admittedly necessary governance themselves. One could speculate that the cost of personal regulation would be much less than the cost of running these bureaucracies if for no other reason than that personal regulation is more direct and therefore more particular.

As with privatizing the currency, there may be doubts as to whether an economy can survive without government regulations and safety nets. How can depositors be sure that their money is used in an ethical and secure manner? How can investors be certain that companies are not hiding important business facts from them? How can consumers know that they will not be taken advantage of by towering corporations?

To be sure, privatizing regulation can only work if we are certain that individuals are capable of commanding the system and all its powerful forces. Otherwise, we will only return to the days of the robber baron and private monopolies. Taking an overview of the condition, however, we can see how great the power held by individuals is when they assume responsibility for their own actions. The idea is not to get rid of laws but to localize them and make them relevant. It is to stress, as Elinor Ostrom puts it, "rules in use" as opposed to "rules in form° " —that is, rules devised by the people and community and suited for their needs as opposed to those devised by government officials and enforced as a way to maintain hierarchy.

First, freeing currency compels individuals to be economically self-controlled and restrained. The risk of losing their money means that depositors will take more interest in where their money comes from and where it goes; they will not take money printed by fiat, and they will be less likely to deposit money in banks that do not guarantee its return. As a result, banks will be discouraged from printing money by fiat on the one hand or from investing deposits on the other. Ultimately, self-restraint by the customers compels banks to increase reserves and reduce risky behavior. It is possible—for a time after the credit crisis of 2008, banks were riding at around 90% reserves, all before the financial reform package was posted on the docket.

Of course, some individuals will choose to take money printed on a whim. It may come in handy in an expanding economy when credit is dear, but the consequences of such a risky endeavor will make the practice less favorable and much less common. Producers and retailers will be inclined to deny payment via these currencies, and self-regulation will guard against most of this kind of trouble.

So too will there be individuals who deposit their money in banks with low reserve requirements, as there will always be investors willing to take on added risk for the prospect of greater returns. In a self-regulated system, these kinds of investments will still exist and may even flourish, only not as bank deposits; they will be identified as what they are—investments in some sort of mutual fund.

It must be acknowledged that the system as it stands does not eliminate risky behavior, as is often presumed. The thought is that government regulation inhibits banks and corporations from leveraging beyond their ability and taking on chancy investments. Reality cannot be further from this fantasy. If anything, banks and corporations have grown riskier under the support of government regulation. The inclination to moral hazard augments as control expands.

Nor do safety nets, as they stand today, prevent innocent bystanders from being harmed. The consequences of the recent banking and housing crises are sufficient to show that nearly everyone in an economy can be hurt in the event of a crash, especially those farthest from the cause. Even those with great credit ratings and sound work history had trouble refinancing after the collapse restricted lending. In all arenas, federal regulations and safety nets simply exasperate the already present tendency to create bubbles and attempt to place the burden on others. Those with close ties to the regulators have the luxury of enduring the fallout, if only because they have direct access to the loopholes and recovery funds.

Only individual and personal regulation can prevent the kind of systemic collapse and hardship seen in the 2008 downturn because only the individual can take into account all the factors that may affect him. Sure, occasional failure on the personal plane is as inevitable as memory loss, but it is much less likely than failure on the interpersonal or impersonal level. In the end, it is much less maddening to lose money, time, or effort because of one's own mistake than because of negligence by some anonymous stranger.

Self-regulation, like self-governance in general, is a form of polycentric order and flourishes naturally in response to any kind of social circumstance. American lawyer and writer Tom W. Bell pointed out that this kind of natural law has become manifest in communities around the West in the last century in response to increasingly abstract and out-of-touch federal governments. As Bell has shown, what he calls 'polycentric law' is thriving in three vital aspects of modern life: arbitration (with alternative dispute resolution firms), community organization (with homeowners' associations and gated communities), and the Internet (with just about everything having to do with it). In these and other areas, individuals and groups have organized and created rules that stipulate shared ideals and help to establish order, all in effort to fill the absence of coherent state laws or to counter unjust government action. In general, the pattern has been clear: Where the state has been lacking, private interests have stepped up to fulfill the need for order.

The article to read is "Polycentric Law in a New Century" by Tom W. Bell: *http://www.cato.org/pubs/policy_report/bell20n6.pdf*

The book to read is Elinor Ostrom's *Governing the Commons* (1990), in which the author provides empirical studies of societies that have produced sustainable rules in use and an analysis of success and failure.

Streamlining the State

Without control over the money supply, the Juggernaut becomes an entirely different creature. Practically all of the problems that we see harbored by the modern welfare state will suddenly and almost magically disperse, primarily because, when the state no longer has control of the money supply, it cannot inflate the money supply on a whim and so cannot disrupt the economy as a whole by any significant means. The state's central functions in the form of fiscal policy become limited and focused, quite as they were intended at the founding.

This might well seem like a tragedy to statists who believe that the only way to save mankind is by allowing the government to exercise infinite power. But there are two important consequences of reduced power that everyone can agree would be a boon to the system and mankind as a whole. The first involves balancing the budget, a goal that all must acknowledge as a valuable endeavor, especially with regard to the vast United States financial system; the second, which might be more universally agreeable than the first, involves getting rid of the swarm of special interests, lawyers, and lobbyists that hover around Capitol Hill, paralyzing its functions and interfering with its true objectives. Who wouldn't want the state to function as best it could?

To regard the second consequence first, consider the major source of parasitism in the modern economy. As touched on above, the only real source of government power comes from its control of the economy, and the greatest control it has over the economy is its control of the currency. The more control it holds over the money supply, the more it can dictate what its citizens can buy or sell and thus what they can do in general. As such, a broad denationalization of money will therefore substantially reduce the power of the government. Once that power is reduced, a flood of changes will occur all but automatically, leaving the state a mere shadow of what it is now at its apex.

Streamlining the state would most likely begin with a spontaneous dismantling of institutions and programs. Lobbyists, legislators, and litigants all swarm around Washington and local capitals like vultures for the simple reason that that is where the money is. The convoluted mechanisms they create to extract a little money here and a little more money there are only effective when there are large amounts of money piled up and waiting to be spent, as is the case in these capitals.

But once government power is reduced, interest in government programs will lessen. No longer will the three 'L's—legislators, lawyers, and lobbyists—be interested in constructing elaborate political machines to extract superfluous funds from the system because there will be no superfluous funds to extract. When the government is incapable of sending billions of dollars to any group or project it pleases, and is likewise powerless in dictating how private individuals and companies use their resources, then there is very little incentive to attempt to manipulate the actions of that government one way or another.

Thus, when government loses its power to control the economy, it will suddenly and spontaneously shed a thick crust of parasitic clingers-on. Only then can it again function as it was designed. The irony with the federal government has been, the more powerful it has become, the less capable it has been of its basic functions—to defend its citizens' natural rights. Without limitless power over the economy, special interests will look elsewhere for their funding and corrupt administrators will not have the power to lead the state astray; their jobs will be laid out for them, cut and dry, and so the government will be able to perform its basic functions.

This brings us to the first and more direct benefit of reducing the state's monetary power—the ability to effectively control the budget. To be sure, the lack of inflationary power will leave any rational government rather handcuffed in the effort to deficit-spend. This is important because, as we have seen in the last thirty years, the government's ability to spend more than it takes in has nearly always led it to do just that. Since the strictly fiat currency was introduced, the government has shown little indication of offsetting spending with one mode or another of raising revenue. Simply, the ability to inflate the money supply has equaled price inflation that can only be stopped by removing the ability in the first place.

Naturally, this will mean a reduction in spending and thus a reduction in government programs and initiatives. And this is where reform becomes difficult on a sentimental level. Everyone can agree that cutting excessive government programs and getting rid of parasitic clingers-on will be healthy for the country, but who is to decide what is excessive and what can be cut? Medicare and Social Security are perhaps the weightiest and most cumbersome government programs active today, and they present perhaps the most troublesome prospects for maintaining solvency; yet no retiree or elderly medical patient is willing to give up his benefits just like that. All government programs come with the same natural resistance. Tobacco farmers might think that corn farmers are fine on their own and don't need subsidies, but corn farmers contend that their livelihood depends on government funds. They will point to subsidies given to tobacco farmers as superfluous and demand that those programs are the ones to be cut. Across the board in the Welfare State, the same argument will be made—'Cut any program except for mine, for mine is my only mode of survival!'

To begin cutting government programs, then, there must be an objective process that all can agree will identify the counterproductive and inefficient enterprises and help facilitate their elimination. Reformers in Western countries can look to New Zealand, which has recently reduced the size of its government by about 50%, all by analyzing effectiveness and getting rid of burdensome strains.

As the leader of the reform movement and then-member of parliament Maurice McTigue explained, the process was a matter of shifting focus. Whereas the government had judged the success of its programs by the mere expenditure of moneys, it would now actually look at what that money was being spent on. The central component to all of the country's reforms was a concerted effort to shift attention from notional measures to concrete results. Parliament began to focus not on how a given agency spent money or whether it was spent in accordance with appropriation, but on what benefits arose from the agency's activity. When parliament looked at the government programs in this new light, it found that many agencies saw no benefit to their action and often didn't know what benefit they were supposed to achieve.

By asking three simple questions, McTigue was able to assess whether a given agency should be reduced, allowed to remain as it was, or cut altogether. The questions were: (1) What do you do? (2) Is it successful? and (3) What should you be doing? Given the Keynesian atmosphere in New Zealand at the time, it is understandable that many agencies didn't know what their purpose was and were admittedly unsuccessful. Such programs were designed merely to circulate money, even if they didn't produce any substantive rewards. In these cases, it was a matter of course to reduce the size of the agency or to get rid of it entirely.

While studies claim different data and show varying results, the overall picture can be seen in the reduction of national debt as a percentage of GDP from a peak of 50% in 1991 to around 20% in the aughts, and the increase in overall employment from around 1,550,000 in 1985 to around 1,850,000 in 2001. In an attempt to 'out-Thatcher' Margaret Thatcher, the success of New Zealand's privatization efforts could perhaps best be seen in the falling prices of goods and services that were formerly only available through state-owned enterprises. Studies show that the privatization of Telecom New Zealand brought customers an estimated $500 million in savings, and that the privatization of New Zealand Rail has benefited the economy by almost $10 billion[*].

Cutting programs is the most powerful tool in streamlining the state and can be made less abrupt by means of incremental phasing out as well as progressive privatization of state functions. New Zealand reforms extended to programs that were classed as 'inefficient but still useful' by simply holding these agencies more accountable. In many cases, agencies had revenue streams and were capable of standing on their own without national assistance. Via the State-Owned Enterprises Act, the country established a requirement for these otherwise independent businesses to be profitable and pay taxes just as any other business would. In this way, New Zealand ushered state-run programs to self-sufficiency and effectively privatized a large portion of the government.

Other examples of privatization offer various methods of shifting useful state programs to more efficient and profitable businesses. Opening up monopolized industries to competition, contracting private businesses to do the work, public-private partnership, commercialization, and voucher systems are all ways for government programs to move gradually to a more accountable and thus independent arrangement. From these schemes, complete privatization can be a smooth and seamless process.

The prototypical example of privatization on a municipal level was seen in Indianapolis, Indiana during the 1990s when Mayor Stephen Goldsmith reversed a decades-long trend of swelling government and economic stagnation. Goldsmith's method relied on privatization as a means of making state operations less wasteful and more competent. Seventy-five city services were opened to competition over the course of Goldsmith's eight-year tenure, which ended up cutting 43% of the public workforce and trimming the budget by $480 million. The Indianapolis population had shrunk from the 1970s to 1992 by about 15,000 people; by the end of Goldsmith's term, the city had grown by 50,000 inhabitants, thanks in large part to the revived economy and the tapering government bureaucracy.

The book to read on how to systematically disassemble the Welfare State, short and only mildly technical, is *A Blueprint for Prosperity* by Robert Donovan.

The article to read on the privatization of Indianapolis can be found at The Mises Institute:
Case Study: "Indianapolis, Goldsmith" (*http://mises.org/story/2866*)

The site to browse is Downsize DC:
www.downsizedc.org/

Modernizing the System

Once the state has been streamlined, it will be able to perform its tasks, whatever they may be, efficiently and effectively. Only at that point will it be possible to fine tune the system and bring mechanisms such as the voting and legislation processes up to date. As the earlier stages of reform will change the appearance of the state, modernization may or may not be necessary for certain elements. The following, then, are sketches of what might be employed once the government has been trimmed to its core.

Refine voting districts. Upon decades of changing voting laws and shifting interests, the voting process has become so distorted as to make practically ineffectual any significant movement for change. One prime example can be seen in the way politicians in power have redrawn voting districts to grant their parties a greater likelihood of winning in subsequent elections. In industry jargon, this is called 'gerrymandering'. Districts end up looking like mangled organisms with tentacles spread into crevices and squished between other districts so that areas with mixed voting interests are divided and subdued. The populations of each district are equivalent, but their arrangement skews elections in favor of the ruling party, resulting in more incumbent victories and a more daunting task for campaigning challengers.

The first step in modernizing districts, then, would be to redraw them so that they are even in population and reasonably aligned. In addition to helping to limit the incumbents' advantage, redistricting will give individual voters more influence. The idea is for every vote to count, not for the individual voter's input to be overwhelmed by the gerrymandered majority.

Apportion representation. Districts should also be redrawn to reflect population growth. That is, districts should be redrawn every ten years or so to encompass roughly the same number of constituents and to ensure an equal level of representation. As population goes up, so too should the number of districts and representatives.

This had been the protocol from the founding until 1911 (note the year), when Public Law 62-5 put a cap on the number of representatives in Congress at 435. Since then, save for a four-year period when the number of representatives was increased to account for the inclusion of Alaska and Hawai'i, the House of Representatives has stayed at a consistent number notwithstanding the skyrocketing population.

A clause in the Constitution states that the number of representatives should not exceed 1 for every 30,000 people, perhaps to limit one state's influence over another and to keep the number of representatives relatively high. The number 30,000 was devised as a round measure of the limits of representative power. In 1911, the ratio was around 211,000 constituents per representative; today, the ratio is around 700,000 constituents.

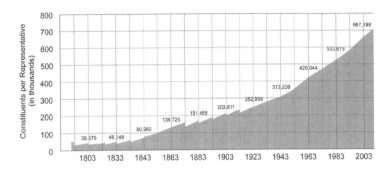

Fig. 33—Average Population per U.S. House District 1790-2010.

One may assume that logistics played a chief role in limiting the number of representatives in the House. At the time of 62-5, the Capitol could not accommodate many more congressmen than it already did. Today, the estimated number of representatives needed to meet old proportions would be around 10,000. Of course, with modern techne the problem of overcrowdedness can be sufficiently eliminated. Activists at Thirty-Thousand.org suggest establishing four or more evenly divided chambers that convene not in Washington, D.C. but in other designated areas closer to the representatives' home states. This would be a vital step in the effort to build a polycentric society. In effect, there would be not one single federal government but several components that operate on their own in the interest of their region. Internet conferences could assemble all the representatives when needed.

Expanded representation would have the primary cost of added administration. With an increase of nearly 10,000 representatives, those costs could be quite significant. Taking into consideration, however, the fact that these representatives would have fewer constituents to speak for and fewer obligations in general due to the reduced role of government, the costs would likely be tempered. Lower campaigning costs due to smaller districts would add to the benefit.

The true advantage gained in the pluralism would be a chamber more directly representative of the population. Incumbents could not lock up seats as easily, a greater number of political parties would gain access to the representation, and bribery would become nearly impossible due to the scope of Congress. This last was one of the main reasons the founders wanted so many representatives included in the House to begin with. Altogether, a return to the 30,000 quotient would allow for a much more effective standard.

> The site to browse is Thirty Thousand:
> *www.thirty-thousand.org/*

Internet voting. New techne should profit the voting system in general with the introduction of electronic balloting and, eventually, Internet voting. The benefits are clear—there is no more efficient and reliable form of polling and calculating than the Internet. Access to the polls, voter harassment, and the technical shortcomings of paper balloting (exempli gratia, hanging chads) are all aspects of old systems that can be overcome with the establishment of the new Internet voting mechanism.

Drawbacks to any such plans revolve around the prospect of voter fraud. It is theoretically easier for a hacker to go in and change a thousand digital votes than it is for a bandit to steal a bag full of paper ballots for one candidate and replace it with a bag full of ballots for another.

This is an understandable concern, though one that is rather naïve in its assumptions. While computer balloting is certainly liable for fraud, it cannot be said that paper balloting persists without risks. One hears of bags of ballots that are left at polling places without being tabulated even as recently as the 2008 presidential election. And there is no reason to suppose that just because ballots are electronic they would be insecure or somehow open for the average hacker to manipulate. Systems of security can be established that match and exceed the current forms of protection paper balloting maintains. After all, banking and other official Internet traffic has proven to be reliable and secure when the necessary precautions are taken.

Automatic expiration of laws. Under the current system, all laws remain in effect until they are repealed or until a given time expressly indicated in the law through a 'sunset clause'. This means that unless a law includes an expiration date in its text, it will remain active until legislators make the effort to strike it from the books. Legislators, naturally inclined to generate new laws rather than to repeal old ones, allow outdated and often ridiculous laws to stay on the books without notice. As a result, those books continue to grow and the people become increasingly overcriminalized.

The solution is to establish the standard of an automatic sunset for every law passed. Laws that are currently on the books could be given a grace period before facing elimination, upon which legislators would have to revisit, revise, and reinstate to keep the law on file. Imagine a country in which every law is pertinent and up-to-date—a far stretch from the current state of affairs.

Benefits would be twofold: First, the ridiculous laws that have remained on the books for decades unused would pass into the archives without much ado, thus alleviating the law books of an immense amount of dead weight. Second, legislators would be responsible for reviewing and renewing every law that nears its expiration. This would, in effect, keep politicians occupied with discerning the fundamental legislation that is most necessary to keep the country running. Not coincidentally, these legislators would also have less time to conjure up new laws to pass. Even if they did find time to do so, they could not guarantee that the next generation would be so dedicated. Ultimately, the volume of laws would be trimmed significantly.

Questions as to how long laws should remain active before the automatic sunset and whether some laws deserve a longer life span than others must be considered. It is also necessary to assume a phased approach in addressing the laws currently on the books. Essentially, every law must be revisited, which will unfortunately take a tremendous amount of time and effort.

The bottom line is that an innovative, technically advanced nation should be able to employ its most sophisticated instruments in its own administration. Once the weight of the bureaucracy is lifted, the state can begin to implement modern institutions as the techne improves and, in so doing, fix the system in a lasting way.

4. TRANSCENDING
THE SYSTEM

FOR FIVE HUNDRED YEARS or so, improvements in economic techniques have afforded Westerners an unrivaled standard of living. What used
to be the finest luxuries in the world, available to only the wealthiest monarchs, have become expected for the average citizen, especially in America. Running water, plumbing, high-definition televisions, mobile Internet
phones, and 3-D action-packed blockbuster movies are luxuries that even
the poorest Americans have general access to. Most in the middle-income
range enjoy still other luxuries from around the world that would have been
unthinkable a hundred years ago, such as a daily dose of Guatemala Casi
Cielo coffee, an occasional night at the best Japanese Kobe beef grill, and a
once-a-year trip to their favorite tropical destination. Not even Louis XVI
and Marie Antoinette could have demanded such extravagance.

As we have seen, however, the technical improvements that have produced this opulence have also bound Western Civilization in a web of inter-
connectedness that has in significant ways lowered the standard of living.
Based in specialism and division of labor, modern economic techniques
have closed the frontier and imposed a strictly competitive system in which

an individual's actions necessarily affect everyone around him, and everyone else's actions impact him just as much. In such a claustrophobic state of affairs, the only solution has been to produce an all-providing government, which has in its own way tightened borders and restricted liberties. One can trace the modern era's progress from industrious self-sufficiency to interdependency, to a closed economy of strict competition and finally to an ever-expanding protectorate state. The pattern takes us from a condition of extensive individual freedom to one of evermore suffocating restrictions and coercion. And so, as the standard of living has increased in many important ways, modern life has become more strenuous and problematic as well.

To take a few examples of this lowered standard of living, regard the daily activities of the average American. Typical office workers must sit in bumper-to-bumper traffic for hours every day to work and earn the income needed to purchase the luxuries mentioned above; average city dwellers must cram into rodent-infested quarters to have access to their high-paying salaries; and, everywhere one turns, there are people crowding around, getting in his way, and trampling over him on their way to their own high-rise offices and cramped, rodent-infested homes.

Ultimately, every modern man must face the depleted morale that Smith warned was the downside of specialism. When one's tasks are so abstracted from his nature that he does not recognize their value, he grows numb to that nature. It has come to a point where specialism and the division of labor have so distorted modern man's perception that he can hardly enjoy the luxuries that he has worked so hard to obtain.

The attitude most have toward amenities like flowing water, plumbing, and even high-definition television is one of apathy and at best expectancy—the plane traveler curses the airline when his Wi-Fi fades for five minutes; the young professional cries in frustration when Starbucks is out of her favorite latte flavor. We assume that we will have these things on demand, and when they are withheld from us for some reason, it is cause for distress and protest. Even when it comes to rarer luxuries, such as the view from a Maui hotel room or the smooth ride of a luxury sedan, true appreciation is hard to come by. It can be surmised that, no matter how advanced a culture, good taste has always been a scarce commodity.

Here we find the source of the progress paradox, the bizarre state of affairs in which an increase in standard of living leads to a reduction in happiness; and higher productivity, higher salaries, and a greater abundance of luxuries all lead to a boom in claustrophobia, loss of purpose, and an increase in clinical depression. The better life seems on paper, the worse it seems in reality, and, as technology continues to improve and populations continue to grow, the paradox only intensifies.

By this point, we can identify the culprit—the paradox is ingrained in the system itself. In order to attain the level of great wealth we have come to expect, we have subscribed to a system of highly specialized division of labor and so have developed an interdependent network of persons and institutions that has become more demanding than it is rewarding. Whence the paradox—the system is needed to alleviate our troubles, and at the same time it is the main source of them; to increase our standard of living, we have had to decrease it.

Since the problems are rather inherent in the system, we cannot be satisfied with the prospect of simply working within it or even fixing it so that it functions optimally. These approaches will help to ameliorate some problems but cannot by themselves detach us from all our difficulties. These problems will be with us as long as we are dependent upon each other for necessities, and so we will not be rid of them until we embrace self-sufficiency and personal responsibility. Only then can we begin to imagine renaissance, a rebirth of the human character and spirit. Only by transcending the system entirely can we achieve our true goal of autarchy.

Now, the skeptic will point out that simply abandoning the system would leave us in no better position than the one we're in today. While completely rejecting the interdependent mode of life would eliminate suffocating crowds, cut-throat competitiveness, and dehumanizing conditions in one sense, the absence of the system would mean a return to pre-modern utilities, the loss of our nearly infinite consumer choices, and vulnerability to the forces of nature. As one economist put it, "Self-sufficiency is the road to poverty°." And so, in following with the paradoxical rise of modern economics, reversing modern economics would decrease the standard of living in order to increase it.

As a result, completely abandoning the system will never be a satisfactory solution. But, given our level of technical achievement, we may be able to overcome the system's faults without deserting it entirely. We have reached a point where we can overcome the crowdedness and aimlessness of the modern economy, not by abandoning modern technology and social resources altogether, but by using them; we can use the system in order to transcend it. The proposal, then, could be described in the way that Ernest Hunter Wright described Rousseau's motto: not *back* to nature, but *forward* to it.

The clearest example rests in the Internet, an advance whose uses we are only now beginning to fully appreciate. In the old model of economic interaction, the consumer, producer, and retailer would all have to convene at a single, physical location to perform any kind of exchange. Thus, all would have to live in close proximity to the others or else expend a great deal of resources in order to connect via proxy. In the new model, none of the participants need to leave their homes. All that is needed is the hire of a specialized distribution service like FedEx or UPS. Whereas the old paradigm required people to be together, whether it was in accordance with or against their individual wills, the new archetype allows all parties to conduct business without the inconveniences of the central meeting place. Suddenly, the hustle and bustle of the marketplace is no longer required, the pressure of having to meet face-to-face is relieved, and the difficulties posed by relying on others involved in a transaction are all eliminated in lieu of a smooth, comfortable exchange.

This is a simplistic proof, of course, and there are several other elements to consider (exempli gratia, the extra costs of producing and maintaining the Internet connection, the longer distribution routes, et cetera), but in general we can see how technology, and in particular the Internet, can be employed to alleviate the strains of the modern economy. Telecommuting, or the practice of working from one's residence, is another seemingly instinctive application of the Internet that can reduce and even eliminate downsides of the city life, such as dealing with rude and uncivilized office mates or a tedious commute.

The modern society, with all its complex interdependency, was necessary for the Internet to be made possible. But, now that we have it, we can use it to retreat from the hectic world of city life and reach a place of detached tranquility. We can use technology to transcend the system.

The modernist will argue that there are benefits to the city that cannot be established in a virtual setting no matter how effective the technology. Many will contend that having millions of people within walking distance is in itself a positive aspect of the modern city life. To them, it is the thrill of the bustle, the diversity of personalities, and the feeling of closeness that makes the city so appealing.

And, while this city dweller cannot understand the rationale that actually seeks out the commotion of the subway or the jumble of a crowded shopping mall, he cannot dispute another's preferences. If that is what they want, he is not inclined to withhold it from them. But only by offering a valid alternative in the form of an economically sound detachment can we make the city a completely voluntary and thus deliberate social construct rather than just a hectic and taxing frustration.

Big cities possess enough allure to remain relevant well into the future. But they can only be a desirable and beneficial mainstay if there is a valid alternative available for those who do not seek the city's haste. Once such an alternative does exist, even the drawbacks of city life can be taken without much distaste. Nineteenth-century London, for instance, was huge, growing, and completely covered in the soot of its burgeoning factories. But, strangely, people who lived there loved it, accepted the odd stench of the pollution, and even wrote verses that alluded to its charms°. They were enamored by the city life, even its nastier elements, because they always had the option to leave and secure a regular life in the country. They could love the city because they were not in any way coerced into loving it; it was a choice, and one that many people made intentionally.

Indeed, if there are alternatives to interdependency, everyone benefits. It can be argued that freedom from the masses is a true prerequisite for appreciating the value in those masses. Only when an individual or group is no longer reliant on others can they truly benefit from them; only when one is free can he take advantage of the industry, trade, and cooperation inherent in the modern economy.

The direct aim, then, in reviving autarchy is to reintroduce the self-sufficient life known before modern times. Technical advance has made that prospect not only as promising as modern living with the wide availability of modern conveniences, but also more economically advantageous by providing greater access to ends that all men find truly valuable.

Cultivating Self-Sufficiency

If we can agree that an open economy is the real solution for the troubles of modern civilization, then we can summarize our quest with the following logic: An open economy is possible only when its participants are engaged in it entirely by choice; only when every participant is involved in a system of exchange by his own volition can that system truly be open and free; and only when one is capable of supporting himself can he make his own decisions and truly choose one action over another. When one is not self-sufficient, his decisions will always be influenced by others, and so it is impossible for him to make any real choices on his own. In short, an open economy comes from self-rule, and self-rule comes from self-sufficiency. Thus, the path toward the open economy and the resolution to our problems comes in the form of a widespread establishment of self-sufficiency.

Now, one might argue that most Westerners, and certainly most Americans, are self-sufficient already—they have jobs, earn incomes, buy their own food, support their families, and accumulate their own savings in order to pursue their own happiness. They do not beg others for food, panhandle for change, or solicit the government for bailouts. Most people are resourceful, productive, and considered to be largely self-sufficient.

But this is to say that one can be self-sufficient without obtaining his own food or preparing it, or even knowing where his food comes from or how to prepare it; that one can be resourceful even when half his life is spent doing work that someone else told him to do, for someone else, and under someone else's supervision; and that one can be productive when his product is a small component of a seemingly meaningless mass of zeros and ones that someone else pays for and uses. It is to say, in short, that someone can be self-sufficient even though he relies on other people for just about everything he thinks and does.

Of course, there is no doubt that an industrious young professional who graduates from Harvard Business, makes six figures on Wall Street, buys a townhouse on the Upper East Side, and starts a family is in many ways self-sufficient. He has the initiative and the intellectual wherewithal to provide what the modern world demands, yet he requires countless other individuals to help him with everything from the basics of procuring his food and building his home to the more complex transactions that fortify his bank accounts. He is certainly self-sufficient in a few important ways, but, in most aspects of his life, he is reliant on many other people. Without the system, he would perish.

True self-sufficiency covers all facets of life, from satisfying one's basic needs of food, rest, and shelter, to the more intricate and personal needs of esteem and self-actualization, as Maslow described it. In order to have a renaissance in our culture, then, its people must endeavor to be self-sufficient in all of these aspects of life. Of course, it is not necessary to actually do everything on one's own, from raising farm animals to building complex electrical gadgets to manufacturing linen suits; to attain self-sufficiency, it is only necessary to be *able* to provide these necessary things on one's own. The distinction rests in the ability. Whereas the modern city dweller needs all of these things to survive, he has no way of producing them himself—he has only the ability to do one thing, the specialized task he went to school for so many years to master. A truly self-sufficient person is able to do all of the things he needs to survive and prosper by himself—from raising the farm animals he might use for food to the processes it takes to procure cotton and manufacture linen apparel. As long as he can do all of these on his own, he is self-sufficient and is therefore capable of autarchy.

As can be reasoned, this kind of self-sufficiency begins with education. Before one does something, one must know how to do it, and this is where the first major step in attaining self-sufficiency comes in. The modern education system is geared to providing the modern citizen with knowledge about living in the modern system; that is, it is designed to socialize students and prepare them for a life of specialized work among millions of others. Lessons are built around the teaching of a single occupation so as to provide the student with the best handle on making a living in the modern economy. Any lesson not directly related to the student's career is offered as a mere 'elective'. And so it cannot be a surprise that, other than their primary focus, graduates know very little upon entering the job market. They certainly are not taught how to provide for themselves on a fundamental level.

And yet, despite the deficiencies in the modern education system, lessons on the basics are not too far removed for anyone. Most basic information in this area comes either in the form of novelty survival guides or off-grid living websites, both of which can be rather enlightening and easy to access. Other, more attractively packaged goods are also being produced that underscore the value in self-sufficient living. One recalls Conn and Hal Iggulden's *Dangerous Book for Boys* as an attempt to revive the kind of hands-on, organic learning necessary for a capable, well-rounded boyhood. This type of learning was not long ago part of the core curriculum for children of all backgrounds, as can be evidenced by the pervasiveness of the handbooks for Boy and Girl Scouts in America prior to 1960. The idea was for children to learn about the real substance of life, nature, and the basic mechanics of the world. The Igguldens claim that these lessons are integral for an adventurous and enjoyable education. The case could also be made that only with sound expertise in these basics can one truly be self-sufficient and thus capable of self-rule.

There is no limit to the education one can attain these days, and this student cannot begin to convey the kinds of information needed to begin the process toward self-sufficiency. All he can do is acknowledge the fact that today, with the help of modern techne and especially the Internet, everyone can have access to information, tutorials, guides, and complete courses dedicated to just about anything—how to tie a knot, what the best method is for curing a skin, how to speak in Japanese or Spanish or Latin, how to bake a loaf of bread, how to catch and prepare a lobster, how to track animals, how to navigate by use of the stars, and so on. There is no limit to the knowledge available because there is no practical limit to the amount of information that can be stored online. And most of it is free.

Google 'self-sufficiency' for scores of web sites providing information, stories, and case studies on living self-sufficiently.

The book to read is *Back to Basics* (2008) by Abigail R. Gehring.

The objective viewer is absolutely astounded by the potential of this mechanism. The obvious and most powerful aspect of this tool is the wide, instant dissemination of information. Like the printing press five hundred years before, the Internet has refined the dissemination process and expanded the potential audience for all ideas. As the printing press pushed an idea's boundaries to the edges of a country and even a continent, the Internet has eliminated boundaries altogether. We are rapidly arriving at a place where the average individual can have access to all the information that has ever been formulated in the history of the world, and that is especially true for basic, universal knowledge such as that needed for self-sufficiency.

Detaching from the System

The most precise and direct way to make use of this knowledge is by applying it directly to one's own life. And, while most practical survival techniques cannot possibly be used in the modern city life, technical advances have made it possible to move away from major metropolises or at least to change the environment within them in order to better make use of autonomous know-how.

This push away from large cities has come almost as naturally as the move toward them over the last several centuries. Cities have grown throughout the modern era, but so too have they repulsed their inhabitants and caused many to move away to the country to find escape.

Almost from the moment the frontier closed, one could see this countervailing force throughout culture and especially in America, where it was most evident in the romanticism of the Wild West. First seen in the paintings of Frederic Remington, then in the dominant Western film genre and even in classical music with the work of Aaron Copland, America's undying devotion to the idea of the West showed how powerful the longing for freedom has been and still is in the country's spirit. And it was not limited to the romance of artists. The introduction of the automobile and the subsequent flight to the suburbs seen from the 1940s to the '70s had as its central premise the same notion of fleeing the restraints of the city, being independent, and cultivating a family apart from the masses.

Of course, this urge to fly westward has always been somewhat disingenuous. Though Americans dreamed of the freedom of the open country, they knew that it was no longer practical. The city was the only real frontier, and so it was there that Americans had to live and work. Suburbanization, as a national event, was itself dependent on the automobile and commuting to and from the city, a process which came with a slew of environmental, social, and cultural problems. The veneer of self-sufficiency was there in the supposed home ownership, the front lawns and white picket fences, but the suburbanites relied on the city just as much as their city-dwelling predecessors. And, since the daily routine included a resource-consuming commute, as well as drives to the local supermarket and shopping mall, it could be said that the new suburbanites relied on the system a great deal more than their predecessors, who could at least walk to work and to the marketplace.

True self-sufficiency requires complete detachment, not only living miles from the city center, but also working and consuming far from the city as well. In principle, self-sufficiency means doing all of these things—or at least having the ability to do all of them—locally. Self-sufficiency means being independent from the system in every aspect. To this end, again, the value of the Internet cannot be underestimated. If there is a single mechanism that is capable of ushering in a new renaissance, it is the network of ideas freely presented and exchanged online. Its central effect—any piece of information accessible anywhere in the world—has meant nothing less than a complete revolution in thought and action. As a result, it is now possible to work, live, and socialize—to enjoy all rewarding aspects of society—even when one is miles away from that society.

Formerly, to be detached from society and especially from the city life meant to be detached from most major means of production, from arts and culture, and from science and progress. Now, detachment means one can keep up with all of these without the interruptions or distractions of the city life. Detachment has all the benefits and little or no drawbacks.

Telecommuting, teleshopping, and telesocializing have distilled old ways of doing things so that only the most important aspects remain, allowing the average individual or family to escape from the confines of the metropolis without extending the system. Of course, many of these activities can be done within the confines of the city. I once telecommuted from a home that was five miles from the office, down the block from high-rise corporate headquarters, and across the street from a shopping mall. Being able to eliminate the commute to and from work, however, meant that I was detached to no small degree and could secure at least some element of self-sufficiency.

Doing It Yourself

Moving away from the system is a good first step, but if one still relies on a complex society to satisfy his needs, then not much is accomplished. For example, one might be able to shop via the Internet, but, if he gets the electricity he needs to run his computer from a nearby municipal electric company, and relies on an army of specialized workers to build his consumer goods and a fleet of distributors to deliver them, he hasn't detached himself in any long-term, sustainable way. To make the move to self-sufficiency, then, he must do all of these things on his own and with his own local power.

This isn't as far-fetched as it may seem. Doubtless in reaction to the mind-numbing conditions of the modern economy, and perhaps in part due to the recession, the do-it-yourself ethos has become rather popular in recent years. Most household chores, such as laundry, washing dishes, and mowing the lawn, have always been part of the do-it-yourself repertory. Nowadays, it seems that homeowners are getting bolder with their projects and expanding into plumbing, automobile mechanics, fixing cabinets, and other endeavors that would make Bob Vila proud. As another do-it-yourself show host has indicated, people are picking up caulk guns and screwdrivers when they would never have done so in the past. It is as if the typical chores of yesteryear have suddenly become enjoyable again. Certainly, the feeling of satisfaction that comes with a hands-on effort is well appreciated in the modern specialized world.

One crucial aspect of this trend is the wider availability of time and the lower availability of money. When a homeowner's budget is tight, hiring professionals becomes a luxury and spending time on a project oneself begins to look like a sound economic move. As can be expected, technology and the Internet have also made such endeavors much more feasible. With websites like eHow.com and DoItYourself.com, learning how to change your oil, unclog a drain, or build a deck becomes easy and straightforward. Granted, one is reliant on the Internet and the other people who have posted tutorials on the sites, but the key for most do-it-yourself projects is not having to pay for someone else to do the actual work. It can be done on one's own time and under one's own power, which is the first essential step in doing it yourself.

This is quite a ways from the kind of self-sufficiency of a Robinson Crusoe or Henry David Thoreau. To be able to fix a leak under a sink is entirely different from, say, building a house and maintaining one's own food source. But, as wild as it may seem, the do-it-yourself mentality can extend pretty far, such that an individual or family could actually become self-sufficient in the vein of Crusoe or Thoreau without departing too much from their normal lives. And, with enough technical advance, it may be possible to extend the do-it-yourself ethos to complete self-sufficiency without losing comfort or convenience in the least.

To examine the potential of a complete do-it-yourself lifestyle, it will be constructive to survey the various human needs and the individual techniques available to fulfill them. Naturally, most of these techniques are rudimentary. The sophisticated city dweller might scoff at the primitive style of some of these methods, and yet he can still take comfort in knowing that they can and will be improved upon as interest in them grows, until the technology progresses to a point where they can all be as effective and efficient as modern municipal processes.

Nor are such techniques to be reserved for isolated hermits living 'off the grid'. Self-sufficiency at its most basic level is the *ability* to provide for oneself. As long as one has that ability, then he is able to decline interaction that he knows cannot benefit him. He can and often will make use of specialism, labor division, and trade, as Westerners have done throughout the last few centuries. The difference will be that his participation will be based in voluntary action and mutual gain, not obligation; in cooperation, not bondage.

Doing it yourself can consist in doing a few things here and there that one would otherwise have hired a large conglomerate corporation to do, or it may involve a rigorous effort to become wholly self-sufficient. It could mean growing a garden of herbs and spices and a few easy crops or developing a full-fledged farm capable of supplying a family with enough foodstuffs to last a year, plus some extras to trade with neighbors. The point is to move in the direction of self-sufficiency and localism, and to remember that every increment helps. The following concepts are at the very core of the enterprise. While just a basic overview is provided here, greater detail can be found in external sources for each.

Staking a claim. To exist at all, one must occupy some area of space, and that means that the first step in self-sufficiency is acquiring and maintaining land. Now, this land can be anywhere as long as its ownership is protected by common law. Ideally, it is capable of supplying its owner with natural resources such as fertile soil in which to plant crops, raise timber, and harvest metals. Naturally, the wider the plot and the more diverse its resources, the better it will be in providing for its inhabitants. As such, it is likely that a move away from the city will be essential in obtaining a truly resourceful plot.

Reasonably, acquiring land will be a costly endeavor. Anyone aiming to purchase acreage near cities should be willing to pay upwards of a million dollars, which would require a tremendous amount of saving or a bank loan, neither of which will seem very enticing to a do-it-yourselfer looking to grow more independent. The further away from cities, however, the lower prices are.

LandCentral.com provides a list of "cheap land" available across the country which makes the possession and maintenance of large expanses of land very accessible. For instance, a seven-acre plot near Van Horn, TX, goes for under $4,000; five acres located south of Fort Garland, CO is for sale at under $5,000. The mere thought that one could escape modern living and actually make a completely independent life for a few thousand dollars is in itself a liberating thought. As alluded to on earlier page, the amount of unoccupied land in America has increased since the close of the frontier, meaning that there is a greater supply of land than ever before. It would take only a higher demand to make use of it.

> The site to browse is LandCentral:
> *http://www.landcentral.com/*

Securing a water supply. As the most essential aspect of survival, water supply is perhaps the most essential component of self-sufficiency. Depending upon one's location, an individual or family can harness enough water on one's own property through natural sources alone. By constructing a well or rainwater collection and storage system, the natural environment can satisfy most needs. Even the desert supplies some cycle of precipitation—usually in torrents—that can be accumulated and kept during droughts.

Of course, unless one's water supply is the spring on a mountaintop, it will need to be transferred for use and purified for drinking and food preparation purposes. The pumping, storing, filtration, and heating mechanisms needed are similar to those found in modern households if one is willing to use manufactured goods and electronics in the process. Other options are available for those who want to exclude all such techne and don't mind dirtier water and colder showers.

> The site to browse is Back Woods Home:
> *http://www.backwoodshome.com/articles2/yago71.html*

Growing a garden. Food is perhaps the easiest element of the do-it-yourself lifestyle because it is still rather natural in spite of the modern economy. Broccoli still grows out of the ground, and apples grow on trees. A push toward organic farming has also revived the completely natural process, which anyone can institute locally given a plot of land and access to source plants and animals. Most essential nutrients for a moderately sized family can be obtained from the harvest of a ten-by-ten garden. To diversify the diet and ensure year-round supplies, those dimensions will need to be expanded and the possibility of trade introduced.

There is no limit to the amount and variety of food one can produce oneself. Vegetables, fruits, grains, and nuts are the core of the small farm, but milk, eggs, and meat can be added if one is not too wary of getting close to animals, and luxuries like spices, honey, jellies, juices, beer, and wine are also rather easy to procure.

The sites to browse are:

Life Unplugged:
http://www.lifeunplugged.net/gardenpantry/default.aspx

DoItYourself.com
http://www.doityourself.com/stry/growing-prawns-with-aquaponics

Back Yark Aquaponics:
http://www.backyardaquaponics.com/

Gardening facilities can be put together to afford home gardeners an even more abundant harvest. Greenhouses might be erected in cold climates, for instance, to provide a place not only for tropical vegetation but also for fruits and vegetables that grow during the winter season, such as oranges and artichokes. Aquaponic and hydroponic systems have also become a fairly reasonable way to procure food in a controlled, compact way. By using self-contained water environments, they allow the farmer to cultivate essentials like lettuce, broccoli, strawberries, and bananas, as well as catfish and prawns, among other delicacies, all within the confines of a small backyard or vertical farm. Yet a home garden doesn't have to be as extensive as these last few options. Even a small garden with a few items helps one to withdraw from the system to some degree. Every little bit makes an impact.

Creating a wardrobe. Perhaps one of the most appealing aspects of modern living is the wide availability of new, comfortable clothing, available for near nothing. And, in what might be the most ironic aspect of modernity, current fashion has completely abandoned this luxury in favor of old-looking, uncomfortable wares, almost as if the luxury is so abundant that people have rejected it to live more ruggedly. Whatever the cause may be, it has come to a point where anyone who has access to cloth and sewing instruments can create highly fashionable apparel.

The trick in becoming a do-it-yourself fashion designer, naturally, is acquiring the cloth and sewing equipment necessary to create the wardrobe. The manufacture of cotton cloth, though it is perhaps the most common variety of fabric, is still a very labor-intensive process that begins with the raising of cotton trees and harvesting of the cotton, and continues with an intricate process of breaking, opening, blending, finishing, carding, drawing, lapping, combing, drawing again, slubbing, and roving, all before the spinning and weaving are endeavored. Each step of the process can be expedited by the use of its own machine which requires its own manufacture—Eli Whitney's cotton gin never seemed so amazing an invention—but can eliminate a great deal of repetitive work and unnecessary toil.

Given such a rigorous procedure, the manufacture of cloth might well be a prime candidate for trade. Once one can obtain enough cloth, however, design and sewing are much easier. With the climate of fashion these

The site to browse is:

Bitwise Gifts:
http://www.bitwisegifts.com/glencoenc/library/flow.htm

days, the do-it-yourself designer might well be able to provide a better product than the top name brands.

Building a house. To live on one's own, one needs to have a place in which to live, and so one of the fundamental aspects of self-sufficiency is building a home. Thoreau's first step was to build a house. Of course, with the size and scope of modern homes these days, such a prospect can be awfully daunting, especially to anyone who is not familiar with engineering or construction. However, putting together a moderately sized dwelling can be very easy and cost-effective (read *Walden* for a practical guide to the process). Even large-scale mansions are feasible with the right resources and dedication.

If the aim is a small or moderately sized abode, it is quite likely that one can find the materials on one's own land. Resources for the structure can be raised on-site in the form of timber and other plant life as well as stones and metals. Wood-framed houses are still the norm for structures under five stories and so can be constructed using locally raised lumber. Stone, homemade bricks, or adobe siding (clay and sand mixed with mud) can be used to fill in the frame using nearby resources and, in the case of bricks, a kiln. Mortar (cement of limestone, clay, or shale) can be obtained from natural supplies, as can paint, stucco, plaster, and glue for interior walls and improvements. Insulation can be provided with straw bales grown locally or acquired via trade. Glass and metalwork for windows and piping will need to be outsourced unless one is extremely ambitious.

More elaborate structures, such as those built by specialized firms, can be produced on one's own as well, though the homeowner will most likely need to trade and outsource for materials and labor, and devote a good deal of his own time to bringing the project to fruition. Given the willingness to trade for these resources and the dedication to undergo the feat, the actual construction process is rather uncomplicated. Homebuilder Carl Heldmann offers a tremendous resource that takes one through the building process step by step, from establishing a budget and pinpointing a plan to raising the beams and installing the lighting.

Again, as with a home garden, just doing some of the steps yourself helps to remove you from the system to some degree. One could lay the tile in the bathroom, install the carpet, or just paint the walls. While doing so won't detach the homeowner from the system entirely, it will provide a sense of independence that can aid in the overall effort to build a localized, polycentric system.

The sites to browse are:

eHow:
http://www.ehow.com/how_2314179_make-bricks.html
http://www.ehow.com/way_5445332_homemade-oil-paint.html

Wonder How To:
http://www.wonderhowto.com/how-to/video/how-to-mix-mortar-for-bricklaying-153890/

BYOH (Build Your Own House):
http://www.byoh.com/

Installing sanitation facilities. Sanitation can be obtained in a variety of ways, from a simple and more natural sawdust toilet and compost pile to a more complex on-site sewage facility. On-site facilities can be rather similar in format to large-scale municipal sewage systems. The process requires plumbing (piping and water-based fixtures such as sinks, toilets, and showers) in addition to a number of containers and processing mechanisms.

The system would look something like this: Indoor plumbing takes wastewater from bathrooms, kitchens, and laundry fixtures to a nearby treatment facility where solids are screened and then deposited in compost piles and the remaining liquids undergo degradation. With the proper precautions in place, such as depositing the waste at a sufficient distance from the other local facilities and a well-designed barrier to seepage, nature takes care of the rest.

Estimates show that on-site wastewater treatment comprises around one quarter of total treatment facilities in the United States, suggesting that it is still an adequate and economical approach. So too have technical advances helped to alleviate common septic problems as well as the pollution that comes with the chemicals used in the process.

The sites to browse are:

AGWT (American Groundwater Trust):
http://www.agwt.org/info/septicsystems.htm

YVW (Yarra Valley Water):
http://www.yvw.com.au/waterschool/seniors/sewerage/sewagetour.html

Generating power locally.   Electric power is, of course, one major aspect of modern living that relies on a complex system. The last and perhaps most useful element to a self-sufficient life, then, is generating power locally. All of the above techniques can be done without electricity, but most can be done much easier with advanced electrical equipment such as an electric water heater, refrigerator, lighting, and, of course, computers.

In recent years, largely spurred by the impulses for renewable energy, several portable, compact power generators have been developed that make local dynamics an effective and economic prospect. Since most options are designed around ecologically sound solar, wind, and water sources, the switch is ecologically friendly as well. Search 'solar panels' on Amazon.com to get a glimpse of the options, which range in cost from a few hundred dollars to several thousands.

There are also possible homemade solutions in the form of wind and water turbines, and, though there is no known way to make solar cells without complex production facilities, the actual panels and wire connections can be built and installed on one's own.

The site to browse is:

Off-Grid:
http://www.off-grid.net/2009/12/08/how-i-built-a-solar-panel-for-100-you-can-too/

Extending Techne

With respect to the do-it-yourself lifestyle described above, purists might claim that it is not enough to simply paint your own walls and grow some parsley, and that living even in this resourceful way isn't really being self-sufficient. They will say that the use of any manufactured good, such as a solar panel, an electric pump, or a refrigerator, is reliant on mass society, and that one cannot truly be self-sufficient without abandoning all such products. To buy these items with money alone proves that one is dependent on others, and the fact that these complex instruments require the output of a multitude of workers means that they are dependent on an intricate arrangement of people not unlike our current system. Even if one detaches from that system geographically, he is still dependent upon it for his well-being and thus cannot make independent choices with regard to it.

Solar panels, for instance, can be an excellent source of electricity, especially for those living apart from a major power grid in the American Southwest, but it is assumed that they can only be manufactured by huge production facilities that require their own unsustainable power sources and a network of specialized workers. Relying on these means that one is as much a part of the system as the average resident of New York or Washington, D.C.

But here a distinction must be made. While no one can dispute the virtues of living in a way that is completely detached from modern civilization and thus without any of its products, it must be said that there is nothing inherently wrong with modern civilization and its products. If a society can avoid the drawbacks of mass civilization somehow, then there is no reason that it should not take advantage of its benefits.

And so the point of self-sufficiency is not to detach from other people in every way or to abandon modern techniques altogether; the point is to establish the ability to live on one's own in order to break down the exploitative Juggernaut. Only when an individual can provide for himself does he possess the ability to reject contracts that he finds unjust or abusive. Indeed, this essay makes no argument against interpersonal interaction, trade, or even the division of labor and specialism. All these techniques provide invaluable luxuries that may well be necessary to sustain the large populations we now have. But they can only be used in the interest of all participants if those participants can survive without them.

There is no reason that self-sufficient individuals and families should not be able to employ these techniques so as to make better use of time and resources, increase productivity, and extend the scope of their wealth. Doing so is just sound economics. No economizing person would discount the efficacy of dividing labor, for example, in a two or three-person association—one person shops, the next person cooks, the third does the dishes, and everyone enjoys a tasty meal. And extending this formula to ten, fifty, or a thousand and fifty people can be just as reasonable. As long as everyone involved understands the process and is willing to accept the consequences voluntarily—in other words, to take responsibility for their own actions within the association—the extension can be gained without a greater threat of mismanagement or exploitation. In theory, such a community could extend to millions or more; given the proper attention to self-sufficiency, there would be no natural limit to this kind of cooperative system.

By the same token, technology is soon approaching a point where this kind of large-scale collaboration might not even be necessary. Within the next few decades, one might predict, the manufacture of agricultural, industrial, and maintenance tools will be so uniform and self-sufficient that industry as we know it will be able to be conducted without interdependence at all. And so, in the interest of fully seeing through the theoretical exploration of this concept, we should examine the prospect of near-future advances that could change the way we think of technology, industry, and self-sufficiency altogether.

There are two converging paths on which this development is progressing. The first is the increasing autonomy of machines. For a century now, manufacturing plants have fine-tuned their facilities so that nearly all of the work that had been done by men is now done by machines and robots. They are more precise, more durable, and more resilient than their human counterparts, and have become much less expensive. The kind of innovations made by Japanese car manufacturers in the 1970s and '80s attest to the kind of efficiency robots can offer.

What's more is that, the more capable these machines become, the less their production is reliant on people, and the less we will have to rely on others to obtain the kind of goods that the modern economy has made possible. This efficacy extends beyond manufacturing plants and into individuals' day-to-day activities. The advance of techne means that, for each person to acquire and make use of the various tools, clothes, and gadgets that he has grown accustomed to in the twenty-first century, he will depend upon a robot and not some other person. In short, highly autonomous and capable robots lead to highly independent people.

For good reason, the increasing capabilities of computers and robots are matter for concern (several worthy science-fiction stories have illustrated such alarm). Without denying these apprehensions, however, it is possible to promote the pure potential lodged in the concept of a perfectly autonomous robot that is able to design, engineer, and manufacture any good desired by its owner, no matter how intricate or complex it might be. If such a robot did exist, for instance, an individual or family could live on their own without losing any of the luxuries of modern life. It may seem far-fetched, but, believe it or not, technology that exists today is leading us in that direction. It can be glimpsed in the automatic guided vehicles used in the military and the service robots used in manufacturing and maintenance.

This brings us to the second converging path, which is the consolidation of all tools, machines, and automated devices into a single application that can read various inputs and put out any number of products. Simply, there are too many desirable goods and services for a single machine to be able to output them all. Robots in automobile plants are stronger and more precise, but they can hardly do more than one or two tasks. To use these kind of robots would mean that each person would need a robot for his car's frame, his tires, his oils, seats, paint, and so on, not to mention a slew of robots for all the other goods he wanted. But the sophistication of computers has brought to light a foreseeable future where a single robot can take care of the production of not only one's car, but also his mp3 player, movie projector, clothing, water pump, solar panels, food, and water. The scope of such a vision might sound fantastic, but the initial steps have already been taken.

Consider, for example, computing in general. To begin, desktop computers were made of a dozen or so bulky electronic components that covered one's desk. Now, thanks to the vision of Xerox Corporation and the initiative of Apple, the desktop computer is a single component with perhaps a few satellites. In computing, the trend is toward the smaller, more compact, and simpler forms. So too will technology in general head in that direction. Nanotechnology promises a way to construct and reconstruct material on a molecular basis. Such a vision is not too far from the picture in which we see computers taking in any number of inputs—not the least fascinating are direct transmissions from the user's brain—and putting out any number of products—filet mignon, three yards of damask silk, a 1965 Ford Mustang, you name it.

Certainly, the specifics of such a machine have hardly been quantified by the author. And, because the development of this kind of machine is still rather far in the future, it is impossible to hypothesize all the contingencies that would come along with it. But its introduction would doubtless change life absolutely. For one, an individual would not have to depend on other people for necessities or luxuries. With the ability to produce anything he wanted, he could survive and thrive on his own and so would be wholly independent from others. That would mean no closed system, no competition, monopoly, or exploitation, and no occasion for government control. In short, such a machine would mean universal peace and prosperity.

It is easy to discount such a vision as naïve. The skeptic might well shrug off the prediction, assuming that oppression would continue in spite of such technical achievements. At least one recent literary work describes the kind of intentional action that would reject the dynamism of a machine like this°. But even the skeptic must admit that the logic is sound. The cause of all great conflicts—war, oppression, slavery, genocide, and so on—is a closed economy in which one can only gain at the expense of another, and the competition for resources that results. The availability of a machine like the one described above would eliminate all of that, leaving only man's inherent desire for companionship and wisdom as compelling forces of interaction.

> The site to browse is Future Timeline, *www.futuretimeline.net*, which offers predictions for the coming decades, centuries, and millennia and is sure to spark the imagination.

Opening a New Frontier

A fundamental aspect of self-sufficiency is land. Without a place to live, to grow crops, and to build a family, it is highly unlikely for one to become independent from others. Land is the essential means of production and thus the essential means of life. The path toward renaissance, then, rests in a frontier, beyond which is free land available for anyone with the will to settle there.

As covered on an earlier page, we can see the power of a frontier in the pure energy emitted over the last five hundred years. It is perhaps one of the most powerful forces in all of human history. The presence of free land available for anyone to settle served as a constant beacon of hope and freedom that drove man toward liberty in the New World and Old throughout the modern era. If we can agree that freedom is at the core of virtuous and prosperous peoples, then we must acknowledge the benefit of such a frontier. And, if we can acknowledge the role that the frontier played in shaping modern civilization, then we must seek out a comparable force in our own time.

Just as the opening of the frontier in the sixteenth century opened the economy in unprecedented ways, calling forth nothing less than a revolution in thought and action, so too would a new frontier open up the modern economy. We've already seen parallels in the opening of the virtual world with the Internet, in which producers are finding new outlets for their products and consumers are finding new avenues of merchantry. The oppression in a given system would no longer seem necessary, and all would suddenly begin working toward a more just social arrangement.

We know from recent experience that expanding our frontier into foreign countries would be a terrible course of action. Not only would we find it ethically reprehensible to impinge upon other peoples, to exploit their land and labor, but such a condition would also be ineffective in providing the kind of self-sufficiency that we seek. By nature, to exploit another's land is to be dependent on them and thus not in any way self-sufficient.

The challenge is to find a new frontier without the threat of encroachment on others. In a world increasingly closed off by growing populations, it is a dilemma that is intensifying with time. Taking a step back, however, we find that there may indeed be a solution within our own borders.

To begin, it must be said that the world is an immense place. The United States alone is exceedingly vast. The passenger of a transcontinental flight will witness a span of earth so wide and varied that it is almost unthinkable for the world to be overpopulated or for there to be a shortage of free land. Simply look down from eight miles high and one will see immeasurable spans of clean, open, and, one might say, free land.

One also sees clusters of cities and towns—streets, houses, parking lots, manufacturing plants, and similar municipal infrastructure—that can seem so expansive that one wonders how so many people can be out there and why they are building so much. But, on the whole, these areas of development are rather isolated compared to the undeveloped, open space. Indeed, survey data show that, since Turner's frontier thesis was published in the 1890s, the uninhabited land in the United States has expanded, not contracted, due to the consolidation of populations into cities. Open land is extensive and is seemingly growing more sizeable.

From even this brief examination, it must be acknowledged that there is at least the potential for expansion into this free land, and that a frontier of sorts exists today within our own country. With improved techne and a streamlined government, it is foreseeable for this internal frontier to slowly become the kind of frontier that pioneers from the sixteenth to the nineteenth century saw in the American West. The greatest hindrance to expansion currently faced by Americans might very well be the thought of having to give up one's standard of living to settle on the frontier, yet advanced techne will help to eliminate that notion, and one can conclude that no place on earth is really uninhabitable with the use of technology that is advanced enough.

It is also difficult to imagine moving to the country and thus escaping one's connection to and sway over the system, but a minimal and streamlined government, one that isn't in control of its citizens' every action, will take care of that impediment.

As with the expansion to the New World and later into the Western United States, the frontier simply needs to exist for it to be a factor in everyone's life. Having the option of self-sufficiency, even when one doesn't pursue it, can influence the thoughts and actions of workers and owners around the world. The frontier must simply be an option, and the economy will open from there.

Diversifying the states. To reestablish a frontier, then, the land need not be a limitless expanse of virgin soil—it need only be sufficient to house a number of influential pioneers whose migration would introduce the possibility of an alternative to the predominant system. Recall that not every

European soul migrated to America in the four hundred years after Columbus. And yet revolution was experienced throughout the West and beyond because of the mere opportunity. To replicate that kind of rebirth, all that is needed is a place for a small contingent to go. The rest of the population who stay behind can benefit from the pioneers' initiative.

Granted the notion that a free market can blossom from even a marginal frontier, it is possible that the land we already have is enough to provide it. All that is necessary is to designate any portion of that land as a place where a free society could be established and government intervention limited to its former role of protecting the free exchanges within that system. Of course, this means that there would need to be an entirely new state formed within the confines of the current nation, one that differs radically from the states that surround it.

Bizarre as it might sound, this notion was actually the crux of the federal system as the Founders envisioned the new country. The idea was that the United States would provide options for its inhabitants represented by the individual states. If an individual or family did not like the laws enacted by the government in Massachusetts, for instance, they could go to New York, Pennsylvania, or Maryland—Roger Williams set the precedent a century before the Declaration was even conjured. In all cases, diversified states would provide options and thus provide the sense of a perpetual frontier.

In the modern United States, with its outsized federal government and Welfare State controlling the nation's economy, the differences between the states have become rather negligible, although some do remain. For instance, some states have high income taxes while others have none. While this difference can equate to several hundreds of thousands of dollars in personal income tax per year, the fact is that federal income tax is so much greater than any given state's that there is no substantive difference. For most Americans, the only real difference between New York and Florida is that one has snow and the other doesn't.

And so the first step to opening a frontier is the diminution of the powers of the central government. If the steps of reform are taken as adumbrated in the previous chapter, we can be certain that the federal government will have minimal influence on the individual states, and so differences between the states will mean much more to individuals, families, and groups.

The Free State Project. In an effort to diversify the states and so provide some form of alternative to the American people, a number of plans have been proposed, all of which can make use of the unused land currently available and work within the framework of the Constitution. The libertarian Free State Project is one such plan. Developed in the past decade, the idea is to recruit a base number of 20,000 liberty-minded individuals to migrate to a given state (the one selected was New Hampshire) and, by means of voting and activism, minimize government interference there. The belief is that, given the right concentration of influence, the state will achieve complete liberty within a generation.

And, it is theorized, such a bastion of freedom could serve as a frontier to the rest of the country. With the kind of sanctuary envisioned by the Free State Project, it could be argued, all Americans would have the option of living in a completely free society if they were so inclined. That alternative would mean that owners and producers across the country could potentially lose their workers and consumer base, and so all workers and consumers would have a new source of leverage. More and more regions would follow the designated Free State's lead, thus bringing about a widespread rebirth of self-sufficient liberty.

Contingent as it is on the designated state's current system, this prospect is not as assured of establishing a frontier as, say, the discovery of a new virgin continent. One major hindrance to such a project's success is the fact that federal laws are growing exponentially and rather quash any liber-

---

The site to browse is The Free State Project: *www.freestateproject.org*

ties that a single state might provide its citizens. But if the reforms mentioned above are administered in the near future, the ability of individual states to create a new frontier is increased exponentially.

Nullification. Despite ever-growing federal presence, the states still hold some power in the equation, and living in one state is not necessarily the same as living in another even though they both fall under the jurisdiction of federal law. The differences that exist between states are substantial, especially in the field of regulation, and can be exploited by the citizens to no small effect. Just as they can vote with their pocketbooks to support or denounce certain corporations, citizens can vote with their feet and move to freer states in order to support those that protect their rights most agreeably.

One feature inherent in our Constitution that might be employed to engender greater independence from the federal government is the act of nullification. At least one prominent scholar, Thomas E. Woods, Jr., has supplied proponents of states rights with a solid history and justification of the procedure. Simply, nullification is a way for state governments, in the interest of their citizens and in defense of the Constitution, to reject or nullify laws that they find unconstitutional. Historical examples are the Kentucky and Virginia Resolutions of 1798 and '99, which protested the Alien and Sedition Acts, and the South Carolina Exposition and Protest, which declared the Tariff of 1828 an unconstitutional "abomination". By rejecting laws that the state finds unconstitutional, state governments can better underscore their commitment to the federation rather than revolting against it. It is yet to be determined whether such a measure could be successful against legislation such as the recent health care reform bill.

The book to read is *Nullification* by Thomas E. Woods, Jr.

Establishing charter cities. Another proposal that comes from a similar stance has been issued by academic Paul Romer in the form of charter cities. The concept is to take an unoccupied plot of land and a charter with the home country, and build a city whose inhabitants are allowed to function under their own rules, id est, beyond the control of the federal power. The intent is that by providing a somewhat protected arena for free interaction, the citizens of this charter city will grow and thrive in a way that citizens of other neighboring communities have been unable to do. With the allure of such a beacon, the rest of the country will see the benefits of the new rules and be compelled to change as well.

The example commonly used is that of Hong Kong, which has been a sort of accidental charter city in its form and effects. Among those effects, according to Romer and others, is the widespread, albeit slow, transition of totalitarian communist China into an increasingly free society and economic powerhouse. The concept can also be seen in the success of notable charter schools, which are based on the same concept of providing an area where a community can develop without the strains of the overarching system°.

Reasonably, Romer's focus is on developing nations such as Haiti, Guatemala, or Angola, which can see the greatest increase in standard of living from such a program. Still, the anxious American does not overlook the potential for such an opportunity stateside. A vision of such a prospect has recently been laid out in Joseph S. B. Morse's political novel, *Gods of Ruin*. Anyone can see that a bastion of freedom in the United States would provide immeasurable energy for the population despite the country's status as already one of the freest, most prosperous nations in the world. Ultimately, a charter city in the United States could provide what other charter cities could not—freedom built on the foundations of freedom, a possibility that redoubles the scope of potential virtue and productivity.

The site to browse is Charter Cities: *www.chartercities.org.*

Discovering new frontiers. Of course, all of the above frontiers are based primarily on land that has already been occupied and controlled, which means that the governments that already preside over them could pose a significant barrier to expansion. It is for this reason that the reader might excuse a brief examination of more advanced and less dependent possibilities. The wide-eyed futurist focuses on two other potential frontiers: water colonies and the colonization of other terrestrial planets.

Water colonies may provide a fine alternative to established land societies at some point within the next century, given a few foreseeable advances in technology, namely mass flotation devices and hydroponic plant growth. Once the technical capabilities are established, water colonies can be a viable alternative for pioneers willing to homestead in the ocean.

This is the aim of Patri Friedman's Seasteading Institute, which claims that the ocean is the natural and direct successor to the nineteenth-century homestead of the American West. With floating cities, one's life need not be much different than it is in the modern world, other than the threat of the occasional rogue wave, and the fact that the catch of the day would be fresher than anything you could get at Anthony's Grotto. Migration would be a matter of using inexpensive water or air transportation, and the living space could be manufactured at a cost not much greater than that of building a home on land. The upshot, of course, is that such an endeavor would essentially expand man's potential living space by 150% around the world.

The colonization of other planets is a much more complicated possibility. Not only would migration consist in costly space travel, but the available destinations don't suit man's lifestyle very much. Mars gets as warm as Antarctica on a winter night and has no atmosphere; Venus is covered in thick clouds of sulfuric acid and carbon dioxide; and Mercury is so close to the sun that SPF googolplex might not be strong enough to avoid adverse reaction. Plans have been sketched out for the colonization of each and could be reasonable pursuits a few centuries hence.

Moon colonization has been proposed as a launch pad for colonization of Mars and seems to be the next reasonable step in space exploration. For other reasons, the colonization of Venus might be the most logical effort in the near future. NASA research scientist Geoffrey Landis has shown that not only does Venus provide an almost identical mass to that of Earth, but it is foreseeable to build aerostatic colonies some 50 kilometers above the planet's surface where the pressure is identical to Earth's and breathable air is abundant. Landis' paper, "Colonization of Venus", is a marvel to read and provides the kind of vision that was perhaps found in the sixteenth century with regard to colonization of the New World. As we can see, it is not only sci-fi novelists who can map out workable solutions to these and other problems—it is becoming real science.

The point to take from this reverie is that the frontier exists somewhere out there, and the only thing stopping us from being able to explore it and thus take advantage of its presence is our own technical and psychological limitations. If we are able to continue the tremendous progress achieved in the last three hundred years or so, then water colonies, space colonization, and methods not even considered yet will become as much a matter of fact for our descendents as the movement west was for sixteenth-century Europeans.

The sites to browse are:

The Seasteading Institute:
www.seasteading.org

The New Mars forum:
www.newmars.com

"Colonization of Venus" (2003) by Geoffrey A. Landis:
ntrs.nasa.gov/archive/nasa/casi.ntrs.nasa.gov/20030022668_2003025525.pdf

Mapping Out the Good Place

In considering the past five hundred years of economic development and all the changes that have taken place, it is easy to lose sight of the truly amazing possibilities that we have before us. While no one will doubt the wild increase in wealth we have seen, the limitations, confines, and over-bearing laws that assail Americans and Westerners from every angle seem to overshadow positive reflections and leave with us only a sense of com-petition, relentless pressure to perform, and a condition that practically eliminates hope, strength, and will. The intent of this last section has been to offer a glimpse at the possibilities that could develop in the near future. If they are given the proper attention, their energy alone can help to make them a reality.

After all, we cannot forget that the Renaissance of classical thought and arts that generated so much energy and brilliance at the outset of the modern era began well before the discovery of any new lands made the Age of Exploration possible. As early as the fourteenth century, glimmers of a rebirth began to flutter through the West, and, indeed, the push to expand and explore was alive and well in the mid-fifteenth century, long before Columbus set out to make his westward voyage.

The lesson to learn from this is that true renaissance takes place in the hearts and minds of men and is available whenever those men are mature and willing enough to seek a better life. As long as we are close-minded and immature in our hopes and dreams, we will be limited to the prisons we have built for ourselves. Once we can break free from our petty needs and the confinement we have manufactured for ourselves, we will have our own renaissance.

Combined with a push toward self-sufficiency, the establishment of a frontier would doubtless provoke a renewed sense of optimism throughout the culture, as occurred in the sixteenth century. Spurred by the discovery of the New World and the promise of free land, Western thinkers made a dramatic turn toward what Thomas More termed 'Utopia', or 'No Place', a fictitious country in which the writer could design his ideal society. Tomma-so Campanella, Francis Bacon, and later even Shakespeare, among others, all participated in the exercise, thus bringing the hopes and visions of a promising new life to the printed page, and, ultimately, to real life.

The renaissance described in this chapter would likely usher in the same kind of literary optimism. After a twentieth-century filled with bleak literature and pessimism defined, if anything, as 'dystopia', a renaissance would return our intellectual attention in the direction of the ideal—what could and should be as opposed to what is and should not be.

Before our culture heads in that direction, it is worth altering the verbiage to reflect the real purpose of the exercise—to map out the ideal, not necessarily what is absent from our current condition, but what our condition could possibly become. Barzun has suggested the term 'Eutopia', meaning 'Good Place', a modification that could differentiate the coming genre from the old. It is with this distinction in mind that one might look forward to the potential literary masterpieces to come. The imaginative will have a hard time quelling the urge to build on such a thought. And, though we cannot be sure what ultimate shape this Eutopia would look like, in conclusion of this study, we can take the time to speculate on some of its more distinct aspects. Here, then, is a truly golden little sketch of the best condition of a people on an island called Eutopia:

We first view this happy place from afar, noting its more prominent features. The ideal community's population is about 60,000 people, enough to provide a wide variety of interests and talent and yet small enough to ensure intimacy with most others one comes into contact with throughout the day. All such communities around the time of Eutopia range between 1,000 to 100,000 people, depending on the topography and abundance of natural resources possessed by the community. The result is a countless number of fair-sized communities linked to others via the Internet as well as old-fashioned high-speed highways and rail. For the most part, teleconferencing and telecommuting make contact with other towns instantaneous and thus make travel solely a matter of leisure and adventure.

Of course, the people of Eutopia like to travel to various places in the world—the fjords in Scandinavia, the Serengeti in Africa, or the Outback in Australia, for instance, or to the moon or space stations for a weekend—the views are worth the expenses. But for the most part, everything they need is within reach right at home. Their friends and family, their favorite restaurants and clubs, their favorite books and libraries, their favorite games and virtual worlds are all accessible from their living rooms.

Given an emphasis on self-sufficiency, total production in Eutopia is lower than it was in the Old World. Most families provide their own necessities and thus have less time for specialized work for trade. Decreasing specialized work decreases overall output. At the same time, Eutopians are more productive because they have fewer distractions, and they are stronger-willed due to their connection to their end products. There is less waste in Eutopia, and fewer goods and services are directed toward making the community work (exempli gratia, there are no hour-long commutes to work, no automobile gas for those commutes, no breakdowns on the side of the road, no headaches due to the breakdowns, and no aspirin for those headaches).

It is reasonable to argue that the higher productivity and reduced waste very well compensate for and possibly overcome any reduced productivity the Eutopians face. Given a happy and industrious populous, anything is possible. There is no reason to think that, in such a community of intentional industrialists, output would not far exceed that of previous cultures' cities, in which citizens had to rise above rivalry and malaise; entrepreneurs had to account for a slew of regulations, licenses, and taxes; and consumers had to hurdle their own regulations and taxes to purchase even the necessities. Citizens of Eutopia have to deal with none of these, and so their volition leads directly to their product.

As a result, their volition is limitless. With no external barrier to their ambitions, Eutopians are inclined to cultivate more innovative ambitions. They are constantly reminded of the absolute vastness of human ingenuity when given complete sovereignty over their means of production and the infinite reward of a more virtuous and productive humanity. For the citizens of Eutopia, there is no barrier to their accomplishments.

A form of money is used, naturally, to reduce the friction of trade, but it is not a very prominent feature in the society. There are several different currencies used in every neighborhood, each having its own value depending on its usefulness in being accepted among the people of the good place. Since there is no national currency, people accept what they believe to be the soundest and most consistent tender. As a result, most currencies, which take the form of zeros and ones in electronic banks, are backed by redeemable gold and silver—a throwback to an ancient time. Strict attention to reserves means that no banks lend out deposits, which means that there are no panics or runs. Most industry comes about via the old-fashioned way of saving, building capital, and investing.

Speculation occurs almost without question as a natural offshoot of money and banking. But the speculation is seen naturally for what it is—risk-taking—and so all risk is assumed by the speculators. At times, these speculators succeed in finding good investments and strike it rich; at other times, their endeavors fail. Either way, they assume the rewards or penalties, and few if any others are affected. But failure is rarely ever seen in this economy because, for the most part, all investors realize the risk involved and take the necessary steps to ensure their investments will succeed.

Responsibility in economic actions leads to a general air of responsibility in all actions; as economic freedom secures political freedom, so too does economic responsibility lead to political responsibility. There is thus little need for military, police, lawyers, or judges in Eutopia. Though, in another light, it could be said that everyone in Eutopia is a guard, policeman, lawyer, and judge. There are laws, but no one relies on a formalized written diktat to rule their lives—common sense rules with a much greater force than any enormous register of legislation anyway.

The laws that exist are minimal, simple, and mostly geared at providing negative freedoms. The most respected is, of course, 'Vulnero Nemo', the Latin for 'Harm No One', the crux of Eutopian law and that of most of its neighbors. Its success, and that of all other laws in Eutopia, is based on the fact that everyone can agree on it—it can be unanimous, and so does not necessitate conformity. For the most part, laws are limited to the natural ones that arise from the organic exchange of thoughts and goods between reasonable men.

In Eutopia, there is no occasion to hurt or exploit anyone since no one is forced to agree to disagreeable terms. Everyone has the ability to be self-sufficient, and so everyone is at leisure to take or reject contracts based on their fairness or their ability to be mutually advantageous. All actions are thus voluntary, and all interaction is based on mutual gain. There is no struggle, no alienation, no hardship. Rather, the open and free society in Eutopia brings forth a flowering of innovation, creativity, and intellect that was unprecedented in past cultures. Focus is centered on virtue, what makes life good, and the kind of joys that interaction between human beings can bring.

Religion, science, the arts, and education are of the utmost importance in this good place, without the constant social pressures of ages past. It is not uncommon for visitors to marvel at the way the citizens continually talk of history and cultural achievements, ideas and philosophical wonders, quite as their descendants did in Jerusalem and Athens, Rome and Venice, Amsterdam and London, Madrid and New York. Like their forebears, Eutopians like to ask the deep questions: What is the nature of the good? What is the meaning of life? Is man capable of self-rule?

To the great satisfaction of the Eutopians, this last question is of primary interest in all discourse. And, as it turns out, it is answered almost always in the affirmative.

COMPENDIUM

I. Wealth

1. Mundus Novus

How the discovery of the New World precipitated a resurgence in the Natural Law (1492 - 1650)

The question that defines the modern era is whether man is capable of self-rule. Prior to 1500, it had been assumed that man was incapable of self-rule, that a system of hierarchy must be established for any semblance of order to prevail. After 1500, with the discovery of the New World, this fundamental assumption was challenged.

The key was the open of a frontier of free land. With an abundance of free land, men could reject the hierarchic system and strike out on their own. The ability to provide for oneself led to the ability to rule oneself; self-sufficiency led to self-rule.

The development of self-rule was a long, complex process met with constant resistance from the start. Reactionary forces were able to maintain feudal systems well into the modern era and even bolstered them to stay relevant. The result was a trend that ran parallel to and countered self-rule, the oppression and destruction of native peoples Africa, the Americas,

Southeast Asia, and Australia. This contradictory development was seen in the economic sphere in the dominant form of policy in the 16th and 17th centuries, Mercantilism, which could only be overcome after the power of the New World could be harnessed completely.

2. The Origin of Wealth
The establishment of private property, industry, and a subjective value
(1550 - 1675)

Where self-rule was able to flourish, economic strength grew as a result, making it an irresistible force in the progress of society. Economically, the development was witnessed in the establishment of property rights. Whereas land and goods had formerly been owned by the lord or king, now it was to be possessed and maintained by the individuals or groups who made use of them.

As individuals assumed ownership, so they assumed the ability to profit from their output, which naturally spurred greater production and, ultimately, greater aggregate wealth. The concept of wealth shifted from being dependent on others to being wholly dependent upon one's own industry.

The stress placed on the individual ushered in the notion that value is subjective. Previous economic theory stated that goods and services had a 'just price' that was the same for all notwithstanding needs and wants. Now it was believed that value could change and that it was dependent on its supply and the consumer's demand for the good or service.

3. Laissez Faire, Morbleu!
From the subjective value to specialism, labor division, and free trade
(1600 - 1776)

Subjective value encourages trade, where two or more are willing to exchange goods they value less to acquire goods they value more. In this way, subjective value means that two or more can gain in a given exchange.

In effort to take full advantage of this mutual gain, Western cultures developed techniques that further exploited subjective value. These techniques rested primarily in specialism and the division of labor, in which individuals and groups focus on the production of one or a few goods in order to optimize output and so are able to offer more for an eventual trade. These techniques, coupled with machine industry and scientific management, increased wealth throughout the West to unprecedented degrees.

Trade also comes with costs, those being, most directly, the cost of trading and distributing the goods, the mental numbness caused by monotonous specialized tasks, and, most importantly, an interdependency that ties traders together. As long as trade is voluntary, an interdependent relationship can remain mutually beneficial.

4. The Abstraction of Wealth
The consequences of the widespread use of money
(1600 - 1800)

In order to better facilitate trade and thus exploit production to its greatest capacity, societies have instated the widespread use of money. Because of its abstract nature, money distorts the economy and changes the notion of wealth altogether.

The widespread use of money democratizes wealth so that it is worth the same no matter who it comes from or what is done to earn it; money also allows for the practically infinite storage of wealth and the simultaneous possession of wealth by more than one party; and, most significantly, money condenses the pursuit of wealth into a single, objective endeavor, in which participants are all seeking the same thing. Given its flexibility and usefulness, money is often rightly regarded as having value in itself and not unreasonably seen as the most important good in the economy.

5. Complexity
The introduction of credit, banking, investments, and insurance
(1650 - present)

Once money is in wide use throughout an economy, institutions arise that seek to produce and augment it as with any other commodity. Through the use of banks, money is circulated, accumulated, and lent out in a process of fractional reserve banking, which grows the money supply and thus the amount of economic activity in a given society. Credit also further entrenches a given society in mutual dependence by uniting persons involved in the process of the multiplying money.

Credit often leads to speculation in the form of lending money without collateral on the promise of future returns. This form of credit introduces money into the economy ex nihilo and so presents a unique form of risk. Speculation is profitable when the economy is eager for such investment, but it fails when the economy is not in want of the investment, typically causing economic distress and often panics and runs on banks.

The pattern witnessed in all investment and especially that of speculation is of boom, bubble, and bust, through which the economy has experienced severe swings in production. Particular instances of this boom and bust are seen in the various manias that have sprung up throughout the West, and the overall effect is seen in the Business Cycle.

II. COMPETITION

1. *The Close of the Economic System*
The economic consequences of the close of the Western frontier
(1800-1890)

After 400 years of economic development, the era's central driving force had come to an end with the closing of the Western frontier in 1890. With this event, the notion of free land, available for anyone to assume had vanished, and so all were left to make due with the system that existed. This effectively brought to a halt and set into reverse many of the vital economic and cultural aspects of the previous centuries.

Economically, the close meant that independence was no longer possible and that to flourish or even survive, one would have to go through other people. This interdependency meant that wealth in general had become controlled and thus limited; the economy had closed.

This condition is best seen in the pressures put on money during the close. Because the people were dependent on each other, they could only achieve what they needed by obtaining and making use of money. The concepts of supply and demand were supplanted by that of effective supply and demand, or supply and demand with purchasing power, the only kind of supply and demand that would have an impact in the closed economy.

The ascent of money meant that everyone in the economy was striving for the same thing, which meant that the old thoughts of mutually advantageous trade had become obsolete, and that one could only gain at the expense of others.

2. Interdependency
From a closed economy to a mutually dependent society
(1850 - present)

While mutual dependency had always been a consequence of modern economic constructs, it had always been optional. With the close of the frontier, it had become compulsory. As a result, the average Westerner's life was growing more and more interdependent with those of others.

By 1900, interdependency was a fact of modern life, and no one could expect to survive without interacting, cooperating, and working with others. This phenomenon is seen in the rapid increase in the service sector and the decline of agricultural and industrial sectors of Western economies.

The psychological effects of interdependency can be summed up in the notion that one's thoughts and actions are all contingent on other people, and that one's personal will becomes secondary to that of the masses. Choices are no longer made of volition, but by the influence of peers, superiors, and society in general.

Interdependency can lead to cooperation and increased production, but, in instances of limited resources, it can also lead to competition and conflict.

3. The Transformation of Wealth
From interdependency to an objective value of wealth
(1870 - present)

The more interdependent people are, the more they are reliant on the agreed means of exchange in their society--money. In the most extreme cases of interdependency, everything one wants to do is dependent on one form or another of an exchange of money. Though all humans desire real wealth in the end, the only way they can obtain that real wealth is by the acquisition and application of money, and so, for all practical purposes, wealth becomes money.

The transformation of wealth from real goods into money can be seen throughout the last century in the various ways in which goods and services have lost value. The introduction of use-and-throw-away goods, multitasking, and the decline of service in a service economy mark the widespread transformation. It can also be seen in the elevation of money as a status symbol and use of monetary statistics to gauge well-being.

Another piece of evidence is found in the shift in attitude toward the rich. With the belief that wealth is money, it is thought that no two parties can gain in a monetary exchange, and that the one who acquires more money is the only one who gains in wealth.

4. The Zero-Sum Problem
The strictly competitive condition and mutually exclusive gain
(1850-1950)

The more desirable money has become in the pursuit of wealth, the more that pursuit has become a strictly competitive endeavor. When everyone is striving for the same thing, such as in a money economy where everyone is striving for money, one can only gain at the expense of another. The pursuit of money is a zero-sum game where one can only win if others lose.

Technically, since the pay-off can fluctuate, it is a non-zero-sum game, but, since the competition between contestants means gain by one necessarily means loss by another, the effect is the same as a technical zero-sum condition. In a money-based economy, all actions amount to part of a strategy in the effort to gain more money. Since all such goals are competitive, the corollary is that another must lose for one to be successful.

Competition has traditionally spurred creativity and encouraged participants to develop alternative and often more efficient and effective methods of production. The Survival of the Fittest applied to the economic realm has meant that only the best and most capable survive the contest. At the same time, competition has encouraged conniving and cheating as an alternative to creativity and innovation. The result has been in many cases dubious and outright unjust advantage of given parties over others.

5. Monopoly

From a competitive condition to the control of wealth
(1870-present)

Competition is seen as positive from the perspective of those who do not have to compete, and negative from the perspective of those who do since the former can enjoy the rewards of the efforts from the latter. The strategy is to monopolize that which people must compete for, money in the modern economy.

The ownership of money can lead to the acquisition of more money. The more desperate one is to obtain money, the more effort one is willing to give in return for it. If, on the other hand, one is able to secure a large amount of money and withhold it from others, one will be able to demand more for the money. Thus, it can be profitable to be rich, even if one is not making use of the wealth.

In a closed system, wealth becomes a matter of relative power over others. Large fortunes and industrial conglomerates are formed to this end. The decades after the close of the frontier saw an exponential growth in the number of conglomerates and trusts.

6. Exploitation

From the consolidation of wealth to the exploitation of the
disadvantaged (1880 - present)

In a closed economy, individuals and companies had become capable of controlling large sums of wealth and thus dictating the terms of contracts with those who did not have similar stockpiles of wealth. Given its altered composition, the economy of the twentieth century could no longer be called a Capitalism, but rather a Vulgar Capitalism.

Exploitation comes in two main forms: pricing consumer goods higher than they are worth, and paying employees less than they are worth. Both are conducted extensively throughout the world, though the latter is more noticeable and reprehensible. A third form of exploitation is pollution or reckless use of natural resources at the expense of the public.

Since contracts are technically based under free terms, consumers, workers, and the public are responsible for their own exploitation. Producers and owners are no more malicious than their victims; they are simply in a better position to take advantage of others. Since consumers, workers, and the public seek the same ultimate goal of wealth, they serve as engines to further entrench themselves in their plight.

III. Government

1. The Great Switch

The argument for large-scale governmental control of wealth
(1910 - 1940)

The monopoly of wealth and resultant exploitation experienced in the Vulgar Capitalism of the turn of the century led reformers to conclude that the laissez-faire form of society was no longer sufficient in providing the people with life, liberty, and the pursuit of property. It was established that an external party must step in and conduct affairs in the economy so as to protect against exploitation and ensure everyone had necessities.

As a result, Western countries shifted focus from negative freedoms, in the form of what government cannot do, to positive freedoms, in the form of what people should be able to do. Taxes were imposed and welfare instruments were established to provide these positive freedoms.

A major aspect of this process in America was the introduction of a central bank, which had been designed to control the money supply and reduce the effects of the Business Cycle. Turmoil partially caused by central bank actions led to the Great Depression in which the Welfare State's role in the economy grew exponentially and became irreversible.

2. New Feudalism
The structure of state government
(1920 - 1970)

Perceived early success of state governments ingrained their place in Western Civilization. The form of state governments differed throughout the West, though all attempted to combine the entire economy into a single enterprise conducted by government officials. This was to bring monopoly to its farthest extent.

The success of state government relied on two premises: that productivity could improve boundlessly with increased scope and that the planned economy could operate as well as the free market. The first has been shown to be false by the unproductive effects of bureaucracy. The second has been shown to be false by inherent deficiencies in planned economies. The deficiencies take two forms: that economies planned by state governments necessarily eliminate the price system and thereby cannot gauge demand and so cannot adjust supply appropriately, and that public officials are not able to put aside personal interests in order to govern the economy justly.

Public officials are like all other humans with needs and wants as well as the potential for errors in judgment. Thus, they are liable like anyone else to succumb to mistakes and corruption. They are also motivated to reward supporters and special interests even when it comes at the expense of their constituents as a whole. The consequences of this are seen throughout Western economies over the course of the last hundred years.

3. The Costs of Transferring Wealth
The constitution of government actions
(1930 - present)

The fundamental action of state governments is to transfer wealth, a process which comes with it many costs, some seen and some unseen. Government transfers wealth in three ways: fiscal policy (taxes and spending), regulation, and monetary policy (control of the money supply through the central bank).

The first cost is to the parties from which government transfers the wealth, which is presumably the rich, though it can easily be deferred to the poor. The second cost comes in the amount of time and resources dedicated to the transfer process and governmental infrastructure. The third cost comes in the form of the distorted economy and the convoluted efforts individuals and companies must make to accommodate the governmental interference.

Evidence of the last is seen in the effects on supply and demand that price controls have, which produce shortages and surpluses of goods and services and ultimately the waste of otherwise useful resources. Government intervention is thought to increase wealth by accelerating the circulation of money, but often ends up directed at the destruction of real wealth.

State control of the economy by means of monetary policy is particularly powerful since it affects the supply and demand of all goods and services. Monetary policy also tends to harm those who are farthest from the government because the benefits of increases in the money supply are experienced incrementally from most connected to least connected to the government.

4. In Perpetuum

The perpetuity innate in a wealth-transferring system
(1950 - 2000)

The process of transferring wealth attracts individuals and groups that seek to gain from the process by influencing state action in their favor. The more money government transfers, the more interest lobbyists take in the government's action, and compels more transfers. Since each transfer necessarily costs others, they are encouraged to join in the lobbying, creating a self-perpetuating cycle of ever-expanding government intervention. Factions within the system work together to generate interest and secure higher contributions.

Mechanisms designed to alleviate strains on the system can only increase government action and thus further this self-perpetuating problem. Attempts at solving the problem add to it and end up making matters worse. The extent of this process can be seen in the exponential growth of rules and regulations that the government has imposed on its people.

5. The Moral Effect of the State

From government intervention to the incapacity for self-rule
(1960 - present)

As government wealth transfers had increased abstract wealth throughout the economy during the mid-twentieth century, the social fabric of the country was degrading. Government action intended to provide for those in need tends to weaken moral capacity and make people more needy of government action. Government agencies tend to create the need that they seek to satisfy.

This is seen in the perpetual status of most government programs, which are implemented to support needy individuals and groups and end up altering their behavior such that they can no longer subsist without the government assistance.

Individuals and companies change their approach in earning income from producing real wealth to becoming too big for the government to allow to fail. Recent financial catastrophes show the effects of an economy infused with state-sponsored moral hazard.

Under control of a planned economy, individuals and groups are given incentive to free ride on the work of others. The goal of social cohesion is replaced by the reality of increased social tension and selfishness marked by the reduction of voluntary charity. Government action renders the society incapable of self-rule and in need of protection by the state.

IV. Autarchy

1. Reassessment
From a closed to an open system
(present)

Proposed solutions to problems rely on the system as it stands, and so tend to add to the problem and thus make it worse. The system is organize in a way in which one can only gain if others lose. A real solution would transcend this zero-sum condition and enable all actions to be mutually beneficial.

Opening the economy would require all those involved to be able to reject the current system as it stands, which means that all must be self-sufficient or capable of providing for oneself. The prospect of self-sufficiency issues three central concerns in an interdependent age which hinge on the likelihood that the modern standard of living will diminish, the improbability of finding a means to transcend the system, and the logistical difficulties of such an endeavor.

2. Working within the System
Relief from the confines of the modern system
(present - 2020)

Relief from the ills of the system must take the form of drawing away from rather than participating in it. So too must these actions be economically sound for participants to justify them.

Efforts that meet these criteria can be listed from most basic to most intricate: simplifying and removing unnecessary clutter from one's life, prioritizing the elements in one's life and designating them as either essential or superfluous, rejecting the call to act in the interest of society and social responsibility, shifting focus on one's economic activities from the spread-out and distant to the local arena, buying from producers that are independent from large conglomerate firms, using one's buying power to create leverage against outsized organizations, storing wealth in the interest of building capital, initiating a business to alleviate bureaucracy, and exercising one's ability to engineer sound leadership by voting.

3. Fixing the System
The process of dismantling the system
(present - 2050)

Reform measures have traditionally relied upon aspects of the system to fix the system, and have thus tended to add to the system they intend to correct. True reform can only come from outside of the system and must take the form of removing obstacles to free enterprise within the system. This process will focus on eliminating governmental barriers primarily because government poses the greatest and most concentrated threat to self-sufficiency. Other threats that have existed in the past can be dealt with better in the absence of government interference.

The reform process begins with the central aspect of all economic action, money. In order to diminish barriers and allow for self-sufficiency, the production, distribution, and possession of money must be unrestricted, which means that no laws should be established against the free administration of money and that the national currency should be abolished to ensure viable alternatives. The Federal Reserve should be dismantled in a five-part procedure that carries the economy from strict dependence on the national currency to private currencies backed primarily by specie.

Regulation should be assumed by local, polycentric organizations as opposed to the distant, central government, the process of which can already be seen in various organizations across the country. State fiscal policy should be streamlined by downsizing and eliminating programs that are economically unsound and counterproductive. Finally, the government should be brought up to date with the use of modern technology.

4. Transcending the System
The possibility of pursuing alternatives to the current system
(present - 2300)

The modern system can be seen as a dual force which has brought both unprecedented standard of living and unprecedented interdependency. In effort to diminish the difficulties posed by the latter, guards must be established to prevent diminishing the former. Using modern technical advances, self-sufficiency can be attained without giving up the benefits of interdependent life.

The Internet provides the key resource in this endeavor in its ability to grant access to a practically infinite source of information, which is the most essential aspect of self-sufficiency. The Internet also allows for individuals and groups to keep in contact with society from afar by enabling telecommuting, merchantry, and socializing.

Other advances have made do-it-yourself projects more reasonable and cost-effective, including securing a water supply, gardening, creating clothing, building shelter, conducting sanitation, and generating power locally. Future technical advances promise to extend the power of individuals by use of autonomous machines.

Self-sufficiency can be bolstered by the introduction of a new frontier. This is possible by means of diversifying existing sovereign states to the extent that all alternatives are made available, the denial of national and international hegemony, and the exploration and settling of new territories beyond the confines of land and the terrestrial planet.

SOURCE NOTES

I. WEALTH

17   *foundation*   Changes in Medieval Europe did occur, embodied in the Great Schisms of 1054 and 1378-1417, as well as the Umayyad invasion of Hispania in the eighth century and the Crusades of the eleventh, twelfth, and thirteenth centuries. These were largely political in nature and dealt with who should be granted the honor of ruling the Occident, not how the rule should be maintained.

22   *Hispaniola alone*   See Carl Ortwin Sauer, *The Early Spanish Main*, Berkley, 1992.

32   *solid knowledge*   See Jacques Barzun, *From Dawn to Decadence*, New York, 2000.

37   *these epochs*   See Achille Loria, *The Economic Foundations of Society*, English translation, London, 1899.

50   *reversed*   See Arthur Vermeersch, "Usury", *The Catholic Encyclopedia, Vol. 15.*, New York, 1912.

55   *abundant*   See Martin de Azpilcueta, *Manual de Confesores y Penitentes*, Salamanca, 1956.

127   *liquidity*   See Raghuram G. Rajan, "Has Financial Development Made the World Riskier?", *International Monetary Fund*, Washington, 2005.

130   suffering   See Jean Charles Léonard de Sismondi, *New Principles of Political Economy, Vol. 1*, 1819.

II. Competition

141   privilege   See Albert Jay Nock, "Henry Geroge: Unorthodox American", *Scribner's Magazine*, 1934.

169   *employment*   See Mack Ott, "The Growing Share of Services in the U.S. Economy -- Degeneration or Evolution?", Federal Reserve Bank of St. Louis, 1987.

179   degrees   See John Meynard Keynes, *The General Theory of Employment, Interest, and Money*, Basingstoke, 1936.

181   *painful*   See Louis Uchitelle, "The American Middle, Just Getting By", *The New York Times*, August 1, 1999.

184   *individual*   From the Constance Garnett translation, Fyodor Dostoevsky, *The Brothers Karamazov*, Part II, book IV, Vintage Russian Library, 1950.

193   *column current*   Credited to syndicated columnist Ellen Goodman (born 1941).

195   *service*   See Staffan B. Linder, *The Harried Leisure Class*, New York, 1970.

198   *something else*   See Walter Kerr, *The Decline of Pleasure*, 1966.

199   *quality*   See Staffan B. Linder, *The Harried Leisure Class*, New York, 1970.

209   *arithmetic*   See Paul Krugman, "For Richer", The New York Times Magazine, October 20, 2002, in which the author argued the simple case that the economy is a zero-sum condition: "And here's a radical thought: if the rich get more, that leaves less for everyone else. That statement -- which is simply a matter of arithmetic -- is guaranteed to bring accusations of 'class warfare.' "

222   *what they do*   See Warren Buffett, *Letters to Shareholders 1977-1983*.

227   *relationships*   See Herbert Spencer, *Principles of Biology*, London, 1864.

229   *story*   As eloquently paraphrased by Will Durant in *The Story of Philosophy*, New York, 1926.

231   *defended*   See Herbert Spencer, "The Morals of the Trade", *The Westminster Review*, April 1859. Also, see Spencer, *Essays: Scientific, Political, and Speculative, vol. 3*, 1854.

257   *Fig. 25*   This notation aims to illustrate wealth distribution in the United States using the Banzhaf Power Index. The population is divided into six equally populous sections (as in Fig. 24) and given a number of 'votes' based on the percentage of wealth that section owns. The first group, the nation's poorest, is given a single vote based on its amount of wealth. Since the last group, the nation's wealthiest, owns 25 times the wealth of the first, it has 25 votes. The number of votes needed to maintain a majority is 19, a number which the wealthiest Americans automatically eclipse.

264   *conglomerates*   These figures are attributed to Joseph Schumpeter in Thomas K. McCraw, *Prophet of Innovation*, 2007. Also see Jesse Markham, "Survey of the Evidence of Findings on Mergers", *Business Concentration and Price Policy, Princeton, 1955*; Ralph Nelson, *Merger Movements in American Industry, 1895-1956*, Princeton, 1959; and Naomi R. Lamoreaux, *The Great Merger Movement in American Business, 1895-1904*, Cambridge, 1985.

270   *possessors*   See Hilaire Belloc, *The Servile State*, London, 1912.

278   *suspicion*   A famous controversy arose in November 2009 when thousands of emails and other documents produced by noted climate scientists at the University of East Anglia in the United Kingdom were made public, revealing apparent misconduct, misinformation, and blurring facts in research and publicity of climate change.

280   *in place*   As recounted by writer John Cassidy in his book *How Markets Fail*, New York, 2009.

III. GOVERNMENT

293   *tyranny*   See Walter Rauschenbusch, "The Ideals of Social Reformers", *American Journal of Sociology, 2*, Sept. 1896.

299   *by law*   See Frederick Jackson Turner, "Pioneer Ideals and the American University", published in *The Frontier in American History*, New York, 1920.

306   *recession*   See Federal Reserve Bank, *Annual Report 1923*, Washington D.C., 1924.

314   *responsibility*   See Eric Hoffer, *The True Believer*, New York, 1951.

316   *it works*   See Lincoln Steffens, *The Autobiography of Lincoln Steffens*, 1931.

322   *website*   The correspondence can be found on the user interface designer Dustin Curtis' blog at *http://dustincurtis.com/dear_dustin_curtis.html*. The subject website, *www.AA.com*, has since been redesigned with a much more user-friendly interface.

323   *1965 to '73*   See Max Gammon, *Health and Security: Report on Public Provision for Medical Care in Great Britain*, London, December 1976.

328   *wants and needs*   A 1911 bill changed the apportionment method in the United States to fix the number of representatives in the House at 435, the default number at that time. The result has been an increase in constituents per representative ever since, despite a clause in the Constitution that states there should be a representative for every 30,000 citizens. The number of representatives had increased from 1776 to 1910, when the average population for each district was around 200,000 people. In 2010, the average population for each district is around 700,000 people.

333   *mankind*   See Frédéric Bastiat, *The Law*, London, 1848.

333   *someone else*   See Ronald Reagan, *First Inaugural Address*, January 20, 1981.

335   *mind-boggling*   See "John Stossel Goes to Washington", *20/20*, written by John Stossel, ABC News, 2001.

343   *generated by ADM*   See James Bovard, "Archer Daniels Midland: A Case Study In Corporate Welfare", *Cato Policy Analysis No. 241*, September 26, 1995.

345   *homemakers*   See Thomas A. Schatz, "Most Outrageous Government Waste", *The Freeman, Vol. 46, Issue 6*, June 1996.

354   *have in view*   William Graham Sumner's essay, "The Forgotten Man", was originally published with the title, "On the Case of a Certain Man Who Is Never Thought Of", as a part of the book, *What Social Classes Owe Each Other*, 1883.

357   *sector*   See Manufacturers Alliance/MAPI, *Economic Analysis*, September 2004, which uses data from the U.S. Department of Commerce, Bureau of Economic Analysis.

366   *the lease*   See John Tierney, "At the Intersection of Supply and Demand", *The New York Times Magazine*, May 4, 1997.

368   *black teens*   See Walter Williams, "Government Sanctioned Restraints that Reduce Economic Opportunities for Minorities", *Policy Review, Vol. 2*, Fall 1977.

383   *few years*   See the Congressional Budget Office's *Budget and Economic Outlook: Fiscal Years 2009 to 2019*, Washington D.C., 2009.

384   *laborers*   See Stephane Fitch, "Gilt-Edged Pensions", *Forbes Magazine*, January 22, 2009.

393   *country*   See the Associated Press article, "Virginia Governor Race a Snapshot of U.S. Attitudes", October 20, 2009.

399   *government*   See Benjamin Disraeli's essay, "Vindication of the English Constitution in a Letter to a Noble and Learned Lord", also published in the book, *Disraeli on Whigs and Whiggism*, ed. William Hutchenson, New York, 1914.

406   *our dreams*   As quoted in "Episode 7: The City and the World", *New York: A Documentary Film*, directed by Ric Burns, PBS, 1999.

406   *doubled*   As quoted by Milton Friedman on Richard Heffner, *Open Mind*, PBS, 1975.

408   *of the city*   As quoted in "Episode 7: The City and the World", *New York: A Documentary Film*, directed by Ric Burns, PBS, 1999.

IV. AUTARCHY

484   *Parnell said*   See the Center for Competitive Politics' press release at *http://www.campaignfreedom.org/newsroom/detail/campaign-finance-institute-analysis-shows-futility-of-reform*.

485   *life itself*   See Hilaire Belloc, *The Servile State*, London, 1912.

488   *'Liberty Dollar'*   See Adam Jefferson Kirby, "The Strange Case of the Liberty Dollar", *Silver Monthly*, 2010, which can be found online at *http://www.silver-monthly.com/1459/the-strange-case-of-the-liberty-dollar/*.

489   *paper notes*   See Judith D. Schwartz, "Alternative Currencies Grow in Popularity", *Time*, December 14, 2008.

489   *hands daily*   See Matthew Beller, "The Coming Second Life Business Cycle", *Mises Daily*, August 2, 2007, which can be found online at *http://mises.org/daily/2640*.

499   *"rules in form"*   See Elinor Ostrom, *Governing the Commons*, London, 1990.

505   *billion*   Two studies that examine the efficacy of privatization in New Zealand should be browsed in: Phil Barry, "Does Privatisation Work?", *Policy Backgrounder*, 2004, which can be found online at *www.nzbr.org.nz/site/nzbr/files/policy/policy-2004/pb_no5.pdf*, and William L. Megginson and Jeffrey M. Netter, "From State to Market: A Survey of Empirical Studies on Privatization", *Journal of Economic Literature*, 2000, which can be found online at *http://www.oecd.org/dataoecd/48/42/1929649.pdf*.

516   *poverty*   Listen to Russ Roberts' podcast, "On Smith, Ricardo, and Trade", *Econ Talk*, February 8, 2010, which can be found online at *http://www.econtalk.org/archives/2010/02/roberts_on_smit.html*.

517   *its charms*   Listen to Noel Coward's "London Pride" (1941), in which the singer delights in the "Grey city, stubbornly implanted, taken so for granted for a thousand years. / Stay, city, smokily enchanted, cradle of our memories, of our hopes and fears".

537   *machine like this*   For those interested in a more elaborate narrative of the development of such a machine and a potential social reaction, read Chapter 98 of the historical fiction, *Monaco*, San Diego, 2008.

543   *system*   See Davis Guggenheim, *Waiting for 'Superman'*, Electric Kinney Films, 2010.

INDEX

Made in the USA
Lexington, KY
06 July 2011